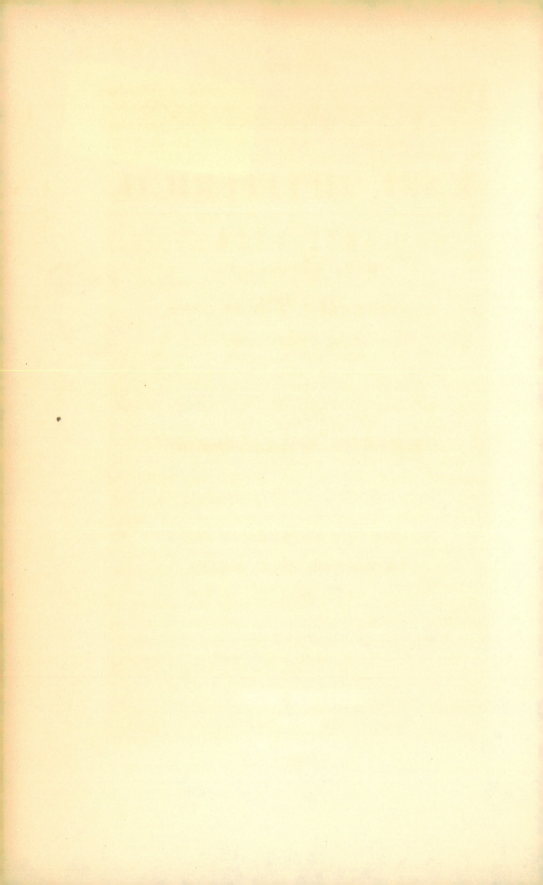

KARL HELFFERICH

1872–1924

KARL HELFFERICH

1872-1924

ECONOMIST, FINANCIER, POLITICIAN

JOHN G. WILLIAMSON

PRINCETON UNIVERSITY PRESS

PRINCETON, NEW JERSEY

1971

Publication of this book has been aided by
the Whitney Darrow Publication Reserve Fund
of Princeton University Press

This book has been composed in Linotype Janson

PREFACE

From the time Helfferich entered public life in 1895 to his violent death in 1924, his life was one of controversy and active participation in great events. As a young economist, he passionately defended the monetary and banking institutions on which he believed German industrial growth and *Weltpolitik* depended. Between 1902 and 1915, he played a more direct role in building the German *Weltwirtschaft*, first as an expert on economic development in the Reich Colonial Office and after 1905 as a leading figure in Wilhelmine Germany's foremost Imperial enterprise, the Bagdad Railway. As a director after 1908 of the railway's parent company, the Deutsche Bank, he was also an important member of Germany's restricted business elite. During World War I, he held a series of high governmental positions: he was Reich Treasury Secretary, Reich Interior Secretary and Deputy Chancellor, secretary of an office to coordinate economic war aims, and the last Imperial Minister to Bolshevik Russia. After the war, he joined the German Nationalist Party, the largest of the right-wing parties in the early years of the Weimar Republic. By the time of his death he had become the most important Reichstag opponent of the ruling majority's economic and foreign policies. Finally, he devised the basic plan by which the catastrophic post-war inflation was ended in 1923. In sum, although only fifty-one when he died, Helfferich had managed to pack an astonishing variety and quantity of activities into his career.

The multifariousness of Helfferich's pursuits was unusual, and in ways revealing of the course German economic and political life took after 1895. Helfferich represents a type that is just the opposite of the cultural pessimists and outsiders so effectively portrayed by Fritz Stern and Fritz Ringer in their books *The Politics of Cultural Despair* and *The Decline of the German Mandarins*.[1] Though by training a mandarin, Helfferich was, if

[1] Fritz Stern, *The Politics of Cultural Despair: A Study in the Rise of*

anything, a cultural optimist and a man who wholeheartedly welcomed the prevailing trends of German economic growth. His acceptance of the Wilhelmine Empire was so complete that he was never able to reconcile himself to the republic which followed it. Since he remained the garrulous intellectual even when a man of affairs, his ideas are much more accessible than is generally the case with such men. A consideration of his career thus helps us to see some of the directions in which the German political and economic elites were developing, why even their more enlightened members were unable to grasp, let alone to solve, the problems that ultimately overwhelmed Imperial Germany, and why they rejected the Weimar Republic when it came in 1919.

The Helfferich biographer has a wide variety of sources at his disposal. Before 1902, there are Helfferich's extensive scholarly and polemical writings, and after 1902, when daily administrative responsibilities began to weigh heavily upon him, a great variety of published and unpublished records. The amount of documentation on his wartime activities, in particular, is overwhelming, and after 1918, when freed from administrative duties, he wrote nearly as much as he had before 1902. A great number of Helfferich's contemporaries also recorded his passage. Because of the positions he held, his undoubted ability, and his provocative personality, he was not a man readily forgotten. What is lacking, unfortunately, are Helfferich's personal papers. Apparently never extensive, they were a casualty of the war. Such letters from him as do exist, however, suggest that the picture of the public man that emerges from available sources would not be changed very much by additional Helfferich materials. The absence of papers hurts most when one attempts to assess the ways in which Helfferich's acts may have reflected the needs of his personality. It is possible to make such assessments without intimate materials, and I believe historians ought to attempt such psychological explorations more often than they do. Lewis Edinger's biography of Kurt Schumacher shows how il-

---

the Germanic Ideology (Garden City, 1965); Fritz K. Ringer, *The Decline of the German Mandarins: the German Academic Community, 1890-1933* (Cambridge, Mass., 1969).

luminating they can be.[2] Although some of Helfferich's acts seem to require something more than common-sense explanations, my own reading in the literature of psychology has proceeded only far enough to incline me to great caution without, regrettably, having provided me with the clues necessary to dispose of the problems of Helfferich's psyche. The picture this biography presents, then, is a straightforward one which concentrates on Helfferich the public man.

In the course of writing this book I became obligated to a number of persons and institutions. As adviser and friend, Professor Hans W. Gatzke supervised this project from its inception and assisted in its completion in ways difficult to acknowledge adequately. Professors Gerald D. Feldman, Frederic C. Lane, and John L. Snell provided me with detailed criticisms of some or all of the chapters of the manuscript. Professors Lewis R. Gaty II, and Helen M. Hunter of the Swarthmore Economics Department read the economics chapters and patiently answered endless questions about their specialties. A different sort of aid came from members of Helfferich's family. His son Friedrich, in particular, offered extensive and detailed criticisms of the penultimate version of the manuscript and helped me to secure some of his father's shorter writings which had previously eluded me. He also provided the photographs of his father and put me in touch with Herr Adolf Schroeter, a younger contemporary of Helfferich's, most recently active as historian. Herr Schroeter subjected the final chapters to painstaking criticism, though in the end we had to agree to differ on many questions.

Important institutional support came from the government of the German Bundesrepublik in the form of a *Dankstipendium* that enabled me to spend a year in Germany; from Swarthmore College in the form of grants for secretarial and publication expenses; and from Princeton Press in the form of a publication grant. I should also like to thank for their assistance the staffs of the Hauptarchiv, Berlin-Dahlem; the Geheimes Staatsarchiv,

---

[2] *Kurt Schumacher: A Study in Personality and Political Behavior* (Stanford, 1965). For some interesting observations about how historians ought to proceed when they lack the more obvious kinds of psychological evidence, see Fritz Schmidl, "Psychoanalysis and History," *Psychoanalytic Quarterly*, 31 (1962), 532-47.

Munich; the Bundesarchiv, Koblenz; the Politisches Archiv of the Foreign Office of the Bundesrepublik, Bonn; the National Archives, Washington, D.C. and the libraries of Bonn University, Johns Hopkins University, and Swarthmore College.

Finally, thanks are due Ruth M. Kimmerer and Eleanor Bennett for their excellent typing, and my wife Lynn, who nurtured the inner and the outer man.

CONTENTS

CONTENTS

LIST OF ABBREVIATIONS

ARR   Anatolian Railway.

"Berichte"   "Akten dem bayerischen Ministerium des Äusserens, Gesandtschaft Berlin, Politische Berichte," in the Bayerisches Hauptstaatsarchiv, Abteilung II, Geheimes Staatsarchiv, Munich, Germany. This file contains reports of the long-time Bavarian minister to Berlin, Count Hugo von Lerchenfeld, which, along with the Lerchenfeld correspondence "Briefwechsel" and "PA" listed below, are a very valuable source for wartime domestic politics.

Bauer "Nachlass"   The papers of Colonel Max Bauer, in the Bundesarchiv, Koblenz, Germany. A few items pertinent to the July Crisis of 1917.

"Briefwechsel"   "Briefwechsel des bayerischen Gesandten Grafen Lerchenfeld mit Ministerpräsidenten Grafen Hertling . . . und mit Ministerpräsidenten von Dandl, 1916-1918," Geheimes Staatsarchiv.

BT   *Berliner Tageblatt.*

"Büro Helfferich"   "Kriegsstelle zur Vorbereitung der Wirtschaftsfragen für die Friedensverhandlungen (Spezialbüro Dr. Helfferich)," in the Deutsches Zentralarchiv, Potsdam, Germany. A few items of value for Helfferich's activities in the winter of 1917-1918. Professor Fritz Fischer was so kind as to allow me to use some of his notes from the Zentralarchiv, which was closed to me in 1961-1962.

DB   Deutsche Bank.

DDF   France, Commission pour la publication des documents relatifs aux origins de la guerre de 1914-1918, *Documents diplomatiques Français* (Paris, 1929ff.). Some documents from the 3rd Series (1911-1914) are of importance for the Franco-German Bagdad negotiations of 1913 and 1914.

"Deutschland" 131   Politische Abteilung, "Deutschland 131: Akten betreffend das Verhältnis Deutschlands zu Russland," Bde. 42ff., in the German Foreign Office, Bonn, Germany. The principal source for Helfferich's activities as minister to Moscow in the summer of 1918.

FO   German Foreign Office.

GP   Germany, Auswärtiges Amt, *Die grosse Politik der europäischen Kabinette, 1871–1914: Sammlung der diplomatischen Akten des Auswärtigen Amtes*, eds. Johann Lepsius, Albrecht Mendelssohn-Bartholdy, and Friedrich Thimme (40 vols., Berlin, 1922-1926). The most valuable printed source collection for Helfferich's activities with the Bagdad Railway, this collection is cited where possible in preference to the originals in the Foreign Office files.

GStA   Geheimes Staatsarchiv, as under "Berichte" above.

"HB"   RI: Reichsinstitut für Geschichte des neuen Deutschlands "[Arndt von] Holtzendorff Berichte [an Albert Ballin]," in the Bundesarchiv, Koblenz, Germany (formerly in the Hauptarchiv, Berlin-Dahlem). This collection, invaluable for Helfferich's wartime activities, consists mainly of reports (*Berichte*) from Holtzendorff in Berlin to his employer Ballin in Hamburg and notes (*Notizen*) on their joint activities when Ballin came to Berlin. For a fuller description of the collection, see Lamar Cecil, *Albert Ballin: Business and Politics in Imperial Germany, 1888–1918* (Princeton, 1967), 249-57, 357-58.

IFA   Erich Matthias and Rudolf Morsey (eds.), *Der Interfraktionelle Ausschuss 1917/18* (2 vols., Düsseldorf, 1959). This is the most valuable single source for Helfferich's activities during the political crises of the summer and fall of 1917.

"Kabinett-Protokolle"   Alte Reichskanzlei, "Kabinett-Protokolle," in the microfilmed records of the German Foreign Office in the National Archives, Washington, D.C. A few items of use for the postwar period. Where possible, microfilmed documents are cited as follows: serial number, if any/

xiii

	container number or filming project designation/frame number, if any.
"Kleine Erwerbungen"	"Kleine Erwerbungen," 45.4, Bundesarchiv. A few inconsequential Helfferich items from the postwar period.
Money	Karl Helfferich, *Money*, ed. T. E. Gregory (2 vols., New York, 1927), a translation of the 6th edn. of Helfferich's *Das Geld* (Leipzig, 1923).
NAZ or *DAZ*	*Norddeutsche Allgemeine Zeitung*; after 1918 the *Deutsche Allgemeine Zeitung*.
"PA"	"Politische Akten, besonders Berichte, Krieg 1914/18," Geheimes Staatsarchiv.
"Preussen" 11	Politische Abteilung, "Preussen 11 secr.: Staatsministerial- und Kronraths-Protokolle," German Foreign Office microfilm in the National Archives. Although very useful for Helfferich's wartime activities, this collection of protocols is incomplete.
Prozess	*Der Erzberger-Prozess: Stenographischer Bericht über die Verhandlungen im Beleidigungsprozess des Reichsfinanzministers Erzberger gegen den Staatsminister a. D. Dr. Karl Helfferich* (Berlin, 1920).
"Reichssteuern"	"Acta Kgl. Bayer. Staatsministeriums, des Königlichen Hauses und des Aeussern: Reichssteuern überhaupt bzw. Beratungen über die Vermehrung der Reichseinnah-

men. Einführung direkter Reichssteuern, Vermögenssteuer. Abgren-
zung der Steuergebiete des
Reiches und der Bundesstaaten,"
Geheimes Staatsarchiv. Invaluable
for the political difficulties that lay
in the way of wartime tax reform.

Reichstagsreden   Karl Helfferich, *Reichstagsreden*
1920–1922   *1920 bis 1922: mit einem Anhang:*
     Reden vom 12. und 14. November
     1919 vor dem Untersuchungsaus-
     schuss der Nationalversammlung
     (Berlin, 1922).

Reichstagsreden   Karl Helfferich, *Reichstagsreden*
1922–1924   *1922–1924: mit einem Lebensbild*
     des Staatsministers a. D. Dr. Helf-
     ferich von Graf von Westarp, ed.
     Jacob Reichert (Berlin, 1925).

RTA   Germany, Reichstag, *Stenograph-*
     ische Berichte über die Verhand-
     lungen des Reichstags: Anlagen zu
     den Stenographischen Berichten
     (Berlin, 1871ff.).

RTV   Germany, Reichstag, *Stenograph-*
     ische Berichte über die Verhand-
     lungen des Reichstags (Berlin,
     1871ff.).

Solf "Nachlass"   The papers of Wilhelm Solf, Bun-
     desarchiv. A few Helfferich items.

Stresemann "Nachlass"   The papers of Gustav Stresemann,
     in Nachlässe, German Foreign Of-
     fice microfilm in the National Ar-
     chives. Scattered items of interest
     about Helfferich from war and
     postwar periods. For an indispensa-
     ble guide to this bulky disorganized
     collection, see Hans W. Gatzke,

	"The Stresemann Papers," *JMH*, 26(1954), 49-59.
"Türkei" 110	Politische Abteilung, "Türkei 110: Akten betreffend die türkischen Finanzen," Bde. 44ff., German Foreign Office.
"Türkei" 152	Politische Abteilung, "Türkei 152: Akten betreffend Eisenbahnen in der asiatischen Türkei," Bde. 35ff., German Foreign Office. Along with "Türkei" 110 above, the most important source for Helfferich's part in the Bagdad Railway. The selective filming of these files undertaken by the University of California unfortunately omitted a number of important items, particularly from the correspondence between Deutsche Bank representatives in Berlin and Constantinople.
UA	Germany, Nationalversammlung, *Das Werk des Untersuchungsausschusses, 4. Reihe, die Ursachen des deutschen Zusammenbruchs im Jahre 1918* (12 vols., Berlin, 1925-1929).
"Untersuchungsausschuss"	Parlamentarischer Untersuchungsausschuss, "Friedensmöglichkeiten Sommer und Herbst 1917: Vernehmung des Staassekretärs a. D. Dr. Helfferich," German Foreign Office microfilm in the National Archives.
Ursachen und Folgen	Herbert Michaelis, Ernst Schraepler, and Günter Scheel (eds.), *Ursachen und Folgen von deutschen*

	Zusammenbruch 1918 und 1945 bis zur staatlichen Neuordnung Deutschlands in der Gegenwart: eine Urkunden- und Dokumentensammlung zur Zeitgeschichte (Berlin, 1960ff.).
"Valuta"	Alte Reichskanzlei, "Akten betreffend Valuta," 2436, Bundesarchiv. A miscellaneous collection of memoranda and protocols relating to the stabilization of the mark in 1923.
VZ	*Vossische Zeitung.*
Weitz "Nachlass"	Papers of Paul Weitz, Nachlässe, German Foreign Office microfilm in the National Archives. Over forty letters from Helfferich to Weitz, mostly from 1908 to 1912, about Bagdad Railway matters.
Weltkrieg	Karl Helfferich, *Der Weltkrieg* (3 vols., Berlin 1919).
"Wk 18 geh."	Politische Abteilung, "Weltkrieg Nr. 18 geheim: Unterseebootkrieg gegen England und andere feindliche Staaten, 1914-1917," German Foreign Office microfilm in the National Archives.
"Wk 18 geh. Adh. 1"	Politische Abteilung, "Weltkrieg 18 geheim Adh. I: Verhandlungen mit den Militär- und Marinebehörden über die rücksichtslose Führung des Unterseebootkriegs, Januar 1916-Januar 1917," German Foreign Office microfilm in the National Archives. The two collections above contain a number of

<table>
<tr><td></td><td>documents of importance on Helf-ferich's fight against unrestricted submarine warfare.</td></tr>
<tr><td>"Wertbeständiges Geld"</td><td>Alte Reichskanzlei, "Akten betreffend Schaffung wertbeständigen Geldes, Währungsbank, Goldnotenbank," 2440, Bundesarchiv. A collection of documents relating to stabilization of the mark in 1923.</td></tr>
<tr><td>Westarp "Nachlass"</td><td>Papers of Kuno Graf von Westarp, in the possession of Friedrich Frhr. Hiller von Gaertringen, Gärtringen, Kreis Böblingen, Germany, who kindly allowed me to use the letters directly to and from either Helfferich or his wife in this valuable collection.</td></tr>
</table>

KARL HELFFERICH

1872–1924

I. BEGINNINGS

Antecedents and Ancestors

Neustadt an der Haardt, Karl Helfferich's birthplace, was founded in the Middle Ages by the Count Palatine of the Rhine. The town was situated in a very exposed location—on the edge of the Pfälzerwald between Kaiserslautern and Speyer. The entire area became a battleground during the upheavals of the religious wars and the struggles for the left bank of the Rhine which followed. By the end of the long Napoleonic occupation in 1815, the Neustadter had seen a bewildering succession of dogmas and overlords come and go. Protestants and Catholics, French and Germans, kings, emperors, and republics—all had ruled. The town was unequally divided in religion, united in its wish for a strong German nation, and more than half-inclined to throw off its new Bavarian rulers to attain it. Moreover, the local nobility was gone, the bourgeoisie was in control. The atmosphere was as free as any in Germany.[1]

The first of the Helfferichs, Karl's great-uncle Gottfried, arrived in Neustadt in 1823 from the lower Frankish region around Frankfurt and Würzburg.[2] This was apparently the original homeland of the Helfferichs, but they cannot be traced with assurance farther back than the 1720's. Most of the Helfferichs before Gottfried were villagers, either artisans or tradesmen, whose numerous progeny had had to leave home to find work elsewhere. But they were adaptable and enterprising. Gottfried's father, Franz Nickolas, became mayor of his adopted village of

[1] On the town's early history, see Veit Valentin, *Das Hambacher Nationalfest* (Berlin, 1932), 7-8, 15-16. See also Kurt Baumann, "Die Kontinuität der revolutionären Bewegung in der Pfalz von 1792 bis 1849," in Johannes Bärmann, Alois Gerlich, and Ludwig Petry (eds.), *Hambacher Gespräche 1962* (Wiesbaden, 1962), 6-8.

[2] For Karl Helfferich's paternal ancestors, see Friedrich Riehm, "Zur Geschichte des Neustadter Geschlechts Helfferich," *Die Pfalz am Rhein*, 16 (1933), 213-16, an account largely based on genealogical studies prepared by Karl's father, Friedrich.

3

Heppenheim near Frankfurt am Main. Gottfried's uncle, Joseph Anton, entered the church, reaching the eminence of *Domkapitular* of Bamberg in 1821. He had earlier achieved some notoriety through his acrimonious participation in the negotiation of the Bavarian Concordat of 1818. The papal diplomat Cardinal Consalvi called him a "zealous man, but too fiery," a description which also suits his nephew fourth removed, Karl Helfferich.[3] Gottfried himself was a merchant in foreign trade as were two of his older brothers, one in St. Petersburg, and the other, Johann Baptist—Karl Helfferich's great-grandfather—in Amsterdam.

Gottfried's affairs prospered in Neustadt's congenial surroundings. In 1832, he was able to take on Johann Baptist's son Carl, Karl Helfferich's grandfather, as an apprentice. Carl, then fifteen years old, had come to Neustadt at an exciting time. On 20 April, his uncle Gottfried and 33 other Neustadters issued a proclamation for a great meeting of national protest, later known because of the place of meeting at the nearby Hambacher Schloss as the Hambacher *Fest*. Aimed at German disunity and weakness and long years of heavy-handed Bavarian rule, the protest was touched off by two years of hard times, the example of Louis Philippe and the French revolution of 1830, and earlier German *Feste*. The Hambacher *Fest*, intended to be the greatest *Fest* of them all, had revolutionary overtones. By the last week in May, a crowd of at least 25,000 had gathered from all parts of Germany. The theme of the speeches was *Freiheit und Einheit*, freedom and unity. Little enough concrete came from all the speeches, but by the time the *Fest* had broken up around 1 June, it had given the authorities a bad fright. The Neustadters resolutely supported their leaders, however, and the Bavarian government was unable to bring anyone to trial before 1833. Only eight were ultimately charged—Gottfried was not among them— and many of these escaped into exile. Although "to be a 'Hambacher' was for many years to carry the taint of high treason about one," the Neustadters themselves evidently considered it

[3] *Ibid.*, 214. Max Bierbaum, *Dompräbendar Helfferich von Speyer und der Münchner Nuntius Serra-Cassano: ein Beitrag zur römisch-bayerischen Kirchenpolitik zum Vollzug des bayerischen Konkordats im Jahre 1818* (Paderborn, 1926), is a history of the settlement and Joseph Anton's part in it.

a badge of honor, since they elected Gottfried Helfferich mayor in 1842.[4]

Two years later, in 1844, Mayor Gottfried married his nephew Carl to Eleonore Schopmann, a Neustadt apothecary's daughter. Carl and Eleonore soon had a son, whom they christened Friedrich Gottfried and baptized a Lutheran after his mother. Like the Helfferichs before him, Carl was himself a Catholic, though to judge by his acceding to his wife's demands a rather easy-going one. Perhaps because Eleonore died before Friedrich was ten, his father became the dominant intellectual influence in his life. Though formally a Lutheran, Friedrich was not particularly devout and followed his father's progressive, liberal views on economic and political questions. Like his father, he was trained as a merchant. When in 1871 Friedrich had the opportunity to buy a small weaving mill in partnership with a certain Jacob Engelmann, however, he took it. Was Friedrich Helfferich's act a declaration of faith in the new German Empire which was founded in the same year? Perhaps, for 1871 was as much a year of economic as of political beginnings in Germany. It was a propitious time for the Helfferichs to turn from merchants into factory owners.

Shortly afterward, the new "industrialist" married Augusta Knöchel, the daughter of a much older industrial family.[5] The Knöchels had been in Neustadt some eighty years longer than the Helfferichs. The first Knöchel to settle in Neustadt, Wolfgang Adam, migrated from the Voigtland, the area around Plauen in Saxony, in the early 1740's; in 1745, he married the daughter of a man who owned a Neustadt paper mill, and shortly thereafter set up his own mill in Schönthal west of Neustadt. The record of the next hundred years is dreary. The Knöchel men all died in their thirties, leaving widows and young sons to run the mill. They were thoroughly plundered during the disorders of the French revolution, and twice, in 1814 and 1835, the mill burned

---

[4] Valentin, *Hambacher Nationalfest*, 15-16, *et passim*.

[5] See Hermann Knoechel, *150 Jahre des Hauses Knöchel im Schönthal bei Neustadt an der Haardt: zur Feier des 150-jährigen Geschäftsjubiläums der Maschinenpapierfabrik von Ph.[ilipp] Knöchel u. Söhne* (Cologne, 1895), for the story of the Knöchels. After 1839, the mill's principal market was the *Kölnische Zeitung* and, after 1882, the *Strassburger Post* also.

to the ground. After the last fire, Karl Helfferich's maternal grandfather, Philipp, and the latter's brother, Fritz, rebuilt the mill on recognizably modern lines, adding machinery in 1838, and steam power in 1857-1858. Philipp, earlier obliged to go into exile in 1833 because of subversive activities, was the driving force for change, and in 1861 he bought out Fritz's interest in the mill. When he turned the business over to his son Theodor in 1865, the way was clear for the extensive modernizations and improvements which the latter carried out over the course of the next forty years. More than a plant modernizer, Theodor was also a progressive and enlightened employer. The comparatively small size of both Neustadt and the plant itself may also have contributed to the allegedly patriarchal relation between Theodor and his workers.

When Neustadt entered the new German Empire in 1871, the town's exciting days were over. Half of the Hambacher ideal had been achieved at the expense of the other. *Einheit* came at the expense of *Freiheit*, although in the southwest the democratic tradition remained strong. In contrast to Neustadt's turbulent political past, however, the winds of economic change had left it comparatively untouched. Trade in the good Pfälzer wines of the Haardt district surrounding Neustadt was the town's principal source of income and still is today. The Helfferichs' weaving mill and the Knöchels' paper mill hardly altered the picture. The town had a population of only 18,000 by 1906 and is less than twice that size today. Since Neustadt has been spared both the ugliness of the industrial revolution and the horrors of modern war, much of it still retains a picturesque, old-fashioned character. Half-timbered houses hem in the narrow streets, making the motorist feel awkward and out of place. It is a place to stroll, a place to stop for a glass of the fine local wine while enjoying the view of the surrounding countryside. In this modest, lovely setting, small factory-owners like the Knöchels and the Helfferichs were important people. Both families had shown more than the usual ability, though nothing remotely approaching genius. They had made their ways from nothing and in the case of the Knöchels had survived some uncommonly hard blows. It was a solid background, promising well for the future.

Youth

On 22 July 1872, Friedrich and Augusta Helfferich's first son was born. They christened him Karl Theodor.[6] At the time, the young couple was less prosperous than later. To help make ends meet, they filled part of their large house with boarders. Money may have been short after the collapse of the *Gründer* boom in 1873; the mid-seventies were lean years for entrepreneurs everywhere. But they were not lean enough to prevent Friedrich and Augusta from following the Helfferich tradition of large families. Young Karl was followed in quick succession by a sister, Emilie, and five brothers. The family's finances rapidly improved. Friedrich Helfferich bought out Jacob Engelmann in 1879 and thereafter ran the weaving mill in his own name. The mill produced then, as it does now, the fine cotton and woolen tricots used to make underwear.[7] Thus, although Karl Helfferich's later statement that "he did not lie in a golden cradle" is true, it is not amiss to say that he grew up with a silver spoon in his mouth. His youngest brother Emil recalled no boarders, and commented: "We never wanted for anything."

Friedrich and Augusta Helfferich provided their children a happy and congenial home. Augusta was easygoing, levelheaded, and good-natured, though shy with strangers, and perhaps less intelligent than her husband. The disputatious Friedrich was interested in politics, literature, and philosophy, and was both more stimulating and more difficult than his wife. A great admirer of the Progressive Party leader Eugen Richter, he was him-

[6] The following paragraphs on Karl Helfferich's early life and education are based on Rudolf Fischer, *Karl Helfferich* (Berlin, 1932), 7; Adolph Scheffbuch, *Helfferich: ein Kämpfer für Deutschlands Grösse* (Stuttgart, 1934), 5-10; and an interview with Emil Helfferich, Karl Helfferich's only surviving brother, on 19 March 1962. The two biographies, while otherwise too laudatory to be of much use, are helpful on Helfferich's early life. In general, Emil Helfferich corroborated the information they provided. Emil's memoirs, which were privately printed and are scarce, say virtually nothing about his brother, doubtless because Emil spent the years of Karl's active career in the Far East; Emil Helfferich, *Ein Leben* (4 vols., 1948-1964).

[7] Over the course of the years, the factory was much enlarged and in 1925 reorganized as a corporation; "Trikotwarenfabrik F.[riedrich] Helfferich A-G., Neustadt an der Haardt," *Die Pfalz am Rhein*, 16 (1933), 205. It remained in the family until 1968.

self a leader of the Progressives in Pfalz. Friedrich encouraged an atmosphere of intellectual freedom in his house, but left no doubt about who was master. The children were successfully instilled with the Protestant virtues of work, sobriety, and discipline, and they all left the parental house with positive feelings toward their parents and authority in general. Karl may have differed from the others, however, in having acquired the driving ambition and the lack of ultimate security that are so often the heritage of the first-born.

Karl was a thoughtful, studious child. In general, he took after his father more than his mother, resembling her only in his shyness with strangers. During his leisure hours, he is said to have read voraciously in the German classics, composed little poems, sketched, and painted in watercolors. He learned the rudiments of piano from a distant aunt. Apparently they quarreled almost immediately, but Karl continued to practice on his own. He was a strong-willed child who took everything seriously. Emil reports that he was inclined to bully his younger brothers. When they played at tin soldiers, Karl Theodor always led the German side, naturally to victory. Sometimes he had to reinforce his own army with levies from his brothers, their objections notwithstanding. It would hardly do for the Germans, and himself, to lose, even if the rules were bent a little. The story is characteristic. One of his biographers claims that he enjoyed sports and excelled at them.[8] He may have enjoyed them, but Emil recalls that he was not very good at them. Karl was not a robust child, and in early pictures he has a delicate look.[9] One certainly does not get the impression of a rowdy, carefree, athletic boy, but of an intense, bookish one, who got his own way more through force of personality than by banging heads together.

Karl's schooling began when he was four. It followed the course usual for the educated German of his day. His first two years in kindergarten were followed by three years in the Volksschule, and after that three more years in Latin school. When he was twelve, he entered the classical Gymnasium in Neustadt, where his six years' attendance presaged his later scholarly tri-

[8] Fischer, *Helfferich*, 7.
[9] Scheffbuch, *Helfferich*, picture facing p. 8.

umphs. He got less than the highest marks only in gymnastics, and his poems were read at school functions. His concentration, rapid grasp of complexities, and astonishing memory, combined with his incisive, forceful style, were the very qualities making for success at this level in school. Some of his qualities as a stylist he apparently owed to the Gymnasium. The Socialist deputy Wilhelm Dittmann asserted many years later that a fellow party member (the journalist, Carl Minster) had acquired at the Neustadt Gymnasium "the same hacked-off, thrusting style as Helfferich."[10] Great things were promised for young Helfferich. One anecdote has it that his history teachers saw in him a second Ranke, his mathematics teacher, a second Gauss.[11] Cloaked in glory, he received his *Abitur* in 1890, a few months after the fall of the first Imperial Chancellor, Otto von Bismarck. Given the liberal political atmosphere in which he was raised, it is unlikely that young Karl was upset by the departure of the *Reichsgründer*. His own future was with the new man, Kaiser William II, and like the latter, his motto was "full steam ahead."

It was in some ways characteristic of the German business classes in the nineteenth century that none of the Knöchels or Helfferichs before Karl had been to a university. No one, however, seems to have questioned Karl's going. Money was no problem, and there were younger brothers to run the mill. Karl was destined for greater things, namely, the upper spheres of the bureaucracy and academia that still marked the apex of the social pyramid for the striving bourgeois. In the fall of 1890, he enrolled as a law student at the University of Munich. Law opens even more doors in Germany than it does in the United States, and it opened more doors then than it does now. Not only potential lawyers but also prospective bureaucrats and academicians

[10] *UA*, v, 11 Oct. 1927, 191. On Minster, later a victim of the Gestapo, see Kurt Koszyk, "Das abenteuerliche Leben des sozialrevolutionären Agitators Carl Minster," *Archiv für Sozialgeschichte*, 5 (1965), 193-226.

[11] "A" [Adolf Stein], *Zwischen Staatsmännern, Reichstagsabgeordneten und Vorbestraften* (Berlin, n.d. [1922]), 72-73. For some interesting insights into the sort of history our young "Ranke" may have been taught, see Horst Schallenberger, *Untersuchungen zum Geschichtsbild der Wilhelmischen Ära und der Weimarer Zeit: eine vergleichende Schulbuchanalyse deutscher Schulgeschichtsbücher aus der Zeit von 1888 bis 1933* (Ratingen, 1964).

studied the law, which included many subjects not ordinarily taught by law faculties in the United States.[12] Economics professors, for example, customarily sat on the law faculty and were usually doctors of both philosophy and law. Since the subject of economics was just coming into its own in Germany as something apart from the law, it was perfectly natural that "law" professors should teach it. Along with law (as we would define it), Helfferich was thus able to sample a good deal else at Munich, including the lectures of the economists Lujo Brentano and Walther Lotz. Characteristically, both Lotz and Brentano sat on the law faculty and were trained as jurists. Helfferich also took piano lessons, filling gaps in his technique left by his premature revolt against his aunt; and for a time he moved in the literary circle around Michael Georg Conrad.[13] He contributed two poems to the latter's magazine, *Die Gesellschaft*, and is said to have written a novel and a novella as well. Neither of the latter has survived, although if one may judge by the poems, the loss was not great.[14] It was altogether the sort of experimental first year one would expect from a bright young man who has yet to find his chosen field.

His second year in Munich was almost entirely taken up with service in a mounted battery of the Third Bavarian Artillery as a one-year volunteer (*Einjähriger Freiwilliger*). Open only to

[12] For a brief discussion of the place of legal studies in the education of future bureaucrats, see J.C.G. Röhl, "Higher Civil Servants in Germany, 1890-1900," *Journal of Contemporary History*, 2 (1967), 101-21. For some telling criticisms of the disastrous preeminence of experts in "codified law" even today, see Ralf Dahrendorf, *Society and Democracy in Germany* (New York, 1967), esp. 149-50, Ch. 15. On the changing role of higher education in German society, see Fritz K. Ringer, *The Decline of the German Mandarins: The German Academic Community, 1890-1933* (Cambridge, Mass., 1969).

[13] Conrad was one of the founders of the "modern naturalist" school of literature in Germany after 1880, the best known representative of which is Gerhard Hauptmann. Lively and quarrelsome, Conrad has been characterized as the "Hutten of the literary revolution." An anti-Catholic who favored secularization of education, he may have strengthened Helfferich's prejudices against Catholicism; at least, it is striking that Helfferich was himself to write a play about Ulrich von Hutten; see n.17 below.

[14] For the poems, see *Die Gesellschaft: Monatschrift für Literatur, Kunst und Sozialpolitik*, 1891 (1891), 195.

those who had completed six years at a Gymnasium and could pay for their keep and equipment, this form of service exacted a minimum of military drudgery in return for a commission as a reserve lieutenant at the end of a year's service. As one Socialist *Einjähriger* conceded: "For the intellectually inclined . . . the institution . . . was a great relief, even if it did have the taint of privilege about it."[15] It was thus not only easier than the normal two years in the ranks, it also meant one could print "L.d.R.," for *Leutnant der Reserve*, on calling cards—a distinct advantage in a society where the officer set the tone. After Helfferich had finished his first year of service, he had only supplemental exercises to complete before receiving his commission.

After his military service, Helfferich abandoned the bohemian delights of Schwabing and Munich for a semester in the more austere Berlin. He shared a room with his brother Philipp, and by all accounts the two exploited the concert season and Berlin family connections to the utmost. Because he had to join the Third Bavarian for maneuvers, however, he returned to Munich for the summer semester. The semester was a total loss academically, but he received his reserve commission at the end of the maneuvers. The maneuvers of 1893 were Helfferich's last, for a bad riding accident in June of that year abruptly ended his military career. His chest was partially crushed, resulting in severe damage to his lungs. For a number of years he had to follow a regimen nearly as restrictive as a tubercular's: very limited physical activity, part of the summer in the pure mountain air of Sils-Maria or Pontresina in the Ober-Engadin near St. Moritz, and part of the winter in the warm south, mostly in Italy or on the Riviera. As a result, Helfferich was pronounced unfit for further military service and dismissed from the reserve in 1899.[16] The enforced exiles of his convalescence later became voluntary ones,

[15] Ernst Niekisch, *Gewagtes Leben: Begegnungen und Begebnis* (Cologne, 1958), 23.

[16] Fischer, *Helfferich*, 11-12; Karl von Lumm, *Karl Helfferich als Währungspolitiker und Gelehrter: Erinnerungen* (Leipzig, 1926), 1-2; *Weltkrieg*, II, 111. Both Fischer and Scheffbuch draw heavily on Lumm, who was a lifelong friend of Helfferich's; see below Ch. 2. The accident may confirm Emil's negative judgment of his brother's athletic prowess.

and Helfferich continued to vacation in these spots, especially Sils-Maria and Italy, until the end of his life.

The physical restraints imposed by the accident made an already shy Helfferich even more withdrawn. Intellectual activity was for a time the only pursuit left open to him, and he devoted all of his considerable energies to it. What the longer-range effects of the accident on Helfferich's psyche were, if any, is difficult to say. The physical blows of 1893 perhaps etched a trifle more sharply a personality whose character was already formed; Helfferich's concept of duty became sterner. It left him little time for idle social pleasures even after he recovered his health. After 1893 his life became his work, and in a very real sense he simply had no private life until his marriage many years later in 1920.[17]

The Student Becomes a Scholar

Helfferich had just about decided to return to Munich, study hard, and take his doctorate in law, with the idea of eventually entering an academic career. After finishing his doctorate, he wanted to take an extended vacation, but his plans for resuming his academic career were extremely vague. Yet he was less satisfied with the law than ever, and the apprenticeship required for a career in the civil service appalled him; he was still at loose ends. Before his return to Munich, however, his parents were visited by an old friend, a woman who was also a good friend of

[17] Emil Helfferich reports that his brother was involved in an unhappy love affair at about this time. He also asserts that the affair inspired his brother's tragic drama, published under the pseudonym F. Erich Helf, *Ulrich von Hutten: Trauerspiel in fünf Aufzügen* (Dresden and Leipzig, 1893); interview, 19 March 1962. This play has a reputation for being more virulently anti-Catholic than it is; Fischer, *Helfferich*, 8-9; Felix Pinner [Frank Fassland], *Deutsche Wirtschaftsführer* (Berlin, 1924), 143. The play is, however, passionately German nationalist in sentiment. Hutten, who seeks to build a free German nation, is thwarted by Catholic princes whose sectarianism seems a less important motivation than their desire to preserve a *status quo* favorable to themselves. Actually, the play would probably upset modern female readers rather more than male Catholics. One of the two ladies in the play is pure, innocent, and dull, and the other, Hutten's erstwhile lover, is passionate, vicious, and weak. She betrays Hutten's plans for revolution to his enemies, sleeping with sundry prelates and princes the while. I am obliged to Herr Adolf Schroeter for locating a copy of this play for me.

the Strassburg economist Georg Friedrich Knapp. She managed to persuade Helfferich that he and Knapp were exactly suited to one another. As it turned out, she was right. Helfferich later said that what he then knew of Knapp did not inspire him. He was not particularly interested in agricultural history or population statistics, Knapp's areas of publication to date. As he later put it, "perhaps because as the son of an industrialist I grew up among the looms and yarn bins, my real interest was the present-day problems of the mightily unfolding German economy."[18] Helfferich set out for Strassburg with considerable misgivings. Had the short train ride been longer, he might not have gone there at all.

Helfferich's first interview with Knapp, despite the warm recommendations from their mutual friend, went badly. Knapp was very reserved. Helfferich's account of his previous accomplishments hardly squared with his professed intention to complete his doctorate by the end of his second semester at Strassburg. Still, since the German doctoral thesis of those days was frequently less than fifty pages, this was less impossible than it sounds. Tactically, however, his taking such a high line was a mistake. Perhaps he was merely trying to hide his nervousness. At any rate, neither charmed the other. Helfferich, accustomed to being taken at his own generous valuation, resented his cool reception, and Knapp summed up his reaction with, "what does he want to study under me for? So far, all he has actually done is brandish a saber!"[19]

Knapp himself, along with Gustav Schmoller, Lujo Brentano, and Max Sering, to name some of the most important men, was an economist of the "younger historical school." Most of them were also *Katheder-Sozialisten*, a sobriquet earned because they held that the state had a positive role to play in ameliorating the condition of the working classes, both urban and rural, and thus integrating them into society. The younger historical school had

[18] For the story of Helfferich's study with Knapp, see his "Lehrer und Schüler," in Kurt Singer (ed.), *Georg Friedrich Knapp: ein literarisches Bildnis: dem Forscher und Lehrer zu seinem achtzigsten Geburtstag in herzlicher Verehrung gewidmet von Freunden und Schülern* ("Sonderheft des *Wirtschaftdiensts*") (Hamburg, 1922), 8-10.

[19] *Ibid.*, 9.

13

arisen in the early seventies in reaction to the more abstract doctrines of classical economics, which, as interpreted in Germany,
left the individual to the tender mercies of immutable economic
laws, and reduced the state's functions to clearing away the
obstacles to the unhindered action of those laws. The scholarly
methods of the classical economists were also repudiated, largely
because of the key position that historical studies had come to
hold in the German scholarly world. The younger historical
school considered that the social and economic institutions of a
nation were an inseparable part of its peculiar historical development. An attempt to explain economic institutions and solve
economic problems through the application of general economic
laws imposed an order that really was not present and suggested
a spurious similarity with outwardly similar institutions elsewhere. The key to the understanding of an institution or problem was a careful examination of its historical development.[20]
Because of the interest these economists had in ameliorating
present evils, the institutions they studied were frequently those
whose history was relevant to such evils, as for instance Knapp's
own work, *The Freeing of the Peasantry and the Origins of the
Agricultural Laborer in the Older Parts of Prussia*.[21] The result
was what would now be called old-fashioned economic history
rather than economics.

Knapp himself was unpolitical, a man who was willing to see
"highly cultivated and well-educated civil servants" continue to
run Germany, using the state as an agent for the removal of the

---

[20] For an excellent guide to the differences among German economists
on questions of methodology and social policy, which are far more complex
than I have made them appear, see Dieter Lindenlaub, *Richtungskämpfe im
Verein für Sozialpolitik: Wissenschaft und Sozialpolitik im Kaiserreich
vornehmlich vom Beginn des "Neuen Kurses" bis zum Ausbruch des Erstern
Weltkrieges 1890-1914* (Wiesbaden, 1967); for the context in which the
economists worked, see Karl E. Born, *Staat und Sozialpolitik seit Bismarcks
Sturz: ein Beitrag zur Geschichte der innenpolitischen Entwicklung des
deutschen Reiches 1890-1914* (Wiesbaden, 1957).

[21] *Die Bauernbefreiung und der Ursprung der Landarbeiter in den älte-
ren Teilen Preussens* (2 vols., Leipzig, 1887). On Knapp himself, see Joseph
A. Schumpeter, *Ten Great Economists from Marx to Keynes* (New York,
1951), 295-97, and for a sampling of his work, his own *Einführung in einige
Hauptgebiete der Nationalökonomie: 27 Beiträge zur Sozialwissenschaft*
(Munich, 1925).

injustices and hardships on which class conflict fed. The scholar's role was "to point out . . . the historical interrelationship of things, in order that the practicing politician, the civil servant, may not be swayed by the vulgar opinions of the day and overwhelmed by one-sided class interests."[22] An extremely effective teacher, Knapp managed to impress these views on many of his students, including Karl Helfferich. At this remove it is impossible to assess the intangibles making for Knapp's teaching success, although the externals of his method were simple enough— he kept his seminar small and ran it with great skill. The liberal economist Lujo Brentano, who once conducted a seminar with Knapp, said he only then learned how it ought to be done.[23]

Helfferich also found Knapp's lectures on the nature of money a revelation.[24] Knapp had a gift for making the student think along with him as he set forth a problem. The hearer did not have the impression "that the solution had been worked out in advance, but felt as if it were being thought out before him, while he himself participated in the mental processes."[25] Clearly an elegant performance. A statement of Knapp's lecture technique is a statement, essentially, of what he considered his responsibility as a teacher: to raise his students to his own intellectual level. His aim was that his students should become his collaborators by realizing their *individual* potential, rather than by turning into carbon copies of himself. He succeeded to an amazing degree. Yet Helfferich's experience also shows the impact of this gifted man on even the strongest personalities.

Helfferich, impelled by desire to overcome Knapp's reserve

---

[22] Knapp, *Einführung*, 107.

[23] Lujo Brentano, *Mein Leben im Kampf um die soziale Entwicklung Deutschlands* (Jena, 1931), 120. On Knapp as a teacher, see Eberhard Gothein, "G. F. Knapp: der Mensch und das Werk," in *Knapp: ein literarisches Bildnis*, 8; Helfferich, "Lehrer und Schüler," 9.

[24] Knapp later achieved his greatest fame as a monetary theorist with his *Staatliche Theorie des Geldes*, which first appeared in 1905 and went through several editions. A highly original work, it was a watershed in German monetary theory. For a detailed analysis, see Howard S. Ellis, *German Monetary Theory 1905-1933* (Cambridge, Mass., 1934), Ch. 2, *passim*.

[25] Helfferich, "Lehrer und Schüler," 9. See also the comments of Knapp's son-in-law, Theodor Heuss; *Erinnerungen 1905-1933* (Tubingen, 1963), 120-21.

toward him, worked hard. Within a few weeks, he had completed a short paper on an aspect of the history of Prussian coinage. Knapp said he liked the paper, but continued his "watchful reserve." Helfferich hence approached Knapp about a topic for his doctoral dissertation with some trepidation. All but refusing him at first, Knapp finally agreed to his doing a study of the German-Austrian Currency Union of 1857. Before the end of the winter semester of 1893-1894 Helfferich had finished. His work was a little over forty printed pages in length. Knapp, with whom Helfferich had not discussed the work in the meantime, accepted it with a surprised, "Already finished?" But he merely shoved it into his desk drawer, and a disappointed Helfferich heard no more of it before he went home for Easter recess. During the vacation, however, he received from Knapp a letter of the warmest praise for his work. Helfferich said later:

> Now the ice was broken. The very next time we met, Knapp discussed the piece with me in the greatest detail. From then on, I had the most thought-provoking conversations with him on the monetary questions then assuming an ever larger place in his interest. I owe to these suggestions a very great deal indeed; they have been decisive for my entire scholarly output, even if the paths I traveled were through differences in temperament and inclination so different from Knapp's that he once referred to himself as a "hen that had hatched out a duck."[26]

In June of 1894, Helfferich received his doctorate in *Staatswissenschaft*—rather than the more usual law or philosophy—with the note *summa cum laude*.

By the end of August 1894, Helfferich had enlarged his original dissertation by two-thirds, entitled it *The Consequences of the German-Austrian Currency Union of 1857*, and sent it to a publisher.[27] The work showed that Helfferich had all the makings of a successful historian: he had mastered a difficult subject matter quickly and presented his findings in a clear, lucid style. Yet

[26] Helfferich, "Lehrer und Schüler," 10.
[27] *Die Folgen des deutsch-österreichischen Münzvereins von 1857: ein Beitrag zur Geld- und Währungstheorie* (Strassburg, 1894).

Helfferich himself claimed the study was "an essay in monetary and currency theory," and here, to modern eyes at least, it has some shortcomings. Helfferich had attempted to establish the essential character of money through an examination of the workings of the Currency Union and the vicissitudes of the union's principal coin, the double silver *Vereinsthaler*, after the dissolution of the union itself. By modern lights he failed. The work was straight economic history of a purely descriptive kind. But he himself would have said he had succeeded. What he called theories were actually legal precedents, and in fact his detailed exposition, which frequently reads like a law brief, simply showed what the German and Austrian governments had in the past considered money to be. His examination revealed that the place the government gave a coin within the monetary system was what determined its monetary character at law. What he had established were some truths about money as a legal institution, rather than money as an economic institution. There were no general lessons in monetary theory.

After finishing his pioneer scholarly effort, Helfferich set off for a well-deserved four months' vacation in Greece. He was now Herr Doktor Helfferich and had established himself, in a small way, in his chosen field.

17

II. POLITICAL ECONOMIST

After Helfferich returned from Greece in late 1894, he visited Knapp in Strassburg to discuss the next stage in his academic career, the writing of his *Habilitationsschrift*. This was the long scholarly monograph German universities required of a man to prove his competence to teach at the university level. His subject was the highly controversial reforms of the 1870's which had introduced in Germany a unified gold currency and a central Reichsbank.

His topic grew quite naturally out of his earlier work on the Currency Union. It revealed, nevertheless, that his interests were diverging significantly from those of most other academic economists. As the son of an industrialist, he did not feel threatened with loss of status by Germany's onrushing industrialization, as economists of the more usual academic or bureaucratic family backgrounds were apt to do. Because he was biased in favor of industrialization, and indeed in favor of the leading sectors of the economy, he was really more interested in analyzing the institutional origins of sound economic development than he was in discovering the origins of the social problems that had arisen with industrialization.[1] He recognized the need for an effective policy to solve such problems, but he was more concerned that Germany develop the economic strength to support the political role in the world for which he considered Germany's cultural attainments qualified it. The *Weltwirtschaft*, in other words, was the foundation for *Weltpolitik*.

[1] On the reaction of the academic community to the "threat" of industrialization, see Ringer, *Decline of the German Mandarins*, and on the social origins of academics, esp. 40-42. On the latter question, see also Alexander Busch, *Die Geschichte des Privatdozenten: eine soziologische Studie zur grossbetrieblichen Entwicklung der deutschen Universitäten* (Stuttgart, 1959), 121-22. On the matters that exercised other German economists see, most conveniently, Lindenlaub, *Richtungskämpfe im Verein für Sozialpolitik*.

For the very reason that Helfferich's professional interests set him off from most academic economists, the government was to take him into its service in 1901. He was never to return to academe. His intellectual concerns thus acquire an interest beyond that which the novelty or the power of his ideas would otherwise lend them. It was not merely a question of his later making policy on the basis of ideas clearly formulated during these years or even a question of his ideas hence being more accessible than those of most contemporary men of affairs, though this would in itself justify a consideration of them. For example, his solutions to the problems of colonial economic development, his wartime policies as Treasury Secretary, and his plan of 1923 for ending the postwar inflation are only three of the more prominent cases where Helfferich can be shown to have acted on the basis, largely, of ideas developed during the years between 1894 and 1901.

But Helfferich's ideas are also important because he spoke for more than himself; otherwise he would never have been co-opted by the bureaucracy. Without making him into some sort of portentous symbol of a Wilhelmine "military-industrial complex," it is still clear that he did strikingly reflect the concerns and interests of the business classes of the Wilhelmine Empire. This was particularly true of his own generation, men who were beginning to reach positions of power and responsibility in the decade before 1914. Even as a young scholar, he was not so much a critic of his society as a vigorous advocate of many of its dominant institutions, the strengths of which his *Weltanschauung* enabled him to see much more clearly than the weaknesses.

Scholarship and Controversy

Upon his arrival in Berlin in December 1894, Helfferich presented his warm recommendations from Knapp to Karl von Lumm, head of the Reichsbank's newly created statistical division and an old student of Knapp's. Lumm gave Helfferich a hearty welcome. Besides being well-spoken for, Helfferich impressed Lumm as a "particularly intelligent man, who knew

19

exactly what he wanted."[2] While Lumm set about getting permission from the President of the Reichsbank, Richard Koch, for Helfferich to use official material on the reform, the latter settled himself into his new home. He rented two furnished rooms at Bamberger Strasse 11 near the heart of Berlin, where he was to live until 1906. His outward circumstances were modest, quite what one would expect of a hard-working, rather sickly young scholar still dependent on his parents for support. After President Koch gave permission in January 1895 for Helfferich to use official material, Lumm provided him with a desk in the statistical division and gave him unlimited access to the reputedly excellent library. Helfferich usually worked from nine in the morning until two-thirty in the afternoon, then ate dinner, usually with Lumm, and went home to work far into the night. Neither character nor health permitted excess of food or drink, nor did he smoke. He later claimed he "never ate until he was full, through lack of time to do so."[3] He clearly did not intend to remain an unknown *Stubengelehrter*, a scholar-in-a-garret, for long.

To supplement documentary lacunae on the comparatively recent events he was studying, Helfferich immediately got in touch with the surviving leaders of the currency and banking reform.[4] The most important was Ludwig Bamberger, who in the seventies had led the reform forces in the Reichstag. Bamberger agreed to allow Helfferich a look at his correspondence with the late Adolph Soetbeer, an economist who had been the principal propagandist for the reform until his death in 1892. The correspondence "opened [Helfferich's] eyes" to the possibilities of scholarly pamphleteering. He determined to take up the fight for the gold standard, the most criticized part of the reform, where Soetbeer had left off. Since the gold standard controversy had originated in the reform itself, Helfferich felt that entering the controversy would divert very little time from his research. His friend Lumm also pointed out that his advocacy "could be of

[2] Lumm, *Helfferich*, 4. Lumm is the principal source of information on Helfferich's personal life during the period 1895-1902.

[3] *Rheinpfälzer*, 7 May 1924.

[4] *Die Reform des deutschen Geldwesens nach der Gründung des Reiches* (2 vols., Leipzig, 1898), I, v-vi.

benefit not only to the cause, but to himself as well."[5] It was true: the fatherland's interests were already meshing nicely with Helfferich's own, as they were so often to do in the future.

Helfferich wrote his articles very rapidly. He usually talked them over with Lumm at dinner, mulled them over later on the same evening, and then dictated them the next morning. His machinegun-style of dictation was so rapid that stenographers had difficulty keeping up. Helfferich would then read the manuscript, pencil in corrections, and send it off to the printer.

The reason the gold standard had become so controversial was that Prussia's traditional landed rulers, the Junkers, had come to see abolition of the gold standard and the introduction of bimetallism as a panacea that would end all their economic difficulties. Hard hit by the sharp decline in grain prices that began in the seventies, the Junkers had successfully exploited their great political influence to secure a variety of subsidies, but not bimetallism. They were also unable to block ratification in 1893 and 1894 of bilateral trade treaties reducing German grain duties in return for reduced foreign duties on German manufactured goods. The Junkers helped, however, to bring down the man responsible for the treaties, Chancellor Caprivi. In part for the very reason that the treaties signified Germany's industrial coming of age, the Junkers rallied all the more fiercely to defend their threatened preeminence. Their first important step was to found the Bund der Landwirte in 1893, an organization designed to generate the mass political support that they had heretofore lacked. They also sought to mobilize other anti-modernist groups who abhorred German progress toward an industrial urban future the ultimate shape of which was ominous and difficult to foresee.[6]

[5] Lumm, *Helfferich*, 12-13.

[6] On the economic difficulties of the Junkers and their response to them, see Kenneth Barkin, *The Controversy over German Industrialization, 1890-1902* (Chicago, 1970), Chs. 1-2; Hans-Jürgen Puhle, *Agrarische Interessenpolitik und preussischer Konservatismus im wilhelminischen Reich (1893-1914): ein Beitrag zur Analyse des Nationalismus in Deutschland am Beispiel des Bundes der Landwirte und der Deutsch-Konservativen Partei* (Hanover, 1967); Hans Rosenberg, *Grosse Depression und Bismarckzeit: Wirtschaftsablauf, Gesellschaft und Politik in Mitteleuropa* (Berlin 1967).

Caprivi's unhappy fate inclined his successor, Count Hohenlohe, to extreme caution. He and his Secretary of the Treasury, Count Arthur von Posadowsky-Wehner, opposed bimetallism but feared the political consequences of taking a public stand against it.[7] Their position became more difficult in 1895 when the English House of Commons passed a resolution calling for an international conference on the currency question. In such circumstances, the services of advocates such as Helfferich were invaluable, because they could act with a disregard for political consequences not vouchsafed to the government. Although Helfferich was not a hired polemicist, the future was to show that monetary virtue, too, has its rewards.

Helfferich's first defense of gold, *Against the Overthrow of the [Gold] Standard*, appeared in March of 1895. Ludwig Bamberger wrote a short introduction to it, saying it was just the thing to set the public straight on the facts. He apparently also helped to get it published.[8] Knapp, however, wrote Helfferich that he thought the latter was making a mistake by entering the controversy, since the fact that he had first come to public notice as a mere "quarreler" would not soon be forgotten. Knapp recommended that Helfferich withdraw from the fray, at least until publication of his work on the currency reform had established his reputation as a scholar. Helfferich's reply is revealing:

> I know very well that it would be better in my own personal interest to await publication. . . . On the other hand, I believe that the general and public interest demands that everyone do his best to block mistakes in monetary policy that are not to be repaired. Unfortunately, those who know the subject and can write are very few in number; this makes the demands on those who can all the greater. All the same, I shall try not to become too deeply involved.[9]

[7] Erich Eyck, *Das persönliche Regiment Wilhelms II.: politische Geschichte des deutschen Kaiserreiches von 1890 bis 1914* (Erlenbach-Zürich, 1948), 154-55. Indispensable for the politics of this period is J.C.G. Röhl, *Germany without Bismarck: The Crisis of Government in the Second Reich, 1890-1900* (Berkeley and Los Angeles, 1967).

[8] *Gegen den Währungsumsturz* (Berlin, 1895).

[9] Lumm, *Helfferich*, 22-23.

But Helfferich did become "deeply involved." Unlike Knapp, however, Bamberger approved highly. To aid Helfferich in his support of gold, Bamberger opened to him the columns of the *National Zeitung* and his other publications and introduced him to many of his political and business associates. Since Helfferich's future was to be so closely tied to these men and their interests, it might be well to note briefly what some of Bamberger's more important associations were. Politically, Bamberger was an ex-National Liberal and a leading member of the Freisinnige Vereinigung. The latter was the right wing of Eugen Richter's Progressive Party, from which it had split in 1893. Unlike the intransigent Richter and his followers, the members of the Vereinigung generally supported the government. The party's foreign policy was *Weltpolitik* and in its domestic policy it stood for the more enlightened and progressive sections of the big business community. Bamberger himself had close ties to the Deutsche Bank, Helfferich's future employer and the largest of the commercial banks, as did Theodor Barth, a party colleague to whom Bamberger introduced Helfferich about this time. For his part, Barth published a number of Helfferich's articles in his journal *Die Nation*, which a contemporary has described as "Germany's most eminent weekly."[10]

Most of Helfferich's currency articles appeared in 1895 and 1896, when the bimetallist controversy was at its height.[11] The arguments of his bimetallist opponents can be reduced to two central propositions. The first was that, because of declining silver prices of goods in terms of gold currencies, the farmers and manufacturers of silver-standard countries enjoyed a substantial export premium. According to the more extreme contemporary

[10] Moritz Bonn, *So macht man Geschichte: Bilanz eines Lebens* (Munich, 1953), 50. On the Progressives before 1893, see Gustav Seeber, *Zwischen Bebel und Bismarck: zur Geschichte des Linksliberalismus in Deutschland 1871-1893* (Berlin, 1965); for the Freisinnige Vereinigung after 1893, see Konstanze Wegner, *Theodor Barth und die Freisinnige Vereinigung: Studien zur Geschichte des Linksliberalismus im wilhelminischen Deutschland 1893-1910* (Tübingen, 1968). See also Pauline Anderson, *The Background of Anti-English Feeling in Germany, 1890-1902* (Washington, D.C., 1939), esp. 98-106.

[11] Helfferich's numerous articles and pamphlets on the currency question (at least sixteen) are listed chronologically in the Bibliography.

versions of the argument, this export premium enabled its beneficiaries to compete successfully even in the German home market. The bimetallists' second proposition was that gold production
was failing to keep pace with increasing demand for money, with
the result that prices were being forced down. Debtors, such as
most Junkers were, were hence forced to pay back cheap money
with dear.

Helfferich's arguments on both questions are in some ways as
dated as those of his opponents. If they are the more convincing it is largely because his careful examination of the facts enabled him to destroy the validity of the examples on which the
bimetallists' generalizations rested. To uphold an unorthodox
position in economics without a sure command of the facts, as the
bimetallists were attempting to do, is impossible. Although Helfferich devoted much effort to considering the effects of changing
exchange rates on foreign trade, his most interesting arguments
were those that dealt with natural costs of production. These
arguments also supported his contention that the gold standard
had not been responsible for the fall in prices since the late
seventies.

Helfferich thought that free silver could not help the German
grain growers, because it did not get at the heart of the problem,
the higher natural cost of production in Germany. The foreign
producers' costs were lower because they farmed cheap virgin
land with cheap draft animals, or, as in the case of Russia, because their own labor was so cheap. Helfferich's careful examination of price movements, wages, and interest rates after 1870 inclined him to think that the fall in agricultural prices was merely
a special case of the more general movement in prices since 1870.
Technological innovations rather than export premia effects or the
relative reduction in the money stock were what had caused the
fall in prices. Actually, he claimed, gold flows in and out of Europe bore no relation to prices, and even after 1890, when gold
production rose sharply, the increased stock had mostly gone into
central-bank reserves and into circulation in countries that had
only recently gone on the gold standard. As he pictured the situation, price movements for the most part originated on the goods

side of the equation of exchange. Monetary influences on price levels hardly existed.[12] When Helfferich's ideas on money and banking are considered below, it will be seen that his future studies in this area merely strengthened the foregoing conclusion.

When Helfferich turned to consider the plight of the Junkers in more detail, his animus against them as a pretentious, anachronistic class emerged clearly. He thought the only real ground for their support of bimetallism was that it would reduce their real mortgage costs. He did not sympathize with what he considered an attempt to bilk their creditors because he thought their own greed and mismanagement responsible for their difficulties. As he explained it, in the seventy-odd years after the Stein-Hardenberg reforms of 1807, the Junkers had done everything possible to exploit the rapidly developing agricultural market. They had added to their lands, mainly by dispossessing the peasants, and spent heavily on capital improvements. Assuming that their incomes would go on rising forever, they had undertaken mortgage obligations which discounted these sanguine expectations dangerously far into the future. But prices fell sharply after 1874. To make matters worse, in their halcyon days the Junkers had also taken up a much grander life style. Helfferich, commenting with a bitterness perhaps natural to the studious bourgeois officer who had served in the less fashionable artillery, noted that his Junker counterparts served "only in the guards and in the cavalry and joined elegant corps [at the universities]—and what that costs is no secret." And not only were they arrogant, they were ignorant, "absolutely incapable of judging the merits of the currency question" or even managing their estates. They had become little more than aristocratic parasites:

> If their income be insufficient to maintain this manner of living, then they claim it is the duty of the state to see that landowner-ship . . . does pay. . . . The landlord sitting over champagne and

[12] Helfferich's earlier arguments on the subject are conveniently collected in his "Wirkungen der gesteigerten Goldproduktion," in his *Studien über Geld und Bankwesen* (Berlin, 1900), 252-61.

crying of want is unfortunately not only a comic figure in our satirical weeklies but a tragic figure of reality.[13]

Like many of his contemporaries in scholarship and business, Helfferich saw in the Junkers an ignorant, presumptuous, backward group that stood in selfish opposition to the dynamic, progressive forces of the nation.

Helfferich's assessment of the consequences of introducing bimetallism was the usual lurid portrayal of "fateful economic and social catastrophe" common to gold-standard propagandists in his day.[14] It was in its way as exaggerated as his criticisms of the Junkers' abilities as agriculturists, for the Junkers were among the more efficient and technologically sophisticated farmers in Europe.[15] But in 1897, English refusal to consider bimetallism effectively doomed it anyway. Helfferich's articles became jubilant.[16] Their number decreased. Bimetallism had ceased to be such a danger, and he was finishing the capstone of his case against it, his massive work on the currency and banking reform.

The work was intended to undercut such intellectual underpinnings as bimetallism possessed and at the same time present a scholarly justification of the reforms of the seventies which had introduced the gold standard. As it was also intended to establish Helfferich's reputation as a scholar, he attempted and largely succeeded in keeping it free of polemical overtones.[17] By the time of completion in 1897, the work had grown to two large volumes,

[13] The above quotations are from *Währung und Landwirtschaft: gemeinfasslich dargestellt* (Stuttgart, 1895), 14, and *Währungsumsturz*, 15.

[14] *Die Währungsfrage: gemeinfasslich dargestellt* (Stuttgart, 1895), 46-47.

[15] John H. Clapham, *Economic Development of France and Germany, 1815-1914* (Cambridge, 1936), 206, 219-21, and Alexander Gerschenkron, *Bread and Democracy in Germany* (Berkeley and Los Angeles, 1943), 79, both note large increases in yield per acre after 1900; but see also Barkin, *Controversy over German Industrialization*, 122-23.

[16] The scornful title of one of these articles, *Das neue Fiasko der internationalen Doppelwährung: englischer Parlamentsbericht vom 22. Oktober 1897* (Stuttgart, 1898), indicates their general tone.

[17] Two of Helfferich's reviewers commented favorably on his success: Wilhelm Lexis, "Zur Geschichte der deutschen Münzreform [A Review of Reform]," *Jahrbücher für Nationalökonomie und Statistik*, 71 (1898), 101; and K. Oldenberg, review of Karl Helfferich's *Reform des deutschen Geldwesens*, *Schmollers Jahrbuch*, 23 (1899), 341.

the first a narrative of the reform and the second a series of essays on related questions. The second volume also contained the extensive statistical apparatus and document collection typical of the "Strassburg School," as Knapp and his students were known. Such a lengthy work from an academic unknown represented a considerable risk for a publisher. Although the book subsequently proved more than able to stand on its merits, it is likely that Knapp helped to persuade his friend Carl Giebel of the scholarly house of Duncker and Humblot to accept the work.[18]

About one-third of the first volume (on the reform per se) was taken up with a careful survey of the monetary conditions prevailing in Europe prior to the reform. This *Vorgeschichte* aimed at answering the question of whether the reform was a "historical necessity," or whether it was a "break in the continuity of the historical development" which had created an "abnormal condition." Helfferich described the chaotic monetary conditions in Germany prior to the reform in tones which make quite clear how much the disorder offended him aesthetically. He also equated a unified currency with a unified government and centralization, whereas a "splintered" currency system was equated with "Balkanization." Helfferich then traced the growth of the demand for currency reform and noted the gold discoveries of the fifties and sixties which made the introduction of the gold standard possible. He thought the change to the gold standard inevitable:

> It is a fact particularly worthy of note that the decisive shift in the standards of the civilized world did not come about through the conscious action of men, but occurred of itself . . . through an *inner necessity*, wholly independent of the wishes and indeed partly against the wishes of those who thought to control monetary developments through laws.[19]

[18] Helfferich only thanked Giebel for accepting the risk; *Reform*, i, viii. Since, however, Lujo Brentano said that Knapp interceded for him with Giebel in 1870, it seems likely that Knapp also did so for his star pupil Helfferich; Lujo Brentano, "Ein Brief," *Knapp: ein literarisches Bildnis*, 2.

[19] *Reform*, i, 3, 82. My italics.

27

Helfferich clearly thought that history had an inner dynamic of its own and, like Bismarck, believed that man could do little more than attempt to perceive its direction and ride with it. Attempts to block the course of historical development or even to influence it greatly were hopeless.

The second major section was on the reform legislation of the seventies. Here again Helfferich's dislike for the centrifugal forces within the new empire emerged quite strongly. He criticized the energy and tenacity with which the *Bundesstaaten*, the individual states of the German Empire, had defended their currency prerogatives: "in these matters their particularism was jealous indeed." The particularist forces in the Reichstag drew their principal support from the Catholic Center Party, "which did not in any case have much use for the Protestant imperium." The Center was supported by the more doctrinaire economic liberals of Eugen Richter's stamp, who favored the banking anarchy then prevailing. These positions came out quite clearly in the debate over the Reichsbank:

> The idea of a Reichsbank [i.e., a central bank] was from the outset as sympathetic to the friends of a unified Reich as it was antipathetic to the particularists; the German-national parties, namely the National Liberals and the Free Conservatives, could be counted on from the beginning as being for the Reichsbank, while one could with almost as much assurance count on the opposition of the particularist parties and groups, namely the Center Party.[20]

All of the anti-bank forces had a common character in Helfferich's mind: like the Junkers, they were anachronistic and did not see where the hand of history was guiding them. In opposing the Reichsbank, they were in a very real sense historically wrong.

In general, however, Helfferich had nothing but praise for the activities of the Reichstag. It worked very rapidly, it eliminated provisions from the draft laws which were harmful, and it insisted upon the incorporation of measures vital to the success of the reform such as free and unlimited coinage of gold, cessation of silver coinage, and the obligation of the Reichsbank to buy

[20] *Ibid.*, 165, 174, 289.

gold; and finally, "the Reichsbank itself had the Reichstag to thank for its existence."[21] But, although Helfferich regarded this Reichstag as far more able than its successors, he said it was no exception to the rule that in complicated matters such as the currency question, only a few of its members could know enough to form an independent opinion. What he admired about this early Reichstag was the expert knowledge of some of its members, but in general, he apparently believed that the experts were often overwhelmed by those acting from motives quite irrelevant to the questions at hand. Implicit in these remarks about the Reichstag was his conception of its functions: it was simply to provide expert criticism of government measures and the funds necessary to carry them out. It had no independent policy-making role of its own.

The last major section of the book discusses the execution of the reform itself. To a modern observer it appears that the government's execution of the reform must have had inflationary effects during the boom prior to 1873 and deflationary effects in the depression which followed—or just the opposite of what was called for. But Helfferich, like most economists and nearly all businessmen of his day, placed the needs of the gold standard above what would now be considered the needs of the economy. The essence of his criticism was thus quite different: it was that, although the government showed great skill in exploiting the French indemnity payments from the Franco-Prussian War to secure the necessary gold, they did not start withdrawing silver from circulation soon enough. This mistake endangered the new gold circulation and prevented the government from unloading appreciable quantities of silver in the strong silver market of 1873. Even after 1873 the tempo of the currency withdrawal was too slow to suit Helfferich. He therefore noted with satisfaction the restrictive measures which were forced on the note-issue banks around December 1874 by their obligation to redeem all their small notes (under 100 marks) by 1 July 1875.

Helfferich also approved the high Reichsbank rates which prevailed from 1874 on, and which were intended to keep the new gold coins in Germany. Except for Vienna, the Reichsbank rate

---

[21] *Ibid.*, 302-303

was the highest central bank rate in Europe.[22] This suggests that the gold standard was dearly bought. The buttressing it apparently required was hardly designed to revive a sluggish economy. But Helfferich was not troubled by such doubts: "The German monetary system has developed since 1885 in an absolutely breath-taking fashion. No one, not even the most zealous advocate of the gold standard, could even have dreamed of such a brilliant upward career." This happy outcome was as much due to the benevolent intervention of events since the conclusion of the reform, which Helfferich dated from the cessation of silver sales in 1879, as to the measures of the reform. The reformers had blindly seized the coattail of history by acting in a way which prevented the sharp rise in world silver production from ruining Germany's currency. To use Helfferich's more flamboyant language: "It was necessary to destroy the so-called parity between gold and silver . . . in order that the gold, and with it the money of the entire *Kulturwelt*, be saved from sharp depreciation." He believed that as knowledge of how "the great and indisputable improvement" in the international monetary situation became "common property" the greater the dangers of bimetallism would appear. But his final conclusion was highly optimistic: "the German gold standard . . . appears today inwardly complete and outwardly secure. With it, the work of the currency reform has been brought to its desired conclusion."[23] It was Helfferich's definitive pronouncement on bimetallism, though not quite his last word.

Habilitation *and a Libel Suit*

With the publication of *Reform*, Helfferich was ready to complete his *Habilitation*, and as soon as the work was off the presses in early 1898, he presented a copy of it to Adolf Wagner of the University of Berlin. Helfferich had already spoken to Wagner

---

[22] *Ibid.*, 384. On the interest rates, see the tables in *Reform*, II, 292-97. For an excellent discussion of Reichsbank policy, see Karl R. Bopp, "Die Tätigkeit der Reichsbank von 1876 bis 1914," *Weltwirtschaftliches Archiv*, 72 (1954), 34-57, 179-221, and esp. 186-88. See also Manfred Seeger, *Die Politik der Reichsbank von 1876 bis 1914 im Lichte der Spielregeln der Goldwährung* (Berlin, 1968), inadequate in its theory but useful for its details.

[23] *Reform*, I, 463-74.

about *Habilitation* once before, in a stormy interview on 10 October 1897. Helfferich handled this interview with his typical lack of finesse. Wagner, a proud and touchy man, pointed out that it was usual to "habilitate" under the teacher one had previously worked for and gratuitously added that he and Knapp had fallen out some years ago. Wagner was a bimetallist and a Free Conservative member of the Prussian Landtag. He estimated that Helfferich's work on the currency reform was not likely to be worth much, but said that he could submit it if he wished. The faculty would judge it. He told Helfferich that he was in for a long wait: "It would be some months before he [Wagner] would have time to prepare a critique of the work." Helfferich was furious. He wrote Lumm: "Wagner could not have chosen a better way to make my decision irrevocable. Now I cannot possibly back down. I have in any event not the slightest doubt that he will recommend my refusal. But I am counting with certainty on the other faculty members not allowing themselves to be influenced by his prejudice."[24] When Helfferich handed over the copy of *Reform* to Wagner, his scholarly fate was in the hands of his faculty committee: Gustav Schmoller, Max Sering, and Adolf Wagner.

Wagner was right about one thing at least. Helfferich's decision to "habilitate" at Berlin was irregular, and he never revealed his reasons for doing so. Among the obvious reasons for his decision were that Berlin was the foremost of the German universities and its economics faculty the most renowned. But it was only partly true that the university was "the intellectual elite guard of the Hohenzollerns." Many influential men around the Kaiser seem to have been more struck by the amount of criticism they received from the faculty, particularly the economists, than by the amount of support it gave the existing order.[25] By 1895, when

[24] Lumm, *Helfferich*, 78-81. According to Knapp, *Einführung*, 5, his quarrel with Wagner was over statistical methods. See also Heuss, *Erinnerungen*, 123.

[25] "Elite guard," Hans Herzfeld, *Ausgewählte Aufsätze: dargebracht als Festgabe zum siebsigsten Geburtstage von seinen Freunden und Schülern* (Berlin, 1962), 285. For the quarrels described below, see Lindenlaub, *Richtungskämpfe*, 56-83, who also documents the animus against the academic economists in industrial circles. For additional insights into the sorts of

the university rejected two liberal economists "on scholarly grounds," things had reached a point where it was possible for Baron Karl von Stumm-Halberg, a politically reactionary industrialist with close ties to the Kaiser, to challenge Wagner to a duel because of heated charges exchanged in the press about the matter. Nor was Stumm the only businessman to assume that the *Katheder-Sozialisten* on the faculty were merely preparing the way for the genuine article. Since Helfferich was not a *Katheder-Sozialist* and was too solid a scholar to be rejected on academic grounds, it seems plausible that his decision to "habilitate" at Berlin was at the very least encouraged by his acquaintances in business and the bureaucracy.

These acquaintances were now more numerous than ever and included some very influential men. By now Helfferich knew most of the men connected with Reich or Prussian finances, in office or out: Rudolf von Delbrück, once Bismarck's right-hand man; the powerful and influential Prussian Finance Minister, Johannes von Miquel; Count Arthur von Posadowsky-Wehner, Reich Treasury Secretary until 1897, when he was promoted to Interior Secretary; Max von Thielman, Posadowsky's successor at the Treasury; and Rudolf Koch, President of the Reichsbank. Helfferich had also come to know many Reichstag deputies representing business interests, the most notable of whom was Friedrich Hammacher. The leading National Liberal of his day, Hammacher was also a prominent member of many industrial interest and other pressure groups, from the Bergbaulicher Verein, of which he was president, to the Colonial Society, and after 1898, the Navy League.[26] Through Hammacher, Helfferich was introduced to Georg von Siemens, head of the Deutsche Bank. Though they differed on many specific issues, these men shared a common conviction in favor of industrial capitalism and *Welt-*

---

petty behavior of which the government was capable in its enforcement of orthodoxy, see Dieter Fricke, "Zur Militarisierung des deutschen Geisteslebens im wilhelminischen Kaiserreich: der Fall Leo Arons," *Zeitschrift für Geschichtswissenschaft*, 8 (1960), 1069-1107.

[26] On Hammacher, see Anderson, *Background of Anti-English Feeling*, 73-78.

politik, and none sympathized with the more extreme claims of either the agrarian Right or the democratic Left. To such men, Helfferich's presence on the Berlin faculty would have been welcome, and it is hard to believe that none of them told him so. For his part, Helfferich may have considered knowing such men, the like of whom were certainly not to be found in Strassburg, an additional reason for remaining in Berlin.

While Helfferich was awaiting the outcome of his *Habilitation*, he unleashed a final broadside at the principal bimetallist propagandist, Otto Arendt. It very nearly ruined his chances. Arendt was a member of the Prussian Landtag, a Free Conservative Reichstag deputy, and editor of the *Bimetallistische Monatsschrift* and a popular weekly, the *Deutsches Wochenblatt*. He owed his scholarly reputation principally to his *International Bimetallism*,[27] which first appeared in 1880 and went through several editions. Because this work contained apparently irrefutable statistical evidence that German silver sales after the introduction of the gold standard had driven world silver prices down (and hence other prices as well), it had converted many to the cause of bimetallism. If Arendt's contentions were true, the reform had indeed created an "abnormal condition," and was not an "historical necessity," as Helfferich claimed.

Arendt had earlier attempted to quash Helfferich when he first appeared on the scene in 1895 with his *Against the Overthrow of the [Gold] Standard*. Arendt patronizingly commented that Helfferich's *Consequences of the . . . Currency Union of 1857* revealed that he was "not without talent," but that his latest effort was an entirely superficial piece, which dodged the issues and rested on "false representations." This was scarcely mincing words, but in order that his meaning might not be mistaken, Arendt concluded: "Given the low intellectual level to which the representatives of the gold standard have sunken, it is natural

[27] *Die vertragmässige Doppelwährung: ein Vorschlag zur Vollendung der deutschen Münzreform* (Berlin, 1880). Helfferich, *Bimetallistische Kampfesart: eine Auseinandersetzung mit Herrn Dr. Otto Arendt* (Neustadt a. d. Haardt, 1895), from which the quotations below are taken, collects most of writings from the early stages of the quarrel.

that the gold standard press is setting up the greatest possible hue and cry for this piece." Helfferich was not one to take anything lying down. He was a hater in the Bismarckian tradition, and one is obliged to conclude that he had the better arguments. This initial skirmish of 1895 soon degenerated into an unedifying exchange of complaints in which each accused the other of not printing his rebuttals as soon as promised.

In July 1898, Helfferich renewed his attack on Arendt with a piece entitled: *Germany's Currency Reform and Silver's Loss of Value: A Few Words on the Bimetallist Writing of History*. Helfferich systematically dismembered Arendt's statistics, finding them "shot through with typographical and other errors." He added that, although he sought not to burden his *Reform* with a "polemic," he intended to expose Arendt for the charlatan he was: "The audacity with which the statistical tables in the book are twisted and punched into the shape necessary to support what Arendt says exceeds by a good deal the boldness of Arendt's sophistical conclusions. What we have here is a blatant case of systematic misrepresentation of the historical truth, and I was not for a moment in doubt that this proceeding had to be mercilessly exposed."[28] Helfferich then proceeded to pick apart Arendt's *Vertragmässige Doppelwährung*, showing how misleading the work was. This led to another mudslinging contest in the press, with both men again accusing each other of failure to print their respective rebuttals.[29] So far as one can judge the substantive issue in the quarrel, the effect of German silver sales on the silver market, Helfferich's contention that the sales were only one of many factors depressing prices was correct. His statistical evidence, based on official material, was certainly more convincing than Arendt's. On the other hand, Helfferich underestimated the psychological effects of German adoption of the gold standard on other countries. France soon followed Germany on to gold, and then a host of other countries. That naturally restricted the

[28] *Deutschlands Münzreform und die Silberentwertung: einige Worte über die bimetallistische Geschichtsschreibung* (Stuttgart, 1898), 6-7.

[29] For most of the documents on this phase of the quarrel and Arendt's own presentation of his case, see Otto Arendt, *Die Ursache der Silberentwertung: an die rechtlich denkenden aller Parteien: eine Antwort für Herrn Dr. Helfferich* (Berlin, 1899).

silver market very greatly and must have driven silver prices down.[30]

Arendt ultimately sued Helfferich and the *National Zeitung* for "slanderous abuse." It was a blunder. When the matter came to hearing on 26 January 1899, Arendt's suit was ignominiously thrown out of court and Arendt himself charged with all costs. Despite the vigor of Helfferich's verbal onslaught, Arendt was admonished that his opponent had not exceeded the usual bounds of propriety. The court also pointed out that since he earlier called the gold bugs "wire pullers" who "swindled the great mass of their followers" he ought not complain. Helfferich's friend von Lumm later commented: "The quarrel had . . . caused no little sensation, and had left the impression in wide circles that the bimetallistic creed of Dr. Arendt was incompatible with the juristic creed of 'good faith.' "[31] Still, Helfferich's own campaign was not much better, at least by modern standards. It was too shrill and too much *ad hominem.* The quarrel was the first notable evidence of Helfferich's view that ends justified means, and that the best way to discredit an idea was to impugn the character of its advocate. He was later to follow the same course in 1919 in his attack on democracy and democratic institutions; a series of books and pamphlets, ranging in tone from polemical to academic, prepared the way for personal onslaught against Matthias Erzberger, then Finance Minister, who, like Arendt, was pictured as the embodiment of the evil ideas which Helfferich was attacking. And history was also to repeat itself in that Erzberger's libel suit, like Arendt's, was in the end unsuccessful.

In the meantime Helfferich's *Habilitation* had gotten nowhere. Wagner had taken until July of 1898 to prepare his critique, and Sering, not to be outdone, took the rest of the year. Toward the end, it was obvious that Arendt's libel suit was causing the delay. The university understandably had no wish to appoint a con-

[30] This was the opinion of both Lexis and Oldenberg in their reviews cited in n.17 above.

[31] Lumm, *Helfferich,* 25-29. Even so moderate a man as Knapp finally decided that Helfferich's methods of fighting Arendt were the only ones possible; *ibid.,* 28. For some interesting speculations on why German scholarly quarrels assume such an acerbic tone, see Dahrendorf, *Society and Democracy in Germany,* Ch. 10.

victed slanderer to its faculty. Some suggested in the fall of 1898 that Helfferich withdraw and accept the job of Syndicus that Hugo Oppenheimer of the bank of Robert Warschauer & Co. had offered him. Helfferich refused to give in, assertingly grimly: "If they won't admit that I have the ability to teach, I mean to have it down in black on white for eternal remembrance."[32] To make matters worse, in November he had a serious relapse of his old injury with severe lung hemorrhages and had to flee to Egypt to recover. He remained there until April 1899. Outward appearances not withstanding, however, Helfferich's chances for *Habilitation* were good. Schmoller made no secret of the fact that he thought the *Reform* a fine work, exactly fitting his conception of economics. Theodor Mommsen, famous historian and author of a book on Roman coinage, also expressed his admiration of Helfferich's work. Both Wilhelm Lexis and Karl Oldenberg, respected names, reviewed Helfferich's work very favorably, commenting on its objectivity, fine literary style, and careful research.[33] Neither thought the work in much danger of being superseded factually, and indeed it remains the authoritative work on the German currency reform. The bureaucracy also took an interest in the matter. Max von Thielmann let Helfferich know that the Prussian Ministry of Culture (in charge of education) viewed his candidacy favorably, as did his own Treasury Office. Rudolf von Delbrück and Richard Koch of the Reichsbank also seem to have done what they could.[34]

Whether by accident or design, the faculty session on Helfferich's *Habilitation* was on 2 February, hardly a week after Arendt's suit had been thrown out of court. Wagner was Helfferich's most serious opposition. He said Helfferich was too much the specialist, having interests that were too narrow, and that Helfferich's presentation of the facts was one-sided. The rest

[32] Scheffbuch, *Helfferich*, 25.

[33] A favorable review from Lexis was the *imprimatur*, since the moderation and soundness of his views made him highly respected. He was also considered one of the foremost monetary authorities among the academic economists. See also Schmoller's later favorable comments on Helfferich as a currency expert; *Grundriss der allgemeinen Volkswirtschaftslehre* (2 vols., Leipzig, 1900, 1904), II, 61.

[34] For the details of the *Habilitation*, see Lumm, *Helfferich*, 80-88.

agreed that there was some substance to the first of these criticisms, but proposed that Helfferich demonstrate the breadth of his learning by giving his trial lecture on a general subject. This was a golden bridge for Wagner, which he refused to take. But Schmoller and Mommsen spoke warmly for Helfferich, and the final vote was 22 in favor, 4 abstaining, and 2 against. Voting with Wagner in favor of rejection was his Free Conservative Party colleague, the noted military historian, Hans Delbrück. Although the latter also accused Helfferich of being a polemicist rather than a scholar, the fact that he had just been disciplined by the government for his criticisms of official policies may have made him less receptive to a man he may have regarded as an official candidate.

Helfferich did not receive the good news until early May. He chose as trial lecture topic Malthusian population doctrines and their lessons for the *Industriestaat*. The topic was accepted in mid-June and 13 July set as the day for delivery. His aim was to carry the war to the enemy: "My intention was to portray the vagueness and general muddiness of Malthusian population doctrines and also the confusion in concepts which occurred when Wagner used them in reference to the *Industriestaat*; from here I meant to lead the discussion to the unclear ideas Wagner and Oldenberg had about the *Industriestaat* itself." His choice was largely a matter of tactics, since he wanted to block any attempt of Wagner "to examine me to death in the discussion period (*Colloquium*)"; he also wanted "to place [Wagner] on the defensive and make the *Colloquium* in the main a discussion of my views." His lecture, the content of which will be considered below, was well received by all except Wagner. Sering and Schmoller made only perfunctory remarks, but Wagner made a speech of rebuttal lasting nearly an hour.[35] Helfferich for once was conciliatory, highlighting areas of agreement and playing down differences with Wagner. Apparently mollified, Wagner voted with

[35] *Ibid.*, 88-89. Since Wagner was shortly to publish the most complete statement of the arguments against the *Industriestaat*, he was well qualified to make such a rebuttal. For a brief summary of Wagner's *Agrär- und Industriestaat* (1901), see Michael H. Tracy, *Agriculture in Western Europe: Crisis and Adaption since 1880* (London, 1964), 92-94. For a full discussion of the matter, see Barkin, *Controversy over German Industrialization*.

the others to accept Helfferich. Helfferich was now a Privatdozent on the faculty of the University of Berlin.

He had reached the lowest level in German academe. For the
first time he was barely independent financially. Since a Privatdozent depended largely on fees collected directly from his students, it was an additional piece of bad luck that Helfferich had
been accepted so late that his courses (on money and banking
and trade policy) could not be included in the catalog for the
winter semester of 1899-1900. His inaugural lecture, "The Effects
of the Increased Gold Production," had, however, an unusually
distinguished audience: Theodor Mommsen and Max Sering
from the faculty, Max von Thielman from the Treasury, Rudolf
von Delbrück, Friedrich Hammacher and other deputies of
liberal economic inclinations, and "leading figures" from the
banking and business world.[36] Was it the enticing nature of the
topic or Helfferich's reputation for brilliance that summoned
these eminent men? One wonders if the lecture had not turned
into a demonstration of the economic elite in favor of their representative at the University of Berlin.

Helfferich, indeed, had great doubts whether a career at Berlin
was still possible. He accordingly considered taking a position
offered him in 1900 at the Kolonialinstitut in Hamburg, and
turned to Richard Koch for help. Helfferich suggested: "The
offer from Hamburg might perhaps be the occasion for the government to make a declaration of their views on me, and that
would help me considerably." He unctuously concluded: "I can
hope for nothing more than the opportunity of remaining in Berlin and thus being able to continue my defense of our money and
banking system."[37] Koch got the message.

Helfferich had taken steps to supplement his meager income
as a Privatdozent by contracting to give a series of lectures in
Hamburg on trade policy. His fortunes took another turn for the
better when the Prussian Culture Ministry asked him in October
1900 whether he would accept an extraordinary professorship at
Kiel. He was also offered a lecture series at the Marine Academy
at Kiel, and that he accepted. Before he could express himself on
the extraordinary professorship, however, the Culture Minister

---

[36] Scheffbuch, *Helfferich*, 26.   [37] Lumm, *Helfferich*, 93.

himself canceled the offer, as he wished to keep Helfferich in Berlin. Helfferich clearly had to be given something in replacement. A short time later, the Seminar for Oriental Languages, an offshoot of the Colonial Division which gave instruction on a variety of colonial and foreign trade matters, asked Helfferich to lecture on trade policy. He accepted. His week was now split in half, the first half being spent in Hamburg and Kiel, and the second half in Berlin. The schedule would have been impossible for an ordinary man, but Helfferich managed to pile considerable scholarship on top of it. He wrote a long introductory essay for a memorial volume of Ludwig Bamberger's writings and speeches on the currency question. The essay bears witness to his respect and affection for Bamberger, and Bamberger showed that he regarded Helfferich as his intellectual heir by leaving Helfferich his excellent library on economics when he died in 1899. Helfferich was also working hard on a text on money commissioned in the fall of 1898. Finally, he managed to find time for a series of essays for a memorial volume commemorating the 25th anniversary of the Reichsbank, as well as some scholarly articles.[38]

The Writings on Money and Banking

Helfferich had begun writing about the Reichsbank in 1898 while awaiting the outcome of his *Habilitation*. After the defeat of bimetallism, the Junkers had directed a part of their anticapitalist campaign against the Reichsbank, the charter of which was up for renewal in 1899. Helfferich's arguments on this question are hardly so singular as to justify extended treatment. His case against the Junkers was entirely conventional, as were the reforms he supported, which had Koch's complete approval.[39]

---

[38] Scheffbuch, *Helfferich*, 26-29; Helfferich, "Bamberger als Währungspolitiker," in *Ausgewählte Reden und Aufsätze über Geld und Bankwesen von Ludwig Bamberger*, ed. Karl Helfferich (Berlin, 1900), 1-158; Germany, Reichsbank, *Die Reichsbank 1876-1900* (Berlin, 1900), to which, according to Lumm, Helfferich contributed anonymously the following articles: "Einleitung," "Notenausgabe," "Diskontpolitik," "Reglung [*sic*] des Geldumlaufs," and "Die Banknovelle vom 7. Juni 1899 als Ergebnis der bisherigen Entwicklung."

[39] His principal works on the renewal of the banking law are the book

Helfferich's passionate defense of the bank explains, indeed, why Koch was so anxious to keep Helfferich close at hand in Berlin.

His defense proceeded from his *Reform* and was based on his usual careful examination of the bank's record. What the Junkers most held against the bank was its alleged discrimination against them and its high interest rates, and their remedy was nationalization. Their intent was to make the bank more amenable to serving the "real" interests of the nation. As had earlier been true of his arguments in favor of the gold standard, Helfferich's arguments on the nationalization question are more convincing than those of his opponents largely because of his superior mastery of the facts. His arguments are thus of interest primarily as additional evidence of his animus against the Junkers, and for what they reveal of contemporary attitudes about the proper relationship between the business world and the bureaucracy, the role of banks as financial institutions, and private property.

Helfferich's case against nationalization is interesting rather than convincing. The idea basically horrified him. He considered that what the Junkers really wanted was to force the bank to make loans "on the no-repayment plan (*auf Nimmerwiedersehen*)."[40] He unkindly added that if things continued as they were, the strong would soon have to band together against the weak. But otherwise his arguments rested on a firm conviction of the virtues of capitalism as an economic system. He considered that a state bank would no longer be able to draw upon the business community for advice and counsel in the way the Reichsbank presently could, because the business community would not look upon a state bank as their "own." Moreover, given the severely

---

Zur Erneuerung des deutschen Bankgesetzes (Leipzig, 1899), the pamphlet *Die Reichsbank: Verhandlungen der Plenarversammlung des deutschen Handelstages vom 14. März 1898: mit einer Einleitung von Karl Helfferich* (Stuttgart, 1898), and the following articles: "Bankdiskont und Notensteuer," *Die Nation*, 14 (1897), 252-56; and "Erneuerung des Privilegiums der Reichsbank," *ibid.*, 15 (1898), 279-81, 295-99, 315-17, and 333-37.

[40] "Privilegium der Reichsbank," 280-81. In point of fact, the Reichsbank was fairly accommodating to landowners and the economically weak; Bopp, "Reichsbank," 45-47, 54. For Helfferich's arguments on nationalization, see *Zur Erneuerung*, 48-68.

limiting juristic training of most civil servants, they could hardly be expected to manage such a bank competently.

Despite the alleged strength of the German tradition of state interference in economic matters, Helfferich considered that the bureaucracy lacked the intimate and detailed knowledge to undertake such interference intelligently. He had, as we have seen in connection with his *Reform*, a very skeptical view of man's ability to plan large-scale activities reaching very far into the future, at least if such activities went much beyond establishing the necessary minimum of an institutional framework. Accordingly, to place extensive economic powers in the hands of the state was not only pointless but harmful. An additional practical argument to his mind was that in time of war, as the experience of the Bank of France in 1870 showed, the fate of a private bank was not tied to that of the state. It might borrow on good terms for the state, even if the latter were bankrupt, and its properties were safe from seizure as reparations. As Director of the Deutsche Bank, Helfferich was later to advance similar arguments to protect the bank's Bagdad Railway from the consequences of the Balkan Wars of 1912 and 1913. These wars stripped the Turks of most of their European territories, from which much of the revenue supporting the obligations of the railway had come. Helfferich reasoned that since the Turkish Public Debt, a private institution, had collected the lost revenues, they could not properly be seized by the Balkan states but still were due the Debt. Such viewpoints also explain the singular outrage with which Helfferich and other businessmen regarded enemy expropriations of German foreign assets during World War I. The specific war aims Helfferich and others were to propose may have been designed to safeguard the German economy from the effect of such seizures in the future.[41]

The reforms Helfferich himself proposed were largely designed to loosen some of the restrictions earlier placed upon the

[41] His clearest statements from this period about the role of the state in economic matters are to be found in his writings on colonial policy cited in n.58 below. For his proposals to compensate the Bagdad Railway for its lost revenues, see Ch. 3 below; and for his war-aims proposals, see Ch. 7 below.

bank which experience showed were either unnecessary or, in the case of various loan and note-issue restrictions, had been outgrown. One of these reforms, the enlargement of the capital of the bank, can best be considered in connection with his ideas on money, but the other, restriction of the note-issue powers of the private banks, deserves mention here. He objected to the way in which such banks issued the maximum legal amount of notes in good times and thus could not meet demands for additional liquidity in bad. That threw the entire burden of meeting such emergencies on the Reichsbank. What Helfferich and his contemporaries failed to see was that this gave the Reichsbank more, not less, control over the financial markets, because the private banks did not have the reserves to oppose the Reichsbank's policy. But Helfferich, like his contemporaries, did not consider that a central bank should, or even could, increase or restrain the tempo of economic activity. As guardian of the currency, the role of the central bank was simply to provide the amount of money, usually by expanding or contracting the note issue, required by the general level of business activity. It was fitting that one who saw money as being a neutral element in the way that Helfferich did would assign a largely passive role to the guardian of the monetary system.[42]

Helfferich had begun his most systematic exposition of the role of money in late 1898. When he left the academic world late in 1901, his book, entitled simply *Money*, was nearly finished, though it was not finally published until 1903. It was not a revolutionary work like Knapp's *State Theory of Money* (1905), but was rather an excellent statement of fairly conventional views. Its strength was its clear exposition and the wealth of historical and technical information it contained. It was extremely popular, going through six editions in German and being translated into a variety of other languages, including Japanese. Helfferich deservedly owed much of his reputation as an economist to the work. But along with its virtues, the work revealed that as a theorist Helfferich had some serious shortcomings. Since a good discus-

[42] For Helfferich's reform proposals and a recent criticism of the assumptions they were based on, see *Zur Erneuerung*, 26-27, 83-96; Bopp, "Reichsbank," 189, 191-92, 214.

sion of these theories already exists, however, we need consider them here only to the degree that they explain Helfferich's outlooks upon economic activity and his future acts as policymaker.[43]

His book is divided into a shorter "Historical Part" and a longer "Theoretical Part." The former covered the development of money and monetary systems and their histories down to the end of the nineteenth century. His studies once again confirmed that deduction was no substitute for historical research in divining the origins of institutions. He hence rejected rationalistic but plausible explanations that men had developed money to eliminate the inconveniences of barter as being on a par with the idea of a social contract: research showed that the facts were different. Indeed, he went to the opposite extreme: "Once one has seized upon the thread of the historical development [of money], then it is easy to formulate the results deductively, and perhaps even to prove that the [actual] developments . . . *were the only ones possible.*"[44]

He thought that the record had clearly established the superiority of metallic standards, with gold at the pinnacle of excellence. He admitted that while the state could secure the acceptance of paper currency, it "will continue to be regarded in practice as an anomaly" and a sign that the state was in serious diffi-

[43] Helfferich, *Das Geld* (Leipzig, 1903). Helfferich revised *Das Geld* in 1910 and again in 1923. A careful comparison of the three editions showed that the addition of new historical material, a few revisions aimed at making the narrative clearer, and a consideration of Knapp were the principal changes from the first to the last editions. There are no important differences between the first and the last edition in the material cited in this chapter. I have therefore generally cited from the 6th edition of 1923 as translated into English and published as *Money* (2 vols., New York, 1927). Howard S. Ellis, *German Monetary Theory 1905-1933* (Cambridge, Mass., 1934), 60-71, 160-62, 253-56, 269, 280, 292, places Helfferich in context and discusses his theoretical shortcomings at some length (esp. 60-71).

[44] "Die geschichtliche Entwicklung der Münzsysteme," *Studien*, 3-4, my italics. A comparison with the section on the origins of money in *Money*, esp. 3-14, shows that the latter is merely more detailed and not so concisely stated as in this citation from "Die geschichtliche Entwicklung." This is but one of many instances where Helfferich took over without essential alteration the substance of an earlier study for the appropriate section of *Das Geld*.

culty; he had no faith in man's ability to use wisely his power to control a paper currency. Nor did later events shake these prejudices. In a book published in 1906 on finance during the Russo-Japanese War, he attributed Russia's ability to borrow so heavily abroad after 1897 and its avoidance of serious consequences after defeat by Japan largely to the success of Sergei Witte, the Russian Finance Minister, in establishing Russian currency so securely on gold.[45] And writing in 1923, in the midst of one of the most drastic and terrifying inflations on record, Helfferich felt more strongly than ever that the prewar years had been a golden age:

> This process of development [of world currency systems] consolidated the monetary institutions of the different countries, and at the same time brought such security and stability in the relations between the various systems that, without the intervention of any connecting links, they presented an orderly and well-established international whole, resting on the common basis of the gold standard. This international monetary machine was an integral part of the entire economic system . . . while at the same time the machine's own working and continued existence depended on the undisturbed functioning of the economic system of the world.[46]

In the "Theoretical Part" of his book, which characteristically was devoted in good part of matters quite remote from theory, Helfferich chose to define money on the basis of its position in the economic order. He considered money one of three "intermediary" goods, the other two being transportation and capital goods as usually defined. He upheld this somewhat novel position by asserting that since money facilitated trade, it was a means of production in the larger sense because it increased the value of goods by abetting their transfer from those with less use for them to those with more.[47] This exalted view of money and transport, it may be said in passing, explains in part the emphasis Helfferich was later to place on the preeminent need for sound

[45] *Money*, 620; *Das Geld im russisch-japanischen Kriege: ein finanzpolitischer Beitrag zur Zeitgeschichte* (Berlin, 1906), esp. 132-33.
[46] *Money*, 208.   [47] *Ibid.*, 277-84.

44

money and adequate transport if the German colonies were ever to be developed. It also explains his tenacious pursuit of monetary and transport controls as a means of securing German economic hegemony in post-World War I Europe, and, in addition, the excessive distrust with which he viewed postwar Allied efforts, particularly as reflected in the Dawes Plan of 1924, to subject German fiscal and transport institutions to such controls. This is not to say that such controls are not important means of influence, only that they were not such powerful instruments of either development or subjugation as Helfferich imagined.[48]

The next two sections of the "Theoretical Part" cover money as a legal institution (characteristically omitted in the English translation) and existing monetary systems, and because of their largely descriptive nature need not detain us. In the fourth and last section, Helfferich discussed the "demand for money," the "supply of money," and the "value of money."

In discussing the "demand for money," Helfferich was principally at pains to set himself off from contemporary quantity-theorists. He denied that such theories revealed anything useful about how much money was demanded in part because they assumed the velocity of circulation was automatically, indeed mechanically, determined by the imperatives of the equation of exchange. This trenchant criticism, unfortunately, was based on certain assumptions which led Helfferich to hold mistaken ideas about the role of banks in the monetary system. It was in fact true that contemporary quantity theories could not accommodate the "cash-saving" devices of the banking system, which, as Helfferich pictured it, reduced the total demand for cash by transferring idle balances to those who needed money. Such transfers speeded "effective" circulation, whereas the use of checks and other credit instruments reduced the demand for money

---

[48] In his *Geld im russisch-japanischen Kriege*, 5, he speaks revealingly of the connection "between financial and military capacity," recognized by both Japan and Russia and the principal spur for their industrialization. What he is doing is to use "financial" in place of "economic" or in the present instance, "economic development." Although he can hardly be criticized for holding oversimplified views on economic development, a field which has come into its own only since World War II, his use of the word "financial" does indicate what sort of influences entered his field of vision and what sort did not.

"through a decrease in the effective rapidity of circulation of money." By modern lights, this is an odd thing to say, but Helfferich's failure, normal in his day, to consider bank deposits money in the usual sense explains it. He used the words "money" and "cash" almost interchangeably and seems to have misunderstood the nature of banking, which he seems to have considered the same in the monetary sense as brokerage.[49]

These misapprehensions about the role of banks explain his advocacy of the second of his proposed Reichsbank reforms, already alluded to above. His proposal was to increase the paid-in capital of the Reichsbank in order that it might make more secured loans in the future. He feared that the bank might at some point have to refuse to make good loans because it had no money to lend. The proposal was based on erroneous contemporary notions about what constituted suitable reserves for a central bank and on how the banking system creates money. Actually, if secured loans had been made legal reserves for the currency the whole problem would have disappeared.[50] Since he did not consider such loans a suitable reserve, the only solution Helfferich could see was to increase the cash reserve available for lending; here, as elsewhere, he clearly identified the coins and notes that left the bank with the coins and notes that had earlier come in.

Helfferich's chapter on the "supply of money" in fact failed to consider bank deposits and role of banks in creating them at all. Only one short section, out of seven, was even on paper money. The others were on the supply of precious metals and their use in industry and as currency. From Helfferich's point of view, his allocation of space was reasonable, since he did not, correctly, consider credit instruments as money under most circumstances. Yet even in pre-1914 Germany bank deposits (if not credit instruments such as checks) were a very important part of the money supply, as now defined.[51]

[49] *Money*, 455-56. See also the strictures of Roy Harrod, review of Karl Helfferich's *Money*, in *Economic Journal*, 38 (1928), 98-101.

[50] For a fuller discussion, see Bopp, "Reichsbank," 50-51.

[51] Lest Helfferich be made to appear simple-minded, it should be pointed out that founders of the American Federal Reserve System also failed to consider bank deposits money and in fact approached their task with as-

The last chapter of *Money* was on the "value of money." In assigning specific levels to the value of money, Helfferich ran into considerable trouble because he persisted in treating money as a commodity subject to the laws of supply and demand like all others. He thought that since as a rule money was the standard from which other goods took their values, its own value could not be measured. The most one could do, he felt, was to chart changes in the value of money, which he attributed mainly to changes in the supply. Because the individual cared but little about the specific number of marks in his pocket, being interested only in their total purchasing power, alterations in the supply of money were soon reflected in price levels.[52] The tendency of all this was to make money, particularly under the gold standard, a fairly neutral element in the determination of general price levels. Most changes in value occurred on the goods side of the equation of exchange, not on the money side. His study of attempts to chart changes in the value of money through price indexes merely reinforced his view that money was the passive element. As he had earlier done in the gold-standard controversy, he emphasized that what indexes with all their deficiencies revealed was that the most important changes were changes in the costs of production, which were reflected on the goods side of the equation.[53]

In arguing that purely monetary influences on price levels were generally exaggerated, Helfferich was correct, but he himself went overboard in the other direction, seriously underestimating the effects of monetary influences. His definition of money left out too much, and his failure to consider the role of banks in the money-creating process meant that some of the most important monetary influences on price levels did not enter his ken.

---

sumptions very similar to Helfferich's. The idea that bank deposits are part of the money supply became established among academic economists only in the late twenties, after Helfferich's death.

[52] For the merits of his views on this question, see Ellis, *German Monetary Theory*, 61, 63, 68, 76.

[53] *Money*, 533. Because of the enormous interest index numbers elicited in post-World War I Germany, Helfferich's treatment of indexes in the 6th edition (1923) was much more detailed than in earlier editions, but the essence of his argument was the same.

Even given his premises, money was hardly so neutral as he made it. He asserted that booms had "no kind of connection" with changes in the money stock. To him, the fact that rising prices and interest rates usually went together proved that money was a neutral element. Money reacted to economic changes, it did not initiate them.[54] He would have been astonished at present-day efforts to control the economy through the exercise of monetary policy. We will see, indeed, that his own ideas about the proper role of the guardian of state finances were —even admitting the distinction between monetary and fiscal policy—quite different. In the concluding summation of his book, entitled "The ideal of a currency with a constant purchasing power," he reiterated his conviction that the gold standard came the closest to this ideal. He admitted once more that a paper currency might seem to meet the ideal more fully, but doubted that man would acquire the skill to manage such a currency very soon.[55] He believed in progress, but had little faith in the efficacy of deliberate efforts to secure it.

These lessons about money were unfortunate ones for a future wartime Treasury Secretary to learn because they made impossible a correct assessment of his responsibilities. It would be manifestly unfair, however, to tax Helfferich with holding views which although mistaken were academically respectable and were not to be successfully challenged until after his death. Whatever Helfferich's theoretical shortcomings, one of his academic critics, the monetary theorist Robert Liefmann, called the book the "best systematic work on money."[56] And Helfferich did make some minor contributions to theory, though none that was particularly important.[57] Still, *Money* was a tremendously erudite

[54] *Ibid.*, 566, 569. Rudolf Havenstein, President of the Reichsbank from 1908 to 1923, shared this opinion. For some of its unfortunate practical consequences, see Bopp, "Reichsbank," 206, and Ch. 10 below. Roy Harrod commented: "He [Helfferich] takes the nominal rate of discount at its face value and argues that because money is often dear in a time of rising prices, the cause of the price change cannot be 'on the side of money.' Indeed certain sentences seem even to suggest a naive confusion between the value of money and the price of money in the money-market sense"; review of *Money*, 99.

[55] *Money*, 620-21.   [56] *Geld*, 6th edn., 552n2.

[57] Ellis, *German Monetary Theory*, 76. Since Joseph A. Schumpeter, *His-*

book and all the more remarkable because Helfferich was under thirty when he finished it. After reading it one can readily understand his continuing fascination with money as an economic institution and the great stress he was to lay in the future on the creation of sound monetary institutions as the foundation for all other economic activity. He combined these ideas with a view of money that made its workings virtually automatic, which is probably why he later was to regard control of a state's monetary arrangements as the first step toward control of all else; he seems to have believed that if its workings were automatic then control of all else automatically followed. If this made money both more and less important than it really was, it was a view Helfferich shared with many of his contemporaries.

Germany and the World

In this early period, Helfferich addressed himself to the problem of Germany's economic future in his *Habilitation* trial lecture on "Malthusian population doctrines and the *Industriestaat*" and in the lecture series on trade policy he gave at Hamburg during 1900 and 1901. During his term in the Colonial Division and shortly thereafter he also wrote a series of articles on the importance of colonies, which, though growing out of his experiences in colonial administration, belong intellectually with the works on trade policy and the industry state.[58] His common concern in all cases was with how Germany could best assert itself as an economic and political power in the modern world.

---

tory of Economic Analysis (New York, 1954), 1081, uses Helfferich's *Geld* as an example of the fact that advances in monetary theory were not penetrating the "common run" of the literature, too much should not be made of Helfferich's contributions to theory.

[58] *Die Malthussche Bevölkerungslehre und der moderne Industriestaat* (Munich, 1899); *Handelspolitik: Vorträge gehalten in Hamburg im Winter 1900/1901 im Auftrag der Hamburgischen Oberschulbehörde* (Leipzig, 1901); and on the colonies, "Die Baumwollefrage: ein weltwirtschaftliches Problem," *Marine Rundschau*, 15 (1904), 641-67; "Die Bedeutung der Kolonieen für die deutsche Volkswirtschaft," in *Verhandlungen des Deutschen Kolonialkongresses zu Berlin am 5., 6. und 7. Oktober 1905* (Berlin, 1906), 571-84; *Zur Reform der kolonialen Verwaltungs-Organisation* (Berlin, 1905); and "Am Scheideweg der Weltpolitik," *Deutsche Kolonialzeitung: Organ der deutschen Kolonialgesellschaft* (1907), 35-40.

Helfferich began his disquisition on Malthus and the *Industriestaat* by condemning the tendency of many economists to judge developments rather than trying to understand them. The reality behind German industrialization was the huge population increase in Germany and other parts of Europe. Most discussions, he said, noted this increase, the rapidly growing dependence on foreign grain which resulted, and then drew on Malthusian doctrines to condemn such dependence and the industrialization which made it possible. Helfferich conceded that if, as Malthus stated, the welfare of a nation depended on its being able to support its population, Germany's situation was bad. But the most Helfferich would admit was that events might eventually justify Malthus's predictions for the world as a whole. Recent events in the industrialized nations directly contradicted Malthus. Population had far outstripped food supply, yet prosperity was rapidly increasing. Within capitalist economies the problem of most men was finding jobs. These the *Industriestaat* provided in abundance. As Helfferich saw it, the Irish depopulation during the nineteenth century was the direct result of a lack of jobs resulting from the adoption of labor-saving farming techniques.[59] Quite different was the situation in England and Germany, where industry was able to absorb both the natural increase in population and the surplus population of the land.

Since Helfferich neither foresaw nor desired a halt in the population increase, he reasoned that further industrialization was both inevitable and desirable. Given those facts, it was important to assure the rapidly growing working classes a share of industrial profits sufficient to allow them to consume an adequate share of the industrial product. If they could not, unemployment was likely. In contradiction to Malthus, who held welfare legislation harmful, Helfferich asserted that such legislation played an important part in assuring the masses a fair share of the industrial product:

[59] Helfferich evidently had the facts wrong about the reasons for Irish depopulation, which was the result of famine and pestilence and was a particularly horrible illustration of Malthusian doctrine; see, for example, Thomas W. Freeman, *Pre-famine Ireland: A Study in Historical Geography* (Manchester, 1957).

50

The proper understanding of these matters . . . shows that a numerous population and the well-being of the masses are not irreconcilables; rather, the amelioration of the working classes sought by the best spirits of our time must ease the path of population increases necessary for any sound and energetic race and thus assure our people its place in the great struggle for existence among nations.[60]

Helfferich's lectures on tariff policy and articles on the colonies covered many of the same points, while placing far greater emphasis on the future position of Germany in the world. In elucidating his views on tariffs, he emphasized that international trade was nothing more than the large-scale "division of labor [that] is the basis of our economic constitution," the function of which was to reconcile natural and artificial differences in resources. In a remark that accurately foretold Germany's economic difficulties during the First World War, he commented: "It can hardly be imagined how much poorer and harder our material existence would be were we ever to be thrown back solely on the resources of our own fatherland." Thus it paid densely populated Germany to concentrate on industry while leaving farming to thinly populated foreign lands. The workings of the doctrine of comparative international advantage had assured that the relative decline of German agriculture was nevertheless accompanied in the decade before 1900 by "the most brilliant development of economic forces," developments which had "excited admirations and envy everywhere in the world"—except among the Junkers. And he noted as proof of the "mighty lifting of economic and material culture . . . which [was] bound up with our so-called *Industriestaat*," the ability of the masses to purchase "nonessentials." Their rising consumption of articles such as sugar and coffee did not mean they were getting "soft" as some critics asserted, merely that for the first time the common man could afford to spend some of his income on luxuries.[61]

In searching for guideposts to the future, Helfferich, good historian that he was, turned to the past. He traced the flaws in mercantilist economic theory which had led to the struggle for em-

[60] *Bevölkerungslehre*, 32.　　　[61] *Handelspolitik*, 10, 35.

pire beginning in 1648 and ending only with the defeat of Napoleon in 1815. He also noted the downfall of Mercantilism, the
victory of free trade in England, and the enormous advantages
which England's timely conversion to free trade had gained the
country. The rhapsodic nature of these passages leaves no doubt
that Helfferich was by sympathy an enthusiastic Manchesterite.
Though German developments differed from English, the German free-trade policy of the sixties and seventies was also the
outcome of natural historical developments. Quite the opposite
was Bismarck's overthrow of free trade in 1879. Helfferich
counted the developments which the protective tariffs ushered
in as "none too favorable." The return to less restrictive policies
with the Caprivi treaties of 1893-1894 set things right again, however, and Helfferich held them in good part responsible for the
post-1894 boom. Since he was proselytizing for the renewal of
the treaties, he may perhaps be pardoned for exaggerating their
salubrious effects.[62]

Helfferich believed that a new age of economic conflict had
begun in the nineties, a struggle for empire similar to that before
1815. But Germany was not a self-contained economic unit rich
in natural resources like the United States, nor was it able to
draw upon the resources of a great empire as the English could.
More than any other nation, Germany had to trade with the outside world to live. The instruments which German foreign
policy had at its command for keeping foreign markets open were
commercial policy, productive colonies, and a strong navy. Helfferich specifically repudiated any notion of autarky; the function
of colonies was to act as a "support for our world-wide economic
interests, as pillars of that greater Germany which exists everywhere that German economic enterprise is active." Nor was the
argument valid that because Germany had gotten along without
colonies and a navy in the past, she could do so in the future: "A
more dangerous and more foolish idea has never been expressed." Even England was shifting away from a policy of free
trade to one of controls, in order to preserve her competitive ad-

[62] *Ibid.*, 57. There would seem to be less reason to excuse Barkin, *Controversy over German Industrialization*, Ch. 3, who wildly exaggerates the
treaties' beneficial effects.

vantage. The alternative was not really *Weltpolitik* or no, the choice was between remaining great or fading away: "Germany would have to give itself over to its fate, and after a short efflorescence of its national powers, resign itself in the future to the role of a continental power, a state of the second rank."[63]

Helfferich considered colonies and trade policy to be mutually supporting. Free trade was no longer possible; a tariff wall had to be erected so that holes could be punched in it in return for others doing the same. Productive colonies merely widened the field for the operation of a successful commercial policy. The right to trade in German colonies could thus be offered, say, in return for a favored trading position in French colonies. There were some raw materials, moreover, that were particularly essential to certain industries, which came largely from one supplier. The most important was American cotton, which was being offered in smaller amounts every year. Helfferich thought some of the German colonies had very good prospects as cotton producers, an opinion shared by most others influential in determining German colonial policy.[64]

To protect the colonies and foreign trade Germany needed a navy. Helfferich doubted that the struggle for empire was likely to proceed peacefully: "Si vis pacem, para bellum." Considering the implications of this idea for commercial policy, he stated: "Political power, above all at sea, has by no means lost its significance as an instrument of commercial policy, even when it need not be actively employed but merely by its mute presence takes away an opponent's desire and courage to do violence to trade." Although in the course of the next decade it was to become unmistakably clear that the construction of a German battle fleet was the greatest obstacle to good relations with England and the most important source of her mistrust of Germany's intentions,

[63] "Die Bedeutung der Kolonieen," 578, 580.
[64] For Helfferich's views on cotton production, see "Die Baumwollefrage." The later colonial secretaries, Bernhard Dernburg and Wilhelm Solf, shared Helfferich's interest in freeing Germany from dependence on American cotton; Harry A. Rudin, *Germans in the Cameroons: A Case Study of Modern Imperialism* (New Haven, 1938), 136, 208. The Cameroons has never become much of a cotton producer. Helfferich, like other contemporary advocates of colonial development, seriously underestimated the difficulties.

Helfferich even in 1919 was not inclined to question the naval policies he had earlier advocated: given Germany's overseas economic interests, navy-building lay "in the nature of things." Considering how backward German naval preparations were in 1900, Helfferich believed English alarm unreasonable and merely a particular instance of the tendency of other European states to regard any German armament measures as a "threat to world peace," while judging their own military spending reasonable measures of self-defense.[65]

At the time he was writing and lecturing on trade policy and the colonies, Helfferich was not unduly sanguine about the prospects for the policies he recommended. He thought that the "crass political power" of the Junkers might well enable them to block trade policies in the interests of the "generality." In the case of colonial policy, too, he thought that those who opposed colonial developments usually did so for selfish reasons. He admitted that his own emphasis on industrialization had its dangers, but he considered them unavoidable and exaggerated by critics. If war were really feared then the bread of the industrial worker should be kept cheap to make him the strongest possible soldier. As it was, the greater numbers of urban workers more than overbalanced whatever slight physical superiority the peasants as individuals might possess.[66]

At this time he foresaw, and his later 1906 study of the Russo-Japanese War confirmed his opinion, that future wars would be short. The danger of being so long cut off from the rest of the world that food supplies ran out seemed remote: "Anyway, what kind of a war would have to be that could block our land and sea frontiers to grain imports?" He thought that "even to consider such a possibility . . . is to look upon our foreign policy with a limitless mistrust." He also cherished enough of the Cobdenite ideal to believe that growing international economic interdependence made war increasingly unlikely: "Where a thousand threads tie individuals together, threads that no one can rip asunder without injuring himself, peace and order rule." He accordingly concluded: "War between two great nations is impos-

[65] *Handelspolitik*, 83-84; *Weltkrieg*, 1, 50-59.
[66] *Handelspolitik*, 165, 194-96.

sible unless the victor is also ready to assume the most frightful kind of economic damage."[67]

In considering the need for an active colonial policy, Helfferich went beyond the need for industrialization as the necessary support for a "perhaps unavoidable *Weltpolitik* on a grand scale" and attempted to provide his people with a cultural mission which would document not only the vitality but also the peaceful character of Germany's world-wide economic activities.[68]

> If Germany devotes a part of its excess strength . . . to this task [of colonial development], it will remove a good part of the mistrust with which people all over the world follow and interpret our every movement. . . . Other nations see our burgeoning power, our rapidly growing population, the expansion of [our] trade and industry, and a spirit of economic enterprise for which no task appears too great; these nations have the distinct feeling that every force requires adequate occupation if it is not to have destructive effects; these nations also have the feeling that Germany so far has found no . . . peaceful occupation for these forces. . . . We appear in the fantasy of other nations as a hungry lion who goes roaring about, seeking the person he will gobble up next.

A perceptive appreciation of how apprehensively other countries regarded Germany's multifarious but apparently aimless foreign activities, this statement is an attempt to quiet these apprehensions by setting the German people a nobler task than the pursuit of wealth and power alone.

An Estimate

The volume and variety of Helfferich's writings attest to the speed and efficiency with which he worked. His work, moreover, is exceedingly clear, readable, and informative. The stock of basic ideas he expressed in the decade after 1895 was to change but little for the rest of his life. Even during this period it is difficult to find cases where he held different views on the same question,

---

[67] *Ibid.*, 197; *Malthussche Bevölkerungslehre*, 25-26.
[68] *Handelspolitik*, 206; "Scheideweg der Weltpolitik," 39.

whereas countless examples could be adduced where he incorporated, almost verbatim, ideas and illustrations from earlier writings into later ones. His wife commented that once finished with something he was disinclined to return to it.[69] This evidently included rethinking his ideas. His intellectual self-confidence certainly contributed to the speed with which he worked and may be part of the explanation for his lack of interest in the larger questions of development that so exercised Max Weber and Gustav Schmoller. A more important reason for his lack of interest in such questions was the empirical and rather uncritical nature of his intellectual interests. He did not want to change the existing system, only to understand it and to help other practical men do so. His aim as a scholar was to provide the man of affairs with the sort of information needed for judging the economic questions of the day—tables of statistics and historical narratives packed with facts.

Helfferich was at his best in economic history. He was an excellent historian and his analysis of price movements, the decline of European agriculture, the benefits of the industrial revolution, and the limitations of price indexes, to name only four examples, sound quite up-to-date. His economic theory was his weakest point. That was true of the younger historical school generally, and also, theory is more subject to obsolescence than "facts." He differed from the senior members of the younger historical school both in his lack of interest in *Sozialpolitik* and his espousal of moderate laissez-faire capitalism. For these reasons and also because of his association with Bamberger, he was often regarded as a throwback to Bamberger's generation. That was true only in a very limited sense. While many younger economists shared Helfferich's sympathy for *Sozialpolitik*, like him they saw the real solution of the social problem in the continued expansion of German industry.[70] If the pie were larger there would be plenty for all. For Helfferich, the problem was to secure a solid basis for industrial expansion by keeping the German monetary system sound and by using political and economic leverage to keep for-

[69] Interview with Annette Helfferich, 11 July 1962.
[70] See, for example, the discussion of Ludwig Bernhard's *Die unerwünschten Folgen der deutschen Sozialpolitik* (1912) in Born, *Sozialpolitik*, 245.

eign markets open. Similarly, because of his concern for these ends, he did not, despite his emotional commitment to laissez faire, advocate unrestrained competition as a good in itself. His goal was to obtain maximum growth from the available resources. He thus favored the creation of a strong central bank, the use of tariffs to protect national economic interests, and other measures of interference designed to create a favorable economic environment. He also favored cartels and, as we will see in the case of the Bagdad Railway, the orderly division of geographical spheres of economic activity with the aim of eliminating wasteful competition.[71]

Helfferich thought that the attainment of the policies he favored would be simple if the power of agrarian reaction were pruned back.[72] Because of the passion with which he opposed the Junkers, he was frequently considered at the time to stand on the Left, but this missed the essence of his position. Actually, he was always to be found defending the *status quo* against reaction while suggesting only modest reforms. He was at odds with the Wilhelmine social order only in thinking that the commercial and industrial classes for whom he spoke should have more voice in political matters than they had. He believed that the bureaucracy was doing a good job of creating a favorable climate for the individual entrepreneurial acts that were so rapidly building German economic strength and hence laying the foundations for German world power. And, although he railed at Junker privilege and influence, he was no democrat himself. He favored the rule of an educated elite, and his ideas of the role of legislative assemblies were accordingly limited. He saw the function of these bodies largely as one of providing expert advice on legislative matters, such as monetary and banking reform where the

[71] For Helfferich's remarks on the positive features of monopoly, see *Georg von Siemens: ein Lebensbild aus Deutschlands grosser Zeit* (3 vols., Berlin, 1921-1923), I, 197; *Deutschlands Volkswohlstand 1888-1913* (4th edn., Berlin, 1914), 47; and for the Bagdad Railway, Ch. 3 below.

[72] Here again, Helfferich's views were widely shared by contemporaries; see Wolfgang J. Mommsen, *Max Weber und die deutsche Politik* (Tübingen, 1959), esp. 23-38, for Weber's similar views on this and other questions such as tariffs and the fleet; and Theodor Heuss, *Friedrich Naumann: der Mann, das Werk, die Zeit* (2nd edn., Tübingen, 1938), 149-50, 160-63.

bureaucracy had little experience or training, and then explaining what had been done to the people. But, like the economic liberal that he was, he viewed anxiously any more government activity in economic matters than was necessary to level the obstacles to economic expansion.

Helfferich had a firm belief that mankind was continually moving toward greater perfection. But progress was mainly the result of unseen agencies—he speaks of "historical necessities"—and only accidentally the result of human interference. Progress was most likely if everyone worked hard in his own area of special competence without consciously seeking the advancement of the commonweal, which was likely to occur in quite unforeseeable ways. His prejudice was for existing institutions, since their continued existence was in a sense their historical justification. Moreover, since German progress was clearly visible, its institutions must be good ones. While small modifications in accord with the general tendency of historical development were sometimes advisable, extensive ones were not. Such attitudes predisposed Helfferich to consider major criticisms of existing institutions captious, and explains why he was so much better able to see the strengths than the weaknesses of Wilhelmine institutions. He was, in fact, open to the charge that Golo Mann levels at other historians of the empire, namely, that he was a "eulogist of the new order."[73] His prejudice for the *status quo* and slow evolutionary change was reinforced by a strong belief in German greatness. Like most of his contemporaries, however, he accepted the idea that violence often accompanied change. He spoke of the "struggle for existence among nations," and assumed the alternative to a successful *Weltpolitik* was national decline. But he did not think Germany destined for such a fate, even though he considered that in the "new struggle for empire" wars were quite possible. As we have seen, however, he assumed future wars would be short, limited affairs, for economic interdependence made long wars an impossibility.

Indeed, Helfferich was not only a man rooted in his times, he was an enthusiastic reflection of them. Unlike the sort of "cultural

[73] Golo Mann, *Deutsche Geschichte des neunzehnten und zwanzigsten Jahrhunderts* (Frankfurt a. M., 1958), 455.

pessimists" or anti-modernist critics so skillfully analyzed by Fritz Stern, Helfferich was before 1918 a cultural optimist and the epitome of modernity.[74] He was an intellectual spokesman for the more enlightened sectors of the business community. Because of his academic training, however, he admittedly held his ideas for more sophisticated and self-conscious reasons than his business compeers can have done. But they supported, and supported with great zeal, the pressure groups, such as the Navy League, that were in general committed to the same sort of capitalist economic growth and *Weltpolitik* that so stirred Helfferich's imagination. To make such an assertion is not to deny the differences that arose over specific issues within the business community between, say, the great commercial banks and the big steel makers, nor those important personal conflicts and rivalries that arose among individuals. It is simply to assert that such rivalries should not be allowed to obscure the existence of a basic consensus in the leading sectors of the business community on the fundamental economic and political questions, nor the fact that Helfferich shared and espoused these assumptions, and in a way that many academic economists did not.

[74] Stern, *The Politics of Cultural Despair*. Ringer, *Decline of the German Mandarins*, is also very good on the sort of alienation that developed within the academic community during these years.

III. *WELTPOLITIK*

From Theory to Practice

In the winter of 1898-1899 when Helfferich was in Egypt recovering from his lung hemorrhages, he chanced to share a dinner table at Shepheard's Hotel in Cairo with a certain Oskar W. Stuebel, a member of the German consular service who was vacationing in the city. As were so many, Stuebel was impressed with Helfferich's "clear and forthright views."[1] After he was appointed Director of the Colonial Division of the Foreign Office in 1900, he decided to take Helfferich into his office to assist in bringing a little order into the disorder prevailing in colonial monetary affairs. When Stuebel talked to Richard Koch about Helfferich, Koch spoke well of the young man, but referred the Director to Karl von Lumm as the person best qualified to assess Helfferich's abilities. That as good as decided it. When Stuebel broached the matter to Lumm at a party at Georg von Siemens's in August 1901, Lumm told him he could not have chosen a better man. Helfferich, pessimistic about his prospects in the academic world, accepted Stuebel's offer. He began work in the Colonial Division on 1 October 1901.[2] Like most new young men in the Foreign Office, Helfferich started as an unpaid assistant on probation. He continued to lecture at the University of Berlin and at the Seminar for Oriental Languages, although he did give up his weekly stint in Hamburg and Kiel.

Helfferich had begun his transformation from scholar to man of action. For the next fourteen years he engaged himself as a servant of the *Weltwirtschaft*, first in the Colonial Office and after 1906 with the Deutsche Bank's so-called Berlin-Bagdad Railway. Although the success with which he pursued these enterprises was a testimony to his personal abilities, it was also

---

[1] Bogdan Graf von Hutten-Czapski, *Sechzig Jahre Politik und Gesellschaft* (2 vols., Berlin, 1936), I, 98.

[2] On Helfferich's entry into the Colonial Division, see Lumm, *Helfferich*, 94.

true that his *Weltanschauung*, scholarly interest in monetary matters, and formal academic qualifications uniquely suited him for the role he was to play. His academic qualifications gave him entrée into bureaucratic circles and created for his monetary ideas a respect not ordinarily accorded the ideas of bankers and other nonacademic monetary pundits in Germany. On the other hand, his active defense of the new industrial order made it possible for bankers and businessmen to accept him as one of their own in a way that they could few other academic economists. He was hence ideally qualified to move easily between business and the bureaucracy and to represent each to the other. Indeed, it is in some ways characteristic that while a civil servant he arranged construction of the only privately financed railways in the German colonies and that while a banker he committed the Deutsche Bank to obligations in Turkey that were difficult to justify as business propositions, but were intended to support German *Weltpolitik*. Although Helfferich's career was hardly average, it was still curiously symbolic of the manner in which the new economic order was opening the way to positions of power and influence for those who were its masters—or servants.

Helfferich's wanderings between business and bureaucracy in these years also determined the sort of friends and enemies he made. Since these connections were to be so important for his political career after 1914, it is perhaps appropriate to say a few words about them here. His years in the Colonial Office acquainted him with most of the men who were to execute official German foreign policy for the next two decades. His fellow apprentice in the Colonial Office, Arthur Zimmermann, later wartime Foreign Secretary and best known for the notorious "Zimmermann Telegram" of 1917, was merely the most notable of such friends. His years with the Deutsche Bank, on the other hand, provided him with a range of contacts roughly delimited by the very fact that he was a director of Germany's largest commercial bank. As such, he was a member of the restricted elite which ran the economy and whose members all knew each other.[3] There

---

[3] One can make such an assertion with confidence even lacking manuscript material. In this respect, of course, Helfferich differed from, say, a Reichstag deputy or newspaper editor. One can say that such persons are likely to

were two main reasons for this. First, a relatively small number of concerns dominated the leading sectors of the economy. Second, the affairs of such concerns were enmeshed with those of their allied banks in a way typical nowhere else. The great banks filled individually needs normally met by a variety of financial institutions: they were commercial, merchant, and investment banks all in one. Unfortunately, Helfferich also made enemies during these years. One of these, Matthias Erzberger, was himself to play a very important political role after 1914. Although like Helfferich a product of the new age, Erzberger was, as we will see, unlike him in virtually every other respect.

German Colonial Development

The story of the German East African monetary muddle, the principal currency problem facing Helfferich, is quickly told. The difficulties dated back to 1890, when East Africa was formally transferred from British to German control.[4] Because the colony's most important economic ties were to India, its monetary unit was the Indian rupee. At the time of transfer, the German East Africa Company was accordingly given the right to mint enough rupees to meet the needs of trade. After 1893 this simple solution to the colony's monetary problems began to cause difficulties, because in that year the Indian government began its effort to stabilize the rupee in terms of the pound sterling, a gold currency. Since the price of silver, of which the rupee was made, had continued to fall, by 1900 the rupee had reached a gold value roughly twice that of the silver contained in the rupee coins. In ten years, the German East Africa Company had seen an oner-

---

know important people, but without manuscript material that is about all one does know. In Helfferich's case, on the other hand, one can be fairly certain that he would have known, for example, the key men at Krupp if only because of the nature of the Deutsche Bank's connections with the steel-maker.

[4] Except where noted below, the history of the German East African currency problem and its solution which follows are based on the collection of memoranda by Helfferich and others in "Aktenstück 354," *RTA* (1903-1905), III, 1990-2028, which contains altogether some 21 separate items.

ous administrative responsibility to mint enough coins to meet the needs of trade transformed into a lucrative fiscal privilege.

If one can judge by the number of coins minted in 1901, nearly double that of each of the preceding three years, the company did indeed succumb to the temptation to make money. Accepting the proposition that "an undervalued currency which has no one in charge of maintaining its value is a monstrosity," Helfferich set about regaining control from the company of issue powers. He acted none too soon. On 7 March 1903, the government of adjoining Zanzibar announced that it would no longer accept German rupees. A hasty support action by the German East African government prevented more than a momentary fall in the German rupee, but the need for further action was unmistakable.

During the summer of 1903, a variety of solutions was discussed. Helfferich conducted the negotiations, in which representatives of the Reichsbank, Treasury Office, and the commercial interests concerned also participated. The first alternative considered was to leave things as they were, only with the German government maintaining the exchange value of the currency. Despite its simplicity, no one favored this solution. The irksome problem of calculating official rupee values in terms of marks, done monthly to five decimal places, would remain, and, more important, the "currency community" with Zanzibar would continue to abet "the commercial hegemony of Zanzibar over German East Africa." To hold the latter opinion was by present lights unrealistic but, given Helfferich's ideas about the role of money in the economic order, to regard control of the monetary system as tantamount to control of trade was perfectly natural.

Such a view, indeed, would seem to have supported the introduction of the mark into German East Africa. This solution was adopted in other German colonies and worked very well. Bookkeeping problems disappeared, and the common currency allegedly fostered ties with the homeland. In the present instance, however, everyone feared that the mark might actually be too effective in cutting the ties with Zanzibar before trade with the mother country could pick up the slack. Because the natives were said to use rupees for making jewelry, Helfferich also feared that they might resent the substitution of the two-mark piece for the rupee. The German coin was lighter than the rupee but was worth more in terms of gold, He also claimed that the government would lose a substantial sum if the existing rupees were redeemed and withdrawn from circulation. It is hard to understand why he did not see that the profits from reminting the old rupees as smaller two-mark pieces would not more than equal the costs of redemption.[5] Perhaps his advocacy of another proposal was the reason.

Both Helfferich and the commercial interests favored a third solution, tying the value of the East African rupee to the mark. But Helfferich and the commercial interests could not agree on the ratio. Both sides' arguments were self-serving, and Helfferich's smelled of the scholar's lamp. For the sake of simple bookkeeping, he proposed the undeniably simple ratio of three rupees to four marks, or 1 to 1.33.[6] This involved a slight appreciation of the rupee, since the existing ratio fluctuated around 1 to 1.38, whereas the businessmen's proposed ratio of 1 to 1.40 involved a slight devaluation. Helfferich also proposed to substitute a new fractional coinage of a hundred Heller for the existing fractional coinage of 64 pesas per rupee. Since the Treasury and the Reichsbank sided with him, he got his way.

His solution to the next problem he had thus created for himself, supplying and maintaining the exchange rate of his new currency, was as bookish as his solution to the currency problem. Foreswearing simplicity, he determined to establish a central bank to do the job.[7] By all accounts, the colony did need a bank of some kind, since the closest facilities were in Zanzibar. Between late 1903 and early 1905, Helfferich successfully negotiated with Berlin and Hamburg commercial houses and banks to get the miniature Reichsbank he wanted.[8] The capitalists were not

[5] He had earlier raised these same arguments in another connection; "Die Vollendung der deutschen Münzreform," in *Studien*, 237-41.

[6] It is hard to see why one ratio would have made for much simpler bookkeeping than another, since each would in any case have required conversion tables.

[7] For the history of the problem and its solution, see "Aktenstück 682: Denkschrift über die Errichtung der Deutsch-Ostafrikanischen Bank, 4. März 1905," *RTA* (1903-1905), VII, 3884-90.

[8] According to Kurt Singer, the negotiations were Helfferich's first official

eager to do their duty. Apparently, only the passage of a bill in 1904 to build a railway in East Africa tipped the scale in favor of the bank, and even then the businessmen exacted a number of special stipulations. The most important was that the bank be granted an unusually long concession, in order that the profits of the later years might make up the expected initial losses.

Although the memorandum to the Reichstag outlining the new currency arrangements dated 19 April 1904 occasioned little immediate comment, the banking memorandum of 4 March 1905 was received with hostility. The youngest Reichstag deputy, Center Party member Matthias Erzberger, singled out Helfferich's monetary arrangements in the course of a general indictment on 8 March 1905 of Germany's colonial stewardship. He attacked what he rightfully described as Helfferich's "wholly unique currency" and forecast trouble for the future. He criticized Helfferich's new bank even more sharply. In this as in other matters he favored the state's intervening actively in the economy when necessary. He accordingly recommended that the Reichsbank should have sacrificed some of its profits to establish a bank in East Africa. Another alternative would have been for the Reichstag to grant the necessary moneys to fund an agricultural credit bank modeled after the Prussian Landschaftsbanken. He most objected to Helfferich's arrangements because they placed monopoly powers in the hands of private interests, namely, the German East Africa Company. He read letters from colonists expressing fears of economic oppression. His monetary and banking criticisms were seconded later the same day by Helfferich's old enemy, Otto Arendt.[9] Although Arendt's criticisms of the bank were not as harsh as Erzberger's, he did emphasize that what colonies needed was the sort of long-term developmental credits which Helfferich's bank was not equipped to provide.

---

contact with his later employer, the Deutsche Bank; Helfferich, *Georg von Siemens: ein Lebensbild aus Deutschlands grosser Zeit*, ed. Kurt Singer (rev. edn., Krefeld, 1956), 194.

[9] *RTV* (1903-1905), VII, 8 March 1905, 5373-75, 5386-87 (Erzberger); 5384-86 (Arendt). For a general appraisal of Erzberger's role in the colonial debates of 1905-1910, see Klaus Epstein, "Erzberger and the German Colonial Scandals 1905-1910," *EHR*, 74 (1959), 637-63, and his *Matthias Erzberger and the Dilemma of German Democracy* (Princeton, 1959), 52-60.

Since Helfferich was the "responsible expert" (*Hauptreferent*), on the currency and banking settlement, refutation of these criticisms was left to him.[10] In his maiden Reichstag speech, he defended his currency arrangements by elaborating on the arguments elucidated above. His defense of the new bank, however, revealed that his implicit assumptions about the role of government in economic development in general and colonial development in particular were quite different from Erzberger's. He said that the difficulty with an overseas branch of any German bank was that such a branch could not adapt to local conditions and meet local needs the way a bank with purely local responsibilities could. While conceding the dangers of monopoly, he held that the important thing was that the great commercial banks were for the first time showing an interest in the colonies. This was the key to colonial development as Helfferich saw it. He believed that the Reich lacked the resources and the skilled people necessary to undertake such development itself. Helfferich, in fact, envisaged development quite differently than Erzberger: whereas the latter wanted the sort of mortgage-credit arrangements appropriate for agricultural development, Helfferich envisaged the sort of close working arrangements between commercial banks and industrial firms which were characteristic of the homeland. In this as in other matters Helfferich thought in terms of trade and industry rather than agriculture.

The subsequent history of Helfferich's new rupee and bank shows that the hostility toward his arrangements was in some measure justified.[11] Hardly a year later, on 16 January 1906, Erzberger attributed the so-called *Maji Maji* rebellion in East Africa in part to the new currency. The new "Helfferich" rupee, worth more in terms of marks than the old, was nevertheless accepted nowhere without the premium of a few Heller. The reason was that, while wages were lowered to take account of the upward revaluation, prices remained the same. Monetary theory in the bush was primitive, but it caught the essential point: the new

[10] *RTV* (1903-1905), VII, 8 March 1905, 5376-79.
[11] See, for example, O. Kobner and Hans Wolff, "Kolonieen und Kolonialpolitik," in *Wörterbuch der Volkswirtschaft in zwei Bänden*, ed. Ludwig Elster (Jena, 1911), II, 133. The authors add: "In recent years the wish that the Reich currency be introduced is heard in increasing measure."

rupee bought less than the old. Helfferich's thoughtfulness in continuing to provide the natives with raw material for their jewelry hence went unregarded. Inclined like Helfferich to over-estimate the importance of monetary factors, however, Erzberger exaggerated the importance of the new money—and German ad-ministrative blunders—as causes of the revolt.[12]

Complaints continued to come in over the years. German rupees and Heller were in chronically short supply, with the re-sult that the old Indian rupees still circulated at par, though hence overvalued. As Helfferich left the Colonial Division in 1906, he cannot be fairly held responsible for these later adminis-trative failures. But the complexities of his scheme made it more than usually difficult to execute, and experience proved that the skill necessary to manage such a small currency system was un-common. Had the mark been introduced in the first place, most of the problems actually encountered would not have arisen, and Helfferich's miniature Reichsbank would also have been unneces-sary. In 1910, Arendt dubbed the bank "that sorry relic of the Stuebel-Helfferich era" and gleefully noted once more that ex-perience had proved that what the colony needed was a bank that could provide long-term agricultural credits, not short-term commercial loans.[13] Although Arendt's strictures, like Erzber-ger's, were exaggerated, one is nevertheless obliged to conclude that Helfferich fell prey to the temptations of empire-building when concocting his monetary and banking arrangements.

Even before he submitted his currency and banking arrange-ments to the Reichstag, however, Helfferich was beginning to turn his attention to other matters. If sound money represented one of the prime economic requisites for development, adequate transportation represented the other. Because geography and cli-mate severely limited the potential of river transport, railroads

[12] *RTV* (1905-1906), I, 16 Jan. 1906, 592. A recent account makes no men-tion of the new currency as a source of difficulties; John Iliffe, *Tanganyika and German Rule 1905-1912* (Cambridge, 1969), Ch. 2, *passim*.

[13] *RTV*, Vol. 259, 3 Feb. 1910, 1024. See also his earlier and later remarks; *ibid.*, Vol. 235, 1 March 1909, 7197; *ibid.*, Vol. 265, 24 March 1911, 5838. It should be pointed out that as a spokesman for settler interests, Arendt was a critic of government policy, which the settlers opposed. His criticisms were anything but disinterested; Iliffe, *Tanganyika and German Rule*, 107, 122.

appeared at the time as the only realistic alternative.[14] But rail-roads are costly, too costly to earn profits very soon in underde-veloped countries. All of the great colonial powers had accepted the obligation to back construction financially. German experi-ence with the most obvious method, state construction and opera-tion, had been very disappointing. It confirmed Helfferich's opin-ion that bureaucrats lacked the skills for such undertakings. The second method, employed in the German homeland and else-where, was for the state to guarantee the interest charges on capital outlays and the minimum operating expenses of a private firm. Despite such safeguards, additional concessions for land and mineral rights, and occasionally harbor facilities, usually had to be offered also. The advantage of this method was that it ac-complished the job at the lowest initial cost to the state. The third method was for a private company to undertake construction and operation using government capital.[15] The aim was to combine the economies of private operation with the benefits of state ownership, of which the most important was that a potential monopoly of economic power was not delivered into private hands.

The most controversial of the railroad projects with which Helfferich was connected was the North Cameroons Railway.[16]

[14] See the arguments in "Aktenstück 776: Entwurf eines Gesetzes be-treffend . . . eine Eisenbahn von Duala nach den Manengubabergen, 4. Mai 1905," *RTA* (1903-1905), VIII, 4487-506. In the event, the truck has proved a better, because cheaper, solution to the transportation problem in the initial stages of development.

[15] The advantages of all three methods were discussed in some detail in "Aktenstück 195: Bericht der [Budget] Kommission . . . betreffend . . . eine Eisenbahn von Duala nach den Manengubabergen, 1. Februar 1906," *RTA* (1905-1906), IV, 3085-106. According to G. Zoepfl, "Kolonieen und Kolonial-politik," in J. Conrad, *Handwörterbuch der Staatswissenschaften* (3rd edn., 8 vols., Jena, 1909-1911), V, 1014, the third method was being increasingly adopted before the war.

[16] The history of the railway which follows is largely based on Anlage ma-terial cited in nn.14 and 15 above, and "Aktenstück 833: Bericht der Kom-mission . . . betreffend . . . eine Eisenbahn von Duala nach den Manenguba-bergen, 22. Mai 1905," *RTA* (1903-1905), VIII, 4820. See also Epstein, "Erz-berger and the German Colonial Scandals," 643-44; Harry R. Rudin, *Ger-mans in the Cameroons: A Case Study of Modern Imperialism* (New Haven, 1938), 239-40; Jolanda Ballhaus, "Die Landkonzessionsgesellschaften," in Helmut Stoecker (ed.), *Kamerun unter deutscher Kolonialherrschaft* (2

The line was intended to be the first segment of a longer road from Duala on the coast north to Lake Chad. In 1902, a concession had been granted a private syndicate to build this line. Like most German colonial railways, it was to be narrow gauge, one meter. Because of difficulties of terrain and climate—much of the annual precipitation of 180 inches comes during the rainy season —construction promised to be expensive, totaling 17 million marks. The syndicate was unable to raise this amount even when the prospective concession was sweetened with land grants and mining rights. Toward the end of 1904, however, Geheimrat Lenz, member of the original syndicate and head of the company that was to build the line, informed the Colonial Office that the Berliner Handelsgesellschaft, one of the great commercial banks, might be willing to finance the line on the basis of a "partial" guarantee.[17] With Lenz mediating, Helfferich bypassed the original syndicate and worked out the financing with the Handelsgesellschaft. It was arranged for the Reich to guarantee the principal of a loan of 11 million to Lenz for the period of construction. After the line went into operation, the Reich was to pay the difference between operating income and interest charges. Sale of preferred shares was to provide the remaining 6 million. The Reich Railway Office checked Lenz's construction estimates and found them acceptable. The costs were, in fact, much lower than those of English and French railways in comparable areas. Although Lenz was allowed a construction profit of 10 per cent, the high risk being held to justify such a figure, Helfferich felt justifiably pleased with his bargain. He had secured construction of the line by a trustworthy firm at an estimate bearing the low rate of interest of 3 per cent. For all the controversy that later swirled up around the plan, it is important to remember that no

---

vols., Berlin, 1960, 1968), II, 163-68. The line never got past the Manenguba Mountains, the remainder of the distance to Lake Chad being traversed by bad roads.

[17] The original syndicate consisted mainly of the founding fathers of the Northwest Cameroons Company, which held the principal development concessions; Ballhaus, "Landkonzessionsgesellschaften," 163. The Handelsgesellschaft was actually the leader of a finance consortium, which included the Diskontogesellschaft, the Nationalbank für Deutschland, a half-dozen other banks, and Krupp; *ibid.*, 163-64.

alternative was ever presented by which the job could be done for less.

By early 1905, the one thing remaining was to secure final approval of the various parties to the agreement. Evidently for the sake of good will, Lenz squared things with the old syndicate in mid-February 1905 with a series of concessions, not all of which were reported to the Colonial Division. A month later, the Handelsgesellschaft and its allied banks granted their approval, and in early May the Bundesrat gave its sanction to a bill embodying the terms of the concession. On 5 May, the bill went to the Budget Committee, and hearings began on the 16th.[18]

The government's foremost critic was again Erzberger, who was of no mind to accede to the government's wish for quick passage. Most of his questions were quickly disposed of. He asked two questions, however, that caused the government much exasperation and trouble. The first was whether the government had tried to get an unguaranteed road built by adding mining rights to the original syndicate's promised land grant. Helfferich replied, correctly, that this approach had been thoroughly explored to no avail, and added that only after "extraordinarily difficult negotiations" had it been possible to reach any agreement at all. Erzberger then asked how the old syndicate was connected to the new company. Colonial Director Stuebel replied that the syndicate had been offered three seats on the board of the new company, but did not mention the other measures by which Lenz had bought off his erstwhile compatriots. One of these measures, payment of 120,000 marks for expenses already incurred, was included in the detailed estimates Helfferich later said he had been prepared to give the committee on request. When later informed that the Conservative Wilhelm Lattmann *had* made such a request, Helfferich said he had "not heard" it.[19] Given the clamor that prevailed in Budget Committee hearings, there is no reason to doubt Helfferich. But it is also true that he blundered in not voluntarily handing out the estimates. On the

[18] See "Aktenstück 833," as cited in n.16 above.

[19] *RTV* (1905-1906), I, 18 Jan. 1906, 638-39. Lattmann is not listed as being present at either set of hearings, but since no one denied his presence, the lists presumably were in error.

whole, however, the hearings went smoothly, and, though the Reichstag adjourned for the summer before a vote could be taken, the Colonial Office had no reason to fear for the future of its project.

Unfortunately for the government, Erzberger spent part of his summer poking into the details of the bargain between Lenz and the old syndicate. What he had been told rang false to him, and he was in any case intensely suspicious of big business. Toward the end of September 1905, he launched an anonymous attack in the *Kölnische Volkszeitung* in which he accused the government representatives of "inexactitudes," the details of which will be considered below.[20] Helfferich replied to the charges with a violent anonymous counterattack in the *Norddeutsche Allegemeine Zeitung*, the government's principal sheet, and succeeded in forcing Erzberger out into the open. Erzberger promised to prove his charges. He did so on 14 December 1905 in a major Reichstag speech.

The speech was merely the first of a number in which he was to set down the failures of German colonial policy in painful and exact detail.[21] He began by remarking that if Germany's future depended on colonies—as Helfferich had asserted a short time before[22]—"then good-bye beautiful German fatherland." He documented how much had been put into German colonies and how little had come out, noted the "precipitate" departure of Stuebel and other worthies from the Colonial Office, regaled his hearers with some old and a few fresh scandals, and scornfully concluded that such a record constituted the "collapse of German colonial policy." He saved his comments on the railway bill for last.

[20] It seems probable that Erzberger got his information from disgruntled members of the former syndicate who were unhappy to see the Northwest Cameroon Company lose so much influence over the affairs of the railway; Ballhaus, "Landkonzessionsgesellschaften," 164, and on Erzberger's campaign, 166-67. Erzberger was careful to distinguish between "inexactitudes" (*Unrichtigkeiten*) and "falsehoods" (*Unwahrheiten*), and expressly stated he was not accusing the government of the latter; *RTV* (1905-1906), 1, 15 Dec. 1905, 399.

[21] *Ibid.*, 14 Dec. 1905, 320-31, and on the railway, esp. 327-31.

[22] Helfferich, "Die Bedeutung der Kolonieen für die deutsche Volkswirtschaft," in *Verhandlungen des Deutschen Kolonialkongresses zu Berlin am 5., 6. und 7. Oktober 1905* (Berlin, 1906), 572.

Sharply criticizing the campaign in the press, he singled out the *Norddeutsche Allegemeine* articles for their "disturbing disregard for the truth." Then, with masterly timing, he produced his most damaging evidence for his earlier newspaper charges, the protocol of the February meeting in which Lenz had bought off the old syndicate. It showed that the syndicate was to receive 360,000 marks worth of preferred stock and 120,000 marks for expenses already incurred. In addition, a certain Konsul René was to receive 55,000 marks for various services rendered.

As Erzberger presented it, the entire scheme looked like a walloping swindle. He claimed that these moneys had been smuggled into the estimates by increasing building costs from an early estimate of 11 million to the final figure of 14.3 million. The government had only itself to blame for this misapprehension, which could have been avoided if Helfferich had given the deputies his detailed estimates the previous spring. Since the estimates also showed the 120,000 marks for previous expenses, he could have saved the government from the charge of mendacity on that item as well. Erzberger also repeated one of his earlier *Volkszeitung* allegations, namely, that the syndicate had been circumvented in negotiating the final agreement—there had been no "extraordinarily difficult negotiations," as Helfferich had stated—and triumphantly abandoned the floor to the government.

Much stung by Erzberger's charges, Helfferich was in a fury when it came his turn to speak.[23] He began directly with the press campaign. He admitted that he had "lit into" Erzberger. He said it was the latter's own fault, however, because he had not revealed himself as a deputy but had "disguised" himself in a "cloak of anonymity." Moving on to the substance of the dispute, Helfferich managed to turn many of Erzberger's charges simply by elucidating in great detail the history of the syndicate's efforts to build the road, the negotiations which had produced the bill considered, and the circumstances surrounding the meeting between Lenz and the old syndicate. At the end of this recitation, the only substantive issue still outstanding was the question of the 360,000 marks worth of preferred stock and the payments to Konsul René. While noting that the government itself had

[23] *RTV* (1905-1906), I, 14 Dec. 1905, 333-38.

learned of these payments only recently, Helfferich took the position that, since the sums were to come out of Lenz's profits, the latter once agreed on were his to dispose of as he saw fit. But the matter *was* embarrassing. Helfferich unfortunately made the mistake of adding that the 360,000 in preferred shares was the "usual provision" for services rendered. Still, by the end of his rebuttal, Helfferich had largely cleared the government of the imputations of mendacity and fraud.

In the debates of the following day, Erzberger seized upon Helfferich's assertion that the 360,000 was the "usual provision" for services rendered. He claimed that some of the recipients were not exactly businessmen, being personages such as the Kaiser's brother-in-law, Duke Günther of Schleswig-Holstein, and Prince Kraft von Hohenlohe-Oehringen.[24] Erzberger held that it was absurd to consider these elegant aristocrats anything more than titled idlers unworthy of public support. He deduced that Lenz's profits were in this instance not his to dispose of as he saw fit. Returning to the matter after the Christmas holidays, Erzberger proposed that the amount of preferred stock be reduced by the disputed 360,000 marks.[25] In the final committee hearings of 25 and 26 January 1906, Helfferich gave in.[26] He also produced the long-awaited detailed estimates and brought Lenz along to explain them in person. The other major change in committee was to reduce the term after which the state could purchase the railway from the originally foreseen 31 years to 21. The bill became law without further significant change on 4 May 1906.

The entire affair left Helfferich disillusioned with the Reichstag and soured on popular legislatures of all kinds. Unless legislators could "subordinate personal interests and views to the commonweal," they merely made things worse by "squandering

[24] For the debates of 15 Dec. 1905, see *ibid.*, 396-404. See also Georg W. F. Hallgarten, *Imperialismus vor 1914: die soziologischen Grundlagen der Aussenpolitik europäischer Grossmächte vor dem Ersten Weltkrieg* (rev. edn., 2 vols., Munich, 1963), II, 38n1. Actually, the business interests of Hohenlohe-Oehringen, at least, were rather extensive.

[25] *RTV* (1905-1906), I, 18 Jan. 1906, 632-36.

[26] *Ibid.*, 637-40, and for Helfferich's surrender in committee, see "Aktenstück 195," 3094-96, cited in n.15 above.

valuable human resources [and] hobbling the administration. . . ."[27] The Reichstag had botched the job Helfferich had assigned it. It had not provided helpful criticism. Helfferich could not conceive of how anyone with Erzberger's modest education and lack of practical experience in finance could have anything useful to say about his East African monetary arrangements. He was also most unwilling to concede Erzberger's claim that the Reichstag was the proper judge of the matters to be brought before it for discussion. Second, he considered that the Reichstag had fulfilled its function of providing funds for the Cameroons Railway in a most unsatisfactory way. For the sake of a few spiteful changes it had delayed construction for an entire year. Finally, instead of explaining the government's program to the people, Erzberger had traduced the motives of its executants. By continuing to hammer away at German colonial "scandals" during the remainder of 1906 and in the election campaign of 1907, "the Center's great colonial sage" had merely compounded his offense.[28]

Helfferich never regarded Erzberger's attacks on his programs as anything more than cynical attempts at self-aggrandizement by means of blocking all colonial expenditures while hypocritically posing as a colonial savior. Although Erzberger's successful exploitation of the colonial scandals did raise him to a political eminence that might otherwise have taken him years to obtain, Helfferich seriously misinterpreted Erzberger's motives. He was unwilling to admit that Erzberger might be acting disinterestedly and according to Christian ethical principals in exposing abuses which none, including himself, were willing to defend. Helfferich was constitutionally disinclined to see good in a man like Erzberger. Their personalities and philosophies of govern-

[27] *Zur Reform der kolonialen Verwaltungs-Organisation*, 26.
[28] "Scheideweg der Weltpolitik," 39. The Socialist Gustav Noske later expressed much the same opinion as Helfferich; Gustav Noske, *Erlebtes aus Aufstieg und Niedergang einer Demokratie* (Offenbach a. M., 1947), 24. On this important election, see George D. Crothers, *The German Elections of 1907* (New York, 1941), and esp. 106-107, for the Colonial Office's unprecedented propaganda campaign for colonial development. Helfferich's colonial writings discussed above, Ch. 2, were a part of this campaign and were favorably noticed by the Kaiser himself.

ment were too different. Helfferich thought that government ought to be in the hands of bureaucrats advised by experts and economic development left to capitalists, whereas Erzberger believed that a democratically controlled government ought itself to assume a considerable role in economic development.

This clash between Helfferich and Erzberger cemented an enmity that was to have important political consequences. Each was an able man and a formidable personality. Each was in the future to make the other a symbol of the evils of the political system he was attacking. Thus Erzberger saw in Helfferich a particularly arrogant manifestation of irresponsible authoritarian Wilhelmine government and a servant of exploitive capitalism. But for Helfferich, Erzberger was a particularly unscrupulous example of the demagogic democratic politico. Their second collision occurred during the wartime political crisis of the summer and fall of 1917. Erzberger led the successful efforts to deprive Helfferich of his office of Vice-Chancellor and himself emerged from the crisis with greatly enhanced influence. In their last battle, however, which culminated in a spectacular libel trial in early 1920, Helfferich as defendant so damaged Erzberger's reputation that he was forced to resign from the very important post of Finance Minister. Helfferich, on the other hand, emerged from the trial as one of the most important leaders of the right-wing opposition to the Weimar majority and its policies. It is hardly an exaggeration to call each the other's worst enemy.

At the time of their first encounter, most of Helfferich's "important" contemporaries considered that he had bested Erzberger. Wilhelm Solf, later head of the Colonial Office, echoed the prevailing opinion in higher circles when he called Helfferich "the most able man in the [Colonial] Division," though he thought Helfferich might have "stirred up Erzberger a little too much" in the December exchange in the Reichstag.[29] Chancellor Bülow evidently did not think so; bureaucrats who could handle debaters as skilled as Erzberger on anything like equal terms were uncommon. Such conduct was also the sort calculated to please the Emperor William, who had a gift for the pugnacious phrase himself. At any rate, Solf reported that Bülow personally

[29] Letter, Solf to Dr. Schultz, 22 Dec. 1905, Solf "Nachlass," 159.

interceded with the Kaiser to secure Helfferich the Order of the Crown (*Kronen-Orden*), second class. Solf added, "Division I-B [personnel] is furious." Helfferich held no other orders and was very young to receive an order of any kind.[30]

"Getting On"[31]

Helfferich's *Kronen-Orden* constituted the final adornment of a very rapid rise in the Colonial Division. By early 1905 he had risen to the rank of Vortragender Rat (reporting counselor), a rank usually reserved for much older and more experienced men. He had quickly established himself as a tireless worker and a tough negotiator. Grasping complicated problems easily, he appeared as successful a man of action as he had been a scholar. Even though some of his East African currency and banking arrangements now seem questionable, what apparently struck Stuebel and his other superiors was the energy with which he had executed them and the vigor with which he had defended them in the Reichstag.[32] Still, his rise might have been slower had he not attracted the attention of the Chancellor, Bernhard von Bülow. The sources are not clear on when this happened, but Helfferich was evidently on a familiar footing with Bülow at least as early as 1904.[33] Whenever the connection was established, it evidently profited Helfferich considerably.

[30] Letter, Solf to Heinrich Schnee, n.d. [late December 1905], Solf "Nachlass," 131. Schnee was still aggrieved decades later; Heinrich Schnee, *Als letzter Gouverneur in Deutsch-Ostafrika* (Heidelberg, 1964), 57-58. For some interesting remarks on "Ordenswesen," see Eugen Schiffer, *Ein Leben für den Liberalismus* (Berlin, 1951), 13ff.

[31] The phrase "getting on" is from Theodor Fontane as quoted in Stern, *The Politics of Cultural Despair*, 130n. Fontane wrote: "You write yourself that 'with a little less "Getting-on" (*Carriere machen*) we could have a little more truth in the world'. . . . And what does Getting-on mean other than to live in Berlin, and what does Berlin mean but to get on?"

[32] According to Helfferich's colleague, Heinrich Schnee, Stuebel lacked both ideas and energy and thus came in time to depend more and more heavily on Helfferich; Schnee, *Als letzter Gouverneur*, 52-53.

[33] Bülow himself claimed to have been introduced to Helfferich by men who, as it happens, were already dead. He also claimed to have introduced Helfferich to the Kaiser, which seems more plausible; Bernhard von Bülow, *Denkwürdigkeiten* (4 vols., Berlin, 1930-1931), I, 219. See also Lumm, *Helfferich*, 40-41; Bonn, *So macht man Geschichte*, 236; *Weltkrieg*, I, 35.

The improvement in Helfferich's outward circumstances paralleled his rise in the bureaucracy, for despite his abstemious character he was not inclined to abjure all material pleasures. For a bachelor of quiet tastes his income after 1902, when his probationary period in the Colonial Office ended, was more than ample for a life of modest comfort. He remained at Bamberger Strasse 11, but refurnished it with his own things. Perhaps the new furnishings included a piano, for he continued to play—as he was to do for the rest of his life—creditably above the usual amateur level. He also painted and sketched, very passably indeed, according to members of the family. Otherwise, his pleasures seem to have consisted mainly of the platonic convivialities of bachelor dinners and official entertainments; essentially, however, his life remained, as before, his work.[34]

By this time he had largely assumed the outward guise familiar from numerous wartime photographs. A meticulous, rather formal dresser, he was above average in height and on the slim side. Although he stood very straight, he was not the sort of man that left contemporaries with the impression of size and solidity, the way his later wartime chief, Chancellor Bethmann Hollweg, did. His clean-shaven physiognomy was striking rather than handsome; "practically all profile," his contemporary Moritz Bonn aptly described it. It was at any rate not a face readily forgotten: large nose, narrow eyes, alert expression, harsh features accentuated by baldness, all combined to convey an impression of quick, hard, calculating intelligence rather than geniality. The owner of the face could in fact be charming enough, though frequently it required continued acquaintance for those softer virtues to manifest themselves.

His workload during these years precluded any very extensive scholarly activities. He was forced to put the finishing touches to his book, *Money*, during his first annual vacation in October 1902. But he wrote a few scholarly articles, contributed some pieces to the *National Zeitung*, and toward the end of 1905 wrote the book already alluded to on state finance during the Russo-Japanese War. He also began collecting material for the biog-

---

[34] He is also said to have been a *Weinkenner*, but he would have been a poor Pfälzer indeed if he had not been.

raphy of Georg von Siemens, the founder of the Deutsche Bank, which Frau von Siemens had commissioned him to write.[35] Ironically enough, the scholarly recognition he had dispaired of in 1900 had also come. As a result of prompting from Koch of the Reichsbank, the Prussian government had conferred on him the title "Professor" in January 1902. He was grateful, but as he said, "It would still have been more of an honor if the title had come from a university."[36] He had not long to wait. Shortly thereafter he was offered a professorship at the Technische Hochschule at Karlsruhe. He felt obliged to refuse, since he had just taken the position in the Colonial Office. In February 1904, he received an even better offer from the Kaiser's alma mater, Bonn University: a full professorship on the faculty of the Staatswissenschaften. It was quite an honor for a man of thirty-one, and there was much shaking of heads in the academic world when he refused it.[37] By 1904, he realized the scholarly life was not for him. He wanted a wider field of action, one where he could shape events. He was acquiring a taste for power.

Whether it was for power, pelf, or simply the chance to employ his talents in the service of a more exciting cause, Helfferich left the Colonial Office early in 1906 to assume the post of Second Director of the Anatolian Railway. The company, technically a Turkish subsidiary of the Deutsche Bank, was the concern responsible for building the famous Bagdad Railway.[38] Helfferich's appointment thus attracted much notice and even more speculation about its meaning. Some held that the Deutsche Bank was merely exploiting Helfferich's official connections and muttered

[35] Lumm, *Helfferich*, 35; Helfferich, *Georg von Siemens*, i, iii-v. The press of his other activities was such that he did not finish the work for twenty years.

[36] Scheffbuch, *Helfferich*, 29; Lumm, *Helfferich*, 94-95.

[37] *Ibid.*, 95-96, and Germany, Kolonialamt, *Deutsches Kolonialblatt: Amtsblatt für die Schutzgebiete des Deutschen Reiches*, 15 (1904), 117, on the Bonn appointment. But then, academics always consider that a man has "fallen" and is wasting his talents if he leaves the academic world.

[38] Legally the Anatolian Railway Company and the Bagdad Railway Company were separate, but the Deutsche Bank dominated the syndicate that held the concessions to both, and the same people in Constantinople and Berlin managed both companies.

about "conflict of interests."[39] Others, including the London *Times*, interpreted the appointment as a sign of increased official interest in the railway.[40] Few doubted that Helfferich's appointment foreshadowed a more active Bagdad policy.

There was something to all these interpretations, though the reasons why the post of Second Director had opened up were prosaic enough: the incumbent, Edouard Huguenin, was being promoted to Director because the former director had retired. In requesting permission of Bülow to offer Helfferich the post, Arthur Gwinner of the Deutsche Bank stressed the need to appoint a first-rate man with both financial and diplomatic talents. He repeated the arguments of the German ambassador in Constantinople, Baron Adolf Marschall von Bieberstein, that the railway was the "foundation of German policy in Turkey," and held it in the "general interest" that Helfferich be released for the position. Bülow fell in willingly enough with the idea, in part because he hoped that if Helfferich were "in some way or other" placed on equal footing with Huguenin, it might blunt growing criticism of the latter. Huguenin, a Franco-Swiss, was said by more extreme critics to be "Frenchifying" the railway.[41] To Huguenin's eventual discomfiture, Helfferich was to be given powers roughly equal to his own. Bülow also interceded personally with Helfferich to persuade him to accept Gwinner's offer rather than a position on the Reichsbank Direktorium proffered him about the same time by Koch.

As the story of his appointment reveals, Helfferich had parted with the official bureaucracy the better to serve official policy. Alternatively, a hostile critic such as Erzberger might have said

[39] In particular, the *Deutsche Tageszeitung*, 2 Aug. 1905, as cited in Hallgarten, *Imperialismus*, II, 46n4.

[40] As cited in Edward M. Earle, *Turkey, the Great Powers, and the Bagdad Railway: A Study in Imperialism* (New York, 1923), 97.

[41] The details about Helfferich's appointment are mainly in Gwinner to Bülow, 9 June 1905, "Türkei" 152, Bd. 35, and Staatssekretär Heinrich von Tschirschky und Bögendorff to Adolf Freiherr Marschall von Bieberstein, ambassador to Constantinople, 22 June 1906, *ibid.*, Bd. 36. On Huguenin, whose daughter married a Prussian officer and who was thoroughly pro-German in sentiment, see Hallgarten, *Imperialismus*, II, 571.

that he merely came out in the open again as a servant of big business after having covertly served it for five years while disguised as an official. The truth was, the line between business and government came to be a rather fuzzy one during the late Wilhelmine Empire, and Helfferich's career, serving the interests of business first as scholar, then as official, and finally as financier, was a sign of how closely the two were becoming enmeshed.

The Bagdad Railway: The Financing of Imperialism, 1906 to 1911

As it happened, the London *Times* was correct about Helfferich's appointment foreshadowing a more active Bagdad policy.[42] Such a policy, in turn, meant that Bülow had embarked on a policy that can with some justice be described as one of "splendid isolation." Earlier efforts to secure British cooperation in the Bagdad Railway, which was, after all, the most important of Germany's imperialist ventures, had failed in 1903. The English, on the other hand, had successfully escaped from their own isolation by coming to terms first with the Japanese in 1902, and then with the French in 1904. German efforts to shatter the entente with the French, which resulted in the First Morocco Crisis, had only welded the entente more tightly. The Algeciras conference, which settled the crisis, made this painfully apparent to all in early 1906. Thus it was natural that Bülow should deemphasize the development of the colonies, as is shown by his notice of 19 February 1906 to the General Staff that the colonies be written off in time of war.[43] It was also reasonable to expend more effort to develop the Ottoman Empire economically, since it had the immense strategic advantage of being accessible by

[42] The best general account of the Bagdad Railway is still Earle, *Bagdad Railway*, though out of date. For the diplomacy of the railway useful supplements are John B. Wolf, *The Diplomatic History of the Bagdad Railway* (Columbia, Mo., 1936), and Maybelle K. Chapman, *Great Britain and the Bagdad Railway 1888-1914* (Northampton, 1943). For the place of the railway in the general context of pre-World War I German imperialism, see Fritz Fischer, *Krieg der Illusionen: die deutsche Politik von 1911 bis 1914* (Düsseldorf, 1969), and Hallgarten, *Imperialismus*.

[43] Iliffe, *Tanganyika and German Rule*, 57.

land in time of war, as the colonies were not.[44] The efforts needed, moreover, to develop the empire seemed likely to bear fruit sooner than similar efforts in the colonies. One might argue, in fact, that since it was impossible politically to limit German naval construction, the most important source of English hostility to Germany, it made sense to concentrate German imperial efforts in the Near East rather than in areas more vulnerable to the British fleet.

By 1906, when Helfferich joined the management of the railway, it had advanced from Constantinople by one branch as far as Ankara and by another, the main line, through Konya to Bulgurlu, a village at the foot of the Taurus Mountains.[45] Although the basic Convention of 1903 provided for construction clear to the Persian Gulf, funds were lacking to finance any further construction, or so it appeared.[46] Since these money problems were what Helfferich was sent to Constantinople to solve, a brief description of them is in order. The root of the difficulty was that during the course of the nineteenth century, the Turks had largely lost control of their state revenues.[47] Tariffs could only be increased if the Powers all agreed, and both tariffs and inland revenues had in good part been alienated over the years to an international body representing European bond holders, the

[44] Helfferich, *Die deutsche Türkenpolitik* (Berlin, 1921), 7-8.

[45] In cases where there is little difference between the modern Turkish spelling and the older Western transliterations of Turkish place names, I have used the modern spelling. In cases where there is considerable difference, or a different name altogether is now used, I have, with apologies to Turkish readers, followed the older spelling but have included the modern spelling in parentheses the first time the name appears. In the case of persons, I have usually followed the older Western transliterations.

[46] For discussions of the March 1903 concessions, see Earle, *Bagdad Railway*, 70-84, and Herbert Feis, *Europe the world's banker: an account of European foreign investment and the connection of world finance with diplomacy before World War I* (New York, 1930), 346-48. For texts of the convention and other supporting documents, see Louis Ragey, *La question du chemin de fer de Bagdad* (Paris, 1936), 128-77.

[47] For a discussion of Turkey's complex financial problems, see Donald C. Blaisdell, *European Financial Control in the Ottoman Empire: A Study of the Establishment, Activities, and Significance of the Administration of the Ottoman Public Debt* (New York, 1929).

81

Public Debt Administration. By the end of the century, the Turks, far from having money to spend on great construction projects like the Bagdad Railway, were hard pressed to meet ordinary governmental operating expenses. Where money for the line was to come from was a puzzle.

Nor was the solution to this financial conundrum simplified by the particular difficulties facing the Germans in Berlin. The same political difficulties that lay in the way of state finance for colonial development made any idea of state subvention of the railway out of the question, however important it may have been for *Weltpolitik*. Moreover, in an era dominated by liberal, capitalist ideas, the state hardly felt able to override the restrictions placed by the stock-market regulation agencies against the sale of Turkish bonds, the amortization and interest charges of which were not guaranteed by the Debt.[48]

Under Arthur Gwinner's leadership, the Deutsche Bank had attempted to solve these financial problems by internationalizing the railway. His aim was to undercut political opposition to measures such as raising Turkish import duties by cutting in the potential opponents of the road, the most tenacious and determined of which was England. Had his plan succeeded, the financing problems would also have been simplified in that London and Paris would have presumably absorbed a substantial portion of the bonds sold to finance the railway. Neither the Turks nor the German Foreign Office had much liking for Gwinner's scheme, but, having nothing better to suggest, they accepted it because the alternative seemed to be no railroad at all. Unfortunately, as has been mentioned, the plan collapsed as a result of English resistance in 1903.[49] None of Gwinner's subsequent efforts met any better success, and by 1906 he too was convinced that Germany would somehow have to build the line unassisted and against stiff English opposition. Baron Marschall, the very able German ambassador in Constantinople, had come

[48] Wolf, *Bagdad Railway*, 20-22.
[49] *Ibid.*, 36-45; Chapman, *Bagdad Railway*, 50-72. The French were not happy with this outcome, as it led the French Foreign Secretary to prohibit the sale of Bagdad bonds on the Paris Bourse. To underline its unhappiness with this decision, the Ottoman Bank agreed to accept 30 per cent of the bonds for the initial section of the railway (Series I).

to this conclusion some time before. His policy was "action, not words." He assumed that the necessary funds could be found and that when construction had gone far enough, the English would have to accept whatever terms the Germans deigned to offer.[50] The history of the railroad between 1906 and 1911 is essentially a history of efforts to implement this policy.

Helfferich may well have been glad that he had taken his sister Emilie with him to manage his household, as his initial efforts as a fund raiser did nothing more than embroil him with his other German colleagues in Constantinople. He was evidently none too tactful about exercising his unusual powers as Second Director, which led to difficulties with Huguenin almost immediately. The latter was soon complaining that far from treating him as a superior, or even as an equal, Helfferich treated him as an inferior. He went on a long vacation and was apparently only with some difficulty dissuaded from resigning.[51] Marschall, too, greeted some of Helfferich's early diplomatic suggestions with acerbity, on one such occasion saying, "It would be nice if the Deutsche Bank, and especially Herr Helfferich, would spare us further instruction. We know exactly what we want and must have, and also have sufficient knowledge of the men and matters involved to get it."[52]

Too much should not be made of these bickerings. It soon became clear to everyone in Constantinople that the most promising source of revenues for the next section of railway from Bulgurlu to Aleppo were the surpluses from so-called "conceded revenues" of the Debt.[53] At the time the Germans sought to obtain these revenues, the Turks were also trying to obtain agreement to an increase in their customs duties from 8 to 11 per cent. But the English would grant the increase only on the condition that it not

---

[50] Marschall to Bülow, No. 60, 25 May 1906, *GP*, xxv, doc. 8633. As Marschall put it, "I count the Bagdad Railway to be one of those matters where one should never speak but only act."

[51] Baron von Bodman, chargé d'affaires in Constantinople, to Bülow, No. 101, 11 July 1906, "Türkei" 152, Bd. 39. Neither Gwinner nor Helfferich seems to have had complete confidence in Huguenin, perhaps because they thought him too much under Marschall's influence; and Huguenin sometimes provided Marschall with information which he did not wish to get back to the bank; Marschall to FO, No. 66, 5 April 1907, *GP*, xxii, doc. 7656.

[52] Marschall to FO, Nos. 268, 270, 14-15 Oct. 1906, "Türkei" 152 Bd. 39.

[53] Gwinner to Huguenin, 18 July 1906, *ibid.*

go to the railway, and would not grant it even then if it seemed likely to free revenues for the railway that would otherwise have to be used for administrative purposes.

This state of affairs was typical of that which the Germans were to face until the time of the settlement in 1913 and 1914 of their disputes with the other powers interested in Turkey. The situation was this. The Turks were always on the verge of bank-ruptcy, needing money not only for long-term capital expendi-tures but for ordinary expenses as well. Thus a three-way strug-gle went on continually, with the English attempting to force the Turks to spend new revenues on administrative reforms of vari-ous sorts, while the Germans and French, sometimes working to-gether and sometimes against each other, attempted to find guar-antee funds for their various projects. In practice, administrative necessities tended to come first; it was dangerous to let salaries for soldiers and civil servants get too far in arrears. This gave the English considerable leverage, which it must be said they ex-ploited very effectively against the Germans.

Indeed, because of delays imposed by the customs-increase negotiations, the need to provide the Turks with administrative advances, and the efforts required to thwart an apparent English attempt to buy a controlling interest in a vital section of the rail-way, negotiations for the next section of the railway, to Aleppo, did not begin until mid-March 1908.[54] Considering the complex-ity of the material under discussion, the talks went ahead fairly quickly once begun.

It soon developed that the Sultan wished to extend the section under consideration another 340 kilometers past Aleppo to Tell Helif. Little more than a geographical designation, Tell Helif was the junction from whence a branch line was eventually to depart for Diyarbakir. In some ways, the Sultan's proposal was better than the original plan to build as far as Aleppo, because it would place the Germans in a commanding position at the head of the Tigris valley. All difficult construction would be to the rear, with only 625 easy kilometers to go before reaching Bagdad. Finan-

[54] Leisurely Turkish business habits may also have contributed. For a hilarious account of these, see Marschall to Bülow, No. 26, 2 Feb. 1902, *GP*, xvii, doc. 5247.

cially, however, the proposal presented serious difficulties, and it was around these that most of the discussion turned. Helfferich and Huguenin handled the actual negotiations in Constantinople, with Gwinner nervously prompting from Berlin. But Gwinner trusted Helfferich's judgment and therefore usually accepted (though with much wringing of hands) the measures which Helfferich and Huguenin thought necessary for the success of the negotiations. Marschall remained in the background, although he sent an occasional telegram to add a little weight to Helfferich's communications with Gwinner.

The first construction and financing proposals reflected the fact that the original plan had been to build only to Aleppo.[55] In early May, these initial proposals had to be abandoned, apparently because they placed too much of a strain on the Deutsche Bank's resources.[56] The scheme the Germans finally adopted to reduce their own financial burdens was ingenious and complex. As it was typical of those to be adopted for the sections of the railway past Tell Helif, it is perhaps appropriate to consider the details of it here.

The essential measure was to convince the Turks that the entire Bulgurlu-Tell Helif section was a unity for construction and financing purposes. A building time of seven years was allowed for completion of the entire section. The Deutsche Bank could therefore use the proceeds from the sale of either of the two series of bonds it planned to issue to begin construction anywhere. The provisions from the Convention of 1903 regulating the payment of the operating guarantee of 4,500 francs per kilometer stated that payment was to commence as 40-kilometer segments were placed in operation. It failed to specify that these segments had to be connected. No compelling need therefore existed to push construction of the expensive sections over the Taurus and Amanus mountains at top speed. It was to the bank's advantage to complete these sections as soon as possible, but the gains from reducing costs by stretching construction time were

[55] Helfferich and Huguenin to Deutsche Bank (henceforth DB), 6 April 1908, "Türkei" 152, Bd. 44.
[56] See, for example, Gwinner to Anatolian Railway (henceforth ARR), 19 May 1908, *ibid*.

even greater.[57] Gwinner planned to issue the first of the new bond series (Series II), worth 108 million francs or Ltq. (Turkish pounds) 4,470,000 at par, in 1909 when construction was slated to begin. He expected no trouble in disposing of the issue.[58] The engineer in charge, Geheimer Baurat Otto Riese of Philipp Holzmann et Cie., planned to combine the initial work on the Taurus crossing with enough inexpensive construction so that the bank could count upon operating guarantees from 400 kilometers of railway from the proceeds of Series II. Helfferich calculated that the surpluses of the conceded revenues would reach Ltq. 355,000 by 1909. This sum was more than adequate to cover the amortization and interest charges on Series II and the operating guarantees for 400 kilometers of railway.[59]

The financing of the second new series of bonds, Series III, and the necessary operating guarantees for the remaining 440 kilometers remained a problem. Helfferich and the others in Constantinople believed that within three or four years, when it became necessary to issue Series III, the natural increases in the guarantee revenues would more than cover the annuities and, by the time the section was completed, the operating guarantees as well.[60] To guard against unforeseen contingencies, the Germans had also persuaded the Turks to pledge as additional security the revenues of the *agnams*, the tax on sheep, from the *vilayets* of Konya, Adana, and Aleppo. Because the *agnams* merely constituted a kind of emergency backing, however, the Turks refused to turn them over to the Debt for collection. This made Gwinner most uneasy, because unless the Debt collected the *agnams* they were worthless as backing for bonds to be sold on the German market.[61] Marschall retorted that Gwinner's fears were unfounded. At the very worst, if the surpluses of the conceded revenues were still insufficient to cover the annuities when the time came to issue Series III, the threat to discontinue construction might make the Turks rather more willing to turn the *agnams*

[57] For the clearest statement of the advantages of the above arrangements, see Helfferich and Huguenin to DB, 28 May 1908, *ibid.*

[58] Gwinner to ARR, 19 May 1908, *ibid.*

[59] Helfferich and Huguenin to DB, 20 May 1908, *ibid.*

[60] *Ibid.*

[61] Gwinner to DB in Turkey, 21 May 1908, *ibid.*

over to the Debt. Since the planned construction program would have left the Turks with disconnected segments of track, Marschall's assumption was doubtless correct.[62] Helfferich repeated the same considerations about a week later, on 28 May 1908, and added that if Gwinner did not give in, the entire negotiation was likely to fail. Gwinner had no choice but to accept the contracts as they stood.[63] When Helfferich and Huguenin signed the new contracts on 2 June 1908, there seemed to be no more obstacles to the completion of the key section of the railway.

In retrospect, the convention of June 1908 left a little to be desired as a business proposition because it placed such heavy demands on the future. If things did not work out as Helfferich and Marschall had foreseen, the railway was going to be in serious financial trouble. But in June 1908 no dangers were in sight.

Helfferich had succeeded brilliantly as Second Director. When he returned home in July it was to assume a Deputy Directorship in the Deutsche Bank's home office in Berlin. By fall of 1908, he was a full director—at the age of thirty-six. In the years after his return to Berlin, Helfferich became increasingly involved in a wide range of the bank's domestic and foreign enterprises.[64] But the Bagdad Railway remained to the very end of his association with the Deutsche Bank the most important and most typical of his concerns, and the narrative will continue to center on it.

As was also to be characteristic of future German triumphs in Turkey, its authors did not long enjoy that of 1908. In July, when

[62] Marschall to FO, No. 140, 22 May 1908, *ibid.*

[63] See n.57 above, and Gwinner to ARR, 23 May 1908, *ibid.* Internal evidence makes it clear that Gwinner's telegram was misdated.

[64] Not all of the bank's manifold interests are equally accessible to the historian, since many of the bank's records were destroyed in World War II. Many of the bank's foreign interests, however, can be traced through Foreign Office documents. For an account which throws much light on the political ramifications of the bank's foreign enterprises, see Fischer, *Krieg der Illusionen*, Ch. 14, *passim*. Fischer is especially helpful on the Balkan and Turkish activities of the bank that were Helfferich's main concern. Some notion of the bank's domestic activities is provided by *ibid.*, Ch. 1, *passim;* Jacob Riesser, *The German Great Banks and Their Concentration in Connection with the Economic Development of Germany* (Washington, D.C., 1911), 432-40, 478-82, *et passim*. As a director of Germany's greatest commercial bank, Helfferich also acquired the usual collection of board chairmanships and memberships, including a place on the Zentralausschuss of the Reichsbank.

Sultan Abdülhamid II seemed as much in control of his chronically unruly subjects as ever, he was upset by a group of young army officers who have come to be known as the Young Turks. In less than three weeks, they had established a "guided" democracy and stripped the Sultan of his power. In the long run the Germans probably stood to lose less from this Turanian upsurge than the other powers. In the short run, however, because the German position had been built on friendship with the Sultan, the events quite justified Helfferich's mournful assessment of the following November: "We have fallen . . . completely beneath the wheels."[65]

Helfferich attributed the German eclipse to a number of other causes as well. First, despite the advice of himself and Marschall, Bülow had backed Austria unconditionally in its annexation of Bosnia-Herzegovina.[66] Second, most of the key German diplomats had been absent at the time of the crisis. Third, "the odium of absolutism is stuck as firmly to us as the aureole of . . . *Parlamentarismus* to the English." Helfferich's findings, indeed, left him rather pessimistic about the future; "England is trumps," he said. He accordingly proposed renewed efforts to reach terms with the English, suggesting the offer of the Bagdad-Gulf section of the railway.[67] His summation was, "we have our work cut out for us."

Marschall was not so inclined to despair as Helfferich. He believed that since the revolution was made by German-trained

[65] Helfferich to Gwinner, 30 Nov. 1908, *GP*, xxvii, doc. 9958; and also for the quotations from the following paragraph. Alfred von Kiderlen-Wächter pointed out very early the positive side of the revolution for Germany; Kiderlen to Bülow, No. 157, 9 Aug. 1908, *GP*, xxv, doc. 8899.

[66] Helfferich to Paul Weitz, Constantinople correspondent of the *Frankfurter Zeitung*, 8 Oct. 1908, Weitz "Nachlass," and *Weltkrieg*, I, 67-68. Helfferich later thought Bülow's "*Nibelungentreue*" to Austria had averted a major war; *Weltkrieg*, I, 71; *Türkenpolitik*, 21.

[67] Colonel Percy H. H. Massy, an Englishman active for many years in Turkey, had earlier presented such ideas to Helfferich. Massy claimed to be acting solely on his own initiative but clearly meant to give the impression of having important backers; Helfferich memorandum on discussion with Massy, 12 Oct. 1908, "Türkei" 152, Bd. 45. Felix Somary claims to have discussed an Anglo-German Bagdad settlement in mid-August 1908 with Sir Ernest Cassel, one of the financiers involved in the Anglo-German discussions of 1903; Felix Somary, *Erinnerungen aus meinem Leben* (Zurich, n.d.), 80-81.

officers, who might well be expected to seek more instruction, Germany's position was more secure than it appeared. He recommended hammering away at the theme that the aims of the new Turkey and Germany were the same and let events take their course.[68] He was also less inclined than the bankers to parley with the English. Although the bankers did discuss matters with the English, things went so slowly the net result was almost the same as if Marschall's advice had been followed to the letter. But the bankers did take a number of other steps to move events in a propitious direction. They participated in the first large loan of November 1908 to the new regime and shortly thereafter established a branch bank in Constantinople.[69] The Germans continued in 1909 to supply the Turks with advances *ad libitum*, as Helfferich put it. He thought these advances politically unavoidable, but by February they were making him decidedly uneasy: "This competition for the good fortune of being allowed to fill the Turkish coffers is bound to lead the Turks to a false estimate of their financial position." By March, he was stating flatly, "this granting of advances can go no further," but it did.[70]

The bankers also moved rapidly to overcome deficiences in the German propaganda organization. Helfferich had taken the first step toward improving German public relations as early as September 1908, when he interceded with Gwinner to secure 9,000 marks for the "expenses" of Paul Weitz, the Constantinople correspondent of the *Frankfurter Zeitung* and a man with extensive contacts in Young Turk circles.[71] After his November 1908 trip, Helfferich pressed Bülow to support a more extensive public relations organization than the bank alone could afford and reported to Weitz that the Chancellor "understands."[72] By early

---

[68] Marschall to Bülow, No. 196, 3 Sept. 1908, *GP*, xxv, doc. 8910.

[69] Correspondence between Helfferich and DB, 3 to 26 Nov. 1908, "Türkei" 110, Bd. 53; FO to Constantinople, No. 1995, 22 Dec. 1908, *ibid.*

[70] Helfferich to Weitz, 5 Feb. 1909, 1 March 1909, Weitz "Nachlass"; correspondence between Helfferich and DB, 20 to 30 April 1909, "Türkei" 110, Bd. 55.

[71] Helfferich to Weitz, 11 Sept. 1908, Weitz "Nachlass."

[72] Helfferich to Weitz, 19 Dec. 1908, *ibid.* By 1910, two of the important papers Helfferich had earlier listed as being in the hands of the English, the *Yeni Gazetta* and *Ikdam*, were printing inspired articles for the Germans;

January 1909, Weitz was getting more money, and though the amounts and means are not clearly indicated, some of the money was evidently transferred through Marschall.[73] On a trip in April 1909, Helfferich also asked the home office for permission to contribute up to 100,000 francs to help an "influential" Turkish group found a newspaper.[74] The Germans were beginning to discover that the revolution was indeed, as a Turk remarked to Helfferich, "the democratization of baksheesh."[75]

By the fall of 1909, the Germans had recovered most of the ground they had earlier lost. The English had helped them. First Sir Gerald Lowther, the English ambassador, repeated the German mistake of committing himself to factions that, as it happened, were on the way out. Marschall ironically commented on his colleague's blunders: "If one wishes to fish in troubled waters, ordinary foresight would seem to demand not conducting this praiseworthy activity in the full glare of an electric searchlight."[76] English precipitateness in pushing for commercial advantages for their own nationals in the fall of 1909, while at the same time denying the Turks the use of a new tariff increase for the Bagdad Railway, did the rest. Curiously, the English only worsened their position by offering to build an unguaranteed railway from Bagdad to the Persian Gulf. While in Constantinople in November 1909, Gwinner pointed out to Hilmi Pasha, the Grand Vizier, what this meant: "[The English] have no interest in a percentage of the Bagdad Railway, but want a geographical division into spheres of influence." Lest the import of his words be lost, Gwinner added: "No builder can build railways in Turkey without subsidies. If he nevertheless does so, it is not a commercial transaction he is engaging in, but a political one."[77]

Helfferich and Fr. E. Neeff to Zimmermann, 4 Aug. 1910, "Türkei" 152, Bd. 51; and Helfferich to Weitz, 16 Dec. 1911, Weitz "Nachlass."

[73] Helfferich to Weitz, 13 Jan. 1909, *ibid.*

[74] Helfferich to DB, 6 May 1909, "Türkei" 110, Bd. 55. Marschall added in a telegram of his own: "I consider it most urgently to be desired that the Deutsche Bank give its consent"; Marschall to FO, No. 215, 6 May 1909, *ibid.*

[75] *Prozess,* 17.

[76] Marschall to Bülow, No. 132, 3 June 1909, *GP,* xxvii, doc. 9600.

[77] Gwinner to Zimmermann, 20 Nov. 1909, *ibid.,* doc. 9976.

In Helfferich's words, English acts "had opened many eyes" to the fact that English friendship was not so altruistic as the English made it appear.[78]

By the summer of 1909, the Germans felt sufficiently confident about the way things were going to order construction begun on the next section starting in November. For a variety of reasons, this was about as early as construction could have begun even if the Young Turk Revolution had not occurred. Despite the anguish the revolution caused the Germans, it did not materially delay completion of the railway. The bankers also reopened negotiations in November over guarantee revenues for further construction. They sought the surpluses of the so-called "divers revenues" of the Debt as guarantee funds, but as Djavid Bey, the Young Turk Finance Minister, refused to grant them for this purpose, nothing much happened.[79] By February 1910, Helfferich was asking Weitz, "developments in Turkey have engendered in me an increasing uneasiness. . . . What is actually going on?"[80] In March, Helfferich and Gwinner in exasperation submitted a long querulous memorandum to the Foreign Office filled with their complaints. They demanded that the "Turks [be] shown with the necessary seriousness that they will not be allowed to trifle unpunished with German rights and interests. . . ."[81] Marschall was so irritated by this blast that he submitted a countermemorandum in refutation. He noted that he was "rather put . . . out" by the tone of the memorandum and commented acidly that the bank had long "enjoyed extensive and very effective diplomatic support for its Turkish undertakings." He dealt with the substantive complaints of the bankers, and cautioned that in the "new Turkey, success can only be obtained through imperturbability, steadfastness, and patience." To use, he warned, "the drastic methods that formerly were usual would compromise the Ger-

[78] Helfferich to Weitz, 23 Dec. 1909, Weitz "Nachlass."

[79] DB to Kautz, Helfferich's replacement as Second Director, 19 Nov. 1909, "Türkei" 110, Bd. 56; Kautz to DB, 21 Nov. 1909, *ibid.*

[80] Helfferich to Weitz, 2 Feb. 1910, Weitz "Nachlass."

[81] Helfferich-Gwinner memorandum, with covering note from Helfferich to Zimmermann, 15 March 1910, "Türkei" 152, Bd. 50. The style of the memorandum suggests that Helfferich was the author.

man cause beyond salvation."[82] The bankers, discomfited, backed down.

By early summer of 1910 most of the matters troubling the bankers had, in fact, been resolved to their satisfaction. Only the most serious problem, the source of money for additional construction, remained outstanding. The question assumed a particular urgency when it was learned late in May that Djavid Bey contemplated negotiating a large state loan in London or Paris. It was feared he might have to pledge moneys that would otherwise be available for the railway. Djavid's negotiations came to nothing, however, and he returned home empty-handed.[83] Resuming his negotiations with the French in late September, Djavid found the French as intractable as ever. Helfferich later characterized the French terms as "tantamount to the erection of a financial control . . . [which] would have subjected Turkey to the fiat of the Western Powers in all economic matters."[84] The Germans desired such an outcome no more than the Turks, and they accordingly let the Turks know that money was available in Berlin. Although the documents seem to show that the Kaiser himself was responsible for this offer, Helfferich privately claimed credit for himself.[85] He explained to Weitz in mid-October that they "were ready to bite into the sour apple if absolutely necessary," but that their hope was to "put some starch into the Turks" and thus force the "Parisians" to offer the Turks "supportable" terms.[86] In short, the French were to do the work while the Germans got the credit.

Such a division of labor proved unacceptable to the French. When reports of the impending breakdown of Franco-Turkish talks began coming in during the third week in October 1910, the bankers hurriedly pulled together a consortium of major Ger-

[82] Marschall to Chancellor Theobald von Bethmann Hollweg, No. 91, 25 March 1910, *ibid.*

[83] DB to ARR, 25 May 1910; Helfferich and Gwinner to Kautz, 22 June 1910, *ibid.*, Bd. 51.

[84] *Weltkrieg*, I, 136. For an excellent summary of the French efforts, see Marschall to FO, No. 346, 8 Nov. 1910, "Türkei" 110, Bd. 51.

[85] See especially Bethmann Hollweg to William II, 30 Sept. 1910, *GP*, XXVII, doc. 10,049, and p. 701n; Helfferich to Weitz, 12 Oct. 1910, Weitz "Nachlass."

[86] *Ibid.*

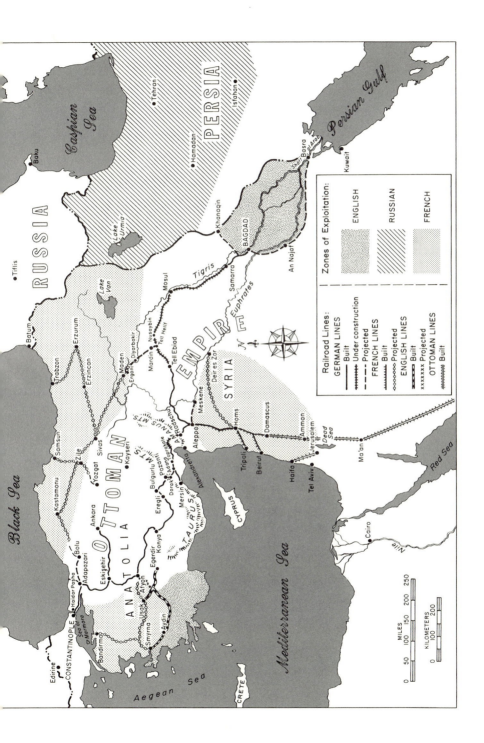

1. The Enemies Chat: Erzberger and Helfferich

2. The Official

3. A Nation Pays Its Respect: Helfferich's Funeral Services in Mannheim

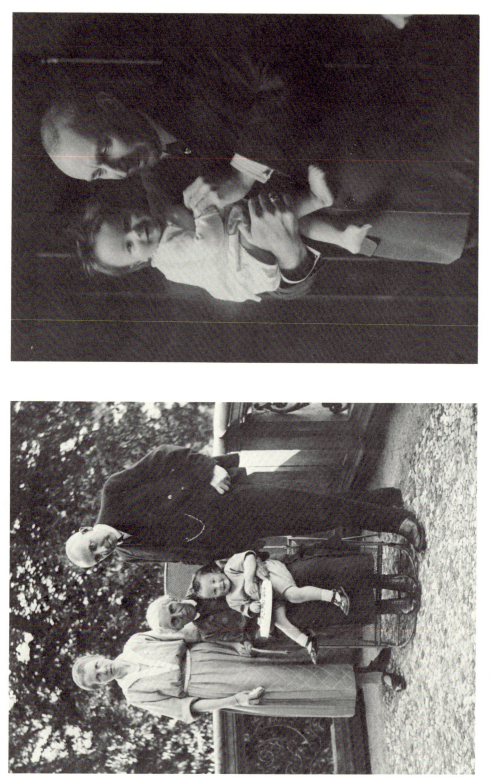

5. Helfferich and Son: Karl and
   Friedrich Helfferich

4. Three Generations: Annette, Augusta,
   Friedrich and Karl Helfferich

man, Austrian, and Swiss banks. On the day of the final collapse
of the Franco-Turkish talks, 25 October, Helfferich wrote his
friend Arthur Zimmermann: "It is likely that I shall have to go to
[Constantinople]. Would you kindly see to it that a seat is reserved for me?"[87] Shortly after Helfferich arrived in the Ottoman
capital, he concluded that Marschall's earlier estimate that "political necessity" demanded a loan "at once" was accurate.[88] The
talks progressed very quickly. In a week Helfferich was writing
Berlin, "Today's *Tanin* carries an article on the unconditional
necessity of the immediate continuation of the Bagdad Railway
to Bagdad. . . . I consider it eminently important that we not only
contract the loan promptly but leave behind the impression of
magnanimous generosity."[89] By 9 November, after what Helfferich described as the "most agonizing negotiations" the contract
was ready to be signed.[90] The bank agreed to provide the Turks
up to 11 million pounds in 1911 and 1912. As the loan was secured by the customs duties of Constantinople, it was usually
styled the "customs loan of 1911."[91] In his final telegram on the
loan, Helfferich requested money for the press. He explained:
"The press expects this according to the usual practice, and we
particularly need a favorable atmosphere on account of our Bagdad plans."[92]

Djavid commented later that Helfferich had acted "with great
intelligence and tact," setting no conditions "inconsistent with the
dignity of Turkey." He grandiloquently described the loan as the
"greatest diplomatic victory" between the Young Turk Revolution and the World War.[93] Marschall was scarcely more restrained. The German position seemed secure as never before,
and his policy of restraint and watchful waiting seemed amply
vindicated. The loan was also a personal triumph for Helfferich,

[87] Helfferich to Zimmermann, 25 Oct. 1910, "Türkei" 110, Bd. 58.
[88] Marschall to FO, No. 265, 29 Oct. 1910, *GP*, xxvii, doc. 10,058; Helfferich to DB, 1 Nov. 1910, *ibid.*, doc. 10,063.
[89] Helfferich to DB, 6 Nov. 1910, *ibid.*, doc. 10,065.
[90] Helfferich to DB, 7 and 8 Nov. 1910, "Türkei" 110, Bd. 59.
[91] The actual transaction was highly involved. For the final arrangements,
see Helfferich to DB, 10 Nov. 1910, *ibid.*
[92] Helfferich to DB (2nd tel.), 10 Nov. 1910, *ibid.*
[93] Earle, *Bagdad Railway*, 225-26.

and one he felt not fully appreciated: "How much work it took and how difficult it was . . . only those who were in on it understand. Even in the Foreign Office . . . they seem to have no adequate conception."[94] Yet the matter had its dark side. The loan stretched the capacity of the German market for Turkish paper past its absolute limits, with the result that issuing additional Bagdad bonds during the first half of 1911 was out of the question. As it happened, this delay was to have important effects.

When the loan was out of the way, Helfferich turned to negotiations for the next section of the railway, from Tell Helif to Bagdad. Once again, Djavid absolutely refused to pledge the surpluses of the divers revenues to the railway. But he did agree that the entire section from Bulgurlu to Bagdad be considered a unit for construction and financing purposes. That meant that the bank could use money from Series II to begin construction from Bagdad north if it desired. As Helfferich drily remarked: "The enormous technical, financial, and political advantages of this solution are obvious."[95] The most serious problem still remained unsolved when Helfferich returned to Berlin in late November. It was where security for the bonds of the three series (Series IV-VI, worth 54 million francs apiece at par) to finance the Tell Helif-Bagdad section was to be found. The question was particularly urgent because Djavid insisted that the bank commit itself to complete the entire section to Bagdad within six years of the time the amended concession was granted. As Helfferich pointed out to Marschall in February 1911, the guarantee revenues then foreseen were some Ltq. 360,000 short of the amount required. Neither he nor Gwinner were entirely convinced by Marschall's argument that according to the terms of the 1903 Convention a *force majeure*—which might mean almost anything—invalidated contracted deadlines. They agreed to Djavid's terms only because "higher, not exclusively financial, considerations prevail."[96]

[94] Helfferich to Weitz, 29 Nov. 1910, Weitz "Nachlass."

[95] Helfferich to Gwinner, 14 Nov. 1910, *GP*, xxvii, doc. 10,017.

[96] Marschall to DB, No. 45, 23 Feb. 1911, "Türkei" 152, Bd. 53; Gwinner to Huguenin, 2 March 1911, *ibid*. Gwinner pointed out that information from a certain Perpagnani showed clearly that if the tobacco tithes were withdrawn from the conceded revenues, the surpluses would hardly cover Series II and III. As the Anatolian tithes would cover only Series IV,

Once the bankers had reluctantly agreed to bite the bullet for the sake of *Weltpolitik*, the remaining issues, which involved the grant of a number of minor concessions to the Germans and a renunciation on their part of building rights from Bagdad to the Gulf, were quickly resolved. On 20 March 1911, Huguenin signed the new Bagdad conventions and handed over the declaration of renunciation for the Bagdad-Gulf section to the Turks.[97] The concessions of 20 March signified a major defeat for England's anti-Bagdad policy, one of the foremost objectives of which had been to prevent the railway from reaching Bagdad.[98] Although the English still had some very effective weapons, particularly the power to withhold the new tariff increase which the Turks so desperately needed, it was now the Germans who could afford to sit and wait. The most that the English could now secure was internationalization of the railway below Bagdad. That was a long way from the international railway which Gwinner had offered them in 1903. Furthermore, there was every prospect that they would have to bargain with the Germans alone and unsupported by their friends. French finance had never opposed the railway, and by March 1911 the Germans were well on their way to a separate agreement with Russia on the Bagdad question.

Kiderlen-Wächter, Secretary of State for Foreign Affairs, characterized the concessions of 20 March as a "spectacular triumph for the German spirit of enterprise and the tenacity of German policy."[99] Helfferich was more restrained. Writing to Weitz in mid-April he said: "The Bagdad contracts represent a good step forward. . . . It is splendid that we have gotten so far and can even begin construction in Bagdad in the near future." But he looked toward the future with some apprehension, as he feared that the guarantee revenues would not increase rapidly enough to meet expected needs. "We must," he concluded, "exploit every opportunity to secure the necessary backing later on."[100] In some

---

Series V, VI, and the operating guarantees for the entire section "are suspended in mid-air."

[97] Marschall to FO, No. 67, 21 March 1911, *GP*, xxvii, doc. 10,037.

[98] Chapman, *Bagdad Railway*, 139-40.

[99] Kiderlen to Bethmann Hollweg, *GP*, xxvii, doc. 10,038.

[100] Helfferich to Weitz, 17 April 1911, Weitz "Nachlass." The Deutsche

ways the concessions of March 1911 resembled Potëmkin's famous villages.

The Bagdad Railway: Some Accounts Are Settled, 1911 to 1914

The French moved almost immediately after the signing of the March 1911 conventions to reach a rapprochement with the Germans. The Ottoman Bank, leader of French economic interests, had formerly hoped that the French government might relent in its refusal to allow French participation in the Bagdad Railway.[101] The bank had apparently abandoned such hopes early in 1910 and, given the failure of French loan negotiations in 1910 and German successes in 1911, decided that its own projects were unlikely to succeed in the face of German opposition. The Germans, on the other hand, were well aware that the French could make it very hard for them to secure better Bagdad guarantees. Finally, Helfferich expressed to Weitz another fear which weighed heavily on both groups: "The rashness . . . with which all imaginable projects are being pursued, without any regard whatever for the financial capabilities of the country, really worries me. Dreadnaughts . . . roads . . . railway projects, harbor construction simply everywhere. . . ."[102]

An exploratory meeting in March 1911 between Helfferich, Gwinner, and Count Georges Vitali, the most important French railway builder in Turkey, went so well that it was decided to hold a summit meeting with the Ottoman Bank. In May the French and German tycoons met halfway in Frankfurt am Main.[103] The meeting was not a great success. Paul Révoil, the new President of the Ottoman Bank, soon managed to create such a poi-

---

Bank credited 15,000 marks to Weitz's account for his services in the conclusion of the March 1911 agreements; DB [Gwinner and Helfferich] to Weitz, 1 May 1911, *ibid.*

[101] DB *promemoria* on French railway plans in Turkey, with corrections in Helfferich's hand, 7 April 1911, "Türkei" 152, Bd. 54. The Ottoman Bank had accordingly accepted 30 per cent of the bonds from Series II.

[102] Helfferich to Weitz, 17 April 1911, Weitz "Nachlass."

[103] DB to FO, minutes of meeting with Révoil, Vitali, and Gaston Auboyneau, 17 May 1911, "Turkei" 152, Bd. 54. See also *GP*, xxxi, doc. 11,499, much abridged.

sonous atmosphere with his continual talk of "compensations" that very little was achieved. Nevertheless, each side at least marked out its positions, which did not differ very much from those eventually agreed to in 1914. The empire was to be divided into zones of construction. In Asiatic Turkey, the French were to have Syria and northeastern Anatolia, while the Germans were to have the Bagdad system and the lines necessary to fill it out. The differences were mostly over exact lines of demarcation. The whole system was to be paid for by establishing a "Caisse de Chemins de Fer" with powers similar to the Debt. To keep the Turks from collapsing under their financial load, a system of priorities was to be worked out, and twelve to fifteen years were allotted for completing the combined Franco-German list of projects. Later, the Germans were inclined to think the talks had gone so badly because Révoil still hoped to realize his program in the face of German opposition. They also darkly speculated that perhaps he had no interest whatever in Turkey but merely "meant to grind his own political axe by fighting the German arch-enemy in Turkey."

Gwinner and Helfferich drew the understandable conclusion that the only way to bring the French to their senses was to block them at every turn. This they did, while themselves following a policy of "temporizing" in their own discussions with the Turks.[104] Although the latter policy eventually drew angry protests from the bank's representatives in Constantinople and the Foreign Office, from Berlin's point of view it was undoubtedly correct.[105] As Helfferich put it to Weitz: "What will come of the insane railroad and financial policies down there [in Turkey] only the gods know."[106] The outbreak of war between Italy and the Ottoman Empire vindicated the bank's policy in a way neither Gwinner nor Helfferich had anticipated. But when Helfferich visited Constantinople in October 1911, he was left no doubt about how unpopular the policy of temporization was.[107]

---

[104] Gwinner to ARR, 23 Aug. 1911, "Türkei" 152, Bd. 56.

[105] See the series of telegrams from 25 Aug. to 17 Oct. 1911, *ibid.*, from Marschall and Franz G. Günther, Kautz's replacement, complaining of the difficult position that Gwinner's directive placed them in.

[106] Helfferich to Weitz, 31 Aug. 1911, Weitz "Nachlass."

[107] Helfferich to DB, 26 Oct. 1911, "Türkei" 152, Bd. 57.

The most he would consent to, however, was to provide Weitz with a substantial sum, up to 100,000 francs, for the purpose of creating a favorable press.[108] Otherwise, he and Gwinner preferred to let things drift. By early 1912, all thought had been abandoned of issuing the bonds of Series III or the second installment of the 1911 customs loan.[109] The pace of construction was slowed.[110] By midsummer, Helfferich was writing Weitz: "I have a feeling that the market for Turkish securities will not stand any more very severe tests."[111] A vain hope: the Turks made peace with Italy only to be set upon by the Balkan League in October 1912. When an armistice temporarily ended the war in December, the political and financial position of the Turks was much worse. Stripped of most of his European possessions and virtually bankrupt, the "sickman" seemed near total dismemberment.

Although this untimely fate was momentarily averted by an advance from the Deutsche Bank,[112] the Turks' long-term prospects remained as gloomy as ever. The Turks' debt had been all they could manage in 1911. By 1913 it had grown considerably, while the territory which supported it had shrunk by about a fifth. For the Deutsche Bank, solving this problem was essential. Helfferich's solution was ingeniously simple: it was, in effect, to expand the Ottoman Empire to its former size.[113] This financial

[108] Helfferich to Weitz, 16 Dec. 1911, Weitz "Nachlass."

[109] Helfferich to Weitz, 4 Feb. 1912, *ibid.*

[110] For the state of construction activities, see the many detailed consular reports, particularly those of Walther Rössler, the consul in Aleppo; "Türkei" 152, Bde. 58-60, *passim.*

[111] Helfferich to Weitz, 25 July 1912, Weitz "Nachlass." This unfortunately is the last of Helfferich's informative letters to Weitz. The demands upon his time had become too great to permit him to keep up the correspondence.

[112] For the acrimonious correspondence about this particular advance, see the material in "Türkei" 110, Bde. 65-66, 4 Feb. to 5 March 1913, especially Baron Hans von Wangenheim, the new German ambassador in Constantinople, to Bethmann Hollweg, No. 42, 10 Feb. 1913; Helfferich to Zimmermann, 19 Feb. 1913; Günther to Helfferich, 20 Feb. 1913; Generalkonsul Josef Mertens to Bethmann Hollweg, 5 March 1913. See also Hallgarten, *Imperialismus,* II, 372-73.

[113] Helfferich developed his solution in a series of statements, the last of which is the most detailed; Helfferich and Gwinner to FO, 12 Dec. 1912,

conjuring trick was to be accomplished by depriving the victorious Balkan League of all compensations and indemnities and by making it assume a share of the Turkish state debt. Of the possible methods for accomplishing this, Helfferich favored assessing the share on the basis of the income the lost Turkish territories had provided the Debt. He reasoned that since the Turks had alienated the revenues in question to the Debt, the only way the League could acquire them was by despoiling the Debt. Since the Debt was a private organization which represented individuals rather than governments, its property could not according to international law be seized as war booty. Oddly enough, the lost territories contributed a disproportionate share of the Debt's revenue. Helfferich must have found the implications of this disquieting indeed, given the fact that the bonds of Series II through VI were so indifferently secured even in 1911. Because all these bonds held last mortgage claims against the conceded revenues, it would not help for the League to assume only a part of the share of the former Turkish debt. It had to assume the *entire* share.

Helfferich pointed out the precedents for his solution and proposed the following arrangements to avoid the difficulties that had arisen in such cases in the past.[114] He wanted written into the peace treaties between Turkey and the Balkan states the amounts for which the latter were liable and the manner in which such sums were to be paid. The method of payment he preferred was to capitalize the income due the Debt at 4 per cent, which sum was then to be lent to the Balkan League in the form of an international loan guaranteed by the powers. One particular advantage of such a scheme, which Helfferich failed to mention, was that the holders of some rather dubious Turkish paper would suddenly find themselves the possessors of gilt-edged interna-

---

"Türkei" 110, Bd. 65; Gwinner to Prince Karl Max von Lichnowsky, the new German ambassador in London, 9 Jan. 1913, *ibid.*; and "Die türkische Staatsschuld und die Balkanstaaten," *Bank-Archiv*, 12 (1913), 167-75.

[114] The main precedent was the Berlin treaty of 1878. Orhan Conker and Emile Witmeur, *Redressement économique et industrialisation de la Nouvelle Turquie* (Paris, 1937), 46, give the sums that each of the Balkan states was to pay but assert that Bulgaria alone made one payment of 40 million francs, a fraction of what it was supposed to pay.

tional bonds. Among the happy capitalists so favored was the Deutsche Bank, whose vaults were still choked with the unsalable bonds of Series III.

Unfortunately, Helfferich's proposal appealed only to the Foreign Office and to none of the other powers involved.[115] The French thought that their position was adequately secured by the Turks' Asiatic revenues. The Russians even demanded compensation for their Balkan protégés, and it is a fact that the winner of a war does not normally pay the loser. Neither the Foreign Office, nor Helfferich himself, who led one of the three committees which met in Paris during the summer of 1913 for the purpose of unsnarling the financial tangle left by the Balkan wars, was able to get his position accepted.[116] The entire question remained unresolved a year later, when the outbreak of the First World War rendered it wholly academic.

Yet, while the Paris finance conference came to nothing, other negotiations were in progress which had more propitious prospects. The Turks had begun discussions with the English soon after the signing of the 1911 conventions with the Germans.[117] Although the talks went slowly, by early 1913 agreement had been reached on most of the outstanding differences between the two countries. The basis of the final settlement was Turkish agreement that the English control the Basra-Gulf section of the railway in return for English consent to the removal of the sand bar at the mouth of the Shatt-al-Arab. This would permit large vessels to ascend to Basra, which would give the Germans the outlet to the Gulf they sought for their railway. On the other hand, it would keep the Germans off the shores of the Gulf, as the English felt their strategic interests required. The Deutsche Bank was in

[115] See the pessimistic but accurate appraisal of Baron Wilhelm von Schoen, German ambassador in Paris; Schoen to Bethmann Hollweg, No. 174, 6 May 1913, *GP*, xxxvii, doc. 15,208.

[116] Helfferich had been summoned by Schoen as financial consultant. For a résumé of the financial commission's progress, see Baron von der Lancken-Wakenitz, Botschaftsrat in Paris, to Bethmann Hollweg, No. 256, 18 July 1913, *ibid.*, doc. 15,252; Sallandrouze de Lamornaix memorandum on talks with Helfferich, 1 July 1913, *DDF* (3), vii, doc. 246.

[117] For a detailed account of the Anglo-Turk negotiations, see Chapman, *Bagdad Railway*, 141-67.

basic agreement with these terms, as it informed the Foreign Office in a *promemoria* dated 17 March 1913.[118]

The bank's *promemoria* also was the starting point for Anglo-German discussions, well underway in London by early summer of 1913.[119] After Gwinner traveled to London to coach Prince Lichnowsky, the new German ambassador in London, on the more technical aspects of the problem, essential agreement was soon reached on the basis of the formula, suggested by English Foreign Secretary Sir Edward Grey, "you rule over the railways, and we over the water."[120] A number of factors served, however, to prolong the negotiations. Subsidiary issues kept cropping up which both sides wished to settle once and for all. The material under discussion was also extremely complex. As a result, the final agreement was not ready for initiating until over a year later, in June 1914. Helfferich complained early in the negotiations that the agreement foreseen "is rather meager for us" and felt that the Germans were making most of the concessions. His opinion was unchanged six years later:

> In all individual points Germany abandoned well-established rights acquired through honorable and tedious effort. Or Germany gave its consent to the grant of concessions to the English which collided to a greater or lesser extent with its old rights, and it did so solely to reach a *modus vivendi* with England at long last, after a decade and a half of friction and ceaseless negotiation.[121]

But the English were not the only beneficiaries, as the Germans well knew. The agreement promised to remove the railway from politics and to end English resistance to it. The English had also agreed to assist the Germans to secure guarantee funds for construction as far as Basra and were willing, if necessary, to allow the use of customs revenues for this purpose. These were no

[118] DB *promemoria* to FO, *GP*, xxxvii, doc. 14,721.

[119] See especially Chapman, *Bagdad Railway*, 168-203; Wolf, *Bagdad Railway*, 92-96; Cecil, *Ballin*, 88-93; Fischer, *Krieg der Illusionen*, 431-34.

[120] Gwinner (London) to Helfferich (Paris), 12 June 1913, "Türkei" 152, Bd. 62a.

[121] *Türkenpolitik*, 28. Helfferich's strictures were more accurate in regard to oil rights than anything else. See esp. Fischer, *Krieg der Illusionen*, 434-37.

mean advantages, and to secure them, the Germans had right-fully made sacrifices.

But while the *Grosse Politik* provides a very detailed record of *what* the German position was at various points during the Anglo-German Bagdad negotiations, the picture it leaves of *how* these positions were arrived at is a little misleading (perhaps unintentionally). The impression is that the Foreign Office played a much more positive role than it actually did. With outgoing proposals, for example, it was usual for Helfferich to transmit the Deutsche Bank's wishes to his friend Undersecretary Zimmermann, who then drafted a document in the appropriate form on the basis of the information provided.[122] Foreign Secretary Gottlieb von Jagow then signed the document and dispatched it to London. Zimmermann frequently followed Helfferich's "suggestions" to the letter, incorporating large sections of Helfferich's text unaltered into his dispatch. Helfferich was always careful to maintain the proprieties. He "sketched the tenor," or "suggested the basis" for proposals, which could be passed on "if they met with the Foreign Office's approval." Somehow, they always seemed to. When the document arrived in London, Lichnowsky, or more usually his embassy councillor (Botschaftsrat), Richard von Kühlmann, would present the proposal to the English. Lichnowsky did not know much about the Bagdad Railway, but Kühlmann had been familiar with its problems for many years and usually handled matters to the entire satisfaction of the Deutsche Bank.[123] The procedure for incoming English proposals was about the same. A copy was given to Helfferich or Gwinner, and the bankers provided commentary or a counterdraft in the manner outlined above. In cases where the matters in question were purely of concern to German and English business inter-

[122] Less frequently Gwinner addressed a letter to Lichnowsky or Botschaftsrat Richard Kühlmann through Foreign Office channels or the bank addressed an official communication to the Foreign Office. But Helfferich was the favored avenue of communication between the bank and the Foreign Office.

[123] Not always, however; see Helfferich to Zimmermann, 7 March 1914, "Türkei" 152, Bd. 71. Helfferich commented: "Just between you and me, we have the impression . . . that Kühlmann muffed it. It is important that the matter be set to rights as soon as possible. . . ."

ests, the Deutsche Bank sent experts on the matter to London, and the businessmen worked things out for themselves.

Not long after the Anglo-German negotiations started, Stéphan Pichon, the French Foreign Minister, began to wonder if the time had not also come for a Franco-German settlement. He feared that, while Turkish fiscal vicissitudes had placed the Bagdad Railway in a precarious position, the agreements were proceeding sufficiently rapidly that the French might be forced to bargain with the Germans in isolation. Since the 1911 talks had collapsed because the French were unwilling to reach terms, this new readiness to talk was promising. Helfferich conducted the initial talks while in Paris during May and June of 1913 for the Balkan finance meetings. Both Helfferich and Révoil marked out their positions with their accustomed asperity. Although the meetings did little to settle the territorial questions outstanding between the two groups, it was agreed that, in Helfferich's words, there must be a "clean break" between the French interests and the Bagdad Railway.[124]

Further negotiations in Berlin during August and September between a German negotiating team led by Gwinner and Helfferich and the French settled the details of territorial conflicts— the disputed lines were split roughly in the middle—and the liquidation of French Bagdad interests.[125] The French also agreed to a series of future financing arrangements most favorable to the Germans. If those concerned could be persuaded to accept the new arrangements, the Germans' financing worries were over at least as far as Bagdad, and probably beyond. The Germans had in effect traded concessions for lines they could not afford for guarantees for those that they could.[126] Unfortunately

---

[124] Helfferich, *Siemens*, III, 145; Helfferich *promemoria* to FO, 23 July 1913, *GP*, xxxvII, doc. 14,932. The *DDF* provides a much more complete record than the *GP*. See *DDF* (3), vII, docs. 246, 275, 302, 448, and 478.

[125] DB memorandum and "Note annexé" on talks of 19-20 Aug., 30 Aug. 1913, "Türkei" 152, Bd. 63, and "Échange de vues" and two annexes, 24-26 Sept. 1913, *ibid*. The disputed lines were: 1) Sivas-Diyarbakir; 2) Yozgat-Zile; 3) Kastamonu-Bolu; and 4) Aleppo-Meskine.

[126] DB memorandum to FO, 17 Sept. 1913, "Türkei" 152, Bd. 64. See also "Anlage" to *GP*, xxxvII, doc. 14,943. The memorandum speaks with relief at being freed from the obligation to build the "expensive and technically

for the Germans, the agreement came unstuck almost immediately. As Maurice Bompard, French ambassador to Constantinople,
expressed official opinion: "The French came off so short because
there were no diplomats present to advise the French nego-
tiators."[127] The French therefore resolved to win back what they
could in the high-level diplomatic talks that were to ratify the
agreements between the French and German financiers.[128]

These new talks began in November 1913. Zimmermann, Friedrich von Rosenberg, and Helfferich handled the German side, although before Christmas, Helfferich's function consisted mainly
of prompting Zimmermann and Rosenberg from the wings. The
talks soon ran aground on the question of a line from Aleppo to
Meskine, itself unimportant but sought by the French as the
northern border of their Syrian zone of exploitation. As the Germans wanted a neutral zone which extended farther south, Helfferich stubbornly refused to give in.[129] On 2 February 1914, after
spending much of January in utterly fruitless talks, Helfferich
remarked in exasperation that, if the French continued to insist
on their demands, "it would be better to break off the pour-
parlers."[130] Last-minute intervention by Jules Cambon, the
French ambassador in Berlin, with Bethmann helped to save the
situation.[131] The Germans abandoned their opposition to French
demands in Syria, and on 15 February the Franco-German agree-

---

difficult Sivas-Diyarbakir line," while at the same time complaining of the
harmful effects to Germany's political position.

[127] Wangenheim to FO, No. 628, 1 Nov. 1913, "Türkei" 152, Bd. 65. But
no diplomats were present on the German side either.

[128] Charles Dumont, Finance Minister, to Pichon, 4 Oct. 1913, and Maurice
Paléologue, Political Director in the Ministry for Foreign Affairs, to Dumont,
6 Oct. 1913, DDF (3), VIII, docs. 257, 272.

[129] Zimmermann memorandum on talks with Jules Cambon, the French
ambassador in Berlin, 16 Dec. 1913, and Helfferich to Zimmermann, 14 Dec.
1913, which formed the basis for Zimmermann's discussions with Cambon,
"Türkei" 152, Bd. 67; Cambon to Zimmermann, 20 Dec. 1913, and Helfferich's comments, same date, ibid.

[130] Cambon to Gaston Doumergue, French Premier and Foreign Minister,
16 Feb. 1914, DDF (3), IX, doc. 315.

[131] Ibid. For Cambon's fears about German encroachment in Syria, see
Cambon to Pichon, 27 Nov. 1913, ibid., VIII, doc. 537.

ment was initialed.[132] Although German financial gains were slightly more modest than those foreseen the previous fall, the French press was nevertheless very "subdued" in its estimation of the agreements. André Tardieu's *Temps* launched a "real jeremiad" against the "lamentable results of French policy in the Orient."[133]

The agreement upon which all else depended, however, was that between Germany and Turkey. Talks had begun in a desultory fashion in August 1913, but did not really get down to business until Djavid Bey arrived in Berlin early in November. Things went badly from the beginning. On 4 December, Helfferich wrote Zimmermann: "It would be very desirable if you would give Djavid a talking to, and the sooner the better." He also included a memorandum signed by Gwinner and himself that developed the bank's position at some length.[134] The main problem was that costs had risen greatly since the signing of the original concession in 1903, while the market for Turkish securities had gotten much worse. With the French out of the railway, a new financing consortium would have to be formed, and unless the lines showed some prospect of profit, that promised to be very difficult to do. The bankers thus sought a higher interest rate on all existing Bagdad obligations, operating guarantees for some presently unguaranteed lines, and a change in the operating-guarantee provisions which would provide the bank a profit of 1,000 fr. per kilometer. The difficulty was that while Djavid admitted in principle that German demands were just, he would not accept German remedies, and his own proposals were "wholly insufficient." Zimmermann gave Djavid the requested

[132] Helfferich to Rosenberg, and text of 15 February agreement, 19 Feb. 1914, "Türkei" 152, Bd. 70.

[133] Schoen to Bethmann Hollweg, No. 39, 17 Feb. 1914, *GP*, xxxvii, doc. 14,998. Helfferich and Lancken had earlier been of the opinion that the good press the Germans enjoyed in the late summer and fall of 1913 was due to Vitali's heeding Helfferich's admonition that a press war would ruin the chances for a settlement. They thought Vitali had simply bought off Tardieu "for a few hundred thousand francs"; Lancken to "lieber Freund," 8 Oct. 1913, "Türkei" 152, Bd. 65.

[134] Helfferich to Zimmermann, and Gwinner and Helfferich to FO, 4 Dec. 1913, *GP*, xxxvii, doc. 14,965.

"talking to" the day he got Helfferich's note, but the Turk remained intractable and returned shortly thereafter to Constantinople.

It cannot be said that matters ever progressed much beyond this initial statement of positions. Djavid delayed the resumption of talks first with one excuse then with another, and finally wore down the Germans to the point where they agreed that the talks could continue in Constantinople, rather than in Berlin as originally planned.[135] Even after they recommenced late in May, Djavid proved most unaccommodating. In mid-July 1914, the bank threatened to break off negotiations and suspend construction of the railway unless Djavid came to terms. Djavid, on his side, threatened to shift Krupp artillery contracts to Schneider-Creusot.[136] In desperation, Helfferich devised a scheme whereby the German government was to participate in both the financing and management of the railway in the event that it was necessary to suspend negotiations with the Turks.[137] But his *promemoria* detailing these plans was submitted on 20 July 1914, when the Foreign Office was too taken up with the Sarajevo crisis to pay much attention to such subaltern matters. When war broke out less than two weeks later, agreement still had not been reached.

The Bagdad Railway: An Assessment

After 1912 the bankers assumed almost complete control over Germany's Bagdad Railway policy. There were a number of reasons for this, none particularly sinister. Between 1903 and 1911 the Deutsche Bank had always been ahead of the Foreign Office in its readiness to come to terms with the English, the railway's principal opponents. Baron von Marschall, the dominant influence in the official Bagdad policy, was less impressed with the financial difficulties which weighed so largely with the bank and

---

[135] The principal objective reason for delay was the need to negotiate a state loan with France. For the terms, see *GP*, xxxvii, 610n***. Ahmed Djemel Pasha, the Minister of Public Works, correctly described the French terms as "annihilating"; *Erinnerungen eines türkischen Staatsmannes* (Munich, 1922), 77-79. See also Fischer, *Krieg der Illusionen*, 439-41.

[136] Wangenheim to FO, No. 350, 18 July 1914, *GP*, xxxvii, doc. 15,041.

[137] See *ibid.*, 638n**, for summary.

refused to consider a settlement with the English until construction as far as Bagdad was assured. With the signing of the concessions of March 1911, the time which Marschall had set for negotiations had come, but the international disturbances of 1911 and 1912 delayed their commencement. At a higher level, before 1912 both Bülow and Bethmann would have preferred to include a Bagdad agreement in a more general Anglo-German settlement. After the collapse of the Haldane negotiations in 1912, however, Bethmann was willing to accept a Bagdad agreement alone in the hope of some improvement in Anglo-German relations. When negotiations with the English finally began in 1913, both the government and the bank were united in their determination to achieve a settlement if at all possible. The same frame of mind also guided negotiations with the French and the Turks. Once talks actually began, the bankers were bound to play a large role, for it was they, not the government, who held the concessions and bore the financial risks of the enterprise. These considerations applied particularly to the negotiations with the French and the Turks, in which the aim in one case was to arrive at a *modus vivendi* between the French and German financial interests, and in the other, to secure from the Turks the financial guarantees which would make the Bagdad Railway once again a profitable enterprise.

Helfferich and Gwinner nevertheless dominated the proceedings to a far greater degree than might have been expected, apparently because the diplomats who so long had guided the Bagdad policy were gone. Marschall and Kiderlen died in 1912, and Count Paul von Wolff-Metternich, long-time ambassador in London, was forced into retirement. All three, and especially Marschall, knew the problems of the railway in detail, had decided ideas on what the situation called for, and were forceful enough to play a major role in deciding what the bankers must concede and what they must not. Neither Jagow nor Lichnowsky knew very much about the railway, nor were they as forceful personalities as Kiderlen and Marschall. Baron von Wangenheim, Marschall's replacement in Constantinople, was superior in both respects, but he was remote from the two most important centers of discussion, London and Berlin, and did not have the prestige to interfere successfully from afar as his predecessor might have done. Thus matters in the Foreign Office were left largely to Helfferich's "lieber Zimmermann" and to Rosenberg, also a close acquaintance of Helfferich's. Helfferich had also been on an excellent footing with both Kiderlen and Marschall, but both were much older and more experienced than he. They were less inclined to follow Helfferich's advice and he was perhaps less inclined to offer it. He was far more comradely with Zimmermann. Zimmermann depended heavily upon Helfferich for advice in economic matters, apparently had few ideas of his own on the Bagdad settlement, and was the last man to set Helfferich conditions.[138] When Helfferich arrived in Constantinople in 1906, Marschall had been there nine years and had been connected with the Bagdad Railway even longer. Now the shoe was on the other foot. Helfferich had seven very active years with the Bagdad Railway behind him in 1913 and knew more about it than anyone in the Foreign Office. He knew to the last detail what he wanted, while the Foreign Office knew mainly that it wanted the matter settled in a way satisfactory to Germany. It trusted Helfferich and Gwinner to find such a solution.

Helfferich was up to the task, for from the outset his role was that of contriver of solutions. Marschall gave his initial efforts in 1906 some rough treatment because of the faulty political judgments upon which the proposals rested, but as time went on he met with fewer rebuffs. How much his political judgment had improved is open to question. His July 1914 proposal to bring the German government actively into the management and financing of the railway was certainly of dubious merit. Even if such a proposal were to secure the necessary Reichstag approval, it would have awakened the gravest of suspicions in England and France and jeopardized the settlements so painstakingly worked out. It must also have raised the severest doubts in the minds of the Turks about the ultimate aims which Germany was following in the construction of the railway. One of the railway's greatest as-

---

[138] See, for example, Zimmermann to Helfferich, 23 Aug. 1913, "Türkei" 152, Bd. 63, asking Helfferich's advice on a question connected with the Benguela Railway, "in order that I may have something by which to judge the answer of the Treasury Office." On the Benguela project, in which the Deutsche Bank was quite involved, see Fischer, *Krieg der Illusionen*, 451-56.

sets had always been that the Turks considered the builders' purpose was to make money rather than to secure control over Turkey. Marschall had always been most careful to encourage this view and to contrast the political altruism of the Germans with the designing policies of the French and English. The care which the financiers took to secure adequate guarantees for the railway encouraged this interpretation, for while the Turks were occasionally unhappy about slow progress of construction, they realized that it was the price of the railway's being a business venture. It is true that the Turks often talked as if they wanted the railway constructed as a gift from Germany, but as soon as construction was pushed ahead without thought of profit, the motives of the builders were bound to be questioned.[139] This was all the truer in a situation like that of July 1914, in which the Turks themselves, not the railway's foreign opponents, were blocking the grant of additional financial guarantees. Helfferich's inventiveness, useful as it was, still wanted the guidance of a broader political viewpoint.

But though Helfferich's political sense of touch was still in some important respects defective, he had nevertheless played a key role in the Bagdad settlements with England and France. These settlements were among the few solid diplomatic successes of which Wilhelmine diplomacy could boast in the immediate prewar period. Regrettably, they came too late for their authors to enjoy them much. On the balance, the Bagdad Railway was probably a political liability to German relations with the other Powers. That is not to say, however, that the railway should have been given up after the failure to internationalize it in 1903. Nearly all of Germany's foreign ventures caused uneasiness and alarm in Entente capitals. The purpose of diplomacy is to smooth such conflicts, and in the case of the Bagdad Railway, German diplomacy ultimately did so.

The financial balance must also fall against the railway. It was probably a sound venture, but its increasing entanglement in politics after 1903 led the bankers to assume fiscal commitments

---

[139] In fact neither the so-called Chester project nor the British offer of 1909 to build the Bagdad-Gulf section without guarantees met with a favorable hearing.

which, the events revealed, rested on overly optimistic expectations of Turkey's future. The bankers' essential miscalculation was not economic—for Turkish revenues did increase about as expected—but political. They failed to foresee the disintegration of European Turkey. Helfferich and Gwinner were agile enough to escape from the difficult position in which this untimely event had placed them by persuading the English and French to assist them in securing additional guarantee revenues. But the settlement with France had its disadvantages, as it meant that the Germans could no longer count on the French placing a third of future Bagdad issues. Helfferich often asserted that Germany could build the railway alone if necessary. Although the statement was doubtless true enough, after 1909 the project unquestionably placed a heavy strain on the resources of the Deutsche Bank available for foreign investment. A successful renegotiation of the basic contracts with the Turks would undoubtedly have simplified the placement of new issues somewhat, but it seems clear that in 1914, when German investment capital was more and more returning to the home market, the market for Turkish paper was at best a limited one.[140]

[140] As late as May 1914 Helfferich warned that floating a proposed military loan to Turkey in Germany would absorb all German funds for investment in Turkish securities. This would prevent the issue of the next series of Bagdad bonds, and since the Deutsche Bank had already advanced 60 million francs for construction, it would have to suspend operations if not repaid; Helfferich and Michalowsky to FO, 29 May 1914, "Türkei" 110, Bd. 72.

IV. FINANCIAL WARLORD

Peace and War

Helfferich's views on German economic development before 1914 are excellently summarized in his little book, *Germany's National Wealth, 1888-1913*.[1] Written to celebrate the silver jubilee of William II's reign, the book rapidly went through a number of German editions and was translated into several foreign languages. A liberal journalist unkindly, but accurately, called the work "courtierly economics."[2] That it was, but it was also more. First, it was one of the most influential early estimates of German national wealth, annual income, and annual economic growth. Corrected now in many particulars, it long remained the "best known" work on the state of the German economy prior to World War I, no mean success for an essay in "courtierly economics."[3] Second, aside from its objective merits, the work reveals much about Helfferich's attitude toward German economic and political developments since the nineties and why, in general, he viewed the future with the optimism that he did.

He portrayed the quarter-century of William's reign as one of the high points of human development, matched (perhaps) only by the Renaissance; a dozen years at the center of German economic life had only strengthened his earlier optimism. In considering the course of German economic development, he traced its progress from the devastations of the Thirty Years' War to the "blood brotherhood" of the wars of German unification, which were "no conclusion, but a new beginning." The Bismarckian era

[1] *Deutschlands Volkswohlstand 1888-1913* (3rd edn., Berlin, 1913), is the one cited from below.

[2] Theodor Wolff, *The Eve of 1914* (New York, 1936), 317.

[3] "Best known" was the designation of no less a person than John Maynard Keynes; *The Revision of the Treaty: Being a Sequel to the Economic Consequences of the Peace* (New York, 1922), 88. For a more up-to-date estimate, see Walter Hoffmann and J. H. Müller, *Das deutsche Volkseinkommen 1851-1957* (Tübingen, 1959), 12-26.

was a time of preparation followed by the "onrushing victorious boom that falls entirely within the reign of our Kaiser" and "has hardly a precedent in world history." Nor would he admit that this economic efflorescence represented an unsound development: "Germany had the most to make up [after unification] in the way of economic development. Since the German people have entered world history, they have stood second to none in moral fiber and strength . . . [they] have taken a leading part in science . . . [and] won a place in the first ranks of literature and the arts."[4]

He then noted the specific technological, organizational, and scientific developments that had made this marvelous economic development possible and sketched the state of the German economy in 1913. He asserted with pride that Germany had overtaken England in iron and steel production, but also noted that the United States was "far ahead of all other nations." He calculated that German national income had nearly doubled since 1896, rising from 23 to roughly 42 billion marks. Although German national income was still less than that of England, it exceeded that of France: "France is the land of the annuity, Germany the land of work." He developed at length the position that the lower classes were the principal beneficiaries of the rise in national income and stated flatly: "The oft-asserted 'plutocratic development' does . . . not exist."[5]

Since Germany had had less time to accumulate capital, however, it stood behind the United States, England, and France in total national wealth. He estimated the total national wealth at between 300 and 335 billion marks and thought that perhaps 8 to 8.5 billion marks out of the total annual income of 42 billion marks was reinvested.[6] With obvious satisfaction, he concluded:

[4] *Volkswohlstand*, 3-6.

[5] *Ibid.*, 63, 100-105. In making some of the foregoing contentions, Helfferich was mistaken. In real terms, German national income had risen from an index value of 63 in 1890 to 100 in 1913; Gerhard Bry, *Wages in Germany 1871-1945* (Princeton, 1960), 17. Helfferich's values were money values rather than real values; or, rather, for him the two were the same, since he denied the existence of inflation during this period; *Geld*, 6th edn., 614-15.

[6] His estimate was low. For the reasons why, see the discussion of his and other estimates in Hoffmann and Müller, *Volkseinkommen*, 23-26.

"Our backward look should make every heart beat faster in pride and joy . . . [and] may contribute to raise German self-confidence to the level of German national strength." Then apparently fearing that this might prove too heady for his readers, he admonished:

> But this survey should also protect us from a vain overestimation of ourselves and from superficial arrogance. . . . Whoever knows history realizes that every great advance creates new and serious problems and carries within it the seeds of its own destruction. . . . While our nation as a whole is running at the highest level economically, we see this very development threatening the moral and physical health of large sections of our population. We see the unified cooperative effort that has made us great threatened by the class struggle and class hatred. We see too often in the place of hard work senseless extravagance and provocative luxury, and in place of a willingness to sacrifice and perform one's duty, greediness and dissipation.[7]

As the foregoing summary of *Germany's National Wealth* reveals, Helfferich was well aware that the existing state of affairs hardly represented perfection. The leading bankers were as a group among the more progressive businessmen in their political outlooks. Their wide-ranging professional concerns, extending across many branches of industry and out into the world, were doubtless in part responsible.[8] Their own labor force was also more tractable than that in most industries. Yet what is striking about Helfferich, a man exceeding most businessmen in both education and intellectual power, is how optimistically he viewed the future. There were a number of reasons for this. His earlier fears that the agrarian right might succeed in committing the

---

[7] *Volkswohlstand*, 124-25.

[8] On this point see Hans Jaeger, "Unternehmer und Politik in Wilhelminischen Deutschland," *Tradition*, 13 (1968), 10. Jaeger accounts for the decline in entrepreneurial participation in the Reichstag after 1890 to a quickening economic tempo and increasing influence of the Verbände. Helfferich's declining interest in institutional politics seems a function of his general satisfaction with the way matters were being managed and his ability to go straight to the bureaucrat responsible if something did not suit him.

government to some folly that would endanger the course of German economic development had proved unfounded. True, as he had learned again to his disgust in 1909, in the course of agitating in favor of Bülow's abortive financial reform, the agrarians and particularists could still block desirable policies.[9] But this was an essentially negative power and did not really alter the fact that high policy was largely geared to the interests of the modern sectors of the economy.[10]

More serious, perhaps, than the threat formerly posed by the Right was that of the Socialist Left. Other than the remarks cited above, Helfferich never said much about this threat, which probably meant he was not particularly worried by it.[11] He thought that events were proving Marx's economic predictions false; prosperity *was* increasing, as the workers themselves could hardly fail to see. Moreover, his own views about the respective roles of the government and the entrepreneur and his convic-

[9] Helfferich, Jacob Riesser, and other liberal bankers and businessmen formed the so-called Hansabund for the purpose of agitating for this and other reforms. On the Hansabund, which never fulfilled the promise of its beginnings, see Jürgen Bertram, *Die Wahlen zum deutschen Reichstag vom Jahre 1912: Parteien und Verbände in der Innenpolitik des Wilhelminischen Reiches* (Düsseldorf, 1964), 102-107; Fischer, *Krieg der Illusionen*, 54-58.

[10] It has been argued recently by Barkin, *Controversy over German Industrialization*, by Herman Lebovics, "'Agrarians' versus 'Industrializers': Social Conservative Resistance to Industrialism and Capitalism in Late Nineteenth Century Germany," *International Review of Social History*, 12 (1967), 59-61, and by others, that Bülow conciliated industry and labor but followed an essentially pro-agricultural policy. Bülow, in fact, recognized that, while the Kaiser preferred the company of landed aristocrats and soldiers, his monarch also wanted Germany to play a great and active role in the world. Bülow survived by neutralizing intrigues in William's conservative entourage, in part with fair words to agriculture and in part with limited economic concessions to it, while simultaneously pursuing a *Weltpolitik* in the interests of industry. Had Bülow been committed to the landed interest, he would scarcely have proposed the sort of financial reforms that led to his fall in 1909. And what was the money needed for? To pay for the domestic and foreign policies of an expanding, if not necessarily expansionist, industrial state. On these questions, see also Gerhard Ritter, *Staatskunst und Kriegshandwerk: das Problem des "Militarismus" in Deutschland* (4 vols., Munich, 1959-1968), ii, 167.

[11] It is perhaps worth noting here that except on financial and monetary questions, Helfferich had very little to say about domestic events in this period. Nowhere, for example, did he comment on either the *Daily Telegraph* affair of 1908 or the Zabern Incident of 1913.

tions about the historically shaped national character of institutions must have made it difficult for him to take the rest of Marx's ideas seriously. As a result, he seems never to have taken the trouble to fathom the meaning of socialism as a political phenomenon.

In 1914, Helfferich certainly had little reason to feel, as he had in the nineties, that men like himself ought to have more of a political voice than they had. A man who could ask a high official in the Foreign Office, the future Foreign Secretary Arthur Zimmermann, to buy him train tickets could hardly be said to lack access to the levers of power. Helfferich, indeed, knew all sorts of *arcana imperii* and had connections in the bureaucracy that were unrivaled.[12] In part these connections were the result of his earlier service in the Colonial Office and his long association with the Reichsbank, and in part they reflected the fact that the foreign concerns of the Deutsche Bank figured importantly in German foreign policy. According to a later critic, another leading banker—not named—complained that whenever one appeared before the government as a banking expert, Helfferich was always there first.[13] This disgruntled financier may have been correct, but in some senses what was significant was that either man was called. In a modern industrial society such as Germany was becoming, the government was increasingly involved in matters in which business had a stake and upon which it was necessarily consulted. This had not been nearly so typical in an earlier day when the main business of the country had been farming.

Helfferich, if he was indeed "always there first," had done much to earn the right. He had supported Bülow's financial reforms with word and deed and written *Germany's National Wealth* to prove to doubters the strength and soundness of the German economy. He had supported the Reichsbank's (misguided) attempts to force the other banks to carry a greater part of the burden of meeting emergency demands for credit in times of

[12] Recent works such as Fritz Fischer's *Krieg der Illusionen* confirm the picture Helfferich presents of himself in the first volume of his war memoirs, *Der Weltkrieg*, as the recipient of all sorts of confidences on the part of those in high places about the great events of the day.

[13] The critic was Josef Andre of the Center Party; *RTV*, Vol. 349, 4 May 1921, 3612.

crisis.[14] He also went to great lengths to prove that the German capital market had survived the tremors coming in the wake of the Second Morocco Crisis of 1911 better than had the French.[15]

He was, in fact, still performing the sort of literary services which had originally provided him entrée into high official circles. Though still no intimate of the Kaiser's, he was now very much a member of such circles himself. In addition to his important role in the Bagdad settlements, other examples testify to the regard he enjoyed. When the possibility arose in July 1914 that the Chinese government might choose a foreign expert to reform its currency, Baron Ago von Maltzan, the German chargé d'affaires in Peking, immediately suggested Helfferich. He said that only such a "capacity of the first rank" stood much chance of being chosen.[16] Bethmann himself had earlier considered Helfferich for the post of Staatssekretär of the Reich Treasury Office when the position fell vacant in 1912.[17] Helfferich's youth (he was forty), Bavarian origin, and usefulness to German national interests as a director of the Deutsche Bank probably all militated against his being offered the position. But he was clearly considered of cabinet potential, and it only wanted the stimulus of unusual circumstance to overcome the objections to his appointment.

Helfferich played a minor role in the final diplomatic ma-

---

[14] Helfferich, "Die zeitweise übermässige Inanspruchnahme der Reichsbank, ihre Ursachen und die Mittel zur Abhilfe," in *Verhandlungen des IV. Allgemeinen Deutschen Bankiertages* (Berlin, 1912), 70-85, 120. The question was controversial because of its implications for wartime economic and financial mobilization. For recent discussions, see Konrad Roesler, *Die Finanzpolitik des Deutschen Reiches im Ersten Weltkrieg* (Berlin, 1967), 24-34; Fischer, *Krieg der Illusionen*, 280-84.

[15] Helfferich, "Deutschlands Finanzkraft in der Morokkokrisis," *Bank-Archiv*, 12 (1912), 17-20. Alfred Landsburg, a noted Berlin banker and economist, called Helfferich's use of statistics to show the respective performances of the Berlin and Paris financial markets extremely misleading; Konrad Wahrmund [pseud.?], *Dr. Karl Helfferich als Gelehrter, Wirtschaftspolitiker und Staatsmann: ein Beitrag zur Geschichte des Untergangs des Bismarckischen Reiches* (Leipzig, 1938), 85-86.

[16] Maltzan to FO, No. A 127, 31 July 1914, *GP*, xxxii, doc. 11,986.

[17] Clemens von Delbrück, *Die wirtschaftliche Mobilmachung in Deutschland 1914: aus dem Nachlass herausgegeben, eingeleitet und ergänzt von Joachim von Delbrück* (Munich, 1924), 163-64.

neuverings before the outbreak of World War I, assisting in efforts to picture Russia as the aggressor, if it proved impossible to keep her out entirely.[18] But he was soon to be engaged in more interesting matters. Late in August 1914, when German arms still seemed invincible, he was summoned to Supreme Headquarters to play Bleichröder to Bethmann's Bismarck.[19] The most immediate of the economic problems on which his advice was sought was the question of how to extract the maximum war contribution from Belgium. In a memorandum for the Kaiser which he submitted in person, Helfferich recommended that the Belgian economy be kept operating at as high a level as possible. He considered that the best way to establish the necessary measure of control was to place all Belgian financial institutions under a German comptroller general. To give the comptroller even more power, Belgian currency was also to be placed under his fiat and a firm ratio established between the mark and the franc. These measures were in important respects similar to those Helfferich had earlier recommended for German East Africa. Their purpose was the same: Belgium was to become a German colony, existing for the benefit of the mother country. Helfferich politely refused the Kaiser's suggestion that he administer his program himself on the grounds that his appointment might cause a stir because of the Deutsche Bank's large Belgian interests. He suggested instead his old friend Karl von Lumm, who was appointed.[20]

While in Koblenz, Helfferich also assessed the amount of war

[18] *Weltkrieg*, I, 188-98; Walter Görlitz (ed.), *Regierte der Kaiser? Kriegstagebücher, Aufzeichnungen und Briefe des Chefs des Marinekabinetts Admiral Georg von Müller 1914-1918* (Berlin and Frankfurt a. M., 1959), 37, entry of 29 July 1914. On official policy, see also Konrad H. Jarausch, "The Illusion of Limited War: Chancellor Bethmann Hollweg's Calculated Risk, July 1914," *CEH*, 2 (1969), 48-76, esp. 67-72.

[19] See Fritz Stern, "Gold and Iron: The Collaboration and Friendship of Gerson Bleichröder and Otto von Bismarck," *AHR*, 75 (1969), 37-46, esp. 38, 40.

[20] Fritz Fischer, *Griff nach der Weltmacht: die Kriegszielpolitik des kaiserlichen Deutschland 1914/18* (Düsseldorf, 1961), 107; Lumm, *Helfferich*, 49-51. Helfferich does not reveal the purpose of his visit in his *Weltkrieg*. For hostile criticisms of Lumm by subordinates, see Somary, *Erinnerungen*, 120-27; and Hjalmar H. G. Schacht, *Confessions of the "Old Wizard": The Autobiography of Hjalmar Horace Greeley Schacht* (Boston, 1956), 120-27.

indemnities which Belgium and France could support after their defeat. Because such an assessment necessarily rested on estimates of national income and national wealth like those he had undertaken for *Germany's National Wealth*, he was ideally qualified.[21] Helfferich continued to advise the government on Belgian economic affairs. In early October 1914, he accompanied Clemens von Delbrück, Secretary of the Interior (Reichsamt des Innern), on a tour of the newly subdued country. Aside from an article which Helfferich wrote about his experiences, the most important result of the trip was to convince Delbrück that Helfferich would make an ideal successor for Hermann Kühn, Secretary of the Treasury Office.[22] Kühn was in fact proving wholly inadequate for his post, hindering all sorts of obviously necessary expenditures through an honorable but obsolete stinginess.

Helfferich himself was having trouble with Kühn in the fall of 1914, because the latter was unwilling to pay for completing the Taurus and Amanus tunnels. The sum involved, 30 to 45 million marks, was small in comparison with the total German war outlay of nearly 2 billion marks a month, whereas the military benefits of completing the tunnels promised to be considerable.[23] Kühn refused to approve the outlay unless General Erich von Falkenhayn, Chief of the General Staff, would vouch for the military necessity of the project. When Helfferich attempted to secure the general's approval, the latter asked how long the construction would require. Helfferich estimated a year, whereupon Falkenhayn allegedly snorted, "Do you really think that the war will last another year?"[24] No money was forthcoming. Kühn also

---

[21] Fischer, *Griff*, 127. Fischer does not give the amounts of the proposed indemnities.

[22] Helfferich, *The Condition of Belgium under German Occupation* (Berlin, n.d. [1914]), which originally appeared in the *NAZ*. See also Count Hugo von Lerchenfeld, Bavarian minister to Berlin, to Count Georg von Hertling, Minister President of Bavaria, No. 611, 17 Oct. 1914, GStA, "Berichte." For Delbrück's account of the trip, see his *Mobilmachung*, 155-64; and the reasons for his objections to Kühn, 69, 77-80, 101-102.

[23] For a reliable account of the Bagdad Railway after 1914, see Ulrich Trumpener, *Germany and the Ottoman Empire, 1914-1918* (Princeton, 1968), Ch. 9.

[24] "Bericht" 839, 5 March 1918, "HB." This was merely one skirmish of a continuing battle in which Falkenhayn successfully resisted the efforts of

"fought tooth and nail" against providing subsidies to the Turkish government, although these were an inescapable political necessity.[25]

To get somewhat ahead of the story, Helfferich discovered after he had succeeded Kühn that being willing to finance the Turks was far from solving the problem of doing so. The difficulty was that the average Turk was reluctant to accept paper money, while the Germans were most reluctant to part with any of their gold stock. The Turks had become somewhat accustomed to the notes of the Ottoman Bank, but that institution was French. Even after Turkey entered the war, the bank successfully resisted issuing notes to finance a German-Turkish war. Although effective coercion was doubtless possible, Helfferich was from the outset against nationalization, the most obvious measure, because it would establish a precedent which might ultimately hurt the Germans as much as the Entente.[26] After a variety of solutions had been proposed and found wanting, Helfferich suggested establishing a new bank of issue—the now familiar solution—which would issue gold certificates on the basis of a one-third gold reserve. The gold reserves were to be held in Berlin, the notes themselves being redeemable in gold at par after the war. For a while it appeared that the Turks might accept this solution, but it was ultimately rejected in the fall of 1915, evidently because the Turks suspected the Germans' motives for proposing it.[27] As a result the financing of the Turks con-

Helfferich, Zimmermann, and others who wished to devote a greater portion of German resources to victory in the east. For the full story, see Karl-Heinz Janssen, *Der Kanzler und der General: die Führungskrise um Bethmann Hollweg und Falkenhayn 1914-1916* (Göttingen, 1967), 42-44, 144, *et passim.*

[25] The quoted phrase is Zimmermann's; "Bericht" 49, 15 Oct. 1914, "HB." See also Bethmann Hollweg to Kühn, 1 Oct. 1914, and Kühn to FO, 14 Oct. 1914, "Türkei" 110, Bd. 73.

[26] "Banknoten für die Türkei," 24 Oct. 1914, unsigned memorandum with corrections in Helfferich's hand, *ibid.*

[27] For the endless bedevilments Turkish finance caused Helfferich, both as a director of the Deutsche Bank and later as Secretary of the Reich Treasury Office, see the voluminous and frequently acrimonious correspondence in "Türkei" 110, Bde. 73ff.; and, more accessibly, Trumpener, *Germany and the Ottoman Empire,* Ch. 8. A history of financial relations between Germany and the other Central Powers would be most useful.

tinued to rest on a series of complex and, from Helfferich's view-point, unsatisfactory expedients.[28]

Helfferich also found time to follow up his earlier glorification of German economic and financial strength. In an article entitled "The German War Loan," he interpreted the first of the great German war loans (of September 1914) as an "event without parallel in history" and a "unique performance."[29] The 4.5 million marks it had raised were a brilliant confirmation of his earlier allegations and contrasted sharply with "French financial embarrassment" and English failure "to attempt" a long-term loan. He attributed German good fortune to the mighty strides that the German economy had made in peacetime, and if his rhetoric was extravagant, his thesis was solid enough at least insofar as it applied to France. His remarks about England were more questionable. He said that if the "last billion" were decisive as David Lloyd George, Chancellor of the Exchequer, "with true British arrogance" had claimed, then England had to go a long way to catch Germany. He added that "Germany alone" had not enacted a banking moratorium, although both England and France had found such a step necessary.[30] He concluded his article on the war loan with a warning to England:

> The English must above all recognize that all plans for forcing Germany economically and financially to its knees will surely shatter against our power and our sense of purpose. . . . We will hold out . . . at the price of the most extreme sacrifices until we achieve a peace which guarantees the present and coming generations of our people freedom and honor, repose and growth.

Although Helfferich held England to be Germany's most dangerous enemy, he did not at first hold England directly responsi-

[28] For Helfferich's later involvement (in late 1917 and 1918) in German-Turkish financial negotiations, see Trumpener, *Germany and the Ottoman Empire*, 339-51.

[29] Helfferich, "Die Kriegsanleihe," *Bank-Archiv*, 14 (1914), 1-4.

[30] Oddly enough, Helfferich had earlier favored a moratorium; Delbrück, *Mobilmachung*, 118-19; Max von Schinkel, *Lebenserinerrungen* (Hamburg, n.d.), 260. The measures Germany took had the same effect as a moratorium; Robert Knauss, *Die deutsche, englische und französische Kriegsfinanzierung* (Berlin, 1923), 56-57.

ble for the outbreak of the war. His first essay on this subject appeared in the *Norddeutsche Allgemeine Zeitung* on 27 January 1915 and was entitled, "The Origins of the War in the Light of the Publications [in the Colored Books] of the Triple Entente Powers."[31] Using the words of Entente statesmen as evidence, Helfferich developed the thesis that Russia was the actual "arsonist," while England and France were the "accomplices" whose decision to save the Entente rather than the peace had ignited the general conflagration. Still, even though picturing Russia as the "arsonist," he placed the ultimate responsibility for the war upon England. The Russians would not have taken the fatal step of mobilizing their armies had they not been assured of French support, and this support would not have been forthcoming unless the French in turn were sure that England stood behind them. Helfferich portrayed Sir Edward Grey, the English Foreign Secretary, as a man "inwardly bound" to France, yet unwilling to commit England to assisting France under any and all conditions. Grey's main problem was finding an excuse for entry into war that would be palatable to English public opinion. The German invasion of Belgium suited perfectly. But England's motives for entering the war were obvious enough. "Commercial envy of a driving economy, instinctive opposition to the strongest Continental Power, and a tradition of suppressing any Continental attempt to secure naval standing" were the real reasons. Though criticized by right-wing journalists because it placed too much blame on Russia and not enough on England, Helfferich's article found favor elsewhere. The Kaiser later told him in the course of an intimate evening shared only by the Empress and Zimmermann that the piece had "pleased him extremely."[32]

Secretary of the Treasury

The day before Helfferich's "Origins of the War" appeared, the *Norddeutsche Allgemeine Zeitung* carried the news of his ap-

---

[31] Helfferich, *Die Entstehung des Weltkrieges im Lichte der Veröffentlichungen der Dreiverbandmächte* (Berlin, 1915). The piece was also translated into English for American distribution: *The Dual Alliance vs. the Triple Entente* (New York, 1915).

[32] "Bericht" 318, 29 Dec. 1915, "HB."

pointment as Secretary of the Reich Treasury Office. Bethmann had offered Helfferich the post a month before, explaining to him that a man young enough to stand the fearful wartime work load of the Treasury Office was needed to replace the ailing Kühn. Bethmann exhorted, "Look on the Treasury Office as your trench." Helfferich later called the offer a "complete surprise," but like most who are thus overwhelmed by fate, accepted his lot gracefully.[33] The astute and well-informed Count Hugo von Lerchenfeld, the Bavarian Minister in Berlin, reported "general surprise" at Helfferich's appointment, but to most the surprise was a pleasant one.[34] Helfferich was unusually young for so important a post, and though it was not unprecedented, appointing a banker Staatssekretär was a little irregular. But most felt that unusual times called for uncommon measures, and Helfferich seemed especially qualified for his new post. He was young and energetic, combined scholarly reputation with years of practical experience in international and domestic finance, and had the appearance of a man who would not suffer bureaucratic obstruction gladly.[35]

Helfferich assumed his new post still believing, as nearly all Germans did, that the end of the war and German victory could not be too far off. His conception of his duties was shaped accordingly. It was quite in line with the list of duties he had prescribed for the "financial warlord" some years before in *Money in the Russo-Japanese War*. His knowledge of economic conditions abroad would enable him better to assist Germany's allies financially and, when the peace terms were being drafted, to assess the indemnities which the nations of the Entente should pay. His knowledge of economic conditions within Germany would enable him to raise money with a minimum of disturbance during the war and, after peace was concluded, carry out a far-reaching reform of Reich finances. In brief, Helfferich saw himself as a second Witte. Unfortunately for Helfferich, it turned out that Germany was fighting a long unsuccessful war, not a short victorious one. Thus, because of the catastrophic inflation which the

---

[33] *Weltkrieg*, II, 112-14.

[34] Lerchenfeld "Bericht," No. 39, 16 Jan. 1915, GStA, "PA."

[35] See, for example, Ernst von Eisenhardt-Rothe, *Im Banne der Persönlichkeit* (Berlin, 1931), 135.

German mark underwent after the war, Helfferich's role as "financial Ludendorff" was often recalled with great bitterness.[36]

Before turning to Helfferich's financial policy and its execution, it seems advisable to add a word on the German state bookkeeping practice of the day, as it differs considerably from our own. There was not one balance sheet but two, one for ordinary expenditures and another for extraordinary, or nonrecurring, expenditures. State revenues were expected to cover ordinary expenses and interest and amortization charges on extraordinary expenditures, which were financed through loans. Since in theory extraordinary outlays were made only for capital improvements, they were self-amortizing. In practice, however, these distinctions were beginning to break down even before the war. By 1914, the state debt exceeded 5 billion marks, and revenues were lagging ever farther behind expenses. Even ordinary expenditures were financed to some extent by loans. This was not especially dangerous, though it was often considered so at the time. With the coming of the war, there was an instantaneous and very sharp rise in expenditures, most of which were placed on the extraordinary budget. All military expenditures, the colonial budget, and a variety of other war-born civilian expenditures were transferred to the extraordinary budget. This meant that only a shrunken civilian budget and the payment of interest and amortization charges on the debt had to be met from ordinary income, everything else being financed by loans. Under this curious system of bookkeeping the budget was considered technically in balance so long as ordinary income covered ordinary expenditures and interest on the debt. Only when it became necessary to finance ordinary expenditures through extraordinary revenues were the books technically in the red.[37]

On 10 March 1915, Helfferich expounded his financial policy in an extended address to the Reichstag.[38] The budget for the

---

[36] The designation was Karl Kautsky's; quoted in Helmut Theisen, "Die Entwicklung zum nihilistischen Nationalismus in Deutschland 1918-1933: eine historisch-soziologische Studie" (Doctoral dissertation, Munich University, 1955), 47.

[37] Walther Lotz, *Die deutsche Staatsfinanzwirtschaft im Kriege* (Stuttgart, 1927), 7-13, provides a good explanation of German budgetary complexities.

[38] *RTV*, Vol. 306, 10 March 1915, 31-45. See also Roesler, *Finanzpolitik*,

fiscal year 1915 (which began 1 April 1915) which Helfferich presented had been largely prepared by his predecessor, but there can be little doubt that he was in agreement with its essentials. He first elucidated the bookkeeping peculiarities of the new budget. Because of the "uncertainty about the duration of the war . . . and the effects of the war on the items in the [ordinary] budget," there was "no adequate basis" for estimating these items. Most were therefore being carried at values budgeted for fiscal 1914. He also called attention to the important items shifted to the extraordinary budget. He then discussed some of the items on the ordinary budget. Sixty-eight million marks were devoted to amortization of the peacetime debt "to maintain the principle, introduced with such difficulty, of planned retirement of the debt." Retirement of the wartime debt, however, "must naturally remain for peacetime." The greatest change was the sum allocated for interest on the debt. Since this was calculable, Helfferich had not carried over the 1914 figure. Wartime borrowing had pushed interest expenses well over a billion marks. Straining at the gnat and swallowing the camel, one might say, Helfferich commented: "I was of the opinion that even in wartime we should avoid the slippery slope of paying the interest on the debt by incurring more debt."

To cover extraordinary expenses, Helfferich called for a credit of 10 billion marks. He asked as well for the deputies' utmost support for the government's efforts to make the current loan drive a success. To anticipate, this drive and the ones that followed were quite successful, and much of the credit for success must go to Helfferich. He greatly intensified the propaganda campaigns which Rudolf Havenstein, the President of the Reichsbank, had instituted, combining press harangues with exhortations from every imaginable tribune. The emphasis of the propaganda was on Helfferich's assertion that every citizen was subject to "financial conscription" which obligated him to do without in order to buy bonds. The network of "signing-up places" was greatly expanded and the methods of payment made as painless as possi-

---

67-70, for a discussion of this budget and the bookkeeping complexities involved.

ble.[39] Though these methods are commonplace now, they were startling enough at the time. A hostile critic described them as being "American-like," an adjective that requires no comment.[40]

Helfferich then made a financial *tour d'horizon* which included all of the belligerents but centered on Germany and England. Another scornful comment on Lloyd George's "last billion" speech reveals the tone of these remarks: "Clausewitz's famous words, 'war is the continuation of politics by other means,' must be translated into English: politics and war are the continuation of business by other means." He contrasted the low war expenditures of the Central Powers with the high expenses of the Entente and went on to compare the stated English policy of financing the war through taxes with the German policy of resorting to loans. Helfferich first pointed out that the English war taxes, "burdensome as they are, constitute only a very modest part of the war budget."[41] In fact, these taxes "did not even suffice" to meet interest charges on wartime borrowing. To pay this interest, the English had been obliged to suspend repayment of the debt, while the Germans, he triumphantly remarked, were not only able to meet interest charges but continue retirement of the debt as well. He deduced: "The compelling necessity for raising new taxes does not exist for us, in contrast to England." This line of reasoning rested on nothing more solid than bookkeeping differences and was arrant nonsense. Since "even the sharpest measures of taxation" could cover but a small percentage of war expenses, he did not wish to add them to the "heavy burdens of war" already borne by the German people. Besides, there was

[39] For the technical details, see Lotz, *Staatsfinanzwirtschaft*, 33-39; and for a sample of Helfferich's publicity, "Die dritte Kriegsanleihe," *NAZ*, No. 252, 11 Sept. 1915. On occasion considerable pressure was evidently brought to bear to make the reluctant sign up; see the later complaints of the Socialist trade-union leader Artur Crispien; *RTV*, Vol. 350, 6 July 1921, 4493. There was nothing, it need hardly be added, particularly "German" about such pressure.

[40] Johannes Fischart [Erich F. O. Dombrowski], *Das alte und das neue System: die politischen Köpfe Deutschlands* (Berlin, 1919), 166. See also *Vorwärts*, No. 141, 23 May 1916, which acknowledged that Helfferich had brought a "modern . . . touch" to the war-loan advertising.

[41] See also "Staatssekretär Dr. Helfferich über die englische Kriegsanleihe," *NAZ*, No. 181, 2 July 1915, one of a number of articles critical of English war finance.

every prospect that Germany would not have to pay: "We hold fast to the hope of presenting our opponents at the conclusion of peace with the bill for this war that has been forced upon us." The remaining third of the speech was a further glorification of German financial and economic virtue reminiscent of his earlier "War Loan" and need not detain us. The speech was well received, although those hoping for radical measures of reform were disappointed.[42]

At the same time that Helfferich was wooing the Reichstag, he was also taking measures to reduce expenditures as far as possible consonant with military efficiency. His actual control over expenditures was rather limited despite the apparent leverage his office gave him. Procurement, procurement policy, allocation of resources, and even considerable revenues were almost entirely under military control, either through the War Ministry, the War Materials Allocation Division (Kriegsrohstoffabteilung), or other military agencies.[43] Helfferich could do little more than check over some of the more important contracts and educate the military on the need for economy. In April 1915, he made a special trip to Supreme Headquarters, presented a view of the financial situation "which did not look so rosy as in [his] Reichstag speech," and demanded that the prevailing motto, "Hang the cost (*Geld spielt keine Rolle*)," be replaced by, "He who honors not the millions is not worth the billions." But as one of the participants of the meeting, General Wilhelm Groener, commented: "The proposed means of economizing are, however, of only slight effect."[44] Helfferich's belief in a short war and his liberal-capital-

[42] The Socialist Hugo Haase, speaking after Helfferich, called for a war profits tax, though as much for political as economic reasons; *RTV*, Vol. 306, 10 March 1915, 47. See also the disappointed comments in *Vorwärts*, No. 76, 17 March 1915.

[43] Otto Goebel, *Deutsche Rohstoffswirtschaft im Weltkrieg: einschliesslich des Hindenburg-Programms* (Stuttgart, 1930), 144-45. On the general problem of procurement see also *Weltkrieg*, II, 127-28, and the fine recent account in Gerald Feldman, *Army, Industry, and Labor in Germany, 1914-1918* (Princeton, 1966), esp. 41-64.

[44] Friedrich Frhr. Hiller von Gaertringen (ed.), *Wilhelm Groener: Lebenserinnerungen: Jugend—Generalstab—Weltkrieg* (Göttingen, 1957), 239. For another such visit see Karl von Einem, *Erinnerungen eines Soldaten 1853-1933* (Leipzig, 1933), 118-19, entry of 1 May 1915.

ist economic orientation made him no more inclined to seek radical solutions to the problem of reducing expenditures than to the problem of raising revenues.

But though economy was the watchword, Helfferich was far from blindly opposing all new expenditures as a simple matter of principle. It was his proud boast that although military expenditures were but little higher when he left office in mid-1916 than when he entered, he had never refused the military a single expenditure that they felt necessary. The sole exception was a battleship that could not have been finished before 1918 or 1919.[45] On the other hand, he encouraged the construction of new industrial plants and the modernization and expansion of old ones through a mixed system of direct subsidies from *fonds perdues*, guaranteed purchase prices, and construction guarantees in areas where wartime requirements exceeded anticipated peacetime needs.[46] He believed that if incentives were adequate the entrepreneurial enterprise which underlay Germany's prewar economic progress could be trusted to squeeze the utmost in production from the economy in time of war.

In some instances he was nevertheless willing to interfere quite drastically in the workings of the free market. He was one of the prime movers in the centralization of all imports and exports under one agency, the Zentraleinkaufsgesellschaft, even threatening once early in 1915 to make a "cabinet question" (i.e., to resign) of the matter.[47] The need was clear if Germany was to receive the maximum of essential imports in return for scarce export goods and foreign exchange. Helfferich also recognized both

[45] *Weltkrieg*, II, 136-39. Admiral Henning von Holtzendorff, Chief of the Naval Staff, may have initiated some of the cutbacks in the construction of surface vessels; "Bericht" 319, 30 Dec. 1915, "HB."

[46] *Weltkrieg*, II, 115-26. Helfferich was "in principle" against direct subsidies; "Notizen," 15 Nov. 1915, "HB." He was even more unfriendly toward paying compensation for wartime losses. For his refusal to compensate colonial enterprises, see "Bericht" 621, 4 April 1917, *ibid.* For his decided lack of enthusiasm toward compensating the HAPAG for its losses, see Cecil, *Ballin*, 238-47.

[47] "Notizen," 9 March 1915, "HB." See also "Bericht" 121, 25 Feb. 1915, *ibid.* For his later efforts, see "Bericht" 147, 30 April 1915, and "Bericht" 308, 19 Dec. 1915, *ibid.* A history of the ZEG would be most useful and would probably throw light on a surprising variety of political and economic problems.

the need for resource-allocation controls—though he thought these frequently went too far—and for food rationing. He held the latter to be a matter of social justice, and so it was.[48] The pity is that he did not see more clearly the social injustice inherent in a wartime system of encouraging desired production through price incentives without at the same time taxing profits drastically. He thus quarreled with the military over their "Hang the cost" philosophy not because he objected to high profits per se but because he thought that through carelessness and ignorance the military spent without regard to value received. Actually Helfferich had no objection to higher than normal profits in wartime because he thought incentives ought to bear some relationship to the extraordinary efforts which the business community was making.

Like most good businessmen, Helfferich had no objection to an occasional speculation. He agreed early in 1915 to subsidize the revolutionary activities of the notorious Alexander "Parvus" Helphand in Russia, although dubious about some of his ideas. He regarded as particularly questionable Helphand's scheme of November and December 1915 to involve the Treasury in an attack on the foreign exchange value of the ruble.[49] Another speculation in which Helfferich played a leading role was the construction of the merchant submarines *Deutschland* and *Bremen* early in 1916.[50] The purpose of these vessels was to smuggle critical raw materials of low bulk from the United States through the blockade. Despite the loss of the *Bremen* on her first voyage, the venture was counted a spectacular success. The sale of dyestuff, chemicals, and pharmaceuticals paid for the construction of both vessels many times over, and the *Deutschland* twice returned with valuable cargoes of nickel, chrome, vanadium, and rubber.

[48] *Weltkrieg*, II, 233.

[49] For the details see Z.A.B. Zeman and W. B. Scharlau, *The Merchant of Revolution: The Life of Alexander Israel Helphand (Parvus) 1867-1924* (London, 1965), 183-84, 203; Z.A.B. Zeman (ed.), *Germany and the Revolution in Russia 1915-1918: Documents from the Archives of the German Foreign Ministry* (London, 1958), 1-10.

[50] The story of the submarines was very fully covered in the *NAZ*; see Nos. 194, 195, 202, 228, 234, 15 July to 26 Aug. 1916, for the *Deutschland's* first voyage, and for more details, Nos. 305, 316, 344, 3 Nov. to 12 Dec. 1916.

Six more cargo submarines were laid down, the costs of construction already paid for out of the *Deutschland*'s first voyage, but diplomatic relations with the United States were severed before the new boats could enter service.[51]

Helfferich's worries about the financial situation were not reflected solely in admonitions to the military for economy. Shortly after his optimistic Reichstag speech of 10 March 1915, he put his office to work drafting new tax legislation. Not only did the public increasingly condemn the injustice of allowing war profits to go untaxed, but Helfferich himself doubted whether indemnities would in fact pay all war costs. His doubts were reinforced by the reflection that new sources of income would be needed to meet the interest on the debt if the war went on very much longer.[52] The finance ministers of the *Bundesstaaten*, alerted by public demands for the taxation of war profits, reached informal agreement shortly after Helfferich's Reichstag speech that no inroad by the Reich into the sacrosanct area of direct taxes was to be tolerated. The finance ministers also agreed that the Reich must be rigidly held to its earlier promise not to repeat the levy of the *Wehrbeitrag*.[53] The hostility of the *Bundesstaaten* to direct Reich taxes was no secret to Helfferich. He therefore developed his plans for new taxes with great circumspection.

Helfferich called the finance ministers to Berlin on 10 July 1915 to outline his program.[54] Presenting his usual optimistic survey of the financial situation, he said that he had reluctantly decided not to request new taxes unless another winter campaign was necessary. Raising indirect taxes alone was sure to excite Socialist opposition and would probably mean the end of the *Burgfriede*,

[51] "Bericht" 311, 30 Dec. 1915, "Bericht" 448, 14 July 1916, "Bericht" 450, 16 July 1916, and "Bericht" 474, 2 Sept. 1916, "HB." See also *Weltkrieg*, II, 128-31. At one point Helfferich called the suggestion that submarines be constructed in the United States "Excellent"; "Bericht" 515, 1 Nov. 1916, "HB."

[52] Dr. Ritter von Wolf, Stellvertretender Bundesratsbevollmächtigter, to Georg Ritter von Breunig, Finance Minister of Bavaria, 10 June 1915, GStA, "PA."

[53] Breunig to Seydewitz, Finance Minister of Saxony, 20 April 1915, GStA, "Reichssteuern." The *Wehrbeitrag* was a one-time capital levy imposed to pay for the great army expansion of 1913.

[54] Memorandum of meeting, 11 July 1915, *ibid.*

the interparty truce which had prevailed from the beginning of the war. In any case the real problem would not arise until after the war, when some means of coping with a debt of at least 70 billion marks would have to be devised. "How this debt is to be cast off," he melodramatically stated, "will be the greatest problem since the beginning of the world." The finance ministers without exception stressed both the necessity for indemnities and the necessity for leaving direct taxes to the *Staaten*. A decent effort was made to conceal the mailed fist, but Helfferich was left in no doubt that the *Staaten* were prepared to fight to the last ditch on the question of direct taxes.[55] Helfferich asserted that he was "in complete agreement" with the finance ministers on the question of indemnities, but cautioned that it might ultimately be necessary to reallocate the nation's tax resources. He mentioned that he was considering state monopolies (in nitrates and tobacco) as a source of revenue and broached the possibility of increasing the Matricular contributions of the *Bundesstaaten* to the Reich. But he made it clear that even if these measures were adopted, the Reich might have to demand a larger share of direct taxes than Matricular contributions presently provided.

Helfferich then outlined his plan. He wished to tax war profits, but since in practice it was impossible to distinguish profits which were a direct result of the war from profits merely earned in wartime, all wartime property increases would have to be taxed. He was opposed to collecting the tax during wartime, but he thought the legislation itself a political necessity. At this point, August Lentze, the Prussian Finance Minister, interjected the comment that as such a tax was confiscatory, a warning was indeed in order: "Perhaps . . . the bill [ought to] be brought in as soon as possible so that people will learn of the measure and can take appropriate steps." Helfferich went on to say that he contemplated a graduated scale of assessment which reached a maximum rate of 15 per cent of the wartime property increase. If the

[55] As late as May 1918, Breunig wrote: "The standpoint of the finance ministers . . . can . . . be summarized: even a one-time independent [i.e., not related to wartime income increases] income tax in whatever form and with whatever restrictions . . . must be counted wholly out of the question, now and forever"; Breunig to Oskar Hergt, Finance Minister of Prussia, *et al.*, 31 May 1918, *ibid.*

property increases were based on income—as would be the case, he believed, with most profiteers—they were to be taxed at doubled rates. He pointed out that although income was being used as a basis for assessment, the tax was not, properly speaking, an income tax. In response to a suggestion that he wait to present the war profits tax until the less popular monopoly and indirect tax measures were ready, Helfferich replied that this was impossible. The draft War Profits Tax Law was nearly ready for the Bundesrat's approval and it "would make a very bad impression" to offer the Reichstag only the promise of a law when it reconvened in August. He added that property increases through inheritance were not to be taxed, nor were corporate profits. Not only would a corporate profit tax constitute double taxation, but it was in practice difficult to get at corporate reserves. If open reserves (i.e., those actually shown on the balance sheet) were taxed, this would merely "throw the door wide open to fraud" since it would be much easier for companies to conceal their reserves than for the tax authorities to discover them. The measure was an extraordinary measure taken to meet an extraordinary need, and in no way a precedent for direct taxation by the Reich. Altogether, it was a modest proposal. No wonder at the end of the meeting Lentze thanked Helfferich for his "clear and *bundesfreundlichen* exposition."

Despite Helfferich's expressed desire to present the Reichstag with a war profits tax draft in the August session, he was unable to reach agreement with the finance ministers on a bill before the Reichstag met. He could thus only hint at the nature of the war profits tax in his address of 20 August 1915. Basically the speech did little more than bring the March address up to date. There was the same justification of basing war finance on loans, the same insistence that new war taxes were as yet unnecessary, the same disdainful comparison between German financial and economic strength and Entente weakness, and the same insistence that the Entente would pay. "The instigators of this war have earned this lead weight of billions; may they drag it down through the years, not we."[56] After the war, when the Germans

[56] *RTV*, Vol. 306, 20 Aug. 1915, 222-29. The "lead-weight" phrase first occurs in one of Helfferich's earliest writings; *Währungsumsturz*, 8.

themselves had to "drag the lead weight," Helfferich's political opponents hung the unfortunate phrase around his neck like the proverbial albatross. If this were not enough, Helfferich also made an unhappy contribution to the *Geld im Lande* myth, according to which the autarky forced upon Germany by the English blockade was a blessing in disguise. Helfferich then contrasted the advantages of Germany's "closed" circulation of money with the monetary difficulties foreign buying was causing the Entente. "When money rolls over the border for the purchase of war materiel and food to supplement insufficient domestic production," he explained, "it does not roll back so easily; the stoppages occur which we observe in the case of our opponents. . . ." This was a cynical repudiation of the doctrine of comparative international advantage and the benefits of international trade of which Helfferich had earlier been one of the foremost prophets. Even while he was publicly boasting of the benefits of autarky, he was privately working to build up German exports and imports, and for what other reason if not "to supplement insufficient domestic production"? A few months later, in March 1916, he privately admitted that he would gladly borrow abroad "if he could only do so."[57]

Although Helfferich's expressed intention to tax war profits was greeted with approbation, it was not until 30 November that the deputies learned more about what was planned. Even at this time Helfferich still disagreed with the finance ministers over the rates of the new tax and so was unable to present the deputies with a bill.[58] But most of the details had been worked out. He promised that war profits "in the very broadest sense of the word" would be taxed but cautioned against considering the tax a "penalty tax" or those who paid it by definition profiteers. Payment of taxes, like military service, was "an obligation of honor" for every citizen. He asserted that actually instances of profiteering were comparatively few and best dealt with through recourse

[57] *Weltkrieg*, II, 151. See also his speech before the Reichstag Investigating Committee of 12 Nov. 1919, in which he related his attempts to place short- and long-term obligations and to buy cotton in the United States; *Reichstagsreden 1920-1922*, 384-86.

[58] *RTV*, Vol. 306, 30 Nov. 1915, 420-23.

to existing legal remedies. How the law was to deal with cases where "excessive" profits had been legally earned, Helfferich did not specify. The tax as he outlined it to the deputies differed little from that proposed to the finance ministers in July. There was one important alteration: excess corporate profits were also to be taxed. Since some of the finance ministers had in July wanted to tax corporate profits, one may suppose that the combined pressure of the Bundesrat and public opinion had forced Helfferich to reconsider his earlier decision. He justified the measure by saying that, although it constituted double taxation, it promised to yield much more than could be obtained if the stockholders were taxed individually after profits were distributed. He might also have pointed out that it permitted taxing undistributed profits, as taxing the shareholders alone did not. To prevent the profits of the second year of war from being divided before a definitive law was passed, Helfferich requested the passage of a *Vorbereitungsgesetz* (Preparatory Law) requiring corporations to place 50 per cent of their *excess* profits in a special reserve out of which the tax would later be paid. He apologized in closing for having no definitive proposals to present, a circumstance which he ascribed to the complexities of drafting a law which intervened "so drastically in every facet of the economy" and to delays imposed by Germany's federal organization. In contrast to his earlier unfavorable opinion of the *Bundesstaaten*, he now referred to them as "the root of our strength." *Raison d'état* was leading Helfferich down some strange paths.

The Budget Committee hearings on the *Vorbereitungsgesetz* occupied the first two weeks of December 1915.[59] Helfferich spent most of his time in explaining the provisions of the bill in detail. There were long discussions of what constituted adequate depreciation reserves in time of war, of the difficulty of distinguishing between profits earned as a direct result of the war and other profits, of the problems of drafting legislation to catch the

[59] "Aktenstück 175: Bericht der [Budget] Kommission über den Entwurf eines Gesetzes über vorbereitenden Massnahmen zur Besteuerung der Kriegsgewinne, 14. Dezember 1915," *RTA*, Vol. 317, 229-51. I have shifted some of Helfferich's remarks, quoted below, from indirect to direct discourse. For a criticism of the law see Roesler, *Finanzpolitik*, 72-74.

profiteer while allowing the honest businessman to go free, and of many other matters. Helfferich warned that the law, though not ideal "as was unfortunately the case with most things capable of practical realization in this world," went about as far as the Bundesrat and the needs of the economy would allow. As was his invariable custom, Helfferich firmly underlined the dangers of destroying economic incentives, but in more explicit terms than usual:

> A prior speaker spoke of the "holy spirit of acquisition." The spirit of acquisition is not holy, but secular and material, an agent, a motivator, that we cannot dispense with in peacetime and most definitely not in wartime. If men were angels, it would be different; but since man acts according to his own interest, we must exploit these interests if we want to win the war. I make no moral judgments but merely take the world as it is.

Helfferich's fears that the committee might demand a tax reserve of more than 50 per cent proved groundless. His talk of the dangers of imposing "burdens so great that our corporations will be no longer viable" misled some committee members into believing that nearly all of the reserve would be taken by taxes—and otherwise of what purpose was it?[60] The *Vorbereitungsgesetz* was reported out of committee and passed the third reading on 20 December 1915 substantially unaltered.

Although the Socialists approved of the war profits tax, the tax would provide little revenue for the coming fiscal year, 1916, and they were therefore curious about how Helfferich proposed to meet the expected deficit in the ordinary budget. In the December 1915 debates over the *Vorbereitungsgesetz* they warned against any increase in the tax burden of the "broad masses," demanded assurances that this was not contemplated, and suggested—in lieu of a general financial reform—levying the *Wehrbeitrag* again. Helfferich tacitly admitted that indirect taxes were planned by "utterly refusing" to accept the proposition that all indirect taxes burdened the masses. But he did promise that the

---

[60] See the Socialist Wilhelm Keil's later complaints; *RTV*, Vol. 307, 22 March 1916, 783-86.

"necessities of life" would not be taxed and also asserted that the war profits tax constituted a "colossal burden" on property increases.[61] While the *bürgerlich* parties generally stood behind Helfferich in the debates of December 1915 and January 1916, even the National Liberals were unhappy when Helfferich announced on 18 January that the tax bills would not be available for study until March when the budget debates actually began.[62] The Reichstag was hardly in a radical mood, but there were a number of storm signals out when it adjourned on 18 January 1916.

Somewhat earlier, Dr. Wolf, a Bavarian plenipotentiary to the Bundesrat, wrote Georg von Breunig, the Bavarian Finance Minister, an alarmed letter about the incipient fiscal radicalism in the Reich government. Opinion was growing in favor of a Reich income tax after the Prussian model. "Certain . . . circles—the Chancellor and . . . Delbrück rather more than . . . [Helfferich] —are said to be in no way hostile to the idea." Lentze, the Prussian Finance Minister, considered the situation "critical."[63] Actually no drastic steps were contemplated. Neither Bethmann nor Delbrück nor Helfferich thought the time ripe for fighting out the question of financial reform. In an apparent effort to conciliate the Reichstag, however, Helfferich modified his program for balancing the 1916 budget. As late as September 1915 and probably for some time thereafter, he hoped to secure a Reich nitrate monopoly, tax increases on tobacco, beer, and spirits, and increases in postal fees and first-class railway fares.[64] By February 1916, all that remained of this program were the increases in the tobacco tax and in the postal fees. In place of the other measures Helfferich substituted a *Quittungsstempel*, a stamp tax levied against nearly all payments of over ten marks, and increases in both the scope and the rates of the *Frachturkundenstempel*, a stamp tax on certain categories of rail freight.[65] Although the

[61] *Ibid.*, Vol. 306, 20 Dec. 1915, 460-65, 491 (Eduard David); 486-87, 491-92 (Gustav Hoch); 465-67, 492 (Helfferich).
[62] *Ibid.*, 18 Jan. 1916, 714, and Ernst Bassermann's (NL) reply, 714.
[63] Wolf to Breunig, 29 Dec. 1915, GStA, "Reichssteuern."
[64] "Notizen," 26 Sept. 1915, "HB."
[65] Helfferich to the finance ministers of the *Bundesstaaten*, 12 Feb. 1916, GStA, "Reichssteuern." Helfferich speaks of his program as if it were un-

Begründungen of both bills speculated, as is usually true, that those formally liable for the tax could "shift" them to the consumer, they were at least less conspicuous than taxes on beer and spirits.[66] Helfferich may also have regarded the taxes as potentially better revenue producers than the taxes on drink.

Helfferich was taking other steps to reduce opposition to his tax program to a minimum. Matthias Erzberger and Karl Herold, another Center deputy, had in January tried to mobilize the *bürgerlich* parties against the acceptance of wartime taxes. They were confident that the enemy would after all have to "drag the lead weight." This attempt came to nothing, evidently because of opposition within the right wing of the Center Party itself.[67] Helfferich still anticipated that the Socialists might vote against his tax bills but wished to have the matter settled before the Easter recess began in mid-April. He feared that if the tax debates ran over into the debates on war credits which were scheduled for May, the Socialists might vote against the credits as well. This would have most unfortunate repercussions abroad and had to be avoided at all costs. On 12 February 1916 Helfferich presented these views to the finance ministers and promised his indirect tax bills within a week. He also requested permission to take the unprecedented step of publishing the essentials of all the tax bills (including the war profits tax bill) in the *Norddeutsche Allgemeine Zeitung* before the deliberations of the Bundesrat were over. He claimed that early publication would give the parties adequate time to study the tax bills, thereby shortening the debates, and would also dispel false notions about how high the rates of the war profits tax were to be. The public believed that

---

known to the finance ministers, which encourages the speculation that the unfriendliness the Reichstag had exhibited toward indirect taxes on articles of mass consumption had forced a last-minute change of plan.

[66] "Aktenstück 224: Entwurf eines Quittungsstempelgesetzes, 13. März 1916: Begründung," 11-12; and "Aktenstück 226: Entwurf eines Frachturkundenstempelgesetzes, 13. März 1916: Begründung," 3-4, *RTA*, Vol. 317. Both documents are numbered internally only. For a survey of all war tax legislation, see Roesler, *Finanzpolitik*, 189-94, and for the 1916 taxes in particular, 105-109.

[67] Lerchenfeld to Hertling, No. 85, 26 Jan. 1916, GStA, "Berichte"; *Weltkrieg*, II, 162-63. But see also Epstein, *Erzberger*, 331-32.

the rates would be very high, a misconception which Helfferich feared might limit bond sales during the fourth war loan drive in March. Although the Bavarians feared that early publication would tie the Bundesrat's hands, Helfferich got his way.[68] On 26 February, the *Norddeutsche Allgemeine* published a résumé of the tax program along with a draft of the *Kriegsgewinnssteuer*.[69]

Helfferich began the tax debates on 16 March 1916 with a defense of his budget.[70] In the twentieth month of war he still used the figures of fiscal 1914 because "accurate estimates could not be carried out under wartime conditions." Helfferich has been justly criticized for this ostrich-like approach to the budget and, with less justice, has been accused of deliberately misleading the German people by using the prewar figures.[71] As it stands, the charge is inaccurate. In fact, he went to considerable lengths to make clear that the ordinary budget for fiscal 1916 would probably show a deficit even after the new indirect taxes were introduced. He specifically stated that the new taxes would balance the budget "only formally." He was at some pains to defend his tax program, which he later admitted was a "patchwork." The program embarrassed him; his tone was apologetic: the taxes were "nothing particularly pleasing" and only "emergency measures." They were justifiable solely because "the politics of finance, like politics generally, is the art of the possible." He emphasized the need for keeping faith with the bond-holder by providing ordinary income to pay the interest on the debt and at the same time cautioned against making overly severe inroads into direct taxes. These taxes were the mainstays of the *Bundesstaaten*, which themselves were confronted with rapidly increasing obligations. It is apparent that Helfferich's basic conception of the problems of war finance had hardly altered during his year in office.

The Socialist Wilhelm Keil made the most damaging criticisms

[68] See n.65 above, and also Lerchenfeld "Berichte" 153 and 166, 16 and 18 Feb. 1916, GStA, "PA."

[69] *NAZ*, No. 56, 26 Feb. 1916. The other drafts appeared in quick succession; *ibid.*, Nos. 62, 66, and 67, 3-8 March 1916.

[70] *RTV*, Vol. 306, 16 March 1916, 768-76.

[71] By among others, Charles Rist, *Les finances de guerre de l'Allemagne* (Paris, 1921), 119-20, and Epstein, *Erzberger*, 331.

of Helfferich's tax program.[72] His heaviest salvos were aimed at the low rates of the war profits tax. When the business world learned the rates, "a hardly suppressed jubilation was noticeable." He conceded that it was necessary to hold rates within limits which permitted the smooth functioning of the economy, but questioned whether such limits had been reached. He pointed out that 3,300,000 small subscribers had paid for less than 4 per cent of the war loan bonds, while 227,000 large signers had paid for over 57 per cent, "a proof of financial strength without parallel." The indirect taxes came in for the usual Socialist criticisms. Keil demanded a renewed levy of the *Wehrbeitrag* and served notice once again that his party expected basic financial reforms: "This shrinking back of the Reich before the power of Prussia cannot go on forever." Defending his bills with familiar arguments, Helfferich asserted that the war profits tax was "an extraordinary expansion of the *Besitzsteuer*" and a "sharp inroad into the area of direct taxation."[73] With the exception of the Progressives, the other parties generally supported Helfferich, but it was clear that the *Burgfriede*, already "riddled with holes" in one deputy's words, was in for another test.

Contrary to Helfferich's earlier hope, the Tax and Budget Committee hearings on his "bucket of taxes" lasted well past Easter and on into the middle of May. Most of the indirect taxes were reported out of committee without major alteration, though with somewhat lower rates. The exception was the very unpopular *Quittungsstempel* which was changed into a *Warenumsatzstempel*, a stamp tax on turnover. As this alteration promised to bring in more revenue, Helfferich did not oppose it. He later claimed to have intended this result all along and said he had refrained from introducing an *Umsatzsteuer* at the outset only for tactical reasons.[74] The great problem was the war profits tax, the subject of most of the committee meetings.[75] The bill emerged in mid-April from the first of two readings in committee with sev-

[72] *RTV*, Vol. 307, 22 March 1916, 780-93.

[73] *Ibid.*, 803-808. Originally passed along with the *Wehrbeitrag* in 1913, the *Besitzsteuer* was a modest tax on property value increments.

[74] *Weltkrieg*, II, 164-65. His logic is unconvincing.

[75] "Aktenstück 320: Bericht der Kommission . . . Kriegsgewinnsteuer, 27. Mai 1916," *RTA*, Vol. 318, 537-633.

eral alterations, the most important of which was the insertion of a *Mehreinkommensteuer*. This was a special tax on private incomes exceeding prewar levels. Helfferich's bill taxed private property increases based on income twice as heavily as property increases from other sources (such as the appreciation of stock holdings), but the deputies still felt that the tax favored the spendthrift and penalized the saver. This was manifestly true, as Helfferich himself admitted. In the face of Bundesrat resistance to anything called an income tax, however, he had seen no way to catch the wastrel. In addition, all schedules of rates were greatly increased, and much to everyone's astonishment, a Socialist amendment calling for another levy of the *Wehrbeitrag* passed with a National Liberal-Progressive-Socialist majority.

This last development did not make Helfferich particularly uneasy, because he anticipated that the National Liberals would follow party discipline and vote against the *Wehrbeitrag* at the second reading.[76] Still, the situation was not very encouraging. When he informed Dr. Wolf of developments, the latter mentioned a Prussian proposal to call a finance ministers' conference. Helfferich was at first quite receptive, Wolf reported to Breunig, but became less so when it struck him that the finance ministers might well present him with binding instructions. That was exactly what Wolf intended. He also hoped to stiffen Lentze, who was showing distressing signs of weakness. Helfferich apparently attempted to shake the resistance of the Bundesrat to the *Mehreinkommensteuer*, but drew nothing but rebukes for his pains. Breunig admonished: "It needs only fresh courage and ruthless energy to make it clear to the party leaders . . . that their opinion rests on false presuppositions [and] that they mistake the popular will and the interests of the state and of the people."[77] But the Bavarians were worried. On 13 May, Lerchenfeld wrote Count Hertling, the Minister-President of Bavaria, an urgent letter summoning him to Berlin to exert his influence on the Reichstag deputies. Lerchenfeld warned that if the Reichstag had its way, Breunig must be allowed more freedom of action. Otherwise Bavaria was likely to find itself in a minority in the Bun-

[76] Wolf to Breunig, 18 April 1916, GStA, "Reichssteuern."
[77] Breunig to Helfferich, 12 May 1916, *ibid.*

desrat against the unreliable Prussia. He added: "We can carry on the fight against democracy only with Prussia. We must not separate from Prussia even if this once it fails us."[78] As it happened, however, Prussia was never put to the test.

The compromise which the committee agreed to at the second reading was in many respects a strange one.[79] Not only were both the *Wehrbeitrag* and the *Mehreinkommensteuer* dropped, but, "throwing the baby out with the bath," as Helfferich put it, the parties also dropped the provisions for taxing increases of private property based on income at double the normal rate.[80] On the theory that national wealth had decreased 10 per cent, however, the tax was levied against all private persons whose property was assessed at over 90 per cent of the prewar valuation. Such were the bizarre expedients to which the Reich was forced, and all because it could not openly tax income. The higher rates of the first reading were retained on both private and corporate income, but even these rates were not high by modern standards.[81] In committee the Socialists refused to vote for the compromise, which had the support of all other parties. They did not substantially alter their position in the debates in the full House but did vote for the war profits tax. This tax was carried by a crushing majority of 313 to 23, the minority consisting of quite disparate elements on the extreme Right and Left.

The Socialists charged that Helfferich's program of taxation lacked "a single new truly creative idea."[82] The charge was accurate enough, but whatever its shortcomings, the Helfferich

[78] Lerchenfeld to Hertling, 13 May 1916, *ibid.*; Hertling answered the summons.

[79] For the compromise negotiations, see Wolf to Breunig, 17 May 1916, *ibid.*; *Weltkrieg*, II, 165-68; Helfferich, *Fort mit Erzberger!* (Berlin, 1919), 28-29.

[80] *Weltkrieg*, II, 166.

[81] The rate for a million-mark increase in assessed property valuation was, for example, 37 per cent of the increase for private persons. For a table of rates for both private persons and corporations, see Roesler, *Finanzpolitik*, 189.

[82] *RTV*, Vol. 307, 1344. See also the *Vorwärts* lead article, "Die Steuermacherei," No. 139, 21 May 1916; Eduard David, *Das Kriegstagebuch des Reichstagsabgeordneten Eduard David 1914-1918*, eds. Erich Matthias and Susanne Miller (Düsseldorf, 1966), 164, entry of 9 March 1916, called the program "deplorable."

budget for 1916 set the course for the future. Count Siegfried von Roedern, who succeeded Helfferich as Secretary of the Treasury in late May 1916, proved quite ingenious at devising new indirect taxes (including one on artificial lemonade and mineral water) and before the war was over had begun to plan for fundamental reform. He was quite unable, however, to break the resistance of the Bundesrat to a Reich income tax and thus was largely forced to follow the precedents which Helfferich had set.[83]

An Estimate of Helfferich as Treasury Secretary

Most students of German wartime finance and politics agree that Helfferich erred in not increasing taxes sharply, especially those on war profits. Political wisdom undoubtedly demanded such a course, for the enormous profits that some were making in a time of general misery were a hateful phenomenon and a source of great bitterness to the vast majority not so favored. To say no more, however, would be to obscure both the real political problems facing Helfferich and the economic effects of the policies he actually followed.

To consider the political side of Helfferich's fiscal policy first, the case against him is nicely summarized in the late Klaus Epstein's assertion that "a great finance minister would have overcome all federalist obstacles and achieved an adequate centralized tax system during the war. . . ." But this was a high fence to ride at. It is true that Helfferich "did not even attempt the task."[84] It is difficult to make a convincing case, however, that a man determined upon immediate reform could have succeeded. We have seen how the Bundesrat greeted the comparatively modest measures which the deputies proposed in the April committee sessions. If Lentze of Prussia occasionally wavered, Breunig and the others did not, and ultimately there was that most backward

[83] See Count Roedern's remarks about the stubborn refusal of the Bundesrat to permit a Reich income tax; "Bericht" 882, 29 May 1918, "HB." In Roedern's behalf, it must be said that he was more aggressive about taxing excess profits than Helfferich. The latter opposed such extensions of the *Kriegsgewinnssteuer* as Roedern sought to make; Feldman, *Army, Industry, and Labor*, 228-30.

[84] Epstein, *Erzberger*, 332.

141

and intractable of all legislatures, the Prussian Landtag, to consider.[85]

Helfferich admittedly had no stomach for such a fight. As a good *Realpolitiker* he thought that he had no illusions and knew a hopeless cause when he saw one. And though he was a dynamic, quick-tempered "man of action," he prided himself on being practical, on "taking the world as it is," on realizing that "politics is the art of the possible," and on recognizing that "men are not angels." Whatever his optimism about Germany's future, however much he idealized the German nation, his view of his fellow man was essentially pessimistic and conservative. Yet even if he had been a "great Finance Minister," willing to cross swords with the Bundesrat, it is hard to see where he would have secured the support needed for success. It would have taken an advocate of genius to have enlisted Bethmann Hollweg for full-scale reforms, to say nothing of the Kaiser. Securing the support of the Reichstag would have been easier, but Helfferich was the last man to do anything to encourage the pretensions or to increase the power of the Reichstag. He was already rather critical of the Reichstag's wartime performance and was to become much more so with time. Moreover, it is certainly questionable whether the already tattered *Burgfriede* would have survived the struggle over financial reform. The course of the controversy over Prussian electoral reform, which began in earnest in 1917, argues that overcoming federalist obstacles to fiscal reform would have been very difficult. The issues which electoral reform raised were far simpler than those raised by fiscal reform, and the need for electoral reform was almost universally conceded, but the problem of electoral reform, too, remained unresolved until the very end of the war.

There were other good political reasons for not taking up

---

[85] On the opposition of the Prussians to financial reform, see Hans Booms, *Die Deutschkonservative Partei: preussischer Charakter, Reichsauffassung, Nationalbegriff* (Düsseldorf, 1954), 69-71. Still very good on the intractable character of fiscal problems in the prewar period is Carl Bachem, *Vorgeschichte, Geschichte und Politik der deutschen Zentrumspartei: zugleich ein Beitrag zur Geschichte der katholischen Bewegung sowie zur allgemeinen Geschichte des neueren und neuesten Deutschlands* (9 vols., Cologne, 1926-1932), IX, 227-56. See also Fischer, *Krieg der Illusionen*, 257-69.

financial reform in 1915 or 1916. Contemporaries thought both the war aims and the unrestricted submarine warfare questions more important than that of financial reform, and despite the way in which the postwar inflation spotlighted the shortcomings of Helfferich's fiscal policy, it is difficult to disagree with this judgment today. Neither Bethmann's refusal to allow public discussion of war aims nor his stand against unrestricted submarine warfare was popular; and in the influential right-wing circles, where the greatest resistance to financial reform was to be expected, his stand on both issues was very unpopular indeed. Was it any wonder that he refused to add to his problems by unrolling the question of financial reform, a question that promised to be as much of a Pandora's box as war aims? It is also well to recall that Helfferich's mistaken fiscal policy did not materially affect the outcome of the war. In contrast, because Bethmann could not block unrestricted submarine warfare, the United States entered the war, which made German defeat well-nigh certain. If Bethmann had to choose a cause, the fight against unrestricted submarine warfare was doubtless the correct one.

A final argument against any very extensive wartime fiscal reform is the fate of the new taxes actually levied. The fiscal authorities of the various states, technically none too sophisticated anyway, had lost many of their best people to the services. The result was, to give only a single example, that one of the most potentially productive of the new taxes, the *Umsatzsteuer*, was evaded on a large scale.[86] The fate of this tax merely foreshadowed the infinitely greater administrative chaos and confusion that came in the wake of Erzberger's tax reforms of 1920 (see Ch. 9 below). Reform was clearly in order, but not during the war.

If one can assume that a major fiscal reform was politically and administratively impossible, the problem of assessing Helfferich's fiscal policies is reduced to judging the economic effects of these policies and his reasons for following them. It must be conceded at the outset that he would probably not have raised taxes very much more than he did even if it had been politically possible. Faced with an unprecedented situation, he failed to readjust

[86] Roesler, *Finanzpolitik*, 125-27.

his thinking sufficiently to understand the fiscal problem that faced him. To a layman, the matter seemed very simple. The debt was rising rapidly. Taxes should therefore be increased in order to bring the budget more nearly into balance. But Helfferich's sophistication in such matters enabled him to see all sorts of reasons for not sharply increasing taxes. He knew that in no major war had any belligerent's tax revenues ever equaled expenditures. He thought that the potentially disruptive economic effects stemming from popular resistance to increased taxes made balancing the budget or even covering the major portion of expenses out of the question. The alternative, of course, was to borrow the money necessary to balance the budget. Although the government was thus able to transfer the necessary resources from the private sector into the war effort, finance through loans was potentially inflationary. That was what Helfferich failed to see.

His researches into the history of money had made him quite conscious of the dangers of inflation but had left him with too limited a view of its origins, a view which his weakness as a monetary theorist reinforced. In the German context, he considered that inflation only occurred when the government financed expenditures by discounting treasury bills with the Reichsbank. He considered this process, in turn, inflationary only to the extent that it proved impossible to fund the short-term debt thus created through the sale of long-term bonds. It was therefore his belief that the tremendous increase in the note issue which occurred at the time of mobilization was not inflationary because the treasury bills against which the notes were issued were funded through the first war loan of September 1914. He believed—with serious qualifications—that inflation began only toward the end of 1916, when it was no longer possible to fund all short-term debt. As he explained it:

> But when the yield from loans fell behind the expenses of war, as was increasingly the case from the fall of 1916 on, a vacuum developed which could only be filled by the state's creating new means of payment—or thus at the price of inflation—or by clamping down with the tax screw. Then at least the necessity presented itself of working against inflation to the greatest

144

possible extent through taxation to reduce its destructive and disastrous effects.[87]

In other words, the damage began after Helfferich left the Treasury.

This explanation of matters is patently inadequate. The wholesale price indexes which Helfferich himself published in his last revision of *Das Geld* (1923) show increases from a base of 100 in 1913 to 106 for 1914, to 142 in 1915, to 153 in 1916, and to 189 in 1917.[88] While Helfferich held indexes in low repute, these figures cannot be ignored. What apparently happened is this. When the war actually broke out, Germany was recovering from a mild recession. Mobilization temporarily disrupted this recovery. Despite the call of a large number of workers to the colors, unemployment among trade-union workers rose in August to 22.9 per cent.[89] Though England blockaded Germany immediately, no particular shortage of goods was for a time noticeable. A few farsighted persons could see that this plenty would not last, but at the time what struck most people was the unused industrial capacity. Because of this excess capacity, the great amounts of money which the government poured into the economy pushed the wholesale average for 1914 only to 106. The fact that it was possible to fund the short bills upon which the note expansion was based is hence largely irrelevant.

This initial slack soon disappeared from the economy. By March 1915, only 3.3 per cent of trade-union workers were unemployed, a figure nearly as low as the 1913 average of 2.9 per cent. In this situation, deficit financing was necessarily inflationary. The wholesale price index rose sharply, reflecting the increasing competition among government, business, and the public for economic goods of all kinds. The fact that Helfferich was again able to fund most of the short-term debt during 1915

[87] *Geld*, 6th edn., 213-14. See also *Weltkrieg*, II, 159.

[88] *Geld*, 6th edn., 620. The impression these summary figures convey is confirmed by the more detailed monthly figures for various categories of wholesale goods in Germany, Statistisches Reichsamt, *Zahlen zur Geldentwertung* (*Wirtschaft und Statistik, Sonderheft 1*) (Berlin, 1925), 16-17, 20.

[89] Leo Grebler and Wilhelm Winkler, *The Cost of the World War to Germany and to Austria-Hungary* (New Haven, 1940), 24-25. For a fuller analysis, see Roesler, *Finanzpolitik*, 150-80.

was irrelevant. In 1915 and 1916, however, the government succeeded in instituting a makeshift system of price and allocation controls, restraining some of the overt inflationary pressures on the economy. Helfferich's admonitions to "honor the millions" also had some effect. In any case, despite a deficit larger than that of 1915 and a continued increase in the money supply, the wholesale index for 1916 was very little higher than that for 1915. With the beginning of the great "materiel battles" of 1916 at Verdun and the Somme, government demand increased very sharply. For reasons yet to be considered, the existing system of price and allocation controls proved inadequate to stem inflationary pressures. The result was a sharp rise in all prices in 1917. Continued deficit financing and the breakdown of price controls were the primary causes of this new inflation, not the failure to fund much of the short-term debt after the fall of 1916.

We must also examine Helfferich's assertion that to finance war expenditures by selling bonds combatted inflation as effectively as raising an equal amount by taxes. Such an assertion is correct only if bond sales and taxes transfer to the government with equal effectiveness aggregates of purchasing power that would otherwise compete for goods in the market place. Most bond sales did not result in such transfers, the limited exception being sales to small subscribers. Many of the latter undoubtedly sacrificed in order to purchase bonds, but such sales represented only a small percentage of total sales. After the outbreak of the war there was a great deal of idle money in the hands of businessmen who found their normal field of activities sharply curtailed.[90] This was particularly true of those in foreign trade. After their existing inventories were sold, they were frequently unable to replace them; nor could they at first employ their idle funds in the stock markets, as the Börse was closed for a time after the beginning of the war. They had thus the choice of leaving their money to collect low rates of interest from commercial or savings banks or investing in 5 per cent government bonds. Each course merely transferred idle hoards from nonspenders to spenders, either to the Reich or to the smaller sovereignties which bor-

[90] On who purchased war loan bonds, see Rist, *Les finances*, 67-70; Roesler, *Finanzpolitik*, 207.

rowed so heavily during the war. As the war progressed these early sources of unemployed funds became relatively less important. Perhaps even from the beginning they were overshadowed by another more important source of funds, the war producers themselves. Because the government paid cash on delivery, most producers found themselves in the unaccustomed position of having credit balances with their banks instead of being in debt as was the rule before the war. Since the government supported the market for its bonds and since they could be used to pay the war profits tax, what better use for idle funds than the purchase of long-term government bonds?

Still, if it was possible to fund most short-term paper until the fall of 1916, why was it not possible thereafter? If one can assume that the sudden increase in military demand embodied in the Hindenburg Program was primarily responsible for the renewed price spiral of 1917, we still have no explanation of why the same percentage of funds was no longer available for the purchase of long-term government bonds. The basic intent of the Hindenburg Program was to mobilize the economy totally in service of the war effort. This end was quite compatible with the fundamental concept of economics, which is that, given a finite amount of resources, one must accept less of one thing in order to have more of something else. Unfortunately, the generals who were the driving force behind the program, Paul von Hindenburg and Erich Ludendorff, tended to translate "total mobilization" into procurement terms simply as demands for the production of more of everything. If their demands were met, however, the generals intended that those who did so should be adequately rewarded: *Geld spielt keine Rolle* was again the watchword. This openhanded approach to procurement apparently had a number of effects. Since the military was now more inclined than ever simply to set production goals without regard to cost, it paid the businessman to bid whatever necessary to secure the human and material resources he required; and this, in turn, encouraged holding larger liquid reserves. Helfferich's remark that short-term government paper found an ever greater market outside the Reichsbank after 1916 was an evidence of this increased liquidity preference. The tendency to hold increasingly large deposits

147

was another.[91] As has been mentioned, this stiff competition for resources soon revealed the inadequacy of the price-fixing mechanism, and prices began to rise. Although the phenomena of inflation were at the time very imperfectly understood, the businessman was well aware that replacement and other costs were rising rapidly. This awareness hardly encouraged the purchase of comparatively low-yield long-term government bonds. Businessmen also wished to be able to redeploy their resources immediately when the war ended. All of these changes were relative, however. The last bond drives brought in as great a number of marks as the first. The foregoing is offered tentatively, and there were certainly other important factors leading to the relative decline in investment in long-term government bonds after 1916.[92]

If long-term loans merely absorbed idle funds which for the most part probably would not have entered the market place during wartime, the question must still be answered whether taxation would have more effectively transferred aggregates of purchasing power from one set of spenders, the business and private sectors of the economy, to another, the government. Helfferich, of course, was far from thinking of the problem in these terms. Although he would undoubtedly have taxed ordinary income could he have done so, he was sincere about the advantages of his policy of taxing war profits "in the very broadest sense of the word." He contrasted favorably his policy of taxing both personal property increases of whatever origin and industrial excess profits with the English policy of concentrating heavily on business and industrial profits.[93] Yet the latter policy was more nearly what the situation required. The apparent appreciation in the value of land, stock holdings, and other property which underlay many "increases" in private fortunes was in part merely a symptom of inflation, though in many cases it also represented profiteers' loot. From the point of view of the economy as a whole such increases in individual wealth were probably not very

[91] *Money*, 229-30; Roesler, *Finanzpolitik*, 141.

[92] The general decline in morale may have been a factor; see Gaertringen, *Groener*, 340, 560-61; *Money*, 594.

[93] *RTV*, Vol. 307, 31 May 1916, 1364.

harmful, whatever their undesirable social and political effects. Industrial and business profits, however, represented to a great extent active purchasing power, and here heavy taxation transferred buying power from one spender to another. Would effective price controls combined with steeply progressive tax rates which reached confiscatory levels on excess profits have dangerously reduced incentives? Helfferich thought they would, but many contemporaries doubted it.

Despite the statement cited earlier in which Helfferich seems to admit the existence of inflation after the fall of 1916, he was actually inclined to doubt that inflation was present in wartime Germany. Because of his limited conception of money, he discusses the problem solely in terms of the increase of the Reichsbank's note issue. The war did not alter Helfferich's earlier view that money was a neutral element in the determination of price levels: the wartime increase in the money supply merely reflected changes on the goods side of the equation of exchange. At the outbreak of the war, a sharp increase in "unproductive consumption" and the "throttling of production" created a strong tendency for prices to rise. The increase in the note issue occurring at this time hardly sufficed to balance the withdrawal of money from circulation. When discussing the price rises occasioned by the Hindenburg Program, he again asserted that decisive changes on the goods side of the equation "would have sufficed" to explain much of the rise in prices. Moreover, an expansion of the circulating medium was also required because of the larger territory under German rule, the increase in the use of notes for domestic payments (as opposed to checks and other such devices), and the large amounts of cash held idle by military paymasters. Helfferich therefore asserted: "It is open to question whether, for the actual period of the War up to 1918, there was in reality any 'inflation' in the sense of an excess cover of the monetary demand by the issue of new circulating media. . . ." The most he would admit was that the continuing issue of notes reinforced the rise in prices to a certain extent. Cost-plus pricing, which pushed up material and wage costs and "thereby . . . increased demand for money," would not have been so possible "if the printing presses had not been at the absolute and unrestricted disposal of the army authorities."[94]

By modern lights, it was a mistake to appoint a man with Helfferich's views on money as a wartime Secretary of the Treasury. His views virtually assured that he would not do the right things. Actually, however, the economic consequences of his errors were not all that desperate, in part because his contemporaries understood inflationary phenomena as little as he. Despite the massive amounts of money continually being created, they retained enough confidence in the purchasing power of the mark to hold increasingly large cash balances. They were, in other words, willing to trade present real income for paper claims against the future. That willingness explains why velocity of circulation continually declined throughout the war, why even as defeat neared the populace began hoarding banknotes, and why, even after price controls began to break down, the wholesale price index had by the end of the war risen to only 2.34 times the prewar level.[95] This relatively modest degree of overt inflation was not enough to disrupt the war effort seriously. It should also be pointed out that while Helfferich was much criticized after the war for his follies while Treasury Secretary, most of this criticism was based on hindsight. It came with especially bad grace from those who had praised his policies during the war.[96] That included most people. Those who opposed his policies at the time, mainly the Socialists, did so for political rather than economic reasons. They wished to tax the profiteer as a matter of social justice, not to reduce inflationary pressures. Given the political realities obtaining and the existing state of economic theory, it is hard to see how anyone could have done very much more than Helfferich. But even within these economic and political limitations, a man more negative than Helfferich toward war profits might have done *somewhat* more.

[94] *Money*, 593-95.

[95] The rises were greatest in industrial products, the least in foodstuffs; Roesler, *Finanzpolitik*, 225-27. Such differences may reflect the relative effectiveness of price controls in the two areas—and a tendency of the official indexes to ignore the black market.

[96] See, for example, the praise of a later critic: Georg Bernhard, *Wie finanzieren wir den Krieg* (Berlin, 1918).

V. SUBMARINES AND
TOTAL WAR

Helfferich's influence soon outgrew his original area of competence, the Treasury Office. Bethmann Hollweg found him a
congenial spirit and a loyal and effective supporter, both within
the cabinet and at Supreme Headquarters. Helfferich warmly
admired his chief, whose greatness as a man and skill as a politician he was in a better position to see than most contemporaries.
He supported Bethmann because he believed Bethmann's foreign
and domestic policies were the only practical ones. In foreign
policy Bethmann sought to assert Germany's position in a manner
that would permit it to develop as a world power, while at home
seeking to achieve evolutionary change within the existing social
order. What distinguished Bethmann from his numerous critics
were the methods by which he attempted to achieve these ends.[1]
His manner was reflective rather than martial, and though able
to act very boldly once determined on a course of action, his
careful weighing of alternatives was often mistaken for weakness.
The flexibility, moderation, and lack of dogmatism characterizing
his political style contributed to the misunderstanding, especially
since Bethmann lacked the political arts that might have enabled him to present a more favorable image to the public. His
great strength lay in his sound political judgment and in his ability as a political bureaucrat to operate effectively within the awkward Imperial constitutional structure. That he so often failed to

---

[1] Fritz Fischer's controversial *Griff nach der Weltmacht* of 1961 greatly
altered the prevailing historical interpretation of Bethmann. Although Fischer
has been much attacked, it seems likely at this stage of the controversy that
his picture of Bethmann as a tough and resourceful politician will stand. The
older view of Bethmann as some sort of philosopher on horseback is hardly
tenable any longer. The best recent appraisal of Bethmann is Fritz Stern's
"Bethmann Hollweg and the War: The Limits of Responsibility," in Fritz
Stern and Leonard Krieger (eds.), *The Responsibility of Power: Historical
Essays in Honor of Hajo Holborn* (Garden City, 1969), 271-307.

get his way is evidence of the obstacles that the cumbersome governmental machinery placed in the path of even the very able.

As a bureaucrat whose forte was confronting the right man with the right argument at the right time, Bethmann found that Helfferich's ability to cook up arguments admirably supplemented his own lack of inventiveness. He also found that Helfferich's "long dialectical discussions of every question," as Jagow later described them, helped to clarify his mind.[2] That was especially true of questions having economic ramifications, and in blockaded Germany few questions did not. In such matters Helfferich's support was invaluable. His economic arguments, supported by masses of detail and yards of statistics, were presented with clarity, force, and assurance. Few of those within government circles, whether bureaucrats or soldiers, could argue effectively against Helfferich on such questions.

Helfferich's words carried additional weight, perhaps, because he was *persona gratissima* with the Kaiser, who liked him and found his "fresh and unaffected directness" pleasing.[3] Helfferich's relations with the Reichstag, though occasionally tense during the budget debates of 1916, were generally good until the fall of 1916. He had encountered some difficulties with the Social Democrats, but that was a fate common to Treasury Secretaries, and in official circles his financial program was recognized as all that was obtainable under existing circumstances.[4] When Clemens von Delbrück's rapidly failing health and growing unpopularity forced his retirement in May 1916, who was better fitted than Helfferich to assume Delbrück's important duties, those of Deputy-Chancellor and Secretary of the Interior?

As Delbrück's "poor appearance" had been a source of comment among insiders for some time, speculation naturally turned to the question of his successor.[5] There was apparently never

[2] As quoted in Johann H. Bernstorff, *Erinnerungen und Briefe* (Zurich, 1936), 121-22. Epstein ascribes the influence of Helfferich's opponent Erzberger over Bethmann to much the same qualities; *Erzberger*, 97.

[3] "Bericht" 412, 14 May 1916, "HB."

[4] Even Wilhelm Keil acknowledged that Helfferich had represented his program in committee "with rare adroitness"; Wilhelm Keil, *Erlebnisse eines Sozialdemokraten* (2 vols., Stuttgart, 1947-1948), I, 349.

[5] Lerchenfeld to Ludwig III, King of Bavaria, "Bericht" 284/LXII, 3 April

much doubt that Helfferich would receive the post. Other than Helfferich himself, who said that Count Siegfried von Roedern (his successor at the Treasury Office) was also under consideration, no one ever mentioned any other possibilities.[6] Reactions to Helfferich's appointment varied. Admiral Georg von Müller, Chief of the Naval Cabinet, noted approvingly in his diary, "A good choice for sure."[7] Others, among them the influential Hofmarschall, Count August zu Eulenburg, felt as Müller did, but worried about finding an adequate replacement for Helfferich in the Treasury.[8] Helfferich himself shared Eulenburg's worries about finding a replacement and also had some doubts about the wisdom of taking over the Interior Office, where the emphasis was on political rather than financial questions. As he later put it, he felt that he was making "a leap in the dark."[9] There was a third school which condemned the Helfferich appointment unreservedly. An expert in finance, Helfferich had deserted the Treasury just when the "real problems were becoming clear" to take a position for which neither his training nor his background suited him.[10] A discreditable "thirst for political laurels" was his only motivation.[11] This does Helfferich less than justice, but there was something to Max Weber's comment that "[Helfferich] fled from the Treasury because he is only a financier, and not a financial administrator, or tax expert, or *Sozialpolitiker*." But in recognition of Bethmann's role in Helfferich's appointment, Weber added: "Bethmann is taking him as support for the 'new course,' which is steering to the left."[12] Helfferich was unquestionably

---

1916, GStA, "PA." For a list of Delbrück's ailments, see his *Mobilmachung*, 197.

[6] See n.3 above.   [7] Görlitz, *Müller*, 176, entry of 11 May 1916.

[8] "Bericht" 413, 15 May 1916, "HB." Zimmermann, one of Helfferich's strongest proponents before his appointment, later complained about his having to conduct the endless and complicated financial negotiations with the Turks; "Bericht" 422, 10 June 1916, *ibid.*

[9] *Weltkrieg*, II, 176.   [10] Pinner, *Wirtschaftsführer*, 146-47.

[11] Fischart, *Das alte und das neue System*, 168-69. See also Gustav Stresemann, "Helfferich," 7 Dec. 1916, draft article for the *Deutsche Kurier*, Stresemann "Nachlass," 6866/3063/219746-54. Stresemann ably summarizes the shifts in opinion on Helfferich down to the date of the article.

[12] Josef Redlich, *Das politische Tagebuch Josef Redlichs, 1908-1916* (2 vols., Graz and Cologne, 1953-1954), II, 120, entry of 6 June 1916.

eager for the post. Even some of his close friends thought that he regarded the Interior Office merely as a "way station" to the Chancellorship.[13] Ambitious Helfferich unquestionably was. He enjoyed the exercise of power and responsibility more than he perhaps would have admitted even to himself. But these qualities are a part of every successful statesman, and it is hard to see anything particularly reprehensible in Helfferich's accepting his new post.

Short of the Chancellorship, Helfferich's new office was the most important civil office in the Reich. As Secretary of the Interior he was not only head of the most important of the Reich's executive agencies, but was also the Chancellor's alter ego (Stellvertreter des Reichskanzlers). In fact, if not in name, he was the Vice-Chancellor and was often informally so styled. According to recent precedent, he should also have become Vice-President of the Prussian Ministry, but since he was the youngest of all the Prussian ministers and a Bavarian, the Vice-Presidency went to Paul von Breitenbach, a man old enough to be his father.[14] The Interior Office was the first new office created after the foundation of the Reich. Over the years it gradually acquired an enormous number of functions, which ranged all the way from administration of the social welfare laws to control of weights and measures and the collection of agricultural and industrial statistics. In the United States its functions would be served by several departments, regulatory commissions, and executive agencies. Even before the war this proliferation of functions had made the Interior Office too unwieldy for one man to control effectively, but all of the Interior Secretaries had successfully resisted every attempt to divide the office.[15] During the war a host of new agencies and the civil administration of the conquered areas

[13] See n.3 above. Both Ballin and Holtzendorff agreed shortly after Helfferich was appointed Secretary of the Treasury that he might be aiming at the Chancellorship; "Notizen," 29 March 1915, "HB." Delbrück thought him a suitable candidate but wished to save him for after the war; "Bericht" 383, 3 April 1916, *ibid.*

[14] Hans Goldschmidt, *Das Reich und Preussen im Kampf um die Führung: von Bismarck bis 1918* (Berlin, 1931), 117-18. The older practice had been to appoint the minister with the most seniority.

[15] Helfferich himself rejected the idea even before he had been officially appointed; see n.3 above.

were added to Interior's jurisdiction, and only the partial loss of control over the regulation of the wartime economy prevented the burden from becoming greater than it was. Materials allocation and other industrial problems were under the control of military agencies and though the War Food Office (Kriegsernährungsamt) was nominally under the Interior Office, Helfferich soon gave up his attempts to control it.[16] He was the last man to head this vast and cumbersome organization.

The Submarine Warfare Controversy

The controversy in which Bethmann Hollweg found Helfferich's support most useful was that over submarine warfare. It was in good part because of the effectiveness of this support that Bethmann selected Helfferich to succeed Delbrück. When the war broke out, Helfferich had no more inkling of the potentialities of the submarine than anyone else. The spectacular early successes of the submarine, however, soon made him a convert to the new weapon. Like most of his countrymen, Helfferich hoped that the submarine might convert England's sea-girt isolation into a fatal liability. While he sincerely objected to the sacrifice of non-combatant lives and the other violations of international law which true submarine warfare entailed, his scruples were somewhat blunted by the "sovereign disdain for international law" with which the English were tightening their blockade of Germany. The English "hunger blockade," too, bore heavily on non-combatants, and if the submarine should prove "an effective means of reprisal," so much the better.[17] Thus it is hardly surprising that Helfferich favored the "submarine blockade" which was imposed upon England in February 1915.[18] While Bethmann

[16] Wilhelm Dieckmann, *Die Behördenorganisation in der deutschen Kriegswirtschaft 1914-1918* (Hamburg, 1937), 11-14; *Weltkrieg*, II, 177-82. The Kriegsernährungsamt was made into a separate Staatssekretariat in July 1917.

[17] *Weltkrieg*, II, 184, 196, 306.

[18] *Ibid.*, 300-306. The fullest accounts of submarine warfare and its diplomatic repercussions for the Allied side are Ernest R. May, *The World War and American Isolation, 1914-1917* (Cambridge, Mass., 1959), and the appropriate chapters of Arthur S. Link, *Wilson* (5 vols. to date, Princeton, 1947-1965), III-V. For the German side, see also Karl E. Birnbaum, *Peace Moves and U-Boat Warfare: A Study of Germany's Policy Toward the United*

had been uncertain just what the neutral reaction to this measure would be, the United States' response was unexpectedly sharp. Though it appeared for a time that the United States would take no action against Germany, a series of incidents culminating in the sinking of the *Lusitania* on 7 May 1915 dispelled this hope. A number of stiff notes from the United States made it quite clear that war was likely to result if submarine warfare was continued in its present form. This eventuality placed submarine warfare in quite a different light and led in the summer of 1915 to a high-level reappraisal of the whole question.

Bethmann himself was not at all sure that submarine warfare would defeat England, but he knew that war with the United States was almost certain disaster. Unfortunately, a skillful and unscrupulous propaganda campaign led by Admiral Alfred von Tirpitz, Secretary of the Reich Navy Office, had convinced most of the public that unrestricted submarine warfare was the key to victory. The danger of American entry into the war was either slighted or, if it was considered at all, American military potential was shrugged off with sardonic remarks about Pershing's sallies against Pancho Villa. The German people approved of the sinking of the *Lusitania,* and to avert an irreparable breach in German-American relations, Bethmann had to move with circumspection. He did so, and by mid-July the worst of the *Lusitania* crisis was over. On 23 July, however, a new American note arrived. Although very sharp in tone, it did assert that Germany and the United States sought a common aim, freedom of the seas. Helfferich was much struck by this statement. He developed his ideas on what it might offer for the future of German-American relations to Bethmann at first orally and then in a letter dated 5 August 1915.[19]

Helfferich's memorandum was the first systematic consideration of the consequences of war with the United States. Since as Secretary of the Treasury he was "not directly involved" with

States, *April 18, 1916-January 9, 1917* (Stockholm, 1958), and Ritter, *Staatskunst,* III, 145-215, 285-385.

[19] The text of the 5 August letter is printed in Alfred von Tirpitz (ed.), *Politische Dokumente* (2 vols., Berlin, 1926), II, 385-95. Original in "Wk 18 geh.," Bd. 3, SA 6.

either foreign or naval policy, he felt that he had to approach the question largely from the economic and financial side. He first emphasized the financial consequences of American entry into the war, developing at some length the difficulties the English were encountering in financing their American purchases. He warned that if the United States entered the war, however, "billions" would become available, and "Entente worries about covering their war needs would be over for the foreseeable future." His second major point was that the German textile industry would be hard hit if American supplies of cotton, for which he was then negotiating, were cut off. Finally, he pointed out some of the political consequences of war with the United States, the most important of which was that many of the small continental neutrals might feel obliged to join the Entente. He accordingly recommended whatever restrictions in submarine warfare as were needed to avoid a break with the United States. He also proposed the positive step of offering to collaborate with the United States to secure freedom of the seas, subject to resumption of "ruthless" submarine warfare if German-American efforts proved unsuccessful within a stated period. He reminded Bethmann that the submarine was, after all, only a means to an end, German victory. If a less intensive submarine campaign would enable Germany to "break the English policy of strangulation," then the submarine would have achieved its end. If, on the other hand, his policy failed, nothing was lost, because an unrestricted campaign could still be resumed.

Neither the Navy nor the Foreign Office showed much enthusiasm for Helfferich's shrewd appeal. The Navy submitted a memorandum in refutation, and Helfferich yet another memorandum rebutting the Navy's "polemic," as he termed it.[20] In general, Helfferich did little more than repeat his earlier arguments, including his initial recommendation of "a temporary and conditional slackening of submarine warfare." The Kaiser, to whom the various letters and memoranda had in the meantime been submitted, noted in the margin opposite this last recommenda-

[20] Helfferich to Bethmann, letter and copy of memorandum, 3 Sept. 1915, "Wk 18 geh.," Bd. 3, SA 6. The Navy memorandum, written by Admiral Bachmann, Chief of the Naval Staff, is in the same file.

tion, "ja," and at the bottom of the memo, "agreed." By providing Bethmann with additional arguments in favor of reducing the level of submarine warfare, arguments to which the Kaiser moreover had proved receptive, Helfferich had increased his chief's ability to resist the importunate demands of the Navy for an all-out campaign.[21] His victory in this first battle of what came to be known as the "memorandum war" had also earned him the right to be heard in future discussions of the submarine question.

Such discussions did not recommence until early in 1916. In the meantime, General von Falkenhayn, increasingly convinced that it was impossible to force a decision on land, had become a convert to unrestricted submarine warfare. The new Chief of the Naval Staff, Admiral Henning von Holtzendorff, had also.[22] As Holtzendorff had been appointed the previous September in part because of his reputation as a moderate on the submarine question, his defection was something of a disappointment to Bethmann. The admiral wished to begin an unrestricted campaign on 1 March 1916, when English grain stocks would be lowest. He charged the political leaders with persuading the United States to permit such a campaign without breaking off diplomatic relations. On 19 February 1916, he gave Bethmann a memorandum which supported his case by detailing the impact the proposed campaign would have on the English.

Helfferich himself still favored an unrestricted campaign only if it were "absolutely sure of success," or if it were possible combine the campaign with continuing diplomatic relations with the United States.[23] When asked by Bethmann to comment on the

[21] The Kaiser took up Helfferich's arguments as his own. In a letter to Tirpitz, he asserted: "America must be prevented from participating in the war against us as an active enemy. It could offer unlimited financial resources to our enemies . . ."; Link, *Wilson*, III, 577n80. Given the Kaiser's receptiveness to Helfferich's arguments, Bethmann may have erred in not showing William Helfferich's 5 August letter when he first received it. Ritter attributes this omission to Bethmann's fear of "the public protests of the U-boat fanatics," *Staatskunst*, III, 179.

[22] For a detailed discussion of Falkenhayn's position on submarine warfare and its relation to his Verdun offensive, see Janssen, *Der Kanzler und der General*, 184-204. For Holtzendorff's complex position, see in addition Birnbaum, *Peace Moves*, 56-57; Ritter, *Staatskunst*, III, 370.

[23] "Bericht" 328, 8 Jan. 1916, and "Bericht" 348, 10 Feb. 1916, "HB."

Navy's latest memorandum, Helfferich made short work of it.[24] He called the Navy's elaborate statistics accurate, but assailed the shoddy logic on which the conclusions were based. In one instance the Navy claimed that the sharp rise in the unfavorable balance of English trade proved how effective the existing submarine campaign was. "If the submarine war were completely effective, thus totally blocking imports and exports, there would be no unfavorable balance at all," Helfferich commented drily. The Navy's case rested on three unverifiable hypotheses: first, that submarine warfare to date had had a great and deleterious effect on England's foreign trade; second, that an unrestricted campaign would triple this effect; and third, that England would therefore have to sue for peace within six months. Helfferich thought that the Navy was asking the wrong questions. What they needed to know was how much English shipping the submarine could destroy within a given time, what relation the destroyed tonnage had to the total tonnage available to England, and what Germany's position would be if the United States and other neutrals entered the war against Germany. If England could not be defeated before the United States fatally overweighed the balance against Germany—which Helfferich implied was unlikely—the Navy's proposals could scarcely be considered.

Armed with the information that Helfferich and other close associates had provided, Bethmann drafted his own memorandum. It embodied Helfferich's conclusions and decisively rejected the Navy's demands. He secured William's assent for his policy in a series of conferences at Supreme Headquarters in early March 1916. Bethmann also succeeded in forcing the meddlesome Admiral Tirpitz to resign, staved off attacks on his policies in the Prussian Landtag, and secured the backing of the Bundesrat. The problem remaining was to secure the backing of the Reichstag in the face of an increasingly virulent and fanatical pro-submarine campaign in the right-wing press. Adroitly transferring the submarine hearings to the relative privacy of closed Budget Committee sessions, Bethmann and Admiral Eduard von Capelle, Tirpitz's successor, presented a solid case for the govern-

[24] Helfferich memorandum, 26 Feb. 1916, "Wk 18 geh. Adh. 1," Bd. 1, SA 20.

ment's policy on 28 and 29 March. Helfferich buttressed this case on the second day with economic arguments.[25] As in the past, he laid great stress on the enormous assistance the United States could provide the Entente. Once the United States was in the war, he warned, "all Americans will have only one fatherland, and they will never rest until we lie prostrate on the ground." He also called attention to the amount of food that the neighboring neutrals were currently exporting to Germany. These supplies were especially needed because the German harvest of 1915 had been extremely poor. If America entered the war, England would doubtless put enough pressure on these neutrals to cut off supplies entirely, and this was sure disaster. As a result of the government's able presentation of its case and Erzberger's successful cloakroom efforts to rally the Center Party behind the government, a Center-Progressive-Socialist majority reported out a harmless resolution which left the government complete freedom of action on the submarine question.[26] The government victory also inaugurated a lull in the violent press campaign for unrestricted use of the submarine.

Unfortunately, the torpedoing of the steamer *Sussex* on 24 March ushered in a new diplomatic crisis with the United States, the most serious to date. Helfferich continued to provide Bethmann with the same loyal and effective support as in the past. By now his influence in the submarine policy was such that his journeys to Supreme Headquarters had come to serve insiders as a mark of how much difficulty Bethmann was having with the pro-submarine forces around the Kaiser.[27] Although Bethmann succeeded in resolving the *Sussex* crisis, it was only to face in the early summer of 1916 a new and exceedingly vicious pro-submarine campaign in the press. Rumors were even circulated that the Kaiser was blocking ruthless use of the submarine because of

[25] Lerchenfeld to Hertling, "Bericht" 302, 7 April 1916, and attached "Niederschrift über die Verhandlungen der Budget Kommission . . . vom 28. und 29. März 1916," GStA, "PA."

[26] Epstein, *Erzberger*, 156-57; Ritter, *Staatskunst*, III, 207-208.

[27] Lerchenfeld, for example, wrote Hertling that Helfferich's departure on one such journey "makes me rather anxious"; Lerchenfeld to Hertling, "Bericht" 385, 2 May 1916, GStA, "PA." See also Görlitz, *Müller*, 174, entry of 2 May 1916.

his English financial interests.[28] And more Reichstag supporters, mainly from the Center, were enrolling daily behind the banners of the pro-submarine forces.

Perhaps foreseeing the day when it would no longer be possible to withstand the growing clamor for the submarine, Helfferich began expressing late in July 1916 a more favorable view of its military potential, though only in the most restricted circles. One rather suspects, though, that he also took this new line in order to appear conciliatory rather than intransigent toward those whose recommendations he continued to oppose. He said in essence that unrestricted submarine warfare was *then* a mistake but implied that it might not be so in the future.[29] First, the new harvest promised to be better than that of 1915. The loss of neutral foodstuffs was hence less dangerous than it would have been earlier. Second, he hoped that growing neutral sentiment against English violations of international law might make it possible to "risk" submarine warfare under "considerably better conditions." The "greatest triumph" for Germany would be to wage an unrestricted campaign while keeping America neutral. He thought 1917 the best time to begin such a campaign unless France or Russia "fell away" from the Entente in the meantime: "then, of course, consideration of America would no longer be necessary."

Helfferich presented these views, at first guardedly and finally in a rather more extreme form, in a series of four high-level conferences held in August 1916. In all of these conferences, Bethmann and Helfferich give the impression of borrowing too heavily against the future for the sake of their policy of staving off unrestricted submarine warfare yet a while longer. In the first such conference of 6 August, for example, Helfferich argued that while England currently had more than a four-month supply of grain, its stocks would be nearly exhausted by spring. He accordingly concluded that it would be foolish to weaken the submarine arm by beginning the campaign prematurely.[30] In the following

[28] Prussian Ministry Protocol, 19 Aug. 1916, "Preussen" 11, 3169/1613/-674904-34.
[29] "Bericht" 457, 25 July 1916, and "Bericht" 466, 3 Aug. 1916, "HB."
[30] Birnbaum, *Peace Moves*, 120-21.

conferences they continued to speak of why this or that objection to submarine warfare "had fallen away."[31] If the purpose of such utterances was to rally support for an unpopular policy by offering the prospect of its future reversal, then one may perhaps conclude that the senior civilians despaired of holding off a policy they considered ruinous very far into the new year.

Bureaucrats vs. Generals: Differing Views of Total War

On 27 August 1916, Rumania declared war on the Central Powers, creating a new crisis on the eastern front. On the following day, Falkenhayn, already fatally associated with the Verdun fiasco, was sacrificed in the name of political expediency.[32] The victors of Tannenberg, Paul von Hindenburg and his Chief of Staff, Erich Ludendorff, officially assumed the Supreme Command. Even from the military point of view, the change was not such an improvement as it was almost universally assumed to be at the time. Falkenhayn lacked the superficial brilliance of Ludendorff, the dominant member of the eastern team, but he had a grasp on reality that often was conspicuously wanting in the latter. Bethmann's relations with Falkenhayn, unfortunately, had never been more than formally correct, and he had long been trying to oust him. Helfferich, too, viewed Falkenhayn's departure with relief. He had had several minor disputes with the general while Treasury Secretary, and, apparently unaware of the complexities of the military situation, regarded Falkenhayn's "mishandling" of Balkan matters as the source of Germany's military difficulties.[33] A visit to Hindenburg's headquarters early in July 1916 only reinforced Helfferich's prejudices. He returned to Berlin full of enthusiasm for the "demigods" of the east.[34] "Demi-

[31] Prussian Ministry Protocol, 28 Aug. 1916, "Preussen" 11, 3169/1613/-674935-42.

[32] For excellent recent accounts of Falkenhayn's fall, see Janssen, *Der Kanzler und der General*, Ch. 24; Ritter, *Staatskunst*, III, Ch. 6.

[33] *Weltkrieg*, II, 91-105; "Bericht" 478, 6 Sept. 1916, "HB." It would appear that Bethmann was also less fully informed of the military situation than he might have been; Ritter, *Staatskunst*, III, 226.

[34] "Bericht" 447, 13 July 1916, "HB"; Görlitz, *Müller*, 207, entry of 29 July 1916. See also Karl F. Nowak (ed.), *Die Aufzeichnungen des Generalmajors Max Hoffmann* (2 vols., Berlin, 1930), I, 126, entry of 30 June 1916; Eisen-

gods" Hindenburg and Ludendorff surely were in the eyes of the public. Bethmann hoped to exploit their popularity to secure moderate measures of his own, particularly a moderate peace. Although his hopes were to be cruelly disappointed, it is difficult to see how, given the generals' extraordinary popularity, Bethmann could have avoided appointing them to the Supreme Command once he had decided to rid himself of the generally unpopular Falkenhayn. Nearly all Germans—with the conspicuous exception of the Kaiser—would have regarded any other appointment as simply outrageous.[35]

Whatever hopes Bethmann may have had for support were dashed almost at once. A Crown Council on submarine warfare had earlier been scheduled for the end of August because both Falkenhayn and Holtzendorff demanded an immediate unrestricted submarine campaign. Now, with Falkenhayn gone, Bethmann apparently looked forward to the council with confidence, as he had some reason to believe that Hindenburg and Ludendorff supported his views on the use of the submarine. On 31 August, the council met.[36] Both naval and civilian representatives rehearsed their now familiar cases, with Helfferich again supporting his stated conclusion that "submarine warfare will probably lead us to catastrophe" with a wide variety of economic arguments. Bethmann warmly espoused these arguments, also mentioning that England might use convoys as a defense against the submarine. But he stated that the final decision depended on how Hindenburg and Ludendorff sized up the military situation. Both of the generals wanted to withhold their decision until the dangerous military situation in the southwest became clearer. Hindenburg left no doubt, however, about where their sym-

---

hardt-Rothe, *Im Banne der Persönlichkeit*, 136-37. Hoffmann, then on Hindenburg's staff, shrewdly surmised that the reason why Helfferich was coming east was to secure support for Bethmann. The ostensible reason, according to Eisenhardt-Rothe, was to clear up difficulties between Interior and *Oberost* over administration of the area.

[35] See, however, Feldman, *Army, Industry, and Labor*, 139-45, who concludes that Bethmann fell victim to his illusions about Hindenburg and Ludendorff.

[36] May, *World War*, 293-94; Birnbaum, *Peace Moves*, 131-37; Arno Spindler, *Der Handelskrieg mit U-Booten* (3 vols., Berlin, 1932-1934), III, 209-13.

pathies lay: "I would be glad if submarine warfare could be waged, and indeed, soon and energetically." Neither general mentioned what effect America's entering the war might have, although both were uneasy about the possibility that Denmark and Holland might do so. In a very real sense, America did not enter their field of vision.[37] It was agreed that Hindenburg would decide when the matter should be discussed again, and after some difficulty Bethmann was finally able to persuade the generals to accept a statement for the party leaders which said that everyone agreed that unrestricted submarine warfare must be postponed.

The import of the generals' remarks was clear. As soon as Rumania was sufficiently subdued they meant to demand unrestricted submarine warfare. Bethmann and Helfferich both seem to have drawn this conclusion and were hardly sanguine about their ability to oppose the generals. Arndt von Holtzendorff, Admiral von Holtzendorff's brother, concluded from remarks made by Bethmann at a Holtzendorff Abend on 14 September 1916 that "the Chancellor seems . . . to reckon that [unrestricted] submarine warfare must come, it is only a question of when."[38] Helfferich and Admiral Holtzendorff continued their argument about the best possible timing for such a campaign, still without reaching agreement. But when Ballin said that "in the end Hindenburg's views would be the decisive ones," both Helfferich and the admiral concurred. Holtzendorff added that should Hindenburg decide "in two weeks" on unrestricted submarine warfare, "the Foreign Office would make difficulties." All (except, apparently, Bethmann) agreed that Jagow had to go.[39] Helfferich's remarks were scarcely those of a man who expected to fight in the last ditch on the submarine question, though perhaps this is attributable to the casual nature of the gathering. Yet while Bethmann's

[37] See especially Gaertringen, *Groener*, 326, entry of 11 Oct. 1916.

[38] "Notizen," 14 Sept. 1916, "HB." For the details on the Holtzendorff Abende and their place in the political and social life of wartime Berlin, see Cecil, *Ballin*, 250-57. Helfferich was a regular guest.

[39] Only a short time later, however, when similar demands were made in the Reichstag, Helfferich feared that letting Jagow go would be construed as a sign of weakness and encourage further demands: "Then perhaps Zimmermann or Helfferich will not suit them, and the government will lose control of things completely"; "Bericht" 488, 21 Sept. 1916, "HB."

remarks were more guarded, their tendency was the same. The emphasis was on the timing of the campaign rather than on preventing it.

The civilians meant, however, to preserve their freedom to maneuver as long as they could, and to do this, they needed the support of the Reichstag more than ever. When the Reichstag convened in the fall of 1916, the submarine question was again quickly referred to the comparative privacy of the Budget Committee. Unwilling to risk his prestige in a defeat, Bethmann left it largely to Helfferich to present the government's case.[40] He was up to the task. His speech of 30 September, fifty typewritten pages long, is a masterly presentation of the arguments against unrestricted submarine warfare.[41] In justification of statements made the previous March in committee, he first discussed German imports from the neighboring neutrals in great detail. Germany had managed to increase its imports from these countries considerably, mostly at the expense of the English. "Could you expect of the Dutch and the Danes that they would increase their exports in this way while we torpedoed their ships without warning, while they received reports, day in, day out, week after week, that such and such a ship was sunk and the crew drowned?" Second, he warned that the effectiveness of a ruthless campaign in frightening neutral shippers was likely to be less than commonly supposed. Many neutral shippers were bound by long-term charters, and their personal feelings about the submarine were therefore not a factor. He also repeated earlier statements to the Crown Council of 31 August about how much shipping the English still had left and about the possibilities of their organizing in yet unsuspected ways to meet the submarine threat. "If we play the card of unrestricted submarine warfare and it does not hold [the trick], we are lost, lost for centuries."

Helfferich's disquisition on the probable effects of America's entering the war made abundantly clear why unrestricted submarine warfare would have such ruinous effects if it failed. After examining the amount of financial assistance which the United

[40] May, *World War*, 296-97.
[41] See *Weltkrieg*, II, 384-89, for a summary. For the complete text, see "Wk 18 geh.," Bd. 22, SA 8.

States could provide, he concluded it to be much greater than the amount which the Entente was then getting. He pointed to just what American steel production, three times that of Germany, meant in terms of war potential. America would also supply troops in large numbers. Germany's difficulties lay "in great part" in the "superiority in human resources" which the Entente already possessed. "Do you think to improve our position by throwing a cultivated land with a strong and mighty race of over a hundred million strong onto the other side?" He scoffed at the notion that the submarine could prevent many American troops from reaching the continent—the Navy had boasted that not a single troopship would reach Europe. The English had so far been able to supply 400,000 men at Saloniki solely by sea despite intense submarine activity in the Mediterranean. And after the war, what would happen then? England would be able to carry on the economic war she dreamed of: "Then we will be the boycotted dog, to whom no one in the whole world will give a piece of bread." These arguments seem in retrospect incontrovertible and were indeed borne out by the events. Yet though Helfferich judged that the speech had made an "impression," he sadly admitted that it did not achieve a "decisive success."[42] The prosubmarine forces were no longer accessible to reason. Unrestricted submarine warfare had become the shibboleth of all those who opposed Bethmann Hollweg's government for any reason whatever.[43]

On 2 October Bethmann and Helfferich attempted to rally support for their policy in a series of conferences with the party leaders, but with little success. Helfferich's further efforts in committee were equally vain. The real decision was being fought out elsewhere, within the councils of the Center Party. Adolph Gröber, a right-wing Center leader who had supported Bethmann the previous spring, now feared the inflammatory effects upon the nation if unrestricted submarine warfare was delayed long-

[42] *Weltkrieg*, ii, 389. For the comments of two who were convinced by Helfferich's exposition, see Conrad Haussmann, *Schlaglichter: Reichstagsbriefe und Aufzeichnungen*, ed. Ulrich Zeller (Frankfurt a. M., 1924), 63-65; and Epstein, *Erzberger*, 160.

[43] May, *World War*, 288-89.

er.[44] Erzberger still opposed the measure, speaking against it in committee and within the party conclaves. But he was now in a minority, and in order to save the unity of the party, he at last acquiesced in a party resolution which called upon the Chancellor to consider the views of the Supreme Command when making the final decision on unrestricted submarine warfare.[45] The resolution further stated that if the decision were in favor of unrestricted submarine warfare, "the Chancellor could be assured of the approval of the Reichstag." In committee all but the Socialists voted in favor of this curious statement. The Center resolution greatly limited Bethmann's area of maneuver, for he could now count on only his immediate entourage to support his submarine policy.

Although Hindenburg and Ludendorff did not demand unrestricted submarine warfare immediately, they had already begun to push in other directions for a more energetic prosecution of the war effort. As Ludendorff, the dominant member of the team, saw the problem he and Hindenburg had inherited, a dangerous military situation had been needlessly aggravated, if not actually caused, by a failure to appreciate the "realities" of total war. Ludendorff's later indictment spared scarcely anyone. Falkenhayn had neglected the building of fortifications in the west and the supply of the troops, the Navy had employed its forces ineffectually, and the civilians had failed to mobilize fully either the moral or material resources on the home front.[46] A position not without some merit, although drastically oversimplified. Ludendorff did perhaps have a more inclusive conception of total war than either Bethmann or Helfferich. In practice, unfortunately, Ludendorff's attempts to implement his ideas on increasing German war potential took too little account of the means and the timing by which his ends, often desirable in themselves, were to be secured. In short, there is considerable justice in Gerald Feldman's assertion that his plans "represent the triumph, not of imagination, but of fantasy."[47]

[44] Willi Bongard, *Die Zentrumsresolution vom 7. October 1916* (Published doctoral dissertation, Cologne University, 1937), 13-14, 54-55.

[45] Epstein, *Erzberger*, 159-60.

[46] Erich Ludendorff, *Kriegführung und Politik* (Berlin, 1924), 110.

[47] *Army, Industry, and Labor*, 150.

This weakness of Ludendorff's is nowhere better illustrated than in his first important foray into high policy, his advocacy of the proclamation of an independent Polish state. Since 1915, both he and Hindenburg had believed that if such a proclamation were issued, the Poles would flock to the colors to fight against Russia in a burst of patriotic enthusiasm. The *Miniaturgebilde* that Ludendorff contemplated was scarcely calculated to arouse such enthusiasm in Polish breasts, but any independent Polish state, however winsome, was likely to thwart any attempt to reach a separate peace with Russia.[48] Bethmann also favored the creation of a Polish state—for rather different reasons than Ludendorff—and negotiations with Austria had been going on for some time. Toward the end of August, however, Bethmann decided that peace with Russia might be near and that the Polish state should not, therefore, be proclaimed until the Russian situation became clear. Nevertheless, when in September the Supreme Command began pressing to issue the proclamation immediately, Bethmann gave in without a struggle. The planning moved into the final stage.

Helfferich's direct connection with Polish affairs was at this time slight.[49] His ideas on Poland differed markedly from Ludendorff's. Throughout the summer of 1916 he had hoped for a separate peace with Russia. Even after Rumania entered the war he continued to believe that peace with Russia was possible once Rumania was subdued. So great were the advantages of peace that he privately said that he was willing to go to great lengths to obtain it. Despite his later strictures about Austria's conduct as an ally, he himself boggled neither at forcing the Austrians to part permanently with East Galicia nor at forcing the Turks to offer Russia free passage of the Straits. If in addition Russian Poland and Courland were returned to their former overlord, he

[48] Werner Conze, *Polnische Nation und deutsche Politik im Ersten Weltkrieg* (Graz and Cologne, 1958), 189, 194-98; Ritter, *Staatskunst*, III, 264-69. The following draws heavily on the excellent accounts of Conze and Ritter.

[49] Although the civil administration of German-occupied Poland lay within the jurisdiction of the Interior Office, Helfferich had little direct contact with Polish affairs if a survey of "Weltkrieg 20 c: Die Zukunft der besetzen Gebiete Polens" is any indication. Ministerialdirektor Theodor Lewald is the Interior Office official whose name appears most frequently.

thought that peace might appeal to Russia. On the other hand, it was a "hopeless beginning" to mobilize the Poles against Russia, and he thought the whole idea of a Polish army "fantasy."[50]

Though the latter insight proved accurate enough, it did not alter the course of events. Bethmann unsuccessfully attempted in early October to delay the Polish proclamation by calling the Supreme Command's attention to renewed signs that the Russians were interested in peace negotiations. Ludendorff refused to wait: "We must act in Poland, there is no patent solution. It is all a question of power, and we need men." On 18 October 1916, the Germans and the Austrians agreed to issue the proclamation "as soon as possible" and the manifesto for Polish volunteers shortly thereafter.[51] Adapting rapidly to the new situation, Helfferich now said that the proclamation should be justified as a "sign of strength," since Russia had "missed the chance" for a separate peace.[52] After some last-minute and again unsuccessful attempts by Bethmann to delay the proclamation, it duly appeared on 5 November and the manifesto for Polish volunteers only four days later. The inept timing of the manifesto, largely attributable to Ludendorff's insistence on haste, destroyed whatever effect the proclamation might have had among the Poles. Helfferich correctly judged the entire episode a "dud."[53]

Bethmann made his last attempt to delay the Polish proclamation because he desired to issue a call for peace in the name of all the Central Powers first. Although Count Stephan Buriàn, the Austro-Hungarian Foreign Minister, had suggested such a step at the conferences of 18 October, the immediate occasion for Bethmann's interest in the matter was a speech which Sir Edward Grey had delivered on 23 October to the representatives of the foreign press. Bethmann and Helfferich misinterpreted this speech to mean that the English were more disunited and more inclined to peace than had been supposed. Bethmann thus fell in readily enough with Helfferich's suggestion that the Central Pow-

[50] "Bericht" 474, 2 Sept. 1916, "HB."

[51] Conze, *Polnische Nation*, 206-15.

[52] Görlitz, *Müller*, 232, entry of 24 Oct. 1916; "Bericht" 510, 25 Oct. 1916, "HB."

[53] "Notizen," 26 Nov. 1916, "HB."

ers issue a call for peace. No terms were to be stated, only a general willingness to negotiate.[54] The Chancellor was becoming increasingly convinced that a general peace offered the Central Powers their sole chance to avert disaster. And with the internal balance of power tipping ever more heavily in favor of the Supreme Command, a successful peace action offered Bethmann virtually his only hope of retaining control of policy. These considerations had already led Bethmann in September to encourage a peace move by President Wilson, but the President had not acted. Helfferich himself had never approved of involving Wilson in the affairs of the Central Powers because he believed that Wilson's previous conduct had revealed him to be a hopeless Anglophile. In September, Helfferich also held the view that England aimed not simply at victory, but was determined "to finish off [Germany] completely."[55] Since he later reverted to this opinion, one must suppose that his optimism in late October about how ready the English were for peace merely rested on his faulty analysis of Grey's speech. It may also be that he still hoped that if the Entente refused the peace offer vehemently enough, the United States might permit unrestricted submarine warfare without entering the war on the side of the Entente.

Bethmann set off at once for Potsdam to gain William's consent for the peace move, and having obtained it, departed for Supreme Headquarters at Pless to secure that of Hindenburg and Ludendorff. Bethmann's peregrinations strikingly illustrate how influential the generals had already become. They had nothing against Bethmann's proposal, but refused to allow the issuance of the Polish proclamation to be delayed. They also asked that the peace offer be preceded by some compelling manifestation of German strength and determination, namely, the Auxiliary Service Law (*Hilfsdienstgesetz*, of which more will be said shortly). Bethmann managed, however, to persuade them that

[54] Wolfgang Steglich, *Bündnissicherung oder Verständigungsfrieden: Untersuchungen zu dem Friedensangebot der Mittelmächte vom 12. Dezember 1916* (Göttingen, 1958), 34-37. Helfferich acknowledged Burián's part in suggesting the peace move, although Jagow later accused Helfferich of taking all the credit himself; *Weltkrieg*, II, 357; Bernstorff, *Erinnerungen*, 117, 121-22.

[55] *Weltkrieg*, II, 351-55; "Bericht" 474, 2 Sept. 1916, "HB."

the law ought to follow rather than precede the peace move. After his return from Pless, Bethmann reluctantly decided that the Polish proclamation and the peace offer would have to be made simultaneously. The next step was to secure Austrian consent to this plan. Buriàn refused to consider this arrangement, demanding instead that the peace move follow the Polish proclamation only at a considerable interval. In the meantime, the Supreme Command decided that the Auxiliary Service Law ought to precede the peace move, and by 5 November, had forced Bethmann to accept their view.[56] This new development promised to delay the peace move indefinitely and ushered in a complicated series of negotiations among the Central Powers over war aims. Should the peace move lead to the negotiating tables, prior agreement on war aims was obviously of vital importance to the weaker of the Central Powers. Helfferich did not participate in these discussions, however, but was instead occupied in preparing the Auxiliary Service Law and seeing it through the Reichstag.

The Hindenburg Program and the Auxiliary Service Law

On 1 July 1916, the British attacked in strength along the Somme. This new campaign, coming as it did on top of the Verdun campaign, created another munitions crisis. The Prussian War Ministry, the agency in overall charge of munitions production, was caught somewhat by surprise. Steel contracts that had been allowed to expire in June had to be renewed helter-skelter in July. Because procurement had never been unified, industry found itself swamped with more orders than it could fill. Aside from its failure to unify procurement (which it intended to rectify), the War Ministry's unfortunate timing on the steel orders was not the evidence of incompetence that its numerous critics in government, industry, and the army alleged it to be. The ministry had bent every effort to increase gunpowder production as rapidly as possible, because powder was the article in shortest supply. All other munitions production was increased only as rapidly as increasing powder supplies permitted, for it

---

[56] Steglich, *Bündnissicherung*, 49-62.

was clearly wasteful to make more shell casings than there was powder to fill them, or more cannon than could be supplied with shells. The confusion in the steel ordering was merely the result of the ministry's commendable if ill-timed attempt to substitute a superior for an inferior grade of steel. Nevertheless, the War Ministry's enemies were able to exploit its momentary vulnerability to launch an attack against it which overturned its sensible policy of tying arms production to powder supplies and deprived it of a substantial measure of its control over war production.[57]

The steel-makers led the assault against the War Ministry. It succeeded because it coincided with the change in the Supreme Command which brought Hindenburg and Ludendorff to power. The steel-makers had a number of long-standing grievances against the War Ministry. They were exasperated by its red tape, they were alarmed by the manner in which it was encouraging worker self-assertiveness in the name of production and industrial peace, and they were irritated by its attempts to reduce costs by controlling their profits. The initial meetings between the industrialists and the War Ministry over what to do about the shell shortage, moreover, had come to nothing, although they did establish that industry wanted unified procurement, the release of skilled workers from the army, and a reduction of government commitments in other (and usually less profitable) areas. Finally, the Verein deutscher Eisenhüttenleute (Association of German Iron Founders) drew up a rather self-serving memorandum, dated 23 August, sharply criticizing the War Ministry and listing their demands. Helfferich, who in general sympathized with the industrialists, had been kept informed of these developments and had coached the steel-makers on how to deal with the War Ministry. At his request, he (along with many others) received a copy of the 23 August memorandum, which he discussed with Bethmann before the latter departed for Supreme Headquarters on 28 August. When Bethmann arrived, he found Hin-

[57] For an excellent account, see Feldman, *Army, Industry, and Labor*, Chs. 3-4, upon which I have drawn extensively in my own analysis of Helfferich's involvement with the Hindenburg Program and the Auxiliary Service Law. See also Ritter, *Staatskunst*, III, 417-33, which places the Hindenburg Program and the Auxiliary Service Law in a more general context.

denburg and Ludendorff "already oriented and determined to act."[58] Their informant was evidently Lieutenant Colonel Max Bauer, an artillery expert who had excellent connections in business circles. He was almost certainly the author of the so-called Hindenburg Program, which called for huge increases in arms production. Bauer's modest rank belied his influence. An old friend of Ludendorff's, he served the latter as an idea man.[59] His program was quite in keeping with the ideas of the industrialists and with Ludendorff's conceptions of total war.

Helfferich found this expressed intention "to act" gratifying. He lost no time in addressing his recommendations to Ludendorff, writing to him on 3 September.[60] He too recommended that skilled workers be released from the army and that purchasing be centralized, preferably under the leadership of "a man of the first rank," not named, from the steel industry. He concluded his appeal with words that revealed his hope of harnessing the energy and prestige of the Supreme Command to achieve ends which the civilians alone had been unable to secure: "I am greatly relieved that the Supreme Command has now taken this important matter in hand. The Supreme Command is the only authority that can influence the War Ministry in this matter with assurance of success." The equivocal reception which the generals gave Bethmann's submarine policy in the meeting of 31 August ought to have warned Helfferich from this summoning of the spirits from the vasty deeps, but it did not. The lesson was not fully assimilated.

Helfferich was soon disabused of the notion that the Supreme Command might be content with the measures he suggested. Hindenburg's letter of 13 September, which Bauer actually wrote, was principally concerned with raising production by

[58] *Weltkrieg*, II, 249-50. At the time Helfferich gave a somewhat different account, which is frequently in conflict with the facts; "Notizen," 23 Nov. 1916, "HB."

[59] Bauer claimed credit for the program in his memoirs, *Der grosse Krieg in Feld und Heimat: Erinnerungen und Betrachtungen* (Tübingen, 1922), 160, and recent authorities accept his claim; Ritter, *Staatskunst*, III, 420; Feldman, *Army, Industry, and Labor*, 150-51, 159. Feldman thinks it "very likely" that Bauer was also the author of the 23 August memorandum.

[60] *Weltkrieg*, II, 255.

utilizing manpower more efficiently.[61] The two most important proposals were to extend the limits of the draft downward from eighteen to sixteen and upward from forty-six to fifty-one, and to establish legal "compulsion to work" for women and others not subject to the draft. Other measures included reducing the number of skilled workers returned from the front to industry (the so-called *Reklamierte*), closing the universities with a few exceptions like the medical schools, retraining injured for war work, cross-training those in nonessential industries, and shutting down the latter. The Supreme Command's stated aim was not only to strengthen the army and raise production, but to bring home to the government and the Reichstag the meaning of total war. What the generals meant to do was "militarize" the home front.[62] "I am sure," the letter concluded, "that if the seriousness of the situation is made clear . . . our people will agree willingly [to these measures]. If they do not, then Germany is not worth the victory." Here too the Supreme Command's timing was probably faulty, for while measures such as it proposed might have been useful in 1914, most of the essential changes had already been made by 1916. Again, some of the measures, which were practicable in a democracy like England or the United States, were not practicable in Wilhelmine Germany. Too much of the population was alienated from the ruling groups and viewed any restrictions on its personal freedom with unconquerable suspicion. There were too few means of redress, and too many abuses had already been committed by the military authorities under the State of Siege Law (*Belagerungszustandsgesetz*). The fear was always present that a right once lost might never be regained.

The Supreme Command's program was not at all what Helfferich wanted. With his assistance Bethmann drafted a rebuttal.[63]

---

[61] Hindenburg to Bethmann, 13 Sept. 1916, in Erich Ludendorff (ed.), *Die Urkunden der Obersten Heeresleitung über ihre Tätigkeit 1916/18* (Berlin, 1920), 65-67. Bauer was evidently the author of most of this early correspondence from Hindenburg; Feldman, *Army, Industry, and Labor*, 172.

[62] Gaertringen, *Groener*, 341.

[63] Bethmann to Hindenburg, 30 Sept. 1916, in Ludendorff, *Urkunden*, 70-76; *Weltkrieg*, ii, 256-58; and for the contents of the Helfferich memorandum on which Bethmann based his reply, see Feldman, *Army, Industry, and Labor*, 174-76.

They accepted the extension of the draft in part, although they pointed out that it was unlikely to help much. "Compulsion to work" was rejected for two reasons. First, nearly all those who could work in war industries were already doing so, attracted by the high wages. Second, there were great moral and physiological objections to forcing women to work. As Helfferich quaintly put it on another occasion, women were "differently organized physically" than men.[64] Furthermore, there were large numbers of women unemployed. The problem was to find work for those who wanted it. The other proposals were also for the most part rejected. Because of the difficulties in relocating and retraining workers, Bethmann expressed doubts about closing down the nonessential industries still operating. Helfferich pointed out that the government already had a powerful weapon against such industries in its power to withhold raw materials. He also cautioned against closing the universities because of the harmful impression it would make abroad. The war would thus appear more than ever a struggle between militarism and democracy. (The impact of such an act on President Wilson, an ex-professor and university president, can be imagined.) Helfferich accordingly proposed limiting action to retraining the wounded and to stopping nonessential construction. Finally, he concluded with a warning which reveals how great the gap between his position and that of the Supreme Command's had already become: "An army suffers itself to be ordered about, but an economy does not." Although Bethmann toned down this warning in the letter he actually sent, Helfferich's admonition was one that the soldiers would have done well to heed.

Such an undramatic approach to the munitions shortage was characteristic of both Bethmann and Helfferich. The latter seldom favored sweeping measures such as the Supreme Command contemplated, but believed in perfecting institutions and procedures already in existence. During October, it appeared for a time that the Supreme Command might content itself with a new office to take charge of procurement and resources allocation while abandoning the extreme measures of manpower control previously sought. Such measures would require the sanction of

[64] *RTV*, Vol. 308, 29 Nov. 1916, 2160.

the Reichstag. Even if approval were given, Helfferich and Bethmann feared an acrimonious debate. Once the new procurement
office, named the War Office (Kriegsamt), was established under
the leadership of General Wilhelm Groener, previously head of
the military railways, developments in the direction of extreme
manpower measures were rapid, however.

On 17 October, Groener, Helfferich, and others discussed
methods by which job-changing could be restricted without
actually repealing the laws of 1867 which granted freedom of employment and domicile. It was agreed that administrative measures would suffice and were less likely to create difficulties with
the Reichstag. Hindenburg confirmed this arrangement less than
a week later in a rather strange letter to the Chancellor.[65] He also
agreed that women could be exempted from the measures finally
adopted. But he demanded that the maximum age for conscription be raised to sixty and indicated that he expected legislation
from the Reichstag, although he left its subject uncertain.
"Should the Reichstag fail to solve this problem, it will be clear
which factions turn a deaf ear to the needs of the state," he said,
adding rather ominously: "On the measures to be taken then I
need not now express myself." When Bethmann journeyed to
Headquarters on 26 October, Hindenburg asked for immediate
manpower legislation.[66] Although Bethmann persuaded him that
such legislation ought to wait, it was clear that the matter was at
best postponed. The time had arrived for working out the details
of the new law.

The discussion of the exact provisions of the new law began on
29 October in the Prussian Ministry.[67] Once again the soldiers
seized the initiative. Groener had ready a draft law with a fancy
title, the Patriotic Auxiliary Service Law (*Vaterländisches Hilfsdienstgesetz*). The draft was very simple, merely being a "skele-
ton law" which stated the obligation of every male not in military
service to serve in some auxiliary service occupation, defined
such occupations in very general terms, and made the War Min-

[65] Hindenburg to Bethmann, 23 Oct. 1916, Ludendorff, *Urkunden*, 78-81.
[66] Steglich, *Bündnissicherung*, 50-51.
[67] *Weltkrieg*, II, 261-64; Gaertringen, *Groener*, 343-45, 555; Feldman,
Army, Industry, and Labor, 198-203.

istry formally responsible for the execution of the new law. Groener, as head of the War Office (which in the meantime had been loosely tied to the War Ministry), was to create the administrative machinery and to write the operating codes through which the aims of the law were to be realized.[68] Helfferich, Groener reports, spoke only of "voluntary measures" and tried to obtain a more limited statement of the powers of the War Office. Few of the ministers favored bringing the law before the Reichstag, and probably least of all Helfferich, who was currently taking a drubbing in the debates about protective custody and censorship. Groener, however, assured of the backing of the Supreme Command, refused to concede much. He justified his proposals by reading the astonished ministers the "gigantic dimensions," as Helfferich put it, of the Hindenburg Program. This was the first time that either Helfferich, or Breitenbach, the Railway Minister, or Reinhold von Sydow, the Minister for Commerce and Industry, had had any inkling of the extent of the Hindenburg Program, although it directly concerned all three. Helfferich bowed to the inevitable and agreed to have his office work up a new draft for future discussions. But he was clearly exasperated by this new example of military highhandedness, and his working relationship with General Groener was off to a bad start.

The following day Ludendorff confirmed the stand his subordinate had taken. "I consider . . . it necessary that a *law* be passed . . . otherwise the extent and significance of the whole question will not be clear to the people." Ludendorff sent a similar message to Bethmann and announced that the law must precede the planned peace offer.[69] After apparently being dissuaded of this idea once again, Hindenburg said on 5 November that there had been a "misunderstanding"; the law really had to precede the peace offer.[70] Helfferich, who learned of Hindenburg's wish on the following day, was furious. It meant that the Reichs-

[68] The establishment of the War Office was not actually announced until 1 November, and Groener officially assumed his new duties only on 3 November; Feldman, *Army, Industry, and Labor,* 190-96.

[69] Ludendorff, *Urkunden,* 81-83.

[70] Steglich, *Bündnissicherung,* 60-62.

tag, adjourned only two days before, would have to be reconvened.[71] Nothing was more calculated to reveal the decisive shift in the balance of power between the Supreme Command and the government.

A month before, Helfferich's friend Arndt von Holtzendorff noted that he looked "rather run down" and commented sympathetically: "I am afraid that he will work himself prematurely *kaputt* in this post, the most thankless in the German Empire."[72] Holtzendorff might well have worried, for his friend was not destined to get much rest in the weeks that followed. Helfferich and Groener held a series of marathon conferences on 7 and 8 November with representatives of the political parties, employer associations, and trade-unions.[73] The talks with the party and union leaders revealed that if the Auxiliary Service Law were presented in the "incomplete" form in which Helfferich's subordinates had redrafted it, trouble could be expected in the Reichstag. Helfferich accordingly had a series of "Instructions (*Richtlinien*)" drawn up for carrying out the law which contained the demanded guarantees of workers' rights. When the matter was considered by the Prussian Ministry on 10 November, it developed that Helfferich was willing to concede the workers more than many of his colleagues, though not so much as Groener would have liked. Groener wanted the "Instructions" incorporated into the text of law itself, and that Helfferich refused to do. He believed that the law had to be kept simple if it were to document the solidarity of the German people. He also thought that if the parties were conceded too much in advance, they would only ask for more. Groener, on the other hand, held that unless the law reached the Reichstag in a form which assured it of speedy and unanimous passage, it was likely to document not the unity, but the divisions, of German society. He later recalled that Helfferich had ridden roughshod over his objec-

---

[71] In 1919, when he wrote his war memoirs, Helfferich was still unhappy about having had to reconvene the Reichstag; *Weltkrieg*, II, 265. See also *Vorwärts*, No. 322, 22 Nov. 1916, which sums up the entire fiasco with the proverb, "To govern is to foresee things."

[72] "Bericht" 504, 12 Oct. 1916, "HB."

[73] The following paragraph is based largely on Feldman, *Army, Industry, and Labor*, 203-14.

tions, saying he "did not know his way around yet," and that "horse trading" with the parties was unavoidable.[74]

In the meantime, the Supreme Command kept demanding haste and more haste, and on the day after the law went to the Bundesrat, 15 November, Hindenburg threatened to resign if action did not come soon. Helfferich, by now fed up with this "furious pushing," offered his own resignation. He did not intend, he told Bethmann, "to work under the whip of Supreme Headquarters." Bethmann made a quick trip to Headquarters and managed to clear up some of the difficulties, and Helfferich agreed to remain at his post.[75]

By 21 November, the Bundesrat had completed its deliberations on the bill. Two days later the Budget Committee of the Reichstag was convened to consider the measure.[76] The hearings went badly from the beginning for reasons which reflect little credit on any of the government representatives. As Groener had foreseen, the Socialists were indeed greatly annoyed at Helfferich for having left out of the bill so much of what they had earlier said was absolutely necessary. Groener, on his part, was so incautious as to speak in a way which hinted that Helfferich's parsimony while Treasury Secretary was partly responsible for the munitions crisis. Stresemann repeated the accusation in unmistakable terms, which particularly galled Helfferich. "I have never seen him so discouraged and upset as today," Holtzendorff reported after the first day's sessions.[77] Helfferich's efforts to rebut the charge of parsimony were disastrous. He chose as his mouthpiece the new War Minister, General Hermann von Stein, a man quite without Reichstag experience. Both his "lackadaisical, cheeky way of speaking" and the content of his speech infuriated the deputies; he failed to follow the text prearranged

---

[74] Gaertringen, *Groener*, 346.

[75] *Weltkrieg*, II, 265-66; Ludendorff, *Urkunden*, 85.

[76] For the details on the Bundesrat hearings and Budget Committee discussions, see Feldman, *Army, Industry, and Labor*, 215-35.

[77] "Notizen," 23 Nov. 1916, "HB." Stresemann's attack may be partly attributable to pique at having been left out of the preliminary conferences at Interior; Stresemann to Helfferich, 17 Nov. 1916, Stresemann "Nachlass," 6825/3063/129638-40.

with Helfferich.[78] The government never succeeded in closing ranks again. While Helfferich was arguing, often pointlessly, to save this or that provision of the government bill, Groener was letting it be known that compromises were possible. The end result was that the government bill was almost wholly rewritten. The "Instructions" were incorporated into the body of the law and several additions were made which went far beyond any compromise with the Left that Helfferich had ever contemplated. The most important addition was a clause (in Article Nine) which stated that a "reasonable (*angemessene*) improvement" in working conditions constituted adequate grounds for changing employment within essential industries. Helfferich correctly anticipated that this provision would encourage the very job-changing that the law was designed to prevent. The second important group of changes was to provide for a variety of workers' committees, to enlarge the proposed arbitration boards in all important auxiliary service industries except the state railways and agriculture, and to provide for a series of conciliation agencies. The third important change was to provide for a permanent Reichstag Committee of Fifteen to supervise the administration of the new law.

Although final agreement had not been reached on a number of important points, the hearings closed on 28 November and the general debates began the following day. The left-wing Socialists, who had separated from the Majority Socialists to form the Sozialdemokratische Arbeitsgemeinschaft (SAG), took the line that the law had no good features and was merely another capitalist attempt to suppress labor. Even the Majority Socialists viewed the law with suspicion. Eduard David said: "Helfferich now says we must work together in the spirit of trust. . . . We cannot give the Bundesrat the trust it demands after the experiences we have had."[79] In retrospect it cannot be said that the government poured much oil on the waters. Groener, for example, when commenting on the wish to write as many safeguards as possible

[78] Gaertringen *Groener*, 347; Lerchenfeld to Hertling, 24 Nov. 1916, GStA, "Briefwechsel."

[79] *RTV*, Vol. 308, 29 Nov. 1916, 2168. On the debates, see also Feldman, *Army, Industry, and Labor*, 235-49.

into the law, was so ill-advised as to say that such measures were useless "unless we carry out the law with common sense." The SAG member Emmanuel Wurm properly judged that this utterance expressed a "fatherly benevolent absolutism, ill-suited to our times." If Groener was patronizing, Helfferich was self-righteous. In reply to a remark made by Ewald Vogtherr of the SAG that effect of the law abroad would not be to shorten, but to prolong, the war, Helfferich said: "Herr Vogtherr has drawn a caricature . . . of this law which is one of the most unbelievable things I have ever heard. . . . Vogtherr does not want a German victory, he wants the very opposite." Vogtherr replied that victory or defeat were not the only alternatives, there was a third: a peace of understanding.[80]

The second reading debates on the next day lasted more than eleven hours. Gustav Bauer began with a statement of the Majority Socialist stand on the bill. Without formally committing his party to it, he defended it against the extreme Left, saying it contained a series of protective measures for the rights of the workers which were "real and valuable." He demanded only the assurance, readily given, that the War Office would help to enforce wage contracts already concluded.[81] In general, the other parties supported the bill as reported out of committee against proposals for extensive amendment from the Conservatives and extreme Left. Helfferich continued to manage the government's case very badly, fighting for tricks that were already lost and creating considerable animosity in the process.

Helfferich did this partly out of desire to "hold the protocol open," since the Bundesrat had not yet deliberated on the bill in its amended form, but much of what he said would have been better left unsaid.[82] In connection with Article Thirteen, which covered the right to form workers' committees, he interrupted

[80] *Ibid.*, 2181-83 (Groener); 2224-25 (Wurm); 2194 (Helfferich and Vogtherr).

[81] *Ibid.*, 30 Nov. 1916, 2198-99.

[82] *Weltkrieg*, II, 268. In a cautious defense of Helfferich written for the *Deutsche Kurier*, Stresemann said Helfferich "talked too much." The general theme of the article was that Helfferich's abilities made it necessary to overlook the shortcomings of his parliamentary personality; Stresemann, "Helfferich."

the debate several times to ask if a certain sentence in the article meant that the workers of the state railways could form such committees. Though informed on each occasion that it did not, he persisted in raising the point. He finally drew the rebuke from the exasperated Stresemann that his point was of a "rather theoretical nature."[83] Helfferich also asked for the striking from Article Nine of the clause stating that a "reasonable improvement" in working conditions constituted grounds for changing employment. Wages and worker interests had been "shoved" too much into the foreground, to the neglect of the general interest. Were it necessary to retain the offending phrase, he wanted a statement of the overall purpose of the law along with it. Later continuing in the same vein, he stated that the workers' committees and arbitration boards constituted "wholly extraordinary progress" for the working classes and that it would "not be easy" for the Bundesrat to accept them. They had also raised "serious doubts" among the munitions producers, doubts which had to be considered if the purpose of the law were not to be thwarted. "Gentlemen, for these reasons I beg you not to overload the ship; add no stones that are not absolutely necessary." Finally, he directed a number of constitutional criticisms at the Committee of Fifteen. He agreed with the Conservative deputy Count Westarp that the committee infringed upon the rights of the Bundesrat to the extent that it sanctioned the measures of the War Office. Technically he was correct, but his viewpoint was one for which no one in the Reichstag except the Conservatives was likely to have any sympathy. Helfferich said he would have preferred Westarp's solution, which was that the Bundesrat pass the necessary ordinances subject to later approval by the Reichstag.[84]

Helfferich's sallies drew outraged cries of indignation from all sides of the House, but particularly from the Left. Wilhelm Dittmann (SAG) said that he had supposed that agreement had been reached with the government during the second reading in committee, yet now Helfferich was reopening all these questions

[83] *RTV*, Vol. 308, 30 Nov. 1916, 2233, 2236-37, 2240 (Helfferich); 2236-37 (Stresemann). The amendment, which was meant to protect the coalition and assembly rights of workers subject to the Auxiliary Service Law, was ultimately accepted.
[84] *Ibid.*, 2246-47, 2260, 2271.

again, and in this "rude manner." He added: "That allows of some rather peculiar conclusions about the promised 'new orientation' after the war." Even Eugen Schiffer, a National Liberal whom the government could usually count upon for support, was "completely out of temper" with Helfferich over the Committee of Fifteen.[85]

Whatever may be said in criticism of Helfferich's miserable parliamentary tactics, however, the final discussions of the bill in the Prussian Ministry on 1 December largely justified his stubborn stand against the demands of the Left. Agreeing in general with Helfferich's disgruntled verdict—"one can almost say that the Social Democrats, Poles, Alsatians, and union secretaries have made the bill"—most of the ministers thought that the bill gave labor altogether too much. But they reluctantly conceded that it had to be accepted, especially after Bethmann told them that yet another telegram had come from Supreme Headquarters calling for rapid passage.[86]

The one serious problem still facing Helfferich appeared to be a National Liberal amendment to provide the state railways with the sort of workers' committees and conciliation boards foreseen in the Auxiliary Service bill. When Helfferich met with the National Liberals after the cabinet meeting, however, he was able to persuade them to withdraw their amendment in return for some minor improvements in the existing railway workers' committees. Less easily satisfied, the Socialists determined to bring in the amendment themselves, and so informed Helfferich that evening. Whether because of fatigue, or bad judgment, or deviousness, or yet some other reason, he failed to make clear to them that he meant to block the amendment at any cost. He had thus created a misunderstanding that in the third reading debates on the following day was to result in a worse row with the Socialists than any he had had so far.

Carl Legien began the debates by announcing that his party, the Majority Socialists, had decided to support the bill but with

[85] *Ibid.*, 2271-73 (Dittmann); 2273 (Schiffer); "Bericht" 533, 2 Dec. 1916, "HB."

[86] On the various ministry and party negotiations of 1 December, see Feldman, *Army, Industry, and Labor,* 241-45.

misgivings. It was their hope, he said, "that the spirit that is manifested in [Helfferich's] speeches, that spirit which seeks to block even the smallest improvement in the law, will not prevail in the execution of the law." Since Legien was no radical, but, on the contrary, a moderate trade-union leader of great influence, his utterance was both a threat and a warning. Without the cooperation of the trade-unions, the Auxiliary Service Law could hardly succeed. This was no secret to Helfferich, who in an attempt at conciliation said that he was sorry that Legien considered him "something . . . of an 'evil genius,'" but claimed that his stand was necessary because the Bundesrat at the time had had no chance to consider the matters under discussion.[87]

Hugo Haase, leader of the SAG, spoke next. After first condemning the Auxiliary Service Law as an "exceptional law against the workers," he turned to the deportation of Belgian workers to Germany.[88] The deportations had begun in November at the behest of the Supreme Command, who saw in Belgian manpower a means of abetting Germany's dwindling manpower resources. The action produced a minimal number of workers and raised a storm of protest abroad, and it was soon to be stopped for these reasons. Though the civilians had not taken the initiative in the measures, Helfferich had apparently not protested the original decision—perhaps he knew it was pointless— and felt obliged to defend the action.[89] His zeal led him to make some rather foolish remarks. He claimed that the deportations were being conducted according to the rules of international law, which was certainly not true. He further asserted sanctimoniously that the deportations were intended to create safe conditions behind the front lines—"there is no greater enemy of order than idleness"—and that the Germans were actually doing the Belgians a favor by preventing their industrial skills from rusting. As if these outrageous statements were not enough, Helfferich all but accused Dittmann, who had come to his colleague Haase's defense, of high treason: "When Dittmann brings up

---

[87] *RTV*, Vol. 308, 2 Dec. 1916, 2286-88 (Legien); 2288-89 (Helfferich).
[88] *Ibid.*, 2290-94.
[89] Ludendorff, *Urkunden*, 124-28. Helfferich favored voluntary recruitment. For an account of this sorry episode, see Ritter, *Staatskunst*, III, 433-50.

these matters on the tribune of the Reichstag, then he too is serving our enemy, whether he means to or not."[90]

Helfferich's next foray into the debates was against the Socialist amendment on the railway workers' committees. In excessively plain language, he threatened that the amendment "would place the purpose of the law in jeopardy. Therefore I am obliged to state that if the amendment . . . is accepted, the law is in fact endangered." Legien's retort was: "It is striking that [Helfferich] . . . should make a declaration that acceptance of our amendment would render the law inacceptable. . . . Herr Staatssekretär . . . you have done the law a very bad service." The amendment was defeated, 139 to 138, but it was a hollow victory for Helfferich. The Socialists drowned him in a flood of criticism. Friedrich Ebert, leader of the Majority Socialists, was vastly irritated with Helfferich for not making his position clear the evening before. He summed up Helfferich's interference in the debates with the rebuke: "The Secretary of the Interior has repeatedly made statements . . . which have not made our stand [in favor of] this law any easier." To make the day complete, Helfferich became involved in an exchange with Georg Ledebour of the SAG, who was more than his match at repartee. Commenting on Helfferich's denial that he had ever stated that including the railway workers' amendment would make the law "unacceptable," Ledebour said that this was the effect of his declaration whether so intended or not. "But if . . . Helfferich cannot judge the import of his own words, he only shows that he is unsuited to his office." Though Ledebour was called sharply to order, at that moment much of the House doubtless agreed with his unflattering conclusion.[91]

The Auxiliary Service Law debates left Helfferich and the Reichstag completely disillusioned with one another. Helfferich was sure that the Socialists were prejudiced against him because he was a former banker. He was genuinely astonished at his treatment and was apparently unable to see why his efforts to get along with the Left, which he recognized was politically essen-

[90] *RTV*, Vol. 308, 2 Dec. 1916, 2294-95.
[91] *Ibid.*, 2312-14 (Helfferich); 2314 (Legien); 2322 (Ebert); 2323 (Ledebour).

tial, had failed.[92] To an outsider, however, the remarks he made in the debates seem reason enough for Alfred Henke of the SAG to call him the "most rabid representative of capitalist interests."[93] Helfferich later complained that his sharp stand against the railway committee amendment was necessary to line up the Center Party against the measure. At the time, he asserted that had he not taken such a strong stand, he would surely have been accused of missing the chance to avoid "this evil."[94] He was probably right about that, though it is possible that if he had been more skillful, the amendment would never have come to the floor at all. Lieutenant Colonel Bauer thought that Helfferich was the only government representative who had shown any firmness, and accused Groener of being too easy-going. Helfferich himself was most unhappy about Groener's performance, and their relations worsened greatly thereafter.[95] There is good evidence that he was partly responsible for Groener's being eased out of his job the following summer.[96]

Helfferich claimed both at the time and later that he would have resigned if the railway worker amendment had been accepted. He apparently did not altogether give up the idea even after the conclusion of the debates, because he felt it impossible to establish satisfactory working relations with the Supreme Command. He was "sick of the whole business," he told Lerchenfeld. If the Supreme Command had not been so precipitate, he probably could have worked out many of the difficulties with the party leaders in advance, and a "wholly different, serviceable law would have been passed." Lerchenfeld recalled to Helfferich the

[92] *Weltkrieg*, II, 271-72.

[93] *RTV*, Vol. 308, 30 Nov. 1916, 2227-29.

[94] "Bericht" 534, 3 Dec. 1916, "HB."

[95] Bauer, *Der grosse Krieg*, 123. In addition to disliking one another, Groener and Helfferich differed fundamentally in their approaches to Germany's wartime and anticipated postwar economic problems. Groener believed in far more extensive controls than Helfferich. He also attempted to draw within his sphere matters traditionally in the hands of the Interior Office, which Helfferich naturally resented; Feldman, *Army, Industry, and Labor*, 295, 297-300, 320.

[96] The most satisfactory account of the intrigue which brought down Groener in the summer of 1917 is *ibid.*, 385-404. But see also Dorothea Groener-Geyer, *General Groener: Soldat und Staatsmann* (Frankfurt a. M., 1955), 63.

difficulties which Bismarck had had with Moltke in the War of 1870, a parallel which probably flattered Helfferich, and encouraged him to remain in office.[97]

A more important inducement for Helfferich to remain was a warm letter of thanks from the Kaiser "in grateful recognition of his brilliant advocacy in the great achievement of the Patriotic Auxiliary Service Law."[98] Did the law deserve such a splendid designation? Helfferich, who anticipated the law's most serious shortcomings, didn't think so then or later, and if the achievements of the law be measured against what its original proponents expected of it, it undoubtedly was a failure.[99] From the opposite viewpoint, that of labor, the law was something of a "bill of rights." It secured for the working man many advantages which he had fought for years to obtain.[100]

"The Rubicon is Crossed"

While Helfferich was busy with the Auxiliary Service Law, negotiations among the Central Powers over the proposed peace offer continued. It proved impossible by early December to reach agreement on a war-aims program, but it was nevertheless decided to issue the call for peace. Buriàn, who had held back earlier, now wished to anticipate a possible peace move on the part of President Wilson.[101] That may also have been a factor in Bethmann's thinking, but other considerations were probably uppermost in his mind.[102] With the end of Rumania now only a matter of time and the Auxiliary Service Law safely through the Reichstag, the Supreme Command's preconditions for the peace move had been met. But the very improvement in the military situation which led the generals to acquiesce in the peace offer

[97] Lerchenfeld to Hertling, 4 Dec. 1916, GStA, "Briefwechsel."

[98] Stresemann to Ballin, 7 Dec. 1916, Stresemann "Nachlass," 6866/3063/-129735-40.

[99] Feldman, *Army, Industry, and Labor,* Ch. 6, analyzes the reasons why in detail.

[100] Ernst Heymann, *Die Rechtsformen der militärischen Kriegswirtschaft als Grundlage des neuen deutschen Industrierechts* (Marburg, 1921), 181-224.

[101] Steglich, *Bündnissicherung,* 124-25.

[102] *Weltkrieg,* II, 359-62, 365. The following paragraph is based largely on Ritter, *Staatskunst,* III, 346-49, and Birnbaum, *Peace Moves,* 234-76.

also made them less interested in it, and more interested in unlimited submarine warfare. The Navy in the meantime had begun a very successful submarine campaign using "cruiser" warfare methods and in December began asking for permission to wage "intensified" submarine warfare. "Intensified" submarine warfare, or unlimited warfare against armed merchantmen only, was little more than a way station for unrestricted submarine warfare and could be expected on the basis of past experience to have the same disruptive effect on relations with the United States. Bethmann therefore had to act on the peace offer before the Navy secured the wholehearted support of the Supreme Command for either an "intensified" or an unrestricted campaign. By 8 December, Hindenburg was already asking that an unrestricted campaign begin at the end of January, but he was persuaded to delay the decision until the results of the peace offer became known. As a compromise it was agreed that if the peace offer was refused, the Navy might begin "intensified" submarine warfare.

Although convinced of the necessity of his peace move, Bethmann was no longer as optimistic about its prospects as when Helfferich had originally suggested it late in October. Since then, Lloyd George, the proponent of the "knockout blow," had become Prime Minister, and similar changes were in the offing elsewhere. What Helfferich's views on the peace move were in these early weeks of December must, unfortunately, remain largely a matter of speculation. He did remark to Lerchenfeld on the 4th that the démarche should be made soon because "too much had already been leaked out" about the plan. Although he sincerely wanted peace, he apparently continued to place his greatest hopes in negotiations for a separate peace with one of the belligerents, most likely Russia.[103] It may be inferred, therefore, that he considered the démarche unlikely to lead to a general peace conference and thought it important primarily as a measure to convince world opinion that the German government genuinely

[103] *Ibid.*, 257. It is not clear from Birnbaum whether Helfferich saw separate negotiations as a means to divide and rule and feared the results of a general conference as Zimmermann did, or whether he simply considered it unlikely that the English were yet ready to agree to general negotiations, or perhaps both.

wanted peace. If the measure succeeded, so much the better, and if it did not, the onus for prolonging the war would then be on the Allied governments.

On 12 December 1916, Bethmann announced the peace offer to the German people in a Reichstag address, and neutral diplomats in Berlin received aggressively worded notes expounding the willingness of the Central Powers for peace. Within a week the unfavorable response of the Entente was known in Berlin. Speaking on 19 December, Lloyd George put his finger on the essential weakness of the proposal, its failure to make any mention of peace terms. Still, none of the Entente responses was as yet official, and even Lloyd George left room in his speech for a reconsideration of the Central Powers' offer should peace terms be named.[104] While the Germans were deciding on the next step, President Wilson made his long-awaited peace overture. Contrary to earlier German hopes, however, Wilson asked the belligerents for "an avowal of the terms upon which the war might be concluded." Apparently wishing to keep Wilson out of any possible negotiations, Zimmermann, Jagow's successor as Foreign Secretary, precipitously rejected Wilson's démarche on 26 December, even before the responses of the Entente Powers were known. Though Wilson was not offended by this rebuff, as might have been expected, Zimmermann's rash act was hardly what one would expect from a man who apparently still hoped to wage unrestricted submarine warfare while remaining at peace with the United States.[105] The act may stand as the first example of the essential frivolity with which Zimmermann handled the United States.

Helfferich was inclined to view the matter more seriously. Discussing Wilson's overture with Admiral von Müller on the day of Zimmermann's reply, of which he was evidently unaware, Helfferich remarked that he was going to try to get Bethmann to call a major conference to work out peace terms. Since he hoped "if possible for the collaboration of the Kaiser," he probably expected to win the Kaiser for more moderate terms than the Supreme Command was otherwise likely to accept. He emphasized

---

[104] *Ibid.*, 249.
[105] *Ibid.*, 268-70, 300-301; see also Ritter, *Staatskunst*, III, 364-65, 655n25; Link, *Wilson*, V, 250.

the need to be "extremely careful" in dealings with the United States, not only to avoid war in the immediate future but also because Germany "could not endure its hostility" after the war. In contrast to Zimmermann, he had abandoned the illusion that unrestricted submarine warfare and peace with the United States might be compatible. He now hoped only that the United States would not regard an "intensified" submarine campaign as grounds for war.[106] Helfferich's desire to present Wilson with peace terms was quite in keeping with his aim of extracting the maximum advantage from the two peace moves. The United States was far more likely to remain neutral if Wilson were convinced that the Central Powers had taken every possible step to reach peace, only to be rebuffed by a militant and vengeful Entente. Given the increasing likelihood that the civilians would not be able to stave off unrestricted submarine warfare, the policy which Helfferich outlined probably represented the last chance to avert disaster but only if, as Helfferich hoped, it actually led to peace negotiations.

Helfferich's ideas were overtaken by the events. As a result of the foregoing developments, the Supreme Command concluded that there was no longer any reason to delay unrestricted submarine warfare. A new memorandum from Admiral von Holtzendorff's office (dated 22 December 1916) calling for such a campaign after 1 February 1917 reinforced the generals' conclusions. A heated exchange of telegrams between Berlin and Pless convinced Bethmann that a conference was advisable, and on 28 December he set off for Pless, accompanied by Zimmermann and Helfferich. Of their reception early on the 29th, Helfferich said " 'ice-cold' is really too mild" a characterization.[107] Neither Hindenburg or Ludendorff deigned to meet the Chancellor at the

[106] Görlitz, *Müller*, 244, entry of 26 Dec. 1916. Zimmermann had said earlier that he resented Helfferich's meddling in foreign affairs, and Helfferich was evidently not as well informed as he had been earlier; "Bericht" 519, 5 Nov. 1916, "HB." For Helfferich's views on "intensified" submarine war, see Stresemann to Bassermann, 28 Dec. 1916, Stresemann "Nachlass," 6834/3061/126049-52, reporting a conversation with Helfferich on the 27th.

[107] *Weltkrieg*, II, 397-98; Bernhard Schwertfeger (ed.), *Kaiser und Kabinettschef: nach eigenen Aufzeichnungen und dem Briefwechsel des Wirklichen Geheimen Rats Rudolf von Valentini* (Oldenburg, 1931), 141-43, 241-45.

station but sent Baron Kurt von Lersner, the Foreign Office representative at headquarters, with the astonishing message that Helfferich could not participate in the discussions. The ground given was that Helfferich, as Secretary of the Interior, was not directly concerned with foreign affairs. This was a surprising development, since Helfferich had visited headquarters not two weeks before and had been cordially received. First Zimmermann, then Bethmann, explained to Hindenburg that Helfferich was the Chancellor's official representative and thus had every right to participate in the conference. Hindenburg candidly admitted that this had not occurred to him and confessed to Bethmann what was really behind his intransigence. Fancied intrigues against Ludendorff and himself were mainly what he was upset about, though he also asserted that "he and Ludendorff had lost all confidence in Helfferich." Bethmann was able to persuade Hindenburg without much difficulty that the generals had been victims of scandalmongering, but the pretensions and assumptions of the Supreme Command nevertheless stood revealed. Bethmann stated that he considered his treatment a serious affront. Helfferich, too, was "very offended" and was taking part in the conference only at Bethmann's explicit request. The Chancellor recommended that Hindenburg apologize. Helfferich, Zimmermann, and Ludendorff were then called in, and Hindenburg "expressed his regrets to [Helfferich] in a very chivalrous way and asked his pardon." This cleared the air somewhat and agreement was soon reached on the submarine question.

The civilians were able to convince the generals that the time for unlimited submarine warfare had not yet come. Bethmann did agree to start diplomatic preparations for the step but still refused to announce the "intensified" submarine warfare which the Navy had proposed as an interim measure. Bethmann wished to delay a decision at least until he knew how the Entente had reacted to Wilson's peace move. Apparently the conference left Ludendorff with the conviction that for the sake of good relations with Bethmann it would be better to let the Navy bear the burden of the campaign for unrestricted submarine warfare. Bethmann and Helfferich, on the other hand, resignedly concluded that they could not delay an unrestricted campaign much longer.

Since the Supreme Command was unreceptive to arguments emphasizing the danger of drawing the United States into the war, reasons acceptable to the generals for delay were about gone. Lersner later said that after the conference Bethmann and Helfferich told him that they "would have to give in" when the generals asked for an all-out campaign. Actually, Bethmann and Helfferich had decided this, inwardly at least, much earlier and not as a result of the conference.[108] Their statement to Lersner was significant because it shows they realized that their efforts at delay had failed and that the measure would come soon.

Their apprehensions were quickly realized. In early January 1917 Admiral von Holtzendorff decided to force the issue. On 5 January he sent Bethmann and Helfferich copies of the 22 December 1916 memorandum which he had earlier sent the Supreme Command.[109] Shortly thereafter, he told Hindenburg that he was coming to Pless to try to persuade the Kaiser. When he arrived, he learned from Admiral von Müller, earlier a foe of unrestricted submarine warfare, that he could now count on Müller's support. Müller had come around to the opinion of his colleague because the Entente's response to the Central Powers' peace offer was so discouraging and because he hoped that the measure might offer Germany a way out of its desperate situation. The military leaders were at last united behind an all-out submarine campaign. When Bethmann telephoned Holtzendorff at Pless on the 8th and discovered the turn events were taking, he determined to go to Pless to fight for his policy. Upon learning of Bethmann's intention, the military chiefs hurriedly agreed that unrestricted submarine warfare had to begin on 1 February, even at the cost of Bethmann's resignation. Holtzendorff for his part had little difficulty in bringing the Kaiser around to his new views. Bethmann meanwhile, not knowing how far things had gone, discussed with Helfferich and Zimmermann the line he should take. They agreed that the decision ought to wait until the

---

[108] Birnbaum, *Peace Moves*, 285-86, however, holds that the decision was the result of the conference. See also Ritter's assessment of the remarks to Lersner; *Staatskunst*, III, 656n35.

[109] The following paragraphs are based on Ritter, *Staatskunst*, III, 376-79; Birnbaum, *Peace Moves*, 304-27; *Weltkrieg*, II, 403-408.

Entente replied officially to Wilson's peace démarche. Both Helfferich and Zimmermann remained in Berlin.

Helfferich immediately regretted that he had not "insisted with the greatest emphasis" on accompanying Bethmann, and he spent most of the night composing a rebuttal to Holtzendorff's memorandum. This he dispatched to Bethmann at 4 o'clock on the morning of 9 January. The greater part of the memorandum was devoted to an annihilating analysis of the impact on English war potential of the shipping losses which the Navy claimed it could impose. Helfferich also reconsidered yet again the impact of American entry into the war. Finally, he counseled patience. The official Entente reply to Wilson's proposal was still unknown. If Wilson encountered a sharp enough refusal, it might still be possible to wage unrestricted submarine warfare without drawing the United States into war. Since English grain stocks would continue to decline until 1 March, there was no need for excessive haste. Sound arguments, but Bethmann did not use them. Even if Helfferich had gone to Pless himself it is unlikely that he could have staved off the decision, although he later professed to believe otherwise.[110] The Supreme Command's insane emphasis on haste prevented either exploring or exploiting the political situation created by the peace moves, although it is highly doubtful that Helfferich's overly sanguine hope of American neutrality *and* "intensified" submarine warfare could have been realized under any circumstances.

Bethmann returned to Berlin early on 10 January. He sent Arnold Wahnschaffe, Undersecretary in the Reich Chancellery, to report on the outcome of the conference. Wahnschaffe told Helfferich simply, "the Rubicon is crossed." "I was most profoundly shaken by this news," Helfferich reports. Indeed he might have been, though it can hardly have come as a surprise. The next decision was a personal one, whether or not to resign. Bethmann himself decided to remain because he feared the effects which his departure would have on Austria and the Socialists. This decision was surely a blunder and a disservice to

[110] *Ibid.*, 406-408. See also Helfferich's long account of the events of late 1916 and early 1917 in Ernst Jäckh, *Der goldene Pflug: Lebensernte eines Weltbürgers* (Stuttgart, 1954), 420-21.

himself, his office, and Germany. Furthermore, it strengthened his personal position nowhere and in time could hardly fail to discredit him with all. Erich Eyck has called the decision "the worst mistake of his political career." "The new policy . . . should have been made by a new man," Eyck concluded.[111] The trouble was, every effort was being made to give the impression that no change of policy had occurred.

Helfferich made the same mistake as Bethmann, with the same results. "It was the hardest decision of my life," he lamented. The passages in his war memoirs in which he explains the sacrifice of his convictions (*sacrificium intellectus*) make painful reading.[112] He asserted that he did not desire to weaken the psychological effects of the unrestricted submarine campaign, that he was aware that he was basing his stand solely on his own opinion about a matter outside his area of competence, and that he hesitated to insist on his opinion when none of Bethmann's other advisers shared it. These reasons carry no conviction. Helfferich recognized that if he remained, he would have "to accept the decision, and stand and fight on the basis of it." Was this likely to strengthen unrestricted submarine warfare as a psychological measure? He had previously marshaled a host of reasons why unrestricted submarine warfare would be disastrous. If he now changed his position he was hardly likely to alter anyone's convictions about unrestricted submarine warfare, but he would condemn himself as an intellectual mountebank. The fall debates had already made him very unpopular in the Reichstag. He could thus expect that in many circles the worst possible motives would be attached to his change of front. Next, his reluctance to insist upon his own opinion in an area outside his competence must be

---

[111] Erich Eyck, *Geschichte der Weimarer Republik* (2 vols., Erlenbach-Zürich and Stuttgart, 1956-1957), I, 22-23. See, however, Ritter, *Staatskunst*, III, 382-84.

[112] *Weltkrieg*, II, 409-13. In his more candid moments Helfferich was later willing to admit that he had erred, and the expression *sacrificium intellectus* is his own; Jäckh, *Pflug*, 387; Ernst Troeltsch, *Spektator-Briefe: Aufsätze über die deutsche Revolution und die Weltpolitik 1918/22* (Tübingen, 1924), 3. Walther Rathenau, however, rather cynically judged Helfferich's confession of the *sacrificium intellectus* to be a means of evading responsibility for a policy that by the fall of 1917 had manifestly failed; *Politische Briefe* (Dresden, 1929), 161, letter, 16 Oct. 1917, to Captain Blankenburg.

considered. Helfferich had never attempted to refute the Navy's estimates of the probable tonnage that an unrestricted campaign would send to the bottom. His case rested upon his estimate of the effects of the campaign on the English economy and on the effects of American entry into the war. He had a better right to make such a judgment than anyone else in the government. He had every reason to resign when his judgment was not accepted, especially in a matter of such life or death importance. His estimate of the consequences of unrestricted submarine warfare proved in fact all too accurate. It was even more true of Helfferich than of Bethmann that the "new policy should have been made by a new man."

Why did a man as intelligent as Helfferich make such an egregious blunder? Though he loved power and responsibility and being at the center of things, he was a man of sufficient principle not to remain in office for purely selfish reasons. One must probably attribute this error to his essentially bureaucratic conception of his office. Rather than looking upon himself as a primarily political figure, he considered himself an expert whose loyalties were to the men who appointed him—Bethmann and, ultimately, the Kaiser. Thus in none of the three cases in the fall of 1916 where he threatened to resign did he carry out his threat. He considered it his obligation to serve his superiors so long as they found his services useful, even if they overrode him on specific questions such as submarine policy and the Auxiliary Service Law. His duty, he said, was to suppress his particular objections "the way a general does . . . when in the drawing up of an operations plan he has failed to secure acceptance of his ideas."[113] Even in the case of the dispute in the Reichstag over the workers' committees, he opposed the measure so stubbornly in part because his colleague Breitenbach, the minister directly responsible for the Prussian railways, was so fiercely hostile to the measure.

But Helfferich also opposed the Reichstag because he considered that it was attempting to usurp policy-making prerogatives that were rightfully the bureaucracy's. The tone of his Reichstag utterances, by turns patronizing, hostile, and aggrieved, revealed what it would have been more politic to conceal, namely, that he

[113] *Weltkrieg*, II, 413.

thought the people's representatives neither competent to know the best interests of the nation nor able to act rationally to secure them. Accurate or not, Helfferich's conceptions offered no adequate basis on which to build a domestic policy, given the democratizing tendencies of total war. The political weakness of Bethmann and Helfferich lay precisely in the fact that as monarchical bureaucrats they now opposed generals who by their victories had created for themselves a genuine national constituency.

VI. NEUORIENTIERUNG

Helfferich was not one merely to accept the new submarine policy in silence. Even before the new policy was announced, his utterances provided the necessary clues to the initiated. The day following the decision, 10 January, he discussed Germany's economic situation with Count Lerchenfeld. Helfferich painted a bright picture for the Count which contrasted markedly with the somber prospects he had presented to Stresemann not two weeks earlier. He also asserted that England had only three months' grain supply left. He deduced that if the submarine war continued to be as successful as it was then, "serious difficulties were bound to arise in all of the Entente nations."[1] A short time later, Helfferich encountered Max Warburg, a Hamburg banker, at a Holtzendorff Abend, and the discussion turned to unrestricted submarine warfare. Warburg tried to convince Helfferich of the "prodigious risk" of the measure, but his arguments fell on deaf ears: "As Helfferich's rejoinders and, even more clearly, his expression showed, he had altered his views, and I had to conclude that it was only a question of a few days before unrestricted submarine warfare was declared."[2]

Elsewhere, explanations of a more formal order had begun. On 15 January, Bethmann briefed the Prussian Ministry on the new submarine policy, and on the two days following, the Bundesrat. Helfferich supported Bethmann's general exposition with economic arguments. He first summarized the poor economic situation of the Entente and then discussed the consequences of unrestricted submarine warfare for Germany. The loss of American food for northern France and Belgium was certain, whether the United States entered the war or not. If the United States did enter the war, Germany's postwar situation would be bad even

[1] Lerchenfeld to Hertling, 10 Jan. 1917, GStA, "Briefwechsel"; Stresemann to Ernst Bassermann, 28 Dec. 1916, Stresemann "Nachlass," 6834/3061/126049-52.

[2] Max Warburg, *Aus meinen Aufzeichnungen* (n. p., 1952), 53.

197

if it won the war. It was hardly a cheerful prognosis. Still, Helfferich said that he thought the grounds for an unrestricted campaign "decisive," and he thus supported the Chancellor's statements "without qualifications." Some doubts were raised about whether sufficient submarines were available for action but Bethmann and Helfferich encountered no serious criticism. When the Bundesrat met again on 26 January to discuss the question, even this slight overt opposition had disappeared. This attitude reflected resignation rather than conviction on the part of the Bundesrat. The day the campaign began, 1 February, Hertling and Baron Karl von Weizsäcker, the Minister-President of Württemberg, privately made "very serious representations" to Bethmann about the new measure. They had, they said, only avoided taking a sharp stand against unrestricted submarine warfare in the Bundesrat because they had not wished to weaken Bethmann's personal position.[3]

The Budget Committee of the Reichstag took an equally equivocal position when presented with the new policy on 31 January and 1 February. "There was no storm," Lerchenfeld noted. Most of the deputies simply assumed a stance of watchful waiting, leaving the responsibility for the new policy to the government.[4] Helfferich's exposition of the new policy, complete with elaborate placards displaying statistics, diagrams, and the like, would have done credit to an advertising man. His rhetoric was equally flamboyant: "By fall the Island Kingdom will sprawl like a fish in the reeds and beg for peace." His use of the same kind of economic arguments that he had earlier used against unrestricted submarine warfare led one committee member to note ironically in his diary: "The statesman must yield to the advocate."[5] Hoch reminded Helfferich of his earlier utterances, but otherwise the astonishment felt at his shift in position was hardly expressed. It existed nevertheless. Erzberger commented with contempt to

[3] Ernst Deuerlein, *Der Bundesratsausschuss für die auswärtigen Angelegenheiten* (Regensburg, 1955), 222, 294.

[4] *Weltkrieg*, III, 31-33. Lerchenfeld commented: "As Your Excellency knows, it is impossible to follow [Helfferich] with pencil. . . . I therefore confine myself to announcing that [he] came to the conclusion: now or never"; Lerchenfeld to Hertling, "Bericht" 102, 1 Feb. 1917, GStA, "PA."

[5] Hans P. Hanssen, *Diary of a Dying Empire* (Bloomington, 1955), 164-70.

Bethmann about Helfferich's "knack with numbers," and Count Westarp, one of the most rabid of the pro-submarine men, noted the "lack of trust" in Helfferich's proof. He was throwing the weight of his reputation as an economist onto the scales in vain.[6] It was not long before parliamentary wits were circulating an atrocious and wholly untranslatable pun at Helfferich's expense. Based on Luther's apocryphal *"hier stehe ich"* ("here I stand"), the pun went: *"Hier statistike ich, ich kann auch anders; Gott Helf er sich! Amen!"*[7] Helfferich continued to defend the new policy with great vigor, not only in the Budget Committee, but outside it.[8] As sinkings rose rapidly in the spring of 1917 to reach a zenith of nearly a million tons in April, his words may have carried more conviction than they had in January. The day of reckoning was only postponed. If the Navy did not make good on its boast to reduce England within five months, the submarine issue was likely to prove a political time bomb.

The "New Orientation": Political Reform

The controversy over submarine warfare had hardly subsided when it was replaced on the political scene by the controversy over political reform. This matter had less immediate effect on the outcome of the war, but its divisive effects in German political life were greater. Indeed, both the submarine and war-aims controversies (see Chapter 7 below) were to a great extent merely reflections of the controversy over political reform. Demands for political reform were hardly new—Helfferich himself had made such demands as a young man—but the war had given them added justification. The old aim of reforming existing injustices had been reinforced by the general realization that the

---

[6] Matthias Erzberger, *Erlebnisse im Weltkriege* (Stuttgart, 1920), 221; Kuno von Westarp, *Konservative Politik im letzten Jahrzehnt des Kaiserreiches* (2 vols., Berlin, 1935), II, 154-55; Veit Valentin, *Deutschlands Aussenpolitik von Bismarcks Abgang bis zum Ende des Weltkriegs* (Berlin, 1921), 301-302.

[7] Jäckh, *Pflug*, 416.

[8] For his utterances in the committee hearings of 21 February, see Lerchenfeld to King Ludwig III, "Bericht" 162/xxxv, 21 Feb. 1917, GStA, "PA"; for 29 March, Bavarian Staatsrat Kohl to Bavarian Foreign Office, 29 March 1917, *ibid.*; for 28 April, Helfferich, *Reden und Aufsätze aus dem Kriege* (Berlin, 1917), 307-19.

German people had earned recompense for their tremendous sacrifices in the form of a greater voice in the destiny of the nation. What the actual reforms were to be was another matter. The driving force behind reform, the Reichstag, principally wanted responsible parliamentary government, a limitation on the control of the crown over the armed forces, and democratization of the Prussian electoral law.

The last of these demands was the key measure on which all else depended. Prussian voters were divided into three classes according to the amount of taxes they paid. A very wealthy man paying a third of the personal taxes of a given district might thus have the first class entirely to himself, a few less wealthy neighbors the second, and all other voters the third. The sharply progressive nature of the Prussian income tax accentuated these divisions. Although this system favored all of the rich, it favored the landlord more than the factory lord. The landlord was apt to be the principal personage of his district, whereas urban plutocrats all lived together in the fashionable city districts. A second factor favoring the landlord was open balloting, which in practice gave him effective control of all the classes of his district. Finally, electoral districting, not much changed since 1848, was weighted heavily in favor of the land. In 1898, for example, 813,560 rural voters from the 55 most sparsely settled districts elected 90 deputies, while roughly the same number of urban voters from the most populous districts elected only 20.[9] Agrarian Conservatives thus dominated the Landtag, and it was they who most opposed other reforms. Moreover, because of its influence over the Prussian Ministry, the Landtag effectively controlled the Bundesrat, the primary legislative body of the Reich. A reform of the Prussian electoral law that would make the Prussian Landtag more truly representative of the Prussian electorate was hence the *sine qua non* for all other reforms.

While Bethmann saw the need for electoral reform, he did

[9] For a good brief description of Germany's constitutional structure and the problems of political reform, see Epstein, *Erzberger*, Ch. 2. For more detailed treatment of the particular problem of electoral reform, see Reinhard Patemann, *Der Kampf um die preussische Wahlreform im Ersten Weltkrieg* (Düsseldorf, 1964); and for the foregoing example, *ibid.*, 11.

wish to postpone consideration of the question until after the war. In order to have a proposal on reform to show the Kaiser at some suitable opportunity, however, Bethmann charged Friedrich von Loebell, the Prussian Minister of the Interior, in December 1914 with drafting a new electoral law. This was setting a wolf to guard the sheep. Loebell's draft was so conservative that it was never seriously considered.[10] Helfferich, too, favored reform and had rather more constructive ideas on the subject than Loebell.[11] Although he also favored delaying reform until after the war, even before assuming his duties as Interior Secretary he concluded that the government would be wise to issue immediately a statement promising reform. He argued that the Socialists had to be won for the "positive work" of government, and not simply permitted to persist in their present attitude of tolerant hostility. This was particularly necessary because the government was asking more and more from the people the longer the war continued, not only in blood but also in taxes. It was up to the government to prevent the Majority Socialists from being undermined by their own radical wing and thus ensure that the troops returned from the trenches "on the basis of our social order." Concessions had to be made and should be promised in the forthcoming *Thronrede* (address from the throne). Bethmann took up Helfferich's arguments as his own, and the promise of reform duly appeared in the *Thronrede* of 13 January 1916.[12] The tactic was successful. After brief but lively debate between Right and Left on the problem of reform, the question disappeared from politics for an entire year.

The question of reform reappeared on the political scene quite fortuitously early in 1917. The spark that eventually ignited the controversy was some minor changes in the Entailed Estate Law (*Fideikommissgesetz*) which were brought before the Prussian Landtag in mid-January. The changes had been long in prepara-

[10] *Ibid.*, 21. See also Ludwig Bergsträsser, *Die preussische Wahlrechtsfrage im Kriege und die Entstehung der Osterbotschaft 1917* (Tübingen, 1929), 12, 79.

[11] *Ibid.*, 99-100; *Weltkrieg*, III, 85.

[12] For the text see Ernst Jäckh and Carl Hönn (eds.), *Schulthess' Europäischer Geschichtskalender* (henceforth cited as *Schulthess*), Vol. 57 (1), 10-11.

201

tion and were not very significant. Not surprisingly, however, anything involving the security of entailed estates was anathema to the left-wing parties.[13] When the Entailed Estate Law had come before the Landtag in 1915, the Progressives announced that they would consider the *Burgfriede* terminated if the law were not withdrawn. The government hastily did so. Delbrück promised that the law would not be brought in again before the end of the war. Yet apparently because of pressure from the Right, Bethmann did allow the law to be brought in again, evidently hoping to blunt the ire of the Left by bringing in a housing bill at the same time.[14] His hope went unrealized, and he candidly admitted later that the action was a "mistake."[15] The Landtag debates of January went comparatively smoothly, but in February there was a stormy full-dress debate on political *Neuorientierung* which may be said to mark the end of the *Burgfriede*. In early March, Bethmann made some conciliatory statements in the Reichstag promising political changes after the war, but whatever calming effects his statements might have had were nullified by the Prussian Herrenhaus (House of Peers). On 9 March, that body rejected a bill for payment of the members of the Prussian Landtag, and did so to the accompaniment of fulminations against parliamentarianism in general and the Reichstag in particular. That the most violent speaker bore the name Yorck von Wartenburg lent a particular piquancy to the episode. Yorck's blast in turn led Robert Friedberg, no Socialist but a National Liberal, to demand in the Prussian Abgeordnetenhaus (House of Deputies; the lower house) a reform of the Herrenhaus. On the same day, 14 March, Bethmann made a speech promising postwar electoral reform and other political reforms. "Woe to the statesman who does not recognize the signs of the times," he said.[16] It was a declaration of war against the conservatives and was universally recognized as such.

[13] Arthur Rosenberg, *Entstehung der Weimarer Republik* (Frankfurt a. M., 1961 [1928]), 134-35.

[14] Bergsträsser, *Wahlrechtsfrage*, 108-11.

[15] Theobald von Bethmann Hollweg, *Betrachtungen zum Weltkriege* (2 vols., Berlin, 1919, 1921), II, 171. Schiffer thought Bethmann had erred because he was out of touch with parliamentary sentiment; *Ein Leben*, 198.

[16] *Schulthess*, Vol. 58 (1), 295-99; Bergsträsser, *Wahlrechtsfrage*, 118-19.

News of the Russian revolution reached Bethmann that very evening, and the details became available to the general public the following day. *Vorwärts*, the great Socialist daily, was quick to draw the lesson of the events in Russia for its readers. Commenting on Bethmann's speech of the day before, the editors stated that his promises of reform were in themselves praiseworthy, but that it would not do to wait until the troops had returned from the trenches. If sufficient bread could not be provided, the people should at least receive recompense for their sacrifices through the introduction of the equal suffrage which the Russian masses now enjoyed. The editors implied that if this demand were met, the Socialists would support a constitutional monarchy after the war. Philipp Scheidemann put the same demands more sharply in a signed *Vorwärts* article, "Time to act," which appeared four days later. The government could ignore these warnings only at its peril. Because of the tremendous impact of the Russian revolution on the German people, the event was more than merely an example of how reforms are achieved in an authoritarian state, it was also a challenge. The Majority Socialists had to meet this challenge or see their followers lured away by the more radical Sozialdemokratische Arbeitsgemeinschaft. For the Majority Socialists, too, it was time to act.

After the Reichstag convened, the pressure on the government increased sharply. On 29 March, both the Majority Socialists and the National Liberals brought in bills for the formation of parliamentary committees to consider political reform. Stresemann echoed the sentiments of all parties as far right as his own when he stated: "The time has come to begin the ordering of things anew, both in Germany and in the *Bundesstaaten*." Lest the import of this be mistaken, he added: "For me and my political friends, the Prussian electoral law is a German question."[17] Helfferich said afterward that Bethmann should have seized this occasion to promise extensive concessions, while simultaneously stating that, because of the work load the ministers and Staatssekretäre were presently carrying, the implementation of the reforms would have to wait until after the war.[18] Although there

---

[17] *RTV*, Vol. 309, 29 March 1917, 2852-58.
[18] "Bericht" 617, 31 March 1917, "HB."

were both constitutional and practical difficulties in the way of his suggestion, Stresemann's speech had put the issue squarely. The need for some sort of government initiative was clear.

Two other events not directly connected with the question of reform gave an added urgency to the need for action. The first was the break in diplomatic relations with the United States. Although this had occurred some time before, it was now clear that war was not far off. When war came—as it did on 6 April—the position of the government vis-à-vis the parties of the left was likely to be weakened still further.[19] The second event which promised trouble was the shortening of the bread ration scheduled for 15 April. The government had already run into difficulties in the Reichstag in the summer and fall of 1916 over food questions, and the reduction hardly squared very well with Helfferich's assurances in the submarine hearings of the previous fall that the German grain situation had improved since 1915. The Majority Socialist Gustav Noske commented with some annoyance in the Reichstag about the bread reductions, which were announced the last week in March, and the government had good reason to believe that protests would go farther than speeches.[20] Helfferich hoped to alleviate some of the popular discontent by doubling the meat ration, but neither Zimmermann nor Bethmann was optimistic about the probable effect of this measure.[21] The winter had been an unusually severe one, made worse by the need to reduce household coal allotments because of transportation breakdowns. It was a bad time to cut the bread ration.

It was in this threatening situation that Bethmann called a meeting of his closest political advisers on 31 March to consider the problem of political reform. Bethmann said that if the Socialists were to be kept in line, something would have to be done about reforming the franchise of the Prussian lower house. Di-

[19] See, for example, the barbed remarks of the Majority Socialist Gustav Noske; *RTV*, Vol. 309, 29 March 1917, 2835-42.

[20] *Ibid.* The government began taking measures against possible disturbances as early as 30 March; Heinrich Scheel, "Der Aprilstreik 1917 in Berlin," in Albert Schreiner (ed.), *Revolutionäre Ereignisse und Probleme in Deutschland während der Grossen Sozialistischen Oktoberrevolution* (Berlin, 1957), 16-17.

[21] "Bericht" 621, 4 April 1917, "HB"; Westarp, *Konservative Politik*, II, 264.

rect, secret, and equal suffrage after the model of the Reichstag law probably offered the best solution, with its radical effects, however, mitigated by a strengthening of the powers of the Herrenhaus. At the same time, of course, agrarian control of the Herrenhaus would have to be ended. Only Helfferich and Roedern wholeheartedly supported Bethmann, with the rest of those present proving to be only tepid supporters or outright opponents of Bethmann's proposals. It was agreed, however, that Bethmann would approach the Kaiser on the matter at the first opportunity.

Bethmann did so the following day but did not actually mention the Reichstag law, probably because he knew that the Kaiser favored less extreme changes. Earlier, William had expressed approval of a "moderately graduated" electoral law, and Bethmann evidently intended to coax him around to the Reichstag suffrage in easy stages. While Bethmann was still with the Kaiser at Bad Homburg, he received a proposal from Adolf Tortilowicz von Batocki, head of the War Food Office, that the Kaiser should promise reforms in an Easter address. The idea appealed to William's sense of theater, and he agreed at once. "The Crown must speak on Easter. After Easter is too late," read his melodramatic marginalia.[22]

Bethmann, determined to seize the favorable moment, called a meeting of the Prussian Ministry upon his return to Berlin. Speed was essential. Easter, 7 April, was only two days off. Bethmann's arguments, which differed little from those presented in the earlier meeting, need not be repeated here.[23] The other members also expressed views which differed little from those expressed on earlier occasions. Change had to come, it was agreed, but there was less agreement about the extent and the timing. Once again, Helfferich proved Bethmann's staunchest supporter. He marshaled an impressive list of arguments in favor of the immediate introduction of the Reichstag suffrage into Prussia. "It has turned out to be a mistake," he observed, "not to have fought this through long ago, [and] now we must decide under pres-

[22] Bergsträsser, *Wahlrechtsfrage*, 27, 131-39.
[23] Prussian Ministry Protocol, 5 April 1917, "Preussen" 11, 3169/1613/-674986-675022.

205

sure." Taking his cue from the Socialists, he said that it was hardly possible to do anything about the food situation or the revolutionary situation in Russia, but something had to be done to reduce the present political tension. He prophesied that otherwise political agitators "would conjure up a storm that we can no longer master." The consequences were clear: "Then we run the risk of losing the war and placing both the state and the monarchy in jeopardy." He admitted that neither the Reichstag nor the Landtag had lived up to the demands made of it but warned that the offer of a plural-vote electoral law (which in his heart he favored) would be worse than no offer at all. But he thought that there was a way to take some of the sting from the Reichstag electoral law, and that was to attach a residence requirement of one year to eligibility to vote. This apparently insignificant addition had proved quite effective in reducing Socialist strength in Alsace-Lorraine. Though he regarded the introduction of the Reichstag law, however embellished, with misgivings, he thought it the only way "to remove the political tinder" from the scene. Furthermore, it was important that the law be not only promised, but actually brought in, in the very near future. If the present districting were retained, he thought that the National Liberals and the Center might well support a law such as he suggested.

Helfferich's analysis of the situation was sound enough. It is possible that, had his appeal been heeded, his solution might have produced the promised results. When put to a vote in the ministry, however, the Reichstag electoral law secured only a one-vote majority, hardly enough to override the known objections of the Kaiser.[24] Bethmann therefore drafted a noncommittal Easter address which merely promised "the abolition of the electoral law based on class." This draft was presented to the ministry on the following day. After the ministry had expressed their approval, Bethmann departed once more for Bad Homburg to secure William's consent to the draft. Though Helfferich found Bethmann's draft "irreproachable" at the ministry session, he soon had second thoughts. Still apparently "on fire with enthusiasm" for the Reichstag suffrage, he discovered that Arnold

[24] Prussian Ministry Protocol, 6 April 1917, *ibid.*, 675025-36.

Wahnschaffe, the Undersecretary in the Reich Chancellory, was of a like mind.[25] Their first telegram to Bethmann proposed only some editorial changes in the draft speech which the ministry had approved, but in their second telegram they made one last attempt to push Bethmann to decisive action. They made three suggestions. Since the Reichstag suffrage was bound to come soon, the Crown might as well earn the gratitude of the country by granting it immediately. Second, some of the Prussian ministers should be replaced.[26] Last, the Herrenhaus ought to be reformed. These were all reasonable proposals, and it is a pity that Bethmann could not act upon them. The Easter message met widespread approval, but it postponed the issue without resolving it.

Helfferich later believed that the Easter message had largely undermined the protest strikes scheduled to coincide with the reduction of the bread ration.[27] There is doubtless considerable truth in his belief, as it is unlikely that the Socialist leadership, including the left-wing leader Hugo Haase, would otherwise have cooperated to the extent that it did in getting the people to return to work. The strike had more significance than Helfferich accords it in his memoirs, because it was the first time during the war that strikers had made political as well as economic demands. The Russian example was beginning to take effect. Under these circumstances, Groener's *Hundsfott* Order of 27 April—so called because of the phrase "whoever strikes while our army stands before the enemy is a dirty dog (*Hundsfott*)"—was especially unfortunate.[28] Helfferich was particularly incensed because Groener issued the order without consulting either Bethmann or himself. Then, after the damage was done, Helfferich had to de-

[25] Magnus Freiherr von Braun, *Von Ostpreussen bis Texas: Erlebnisse und zeitgeschichtliche Betrachtungen eines Ostdeutschen* (Stollhamm, 1955), 104-105, entry of 6 April 1917, referring to Helfferich's state on the 5th.

[26] Bergsträsser, *Wahlrechtsfrage*, 153-55. Bergsträsser is of the opinion that there was much sense in this proposal. The ministry had shown itself to be too badly split to work together much longer. Nor in fact did it do so.

[27] *Weltkrieg*, III, 99-100.

[28] Gaertringen, *Groener*, 362-63. See the remarks of Oskar Cohn (USPD), among others; *RTV*, Vol. 309, 5 May 1917, 3095-99.

fend the action in the Reichstag.[29] In Helfferich's eyes, Groener, with whom he was already at odds over other matters, had acquired one more blemish.

Helfferich was also engaged in more important business, since he was to represent the government at the sessions of the newly formed Constitutional Committee, which were to begin on 2 May. As a result of his preliminary talks with the party leaders, Helfferich was not unduly worried. The demands which he reported to the Prussian Ministry on 1 May were in fact rather modest.[30] According to him, the parties were generally satisfied with the promises made for Prussia in the Kaiser's Easter message and were mainly concerned with the situation in the backward state of Mecklenburg, which did not even have a constitution.[31] The government had already taken up the matter with the minister from Mecklenburg, who reported that the estates were resisting efforts to introduce a constitution. The parties were also demanding a redistricting of the Reich, which had not been done since 1867 (1871 in the south). Helfferich felt that the government would have to give ground on this point. Rather than acquiesce in a general redistricting, which would give too much strength to the parties of the Left, Helfferich proposed that an additional member be added for every 200,000 electors in districts which presently exceeded 300,000 electors. This would meet the justified demand for more representation for the cities, yet limit Socialist power. It was agreed that the government would take the position that it could not interfere in the internal affairs of Mecklenburg and as far as possible would avoid committing itself on electoral redistricting. Helfferich mentioned that the National Liberals and the Center had shown interest in a national supreme court, but that, really, "no party knows today

---

[29] *Ibid.*, 3099-101; "Bericht" 636, 3 May 1917, "HB."

[30] Prussian Ministry Protocol, 1 May 1917, "Preussen" 11, 3169/1613/-675040-50; *Weltkrieg*, III, 100.

[31] Mecklenburg, a small agricultural *Bundesstaat* on the Baltic, was politically dominated by its Junker nobility. Political reform in tiny Mecklenburg was of essentially symbolic importance. What was at stake was the right of the Reichstag to interfere in the internal affairs of the *Bundesstaaten*.

exactly what it wants." He promised to maintain an attitude of reserve, and, in the light of his past opposition to the pretensions of the Reichstag, the promise doubtless reassured the ministers.[32]

Helfferich was astonished when the National Liberals, the Center, and the Progressives, despite earlier assurances, brought in a bill in committee which called for a responsible ministry, a national supreme court, and the countersigning of officers' commissions by a war minister responsible to the Reichstag.[33] In many ways the last request was the most serious of all, as it impinged directly upon the Kaiser's command prerogatives and was therefore likely to be taken as a personal affront. Helfferich merely heard these surprising requests *ad referendum.* But he "made no secret" of his opinion that the deputies had been very tactless in assailing the command prerogatives of the Kaiser immediately after his Easter message. Helfferich did not appear at the later sessions of the committee, sending his deputy, Theodor von Lewald, instead. From all accounts, Lewald was a thoroughly competent man, but according to Stresemann his manner had an "absolutely infuriating" effect upon most of the deputies.[34] Lewald was also too low in rank to make binding declarations for the government. This may have been a deliberate tactical measure on Helfferich's part, since he intended to see that the bill "fell under the table" and did not come up for discussion in the House.[35] In this he succeeded. Neither then nor later did the deliberations of the Constitutional Committee show any tangible results. Helfferich warned the Prussian Ministry on 23 May, however, that it was only because the National Liberals and Progressives had for tactical reasons agreed to the sidetracking of the efforts of the committee that the sessions had not taken a more

---

[32] For instances not already mentioned of Helfferich's defense of the government's constitutional prerogatives against the Reichstag's assaults, see his remarks on the formation of the Hauptausschuss and on protective custody; *RTV*, Vol. 308, 26 Oct. 1916, 1811-12, and 28 Oct. 1916, 1883-85.

[33] *Weltkrieg*, III, 101-103; Deuerlein, *Bundesratsausschuss*, 296-97.

[34] Stresemann, "Helfferich"; also Philipp Scheidemann, *Der Zusammenbruch* (Berlin, 1921), 168.

[35] Lerchenfeld to Hertling, 15 May 1917, GStA, "Briefwechsel"; "Bericht" 643, 10 May 1917, "HB."

dangerous turn.[36] He and Bethmann warned that it was high time to decide on a "definite electoral program."

Although the Constitutional Committee's proposals had "fallen under the table," its expressed intention of limiting the Kaiser's command prerogatives produced the explosion at Supreme Headquarters that Helfferich had foreseen. William sent a warm letter to Lewald praising his forthright defense of the imperial prerogative, while the Supreme Command blasted the supineness of Bethmann and Helfferich in the face of parliamentary pretensions.[37] When the committee proceedings were nearly over, Helfferich and Bethmann journeyed to Headquarters to set things right. It soon developed that William, despite his initial outrage, had taken the entire affair less "tragically" than the generals. He was rather easily persuaded that the course which the government had followed was the correct one. As Helfferich explained it to Lerchenfeld after his return, a sharper stand would only have provoked resistance *à l'outrance* to the government's efforts to prevent the matter from reaching the floor of the Reichstag. Helfferich added that he thought Bethmann's position was firm.[38]

Although Bethmann may have been on a firm footing with the Kaiser, relations between the civilians and the Supreme Command were steadily worsening, and that was what mattered. What Helfferich held most against the generals was their repeated attempts to drive out Bethmann and their unceasing hamfisted interference in civil matters. Discussing the problem with Arndt von Holtzendorff on 10 May, Helfferich first called attention to an "outrageous" anti-Bethmann article which had just appeared in the pan-German *Deutsche Tageszeitung*.[39] "Nothing can be done," he complained, "because the censorship is in the

[36] Prussian Ministry Protocol, 23 May 1917, "Preussen" 11, 3169/1613/-675054-69. See also Patemann, *Wahlreform*, 73-76.

[37] Rudolf Schmidt-Bückeburg, *Das Militärkabinett der preussischen Könige und deutschen Kaiser: seine geschichtliche Entwicklung und staatsrechtliche Bedeutung 1787-1918* (Berlin, 1933), 278-80. For one conservative officer's furious reaction, see Einem, *Armeeführer*, 308-309.

[38] Lerchenfeld to Hertling, 15 May 1917, GStA, "Briefwechsel." I think Ritter, *Staatskunst*, III, 546, exaggerates William's ire. See also "Aufzeichnung zu den Sitzungen des diplomatischen Ausschusses von Dienstag den 8. und Mittwoch den 9. Mai 1917," GStA, "PA."

[39] "Bericht" 643, 10 May 1917, "HB."

hands of the military, and it is simply not to be had for support of the Chancellor's policy." Warming to his work, Helfferich labeled the agitation against Bethmann at Headquarters "the worst and most irresponsible of all." He asserted flatly that the "favorable outcome of the war" depended upon "keeping the mood of the country calm," and concluded: "Instead of the Supreme Command's being grateful to the Chancellor for his magnificent performance, however, they fling clubs between his legs."

As the spring of 1917 progressed, Helfferich also grew increasingly angry about the Supreme Command's perpetual meddling in economic matters that were properly the concern of his own Interior Office. The generals did everything from suggesting methods of organizing the postwar economy and of raising current production to complaining about the coal shortages and the rapid rise in wages and procurement costs.[40] They refused to see that their interference was responsible for much of what they complained of. Earlier, in April, Helfferich had feared that the popularity of the Supreme Command was such that there was little point in taking his grievances to the Kaiser.[41] By mid-June, the coal situation had manifestly reached a point where such considerations were obsolete. Helfferich finally decided that the only solution was to visit Headquarters and take up the matter with Ludendorff personally. Both Bethmann and Zimmermann viewed his departure with uneasiness. He had threatened to make a "cabinet question" of the release of miners from the army, and he was, as Zimmermann put it, "very little loved" at Headquarters. At the height of the submarine crisis in January, Ludendorff had, in fact, called Helfferich a "pussy-footer" and a "weak sister (*Schwachmatikus*)."[42] But to the evident relief of Bethmann and Zimmermann, the meeting between Helfferich and Ludendorff went smoothly. Ludendorff "appreciated" the justice of Helf-

---

[40] See the correspondence in Ludendorff, *Urkunden*, 87-89, 136-39, 177-82, 188-89; Feldman, *Army, Industry, and Labor*, Chs. 5-7, provides the best account of their activities.

[41] "Bericht" 629, 19 April 1917, "HB."

[42] "Bericht" 664, 17 June 1917, "HB"; and for Ludendorff's epithets, Einem, *Armeeführer*, 278.

ferich's proposals and "gave in"; the miners were released.[43] Obviously, this isolated episode hardly constituted a real détente between the generals and the politicians. There is, indeed, every indication that, as June drew to a close, their relations were worse than ever.[44]

It was also because of worsening relations with the Supreme Command that the government had in the meantime been able to make so few plans for the coming July Reichstag session. The events of the spring session, particularly the contretemps in the Constitutional Committee in May, though in the long run not serious, made any immediate fulfillment of the promises of the Easter message difficult and more sweeping reforms impossible. Bethmann had trouble enough just to reassert his position with the Kaiser. Even before the meeting of the Constitutional Committee, he and Helfferich had carefully denied, on constitutional grounds, any intention of appointing Reichstag deputies to posts in the Reich or Prussian governments.[45] As Bethmann explained it to the Prussian Ministry on 1 May, "parliamentary ministers without a parliamentary system are an impossibility."[46] The program for the next Reichstag session that Helfferich outlined on 9 May for the Bundesrat Foreign Affairs Committee thus contemplated only a token meeting for the granting of new war credits. A new electoral law, which Helfferich circumspectly promised would be acceptable to the *Bundesstaaten*, was not to be introduced until fall.[47]

[43] "Bericht" 665, 24 June 1917, "HB." On the coal crisis, see Feldman, *Army, Industry, and Labor*, esp. 261-64.

[44] According to Valentini, on 29 June 1917 both Hindenburg and Bethmann Hollweg asked to resign; Schwertfeger, *Valentini*, 156.

[45] These denials were almost surely made for tactical reasons, for while neither was particularly looking forward to such an innovation, both recognized it would have to come; *Weltkrieg*, III, 102; Bethmann Hollweg, *Betrachtungen*, II, 192. See also Schmidt-Bückeburg, *Militärkabinett*, 284.

[46] See n.30 above. According to Westarp, who had access to official documents, Helfferich submitted a memorandum on 23 April 1917 against the recruiting of Prussian ministers and Staatssekretäre from the Reichstag which is one of the "best things written on the subject"; Westarp, *Konservative Politik*, II, 250.

[47] See n.38 above; also Lerchenfeld to Hertling, 17 May 1917, GStA, "Briefwechsel."

Although Helfferich did not say so in the Bundesrat, he was hoping that by July a "considerable clarification" in Germany's military situation would have occurred and that by fall, or by the end of 1917 at the latest, peace would follow. Whether he was pinning his hopes on peace with Russia or on the submarine campaign, or both, is not clear.[48] Maybe he was only whistling in the dark. The consequences of such a development were certainly alluring to contemplate. The Reichstag would have had no particular reason to make difficulties about the grant of new credits. And once peace was assured, Ludendorff and Hindenburg would no longer be indispensable: Bethmann was not likely to have much trouble in persuading William to accept any sensible foreign or domestic policy once the latter dared to take the field against his increasingly arrogant and insubordinate inferiors. Unfortunately, as the end of June approached it was clear that Helfferich's wishes were not going to be fulfilled. The best that Helfferich hoped for was peace by fall, and that without much conviction.[49] For the moment, however, the government had concrete prospectives of neither peace (to say nothing of victory) nor political reform to offer the deputies in the coming session.

The situation augured very poorly for a peaceful outcome of the session. By mid-June Helfferich was beginning to worry openly about the Socialists' raising "a great storm" against him because of his alleged promises that submarine warfare would force the English to sue for peace by August. Although he may not have made such promises officially, he had said in the budget hearings of April that the results of the submarine campaign could be predicted "with almost mathematical certainty" and that "time works for us."[50] Others agreed that Helfferich would come under attack. Yet as late as 27 June Helfferich still aspired to hold

[48] "Bericht" 643, 10 May 1917, "HB." See also "Bericht" 629, 19 April 1917, *ibid.*; Braun, *Von Ostpreussen*, 129, entry of 30 May 1917, in which von Braun notes that Helfferich "believes that England will be forced to conclude peace by August."

[49] Görlitz, *Müller*, 295, entry of 19 June 1917.

[50] "Bericht" 662, 15 June 1917, "HB," and for the remarks in committee, Westarp, *Konservative Politik*, ii, 159-60.

the sessions to the two or three days necessary for the granting of credits; "a pious wish," said Zimmermann.[51]

That very day, Scheidemann and David, who had just returned from an international Socialist conference in Stockholm, reported to Bethmann that they had found no readiness to compromise in their Western comrades and that the Russians were unwilling to agree to a separate peace on any basis so far proposed by the Germans. For their part, the Socialists demanded that the government accept a program of peace without indemnities and annexations and immediate electoral reform in Prussia.[52] Although Helfferich may not have known on the 27th of these latest Socialist demands, it is still difficult to say why he persisted so long in pursuing the chimera of a short session. Mental and physical exhaustion may have dulled his political perceptiveness. His father had died on 17 May, and he was badly overworked. On 27 June, his press chief, Baron Magnus von Braun, wrote in his diary: "He is suffering from headaches and the deputies keep him very busy. What is more, he is drowning in paperwork and cannot break free to act."[53]

Actually, however, the government was moving as rapidly as it could to meet the Socialists halfway. On 29 June, Bethmann suggested to William that a single Reichstag deputy, Center Party leader Peter Spahn, should be appointed Prussian Minister of Justice, a post for which he was admirably qualified. Although Spahn was in every respect a safe man and a staunch monarchist, William refused.[54] Bethmann also seems to have planned a conciliatory statement about war aims, especially regarding Belgium.[55] It soon became apparent, however, that such steps were hardly likely to satisfy the Socialists. During the conferences of the 30th, with the party leaders about the coming session, Helfferich learned from David and Scheidemann that they wanted a clear

[51] Braun, *Von Ostpreussen*, 107, entry of 27 June 1917, and for Zimmermann's remark, "Bericht" 671, 30 June 1917, "HB."

[52] Ritter, *Staatskunst*, III, 554-55.   [53] Braun, *Von Ostpreussen*, 107.

[54] Görlitz, *Müller*, 298, entry of 29 June 1917. Spahn was appointed in August.

[55] Wolfgang Steglich, *Der Friedenspolitik der Mittelmächte 1917-1918* (Wiesbaden, 1964), 127. Such a statement would have been aimed as much at foreign opinion as at the Socialists. See also Ritter, *Staatskunst*, III, 556-57.

statement renouncing annexationist war aims and another in favor of Prussian electoral reform. Scheidemann also made it clear that he thought the cause of peace might better be served by a new chancellor. The next day, 1 July, he tried to force the government's hand by an aggressive article in *Vorwärts* on *Neuorientierung*. Threatened by the Supreme Command and its allies on the right and now without the prospect of firm support from either the Kaiser or the Left, the government's situation had become precarious. Its only chance for survival was to keep a tight lid on parliamentary developments.

Helfferich meant to resist pressure from the Left to the uttermost. Bethmann's only reaction could be "to refuse all [Socialist] demands," he told von Braun, since "Scheidemann is a really ugly customer (*ganz brutaler Patron*) who will exercise power ruthlessly once he gets his hands on it." He also feared that the Progressives were likely to join the Socialists in pushing for reform in the Constitutional Committee. But though he admitted that almost anything was possible in committee, he believed that with the assistance of the Conservatives, National Liberals, and the Center he could again thwart the efforts of the Left.[56] Reporting on the 2nd to the Prussian Ministry on the party negotiations, he revealed that the Progressives were, in fact, planning to bring in a bill calling for the introduction of constitutions and the Reichstag electoral law in all *Bundesstaaten*. At this time he still thought that he could delay consideration of this bill. He pointed out, however, that the government's position would be considerably improved if he could at least promise more seats for districts with "especially great" population increases. While many ministers agreed with this proposal, they were unwilling to set a definite date for its realization. Bethmann, Helfferich, and other government representatives met again with the party leaders shortly thereafter. Helfferich then discovered that the parties meant to push ahead with parliamentary reform. He duly reported this discouraging new information back to the Prussian Ministry later in the day. The intractable ministers would only agree that if discussion in the Constitutional Committee returned to the Progressives' bill, Lewald was to state that the Reichstag

[56] Braun, *Von Ostpreussen*, 107-108, entry of 1 July 1917.

was not competent to interfere in the affairs of the *Bundes-staaten*, while simultaneously pointing out that steps in the desired direction had already been taken in Hamburg, Mecklenburg, and Prussia.[57]

By this time Bethmann and Helfferich understood that their supposed Conservative-National Liberal-Center bloc was far less solid than they had believed. Stresemann, now the real leader of the National Liberals, had already stated privately that he believed that the coming session would last "at least two weeks," and asserted that "this time the so-called Constitutional Committee does not mean to adjourn again without issue."[58] Even more serious was the action being planned by Matthias Erzberger. Erzberger had made no secret to Bethmann and Helfferich of his dissatisfaction with the results of unrestricted submarine warfare, but he had given them no sign that he would not support the government as in the past.[59] Indeed, when Colonel Bauer wrote Erzberger that he had heard from a Reichstag deputy (not named) that Erzberger had lost confidence in unrestricted submarine warfare, Erzberger specifically denied even that. "In the last weeks I have spoken to no Reichstag deputy whatsoever about submarine warfare," he insisted. He added: "It is really frightful the amount of slander-mongering that goes on these days!"[60] It may be assumed that Bauer's informant was Strese-

[57] Prussian Ministry Protocols, 2 July 1917, "Preussen" 11, 3169/1613/-675113-28, on both sessions. To have two sessions in one day was unusual and probably indicated how seriously the government regarded the developing situation.

[58] "Bericht" 669, 29 June 1917, "HB."

[59] Whether Erzberger had, in fact, warned the government that he meant to attack it was later much disputed. Bethmann, Helfferich, Solf, Spahn, and others claimed that Erzberger had provided no such warning, while the latter protested that he had; *Prozess*, 12, 36-37, 697-712. Solf did admit later that Erzberger had told him in mid-June that he meant to undertake a "démarche" against the government, but for some reason he did not report this news to Bethmann; *ibid.*, 714, 718-20; "Bericht" 660, 13 June 1917, "HB." See also *Weltkrieg*, III, 105-106; Epstein, *Erzberger*, 191n25.

[60] Erzberger to Bauer, 26 June 1917, Bauer "Nachlass." Erzberger and Bauer had already discussed the military situation, which Bauer painted in sombre hues, on the 10th and the 19th. Ritter thinks that Bauer was attempting to use Erzberger as a tool to create a disturbance such as later

mann, since Erzberger told the latter on 19 June that he was planning an attack on Helfferich "because submarine warfare . . . had not fulfilled expectations."[61] A week later, Erzberger telephoned General Max Hoffmann that "his [Erzberger's] patience was at its end" and that he too was for "changing . . . 'certain people.' "[62] "Certain people" may refer only to Helfferich, but in view of Hoffmann's known antipathy to Bethmann it is virtually assured that the phrase also included the Chancellor.

The supposition that Erzberger was aiming at Bethmann as well as Helfferich is reinforced by his flirtation with ex-Chancellor von Bülow. This bizarre alliance dated from the days when the two had worked together in a futile diplomatic effort to keep Italy out of the war. In the spring of 1917, Erzberger had attempted to arrange a rendezvous between the Kaiser and Bülow at Homburg, only to have his efforts thwarted (he thought) by Helfferich.[63] This meeting could hardly have had any other purpose than to reconcile the Kaiser and Bülow and thus make the latter a candidate for Chancellor once again. It must be pointed out, however, that Erzberger also wrote Admiral von Müller on 8 May opposing a change of chancellors at that time.[64] Since Erzberger had heard that a general was under consideration for the post, it is possible that he was merely trying to keep the field clear for his own man. On 30 June, Arndt von Holtzendorff noted an item whose import is almost unmistakable: "This evening Zimmermann is joining the Bülows for dinner, and, astonishingly enough, at Erzberger's. . . . Is Erzberger toying with the idea of raising Bülow on his shield?" Zimmermann did not think so. He reported to Holtzendorff on the following day—the two took morning walks together—that "Erzberger considers the Center

---

occurred in the Reichstag in order to bring down Bethmann; *Staatskunst*, III, 573. Bauer would doubtless have done it for this reason if he had thought of it, but such an interpretation seems to me a little farfetched.

[61] Stresemann to Bassermann, 19 June 1917, Stresemann "Nachlass," 6833/-3061/125825.

[62] Nowak, *Hoffmann*, I, 170, entry of 26 June 1917.

[63] Erzberger, *Erlebnisse*, 40-41.

[64] Görlitz, *Müller*, 284-85, entry of 10 May 1917.

absolutely reliable," the party upon which the Chancellor "can most depend."[65]

The July Crisis of 1917

The hearings of the Main Committee began on 3 July. In order to discourage a general political debate, Bethmann elected to stay away from the hearings and left the representation of the government to his subordinates. This proved to be a major tactical error, since, as Helfferich ruefully admitted afterward, he and Capelle and Zimmermann were all under a cloud at the time.[66] Roedern spoke on the need for new war credits and was followed by Zimmermann and Capelle. Then it was the turn of the parties. Friedrich Ebert spoke first, leading the Majority Socialists in the expected attack on the government, which was more violent, however, than the government seems to have anticipated. "Because of the failure of submarine warfare and of the food supply, trust in the government is completely gone," Ebert asserted. He demanded that the government pledge itself to a program of peace without annexations and immediate introduction of the Reichstag suffrage in Prussia. Next, Erzberger spoke on the need to restore the spirit of unity and common sacrifice of 4 August 1914. In a cautious and pessimistic speech, he ventured the opinion that submarine warfare was unlikely to prove decisive. Helfferich spoke in rebuttal, bringing forth the usual "statistical mumbo-jumbo" to prove that unrestricted submarine warfare would eventually defeat England.[67] He emphasized that everyone had to keep his head, to hold out, since there was actually no chance for any kind of peace except a "peace of capitulation."[68] The hearings of the two following days were essentially repeat performances. Hoch followed up Ebert's thrusts with even sharper attacks, and Helfferich again demanded that Germany remain

[65] "Berichte" 671-72, 30 June and 1 July 1917, "HB."

[66] *Weltkrieg*, III, 106-107. See also *IFA*, I, xxvi-vii, on Bethmann's psychological blunder. The *IFA* is the most useful single source on the July Crisis.

[67] David, *Kriegstagebuch*, 239, entry of 3 July 1917.

[68] For the proceedings on the 3rd, see Fischer, *Griff*, 512-13; *Weltkrieg*, III, 108-109; Hanssen, *Dying Empire*, 194-97; "Aufzeichnung über die Sitzung des . . . Hauptausschusses von 3. Juli 1917," and "Reden gehalten in der Sitzung des Hauptausschusses . . . von 3. Juli 1917," GStA, "PA."

steadfast until a peace "which does not signify our ruin" was obtainable.[69] Helfferich, not realizing how serious the government's position still was, thought the storm was dissipating.[70]

Far from being over, the storm had scarcely begun. On 6 July, Erzberger launched a major assault against the government in a speech which dramatically voiced the fears and doubts of the majority of his countrymen.[71] He first asked the fundamental question whether holding out another year would secure Germany a better peace. He answered with a resounding no: "I do not hesitate to say it: I do not believe that we can obtain a better peace at the end of another year." He then discussed submarine warfare, asking, "Can we rely on Helfferich's calculations?" and finally deciding that the calculations were "incorrect." His case rested on essentially the same arguments that Helfferich himself had used against unrestricted submarine warfare in the fall of 1916. Erzberger concluded with an appeal for peace on the basis of 4 August 1914: it had to be stressed that the war was "for defense only." The Reichstag had to take the initiative: "If it is possible to secure a majority we must draw up a resolution in which we let the government know that we are willing to conclude a peace on that basis [i.e., without annexations]." The speech was a bombshell. Helfferich's rebuttal offered nothing new and did nothing to vitiate the dramatic impact of Erzberger's words. According to Westarp, a friendly witness, the majority of the deputies "hardly paid any attention to it." The effect of Erzberger's speech was the greater because everyone knew about Erzberger's access to official material denied most deputies and his intimacy with the Chancellor. Some, including the titular leader of the Center Party, Peter Spahn, even thought that Erzberger's attack might have been prearranged with the government. Helfferich soon set Spahn's mind at rest on that score; when Spahn asked

[69] Hanssen, *Dying Empire*, 197-201.

[70] *Weltkrieg*, III, 110. See also "Berichte" 674-76, 3, 4, and 5 July 1917, "HB." The tone of the reports, which were based on information given Holtzendorff by members of the government, was "business as usual." Yet on 5 July, David told Wahnschaffe that Helfferich would have to resign; *IFA*, I, xxxii.

[71] Hanssen, *Dying Empire*, 201-207; Westarp, *Konservative Politik*, II, 344-45; Erzberger, *Erlebnisse*, 255-56; Epstein, *Erzberger*, 183-84.

him directly whether Erzberger's assault was prearranged, Helfferich replied in consternation: "I am just as appalled as you!"[72]

The motives behind Erzberger's attack remain somewhat problematical to this day,[73] and Erzberger undoubtedly stops short of the whole truth in his memoirs. As he explains it, his tours of the front during the spring and summer of 1917 and his knowledge of how pessimistically the Austrian government regarded its ability to continue the war led him to believe decisive action imperative. He was also growing worried about the apparent failure of the submarine campaign. He had submitted a memorandum on the question to the Navy in June but received an answer—and an unsatisfactory one at that—only on 3 July. The Navy's experts scarcely deigned to consider the points which the Center deputy had raised, apparently because the latter was not an expert on the matter at hand. In this situation, Erzberger, finding the government's failure to produce a program intolerable, determined to act. He feared that if nothing was done the Majority Socialists might well fail to vote new war credits, and he wished in any case to recreate the spirit of 4 August 1914. To this point, Erzberger's explanation of his actions is believable, but his ultimate intention can hardly have been that which he told Bethmann on the afternoon of the 6th: namely, that he wished to rally a moderate majority behind the Chancellor. Since he had reserved his most acid phrases for the extreme annexationists, his statement to Bethmann had a certain plausibility, especially since he had always supported the government in the past. Nevertheless, it is hardly politic to launch a frontal attack on a government that one is attempting to support, and it is difficult to believe that Erzberger's allegation to Bethmann was not a deliberate attempt to mislead.

Indeed, in the light of Erzberger's earlier statements to Strese-

[72] Wilhelm Ziegler, *Volk ohne Führung: das Ende des Zweiten Reiches* (Hamburg, 1938), 25; *Prozess*, 710.

[73] For a detailed discussion of Erzberger's motives, see Epstein, *Erzberger*, 185-93. Epstein's interpretation differs in important respects from mine and is much more favorable to Erzberger. Epstein should be supplemented by Rudolf Morsey, *Die Deutsche Zentrumspartei 1917-1923* (Düsseldorf, 1966), 54-67, on Erzberger's wartime role in the Center Party. See also Erzberger, *Erlebnisse*, 255.

mann and Hoffmann, it appears probable that he had intended from the outset to bring down Bethmann and Helfferich and replace them with Bülow. He perhaps delayed his attack until 6 July in order to heighten the element of surprise, and perhaps, as he implied, to give the government one last chance to produce a program.[74] Once having determined to act, he was an able enough politician to know the effects his speech would have.[75] His great miscalculation was to assume that Bülow might prove acceptable to the Kaiser. Since Bülow was not, Erzberger had committed himself to overthrow a chancellor whose views on war aims and other political questions were not very different from his own.[76] It must have occurred to Erzberger as he planned his speech that if his effort at playing the kingmaker were successful, the new chancellor would be in his debt. He would thus be raised to a commanding position both within his own party and the new Reichstag majority. Erzberger did emerge from the crisis with a much enhanced position, although his kingmaking was not as successful as he had hoped.

At the time, naturally, Erzberger's motives were a mystery. Hostile observers concluded immediately that Erzberger's attack was a "put-up job," as Arndt von Holtzendorff expressed it, undertaken at the behest of Vienna or the Vatican. Helfferich's press chief, von Braun, also attributed the attack to the "influence of the Austrians."[77] As Ottokar von Czernin, the Austrian Foreign Minister, later claimed credit in his war memoirs for having inspired Erzberger's attack, the idea that the Austrians were behind it came to have a kind of official standing among Erzberger's numerous enemies. Helfferich later said he believed that the attack had been inspired by Vienna, although what he attributed

[74] See Friedrich von Payer, *Von Bethmann Hollweg bis Ebert: Erinnerungen und Bilder* (Frankfurt a. M., 1923), 29-30, on Erzberger's skill in properly timing his attack.

[75] Stresemann noted in a personal memorandum on the July Crisis that Erzberger had asserted on 7 July that he intended to bring down Bethmann; *IFA*, I, 76.

[76] What Erzberger saw in Bülow is at this remove impossible to say. It is hard not to feel, as Ritter (*Staatskunst*, III, 510) implies, that Erzberger was simply taken in by the old fraud.

[77] "Notizen," 7 July 1917, "HB"; Braun, *Von Ostpreussen*, 113, entry of 9 July 1917.

it to at the time is unfortunately unknown. Neither he nor Beth-mann expected it. They were much aggrieved, especially Beth-mann, when their expectations were deceived.[78]

Bethmann moved at once to restore his weakened position. On the afternoon of the 6th he questioned Erzberger about the pur-pose of his speech and received the above-mentioned assurance that he had only intended to rally a moderate majority behind the Chancellor. Although the two parted amicably, it is doubtful that Bethmann found such assurances very convincing. Confer-ences with other party leaders the same evening made clear the need for immediate action on electoral reform in Prussia. The Majority Socialists reiterated the demand that the government agree to the formula "peace without annexations," threatening to vote against new war credits if the government did not. The fol-lowing morning in the Main Committee, Bethmann made his last parliamentary address. It did little to reduce the "indescribable tension," however, because he could promise nothing definite on war aims or Prussian electoral reform.[79] He did state that the government had never departed from the defensive war policy of 4 August 1914, but he refused to make such a declaration in the Reichstag lest it be taken abroad as a sign of weakness. Helf-ferich also addressed the committee, delivering what Conrad Haussmann, a Progressive deputy, mistakenly supposed was his "swan song."[80]

Bethmann had also acted immediately to secure the Kaiser's support, summoning him back from a visit in Vienna. When Wil-liam arrived in Berlin on the morning of the 7th, Bethmann told him that, though the situation was "extremely serious," he still hoped to master it.[81] William was therefore rather puzzled when

[78] *Weltkrieg*, III, 114. Bethmann also attributed the attack to Austrian in-fluences; *Betrachtungen*, II, 224-25. See also material cited n.59 above.

[79] Braun, *Von Ostpreussen*, 111-12, entry of 7 July 1917. For one Socialist's reaction, see David's scornful remarks; *Kriegstagebuch*, 241, entry of 7 July 1917.

[80] Hanssen, *Dying Empire*, 212-14; Haussmann, *Schlaglichter*, 103.

[81] *Prozess*, 731. For William to have arrived so quickly, Bethmann must have summoned him very soon after Erzberger spoke. That would seem to show that he judged the situation to be as serious as it in fact was, and was not so lacking in "political instinct" as Epstein (*Erzberger*, 193) alleges. Although Bauer and Stresemann later stated that Bethmann painted William

Hindenburg and Ludendorff arrived unbidden in Berlin later in the day. Exasperated by this latest attempt to meddle in political matters that lay within the Imperial prerogative, William summarily ordered the generals to return to their post. The abashed generals, who had thought that Bethmann was finished, departed in confusion. Helfferich considered this latest attempt to interfere in civilian affairs intolerable. He told von Braun, who was his principal sounding board during the July Crisis, that he was going to insist on a "clarification" of civil-military relations. "Things cannot go on as they are," he asserted. The following day, Helfferich thought it "not impossible" that Bethmann might survive the crisis. Discussing the possibilities with von Braun, Helfferich estimated that Bethmann would "immediately" command a large majority if he could declare his adherence to the formula "peace without annexations" and if he could persuade the Prussian Ministry to accept the Reichstag electoral law and to allow Reichstag deputies to enter the Reich and Prussian governments. Helfferich may have underestimated the amount of parliamentary feeling against Bethmann and himself, but had Bethmann been able to follow the course which Helfferich proposed within the next two days, it is possible that he might have survived. Helfferich was dubious about whether he could represent such a program in the Reichstag, since "he had previously represented nothing like it." For the moment, it apparently escaped him that he had once been an opponent of unrestricted submarine warfare but was now representing that very policy in the Reichstag. If the analogy struck von Braun, he tactfully kept it to himself. But he did say that if Bethmann remained in office without Helfferich, his doing so would be universally interpreted as "clinging to office," and another crisis would develop within three months.[82]

On 9 July, a Crown Council met to discuss the crucial question of electoral reform.[83] Bethmann began with a long exposition of

---

a rosy picture of the situation, William must have realized that things were seriously amiss from having been summoned; *IFA*, I, 75-81.

[82] Braun, *Von Ostpreussen*, 111-13, entries of 7 and 8 July 1917; the reverse also turned out to be true.

[83] *Kronrat* Protocol, 9 July 1917, "Preussen" 11, 3169/1613/675071-112; *Weltkrieg*, III, 118-19. Bethmann had threatened the Prussian Ministry on

the problem, mainly for William's benefit. Helfferich then discussed the general situation, emphasizing that, while the people had the strength to hold out until victory, the internal disturbances created by the insufficient food supply and the question of electoral reform were sapping its will to do so. The morale of the Reichstag was bad. He had never been willing to concede to the Reichstag the right to pressure the Crown and had always fought such tendencies "with success," but the Reichstag was undeniably the "barometer of the political mood." Therefore, since nothing could be done to alleviate the food situation, it was essential to promise immediately to introduce the Reichstag suffrage. It was not necessary to bring in the actual bill at once, but for maximum political effect the promise should be published. He warned against offering a plural-vote law. It was politically impossible, and in any case a plural-vote law had "no decisive advantages" over the Reichstag law with a one-year residence requirement. When Loebell denied that the effects of a plural-vote law would hardly differ from those of the Reichstag law, Helfferich made no attempt to refute him, merely saying: "If [you] had experienced what I have during the last weeks in the Reichstag, then perhaps you too might think differently." But the outcome of the council was disappointing. The Ministry voted six to five in favor of the Reichstag law, and the Kaiser withheld his decision. He wished, he said, to consult the Crown Prince. Even so equivocal a stand, however, when combined with William's tentative agreement to a modified version of the Peace Resolution (discussed more fully below), meant that Bethmann had come a long way toward neutralizing conservative forces around the Kaiser that had prevented earlier progress toward reform.

Despite the fact that he had been originally summoned by the anti-Bethmann frondeurs, the Crown Prince, on arriving in Berlin on 11 July, proved surprisingly receptive to his father's arguments in favor of the Reichstag suffrage. He also agreed that Bethmann's resignation, which the Chancellor had in the mean-

---

the 8th with resignation if it failed to agree immediately to the Reichstag suffrage; Westarp, *Konservative Politik*, II, 351. For the impact on William of Austrian support of Bethmann, see Ritter, *Staatskunst*, III, 575.

time proffered, be refused.[84] The decision to introduce the Reichstag suffrage into Prussia was announced at a Crown Council held later in the day, and William signed the necessary Imperial Proclamation that evening. Since most of the Prussian ministers had refused to accept responsibility for the measure contemplated, they collectively placed their offices at Bethmann's disposal. The way was open for the appointment of Reichstag deputies to the Prussian Ministry, and Bethmann at last had some solid accomplishments toward domestic political reform to show the parties.

Unfortunately, however, events had already moved beyond the point where Bethmann's triumphs could help him much. Led by Stresemann and Erzberger, the parties were taking an increasingly hostile line toward the Chancellor. Colonel Bauer, acting for the Supreme Command in Berlin, was making an all-out effort to dislodge him. Bauer gave Stresemann to understand on the 11th that Hindenburg and Ludendorff meant to resign if Bethmann did not.[85] The same day, Bauer also arranged interviews for the Crown Prince with members of the various parties. Bauer took great care that those who were to appear were either hostile to Bethmann or, in the case of the Left parties, not active supporters of his.[86] Although the Kaiser and the Crown Prince had agreed earlier that Bethmann was to be retained, the interviews, scheduled for the following day, could have no purpose unless the fate of the Chancellor was once again in the balance. William may have agreed to the interviews in order to rid himself of the responsibility for Bethmann's fate.[87]

Helfferich was less inclined than the Kaiser to abandon the struggle. (Von Braun noted that he was "in a fighting mood such as I have never seen him in before.")[88] During the evening of the 11th, Helfferich, Roedern, and Wahnschaffe held their own inter-

---

[84] Valentini had just spoken to the impressionable Crown Prince at length on the need for these measures; Schwertfeger, *Valentini*, 162-63; Paul Herre, *Kronprinz Wilhelm: seine Rolle in der deutschen Politik* (Munich, 1954), 86-88. But see also Patemann, *Wahlreform*, 93n1.

[85] Bethmann thought Bauer was acting on his own; *Betrachtungen*, II, 232-33. See, however, *IFA*, I, 62n4.

[86] *IFA*, 56n28.   [87] Herre, *Kronprinz*, 88.

[88] Braun, *Von Ostpreussen*, 114, entry of 11 July 1917.

225

views with the leaders of the majority parties.[89] Helfferich made only a few "resigned objections" of a tactical nature to the peace resolution which the parties had in the meantime drafted to express their desire for a "peace without annexations." He also promised political concessions going far beyond those which he had contemplated only three days before. In addition to the introduction of the Reichstag suffrage in Prussia and the appointment of Reichstag deputies to the Reich and Prussian governments, he held out the prospect of more deputies for the underrepresented city districts, the division of Interior into several offices, and the formation of an advisory council which would discuss all important administrative and legislative measures. The council was to consist of five Reichstag deputies, five members of the Bundesrat, and five Staatssekretäre and was to sit under the chairmanship of the Chancellor. Because Helfferich refused to abandon Article Nine of the Reich Constitution, which forbade a Reichstag deputy's sitting on the Bundesrat, the council could hardly be considered a parliamentary cabinet, although Reichstag deputies and former deputies (some of the Staatssekretäre and Prussian ministers who sat on the Bundesrat) would probably form a majority. But as rapidly as political developments were progressing, it was reasonable to expect that Article Nine would not long survive, and the council might well have been a useful bridge between the existing system and true parliamentary government. Although Helfferich also requested that no attempt be made to have a Socialist appointed to the new office responsible for administering the social welfare legislation, this program would have represented an important advance toward democratization.[90]

Conrad Haussmann, who, along with Friedrich von Payer, represented the Progressive Party, thought Helfferich expected that he and Bethmann would survive. That was true, for early the following morning, Helfferich told von Braun that he thought Bethmann's chances were good "unless he [Bethmann] is thrown

[89] *IFA*, I, 45-46.

[90] This scheme, or some variant of it, had been under discussion within the ministries since before 30 June; David, *Kriegstagebuch*, 238, entry of 30 June 1917.

out by the Reichstag."[91] The events of the day (12 July) proved Helfferich unduly hopeful, although the end did not come exactly as he had anticipated.

The same morning, Helfferich, Roedern, and Wahnschaffe made one last effort on Bethmann's behalf, attempting to persuade the National Liberals not to attack the Chancellor in the Reichstag. They informed the party representatives, not altogether correctly, that the other parties had "reconciled themselves" to Bethmann's remaining. Then Stresemann sprang his mine. He asked if Bethmann were prepared to remain in office if the consequence were that the Supreme Command resigned. "Helfferich got terribly excited, pounded on the table with his fist, and said that spreading rumors of that kind was absolutely unheard of," Stresemann later recalled. Helfferich announced that he intended to go straight to Bethmann, and they would telegraph Ludendorff demanding to know if he had made any such statement. Stresemann defended his position heatedly, which prompted Helfferich to apologize for his remarks "several times." He assured Stresemann that his remarks were not directed at him personally. Shortly thereafter, Helfferich departed, and later still Stresemann set out for the General Staff building. According to Stresemann's account, as soon as "they," probably meaning Bauer, heard his report of the meeting, they telephoned his news to the Supreme Command.[92]

It may be, however, that Erzberger had already given the decisive turn to events. During the meetings between the Crown Prince and the party representatives on the morning of the 12th, Erzberger delivered a hostile verdict against Bethmann. According to Bauer's account—he had been discreetly taking notes in the next room—it was all the Crown Prince needed to know. The Crown Prince had too low an opinion of the Reichstag to have taken its views very seriously, but with the Center now aligned with the National Liberals and Conservatives, he could point to a Reichstag majority against Bethmann. The meetings with the

[91] Braun, *Von Ostpreussen*, 114-15, entry of 12 July 1917. Solf agreed that Bethmann might well survive; Solf to wife, 12 July 1917, Solf "Nachlass."
[92] *IFA*, I, 79-80; Schiffer, *Ein Leben*, 196. According to Schiffer, the generals' answer to Helfferich was such that "nothing definite" could be made of it.

deputies were little more than a formality, but then, the Crown Prince and Bauer were merely looking for confirmation of their prejudices. After the meetings, the Crown Prince informed his father of the outcome and said that the Chancellor would have to resign. For his part, Bauer telegraphed Ludendorff about Erzberger's stand against the Chancellor, which Bauer later said "turned the scale" against Bethmann.[93]

Unaware of these last developments, Helfferich still supposed that it might be possible to humble the Supreme Command. The lengths to which the generals were going were, in fact, scandalous, and Helfferich's sense of outrage was fully justified. He told his luncheon companions (Zimmermann, Ballin, Arndt von Holtzendorff, and Admiral von Müller) that in his opinion the Kaiser ought to summon Ludendorff and tell the general that he, William, did not believe a word about the "goings-on" in which Ludendorff was "supposedly" engaged.[94] Furthermore, so far as he was concerned, the entire affair had never happened. Helfferich felt that such an action on William's part would greatly strengthen Bethmann's position, since any further actions against Bethmann by the Supreme Command would constitute a kind of lèse majesté. It is certainly doubtful whether William was man enough to act on this proposal, but, by the time Helfferich suggested it, events had rendered it obsolete.

During the evening, the Kaiser received telegrams from Hindenburg and Ludendorff containing their resignations. The telegrams arrived during a conference between Bethmann, the Kaiser, the Crown Prince, and others, which Helfferich did not attend. Bethmann offered to resign, but it was decided instead to summon the generals to Berlin before making the final decision. After the conference, Helfferich talked to Bethmann about the latter's future. By this time, Helfferich too was ready to give up the struggle. He strengthened Bethmann in his determination

[93] Herre, *Kronprinz*, 88-92; Bauer, *Der grosse Krieg*, 141. The Supreme Command had let it be known as early as the 12th that they intended to resign if Bethmann remained. The events of the day probably at most confirmed in their minds the soundness of their tentative decision.

[94] Görlitz, *Müller*, 302-303, entry of 12 July; "Notizen," 13 July 1917, "HB."

to resign, because he felt that "further collaboration [with the Supreme Command] was in fact impossible."[95] On the morning of 13 July, Bethmann once again offered his resignation, and this time it was accepted. Bethmann may have shown want of "political flair" in the way he resigned; the impression, however, is not so much of political ineptitude as of deep discouragement and exhaustion.[96] Later in the day, Bethmann commented to Admiral von Müller that he felt as if a "great weight had been lifted from his mind."[97] Bethmann, who had served his country as Chancellor almost eight years to the day, deserved better of it than he received. He was dismissed at the wrong time and certainly for the wrong reasons.

In the meanwhile, Helfferich continued the negotiations over the Peace Resolution, first discussing it with Hindenburg, Ludendorff, and Wahnschaffe, and then drawing in the leaders of the conservative parties. All agreed that the resolution as it stood would create a "ruinous impression" abroad and therefore had to be altered or, if possible, completely suppressed. Helfferich and the generals hoped that the latter might be possible. Ernst von Heydebrand and Count Westarp, the leaders of the Conservatives, thereupon suggested that the government's chances of suppressing the resolution would be far better if they said they would dissolve the Reichstag and call an immediate election if the Majority Socialists refused to vote new war credits. Helfferich and Wahnschaffe would not hear of it, pointing out the disastrous effects a Socialist refusal to vote credits would have both at home and abroad. Ludendorff also objected to elections because of their bad effect on the unity of the Army. According to Westarp, the idea of governing without the Reichstag was not "seriously" considered.[98]

A series of discussions with the leaders of the majority parties followed. Hindenburg and Ludendorff did most of the talking for the government side, while Helfferich and Wahnschaffe looked

[95] *Weltkrieg*, III, 128-29.
[96] "Flair," Epstein, *Erzberger*, 200; Schwertfeger, *Valentini*, 164.
[97] Görlitz, *Müller*, 303, entry of 13 July 1917.
[98] Westarp, *Konservative Politik*, II, 468; *Weltkrieg*, III, 130.

on like "a pair of fretful tanners."[99] The generals were apparently very charming, but neither their cordiality nor their summary of the military situation was able to dissuade the deputies of the need for the Peace Resolution. Indeed, Payer and Scheidemann, who Helfferich thought spoke "impressively," soon convinced the generals that the resolution was necessary if rioting, strikes, and other internal disturbances were to be averted. Hindenburg accordingly shifted his attack toward obtaining a more "positive" phrasing of the resolution; he wanted "a little more pepper," he said, in order that the resolution would not be construed as a sign of weakness abroad. After it had been agreed to continue the talks on the next day, the discussions ended. Helfferich thought that this meant that there would be more discussion of the text of the resolution, although Scheidemann stated as he was leaving: "There is nothing more to discuss about the resolution."

Helfferich first learned of the appointment of Georg Michaelis to the Chancellorship from Hindenburg during the afternoon meetings and met the new Chancellor that evening at a reception at Bethmann's. The reception followed a farewell dinner which Bethmann had given for his closest associates, Helfferich, Wahnschaffe, and Count Zech. Judging by the reception Michaelis received, his appointment must have been the subject of much indignant comment at dinner. Valentini, who introduced Michaelis, said that Bethmann was "frightfully excited," but managed to preserve the amenities, which the others did not.[100] Helfferich later wrote that he found Michaelis's appointment "incomprehensible," and told Valentini so most emphatically. He asked Valentini to convey his resignation to the Kaiser and predicted that Michaelis would not last until Christmas.[101] Valentini drily described the evening as "unpleasant." But the tension eased, and Bethmann and Michaelis actually joined forces to persuade Helf-

---

[99] Scheidemann, *Zusammenbruch*, 92-93, and *Memoiren eines Sozialdemokraten* (2 vols., Dresden, 1928), II, 39-40 (in both the meeting is incorrectly dated 14 July); Haussmann, *Schlaglichter*, 127; Payer, *Erinnerungen*, 36-37.

[100] Schwertfeger, *Valentini*, 169-70.

[101] *Weltkrieg*, III, 131-32; Georg Michaelis, *Für Staat und Volk: eine Lebensgeschichte* (Berlin, 1932), 325.

ferich to remain in office until his successor could be chosen and Michaelis was more familiar with his new duties.[102]

The circumstances of Michaelis's appointment are obscure to this day. Bethmann's own choice of successor was Count Hertling, Minister-President of Bavaria, but the latter refused on grounds of advanced age and poor health. None of the civilian chiefs was consulted about the appointment of Michaelis, who was discovered by the soldiers and von Braun.[103] Michaelis was a career civil servant who at the time of his appointment was Food Commissar for Prussia. Here he had called attention to himself in a small way by his direct and forceful manner, which appealed to the soldiers. He was a good enough administrator, but he was totally innocent of political experience. He had never dealt with the Reichstag and knew nothing of foreign affairs, deficiencies which rendered him wholly unsuited to his post.

During the night, Helfferich discovered that Wolffs Telegraphen Büro, the principal news agency, had already received the text of the Peace Resolution. Much frantic telephoning followed, and, although Helfferich successfully prevented the resolution from appearing in other papers, *Vorwärts* ran the text in its morning edition. The paper had acted on Scheidemann's authority, and, as he had intended, his action produced a *fait accompli*. The other majority leaders were rather displeased with Scheidemann's action, as it hardly squared with the previous afternoon's agreement to continue discussion of the resolution. It was agreed, however, that major alterations in the text of the resolution were now impossible. Learning of this before the meetings of the 14th, Michaelis decided to undercut the resolution in another way: he would make a declaration in the Reichstag which would render the resolution "superfluous."[104]

The participants in the late afternoon meeting of 14 July in

[102] According to Zech, Bethmann "determined" Helfferich to remain in office, but it is possible that he did so later and not on the 13th; Walther Rathenau, *Briefe* (2 vols., Dresden, 1927), I, 307.

[103] Braun, *Von Ostpreussen*, 113-16, entries from 10 to 14 July 1917; Görlitz, *Müller*, 304; Schwertfeger, *Valentini*, 168-69; Ritter, *Staatskunst*, III, 583.

[104] *Weltkrieg*, III, 132; Scheidemann, *Zusammenbruch*, 95-96; IFA, I, 84-87.

Helfferich's garden presented "a historic picture . . . : Hindenburg, as if cast in iron, Ludendorff, Michaelis, Helfferich, Erzberger [and other majority representatives]. . . . Hindenburg and Scheidemann shake hands."[105] The externals of the meeting resembled those of the day before. Hindenburg continued to charm the deputies, while Helfferich remained for the most part in the background. Michaelis lost no time in revealing his political naïveté. "Until now I have only run along beside the wagon of high policy like the average man," he said, "and have attempted to keep current like any other newspaper reader."[106] He then developed his arguments in favor of a statement in the Reichstag which would take the place of the Peace Resolution. Of all the deputies present, only Erzberger was even conditionally willing to accept the new Chancellor's proposal. The "supple" Helfferich then suggested a compromise of sorts whereby the deputies agreed to admit minor changes in the text of the resolution which did not affect its basic meaning, while, on his side, Michaelis agreed to make a prearranged statement on 19 July declaring his acceptance of the resolution.[107] A similar meeting on 15 July with the leaders of the minority parties served mainly to familiarize them with what had transpired between the government and the majority parties the day before.[108]

During the days that followed, Michaelis conferred on several occasions with the majority leaders on his forthcoming speech. When the day for delivery of the speech arrived, all outstanding details had supposedly been settled. Nevertheless, when Michaelis spoke, on the 19th, he stated that he agreed with the resolution "as I interpret it." With this addition, he hoped to make the Peace Resolution compatible with whatever annexations German arms might secure.[109] The phrase "as I interpret it," certainly the

[105] Braun, *Von Ostpreussen*, 117, entry of 14 July 1917.

[106] See *IFA*, I, 99-100, for the devastating effect of this utterance on the deputies. See also Payer, *Erinnerungen*, 40-41.

[107] David, *Kriegstagebuch*, 246, entry of 14 July 1917.

[108] Westarp, *Konservative Politik*, II, 469-70.

[109] Michaelis said later that he strayed "unintentionally" from the text; Michaelis, *Für Staat*, 328-29. Contemporary evidence reveals beyond much doubt, however, that Michaelis meant to weaken the resolution and make it thus acceptable to the parties of the Right and the *Heeresverwaltung*;

most notorious of Michaelis's many notorious utterances, was another evidence of the Chancellor's political ineptitude. None of the parties was likely to stick at verbal niceties if annexations actually became possible, as the treaties of Brest-Litovsk and Bucharest later revealed.[110] It was therefore folly for Michaelis to open himself needlessly to the charge of bad faith, conduct of which he was in fact guilty. Before the speech, Helfferich thought that the only way to avoid a "catastrophe" was for Michaelis "to discuss war aims in a way that corresponds approximately to the resolution." He believed that, if this were done, a general political debate might be avoided, war credits speedily voted, "and the impression created abroad that the Reichstag stands united behind the Chancellor."[111] Since the parties were willing to "swallow" Michaelis's fatal insertion at the time, Helfferich's hopes were largely fulfilled.[112] But, assisted by the Conservative press, the majority leaders were not long in discovering that they had been duped. Michaelis was a ruined man before his chancellorship was a month old.

The day following Michaelis's speech, Helfferich gave another of his political soirées. A last-minute inspiration, the party was for the praiseworthy purpose of acquainting the Kaiser with the leading deputies of the majority parties.[113] Helfferich, very loyal to the Kaiser, probably hoped that his monarch would score a social triumph such as Hindenburg and Ludendorff had done less than a week before. Unfortunately, the scheme failed in the execution. The Kaiser made a real effort to put his best foot forward, showing a sincere and flattering interest in the personal affairs of several of the deputies. The Socialist Friedrich Ebert

Lerchenfeld to Sigmund Ritter und Edler von Lössl, Bavarian Staatsrat, "Bericht" 579, 18 July 1917, GStA, "PA."

[110] The day before Michaelis's speech, Scheidemann emphasized that the Majority Socialists were not against annexations, they were only against prolonging the war to secure them; Braun, *Von Ostpreussen*, 118, entry of 18 July 1917.

[111] "Bericht" 680, 16 July 1917, "HB."

[112] David, *Kriegstagebuch*, 249, entry of 19 July 1917. Rathenau, however, writing to Gustav Steinbömer on 26 July, noted that the deputies were already annoyed about the insertion; *Politische Briefe*, 156.

[113] Braun, *Von Ostpreussen*, 119-20, entry of 20 July 1917.

was the most notable recipient of Imperial attentions, a circumstance beyond the realm of possibility before the war. The Kaiser's briefing apparently did not go beyond personalia, however, for his utterances on the political situation were disastrous. Referring to the recent German successes in Galicia, he said, "Where my guards appear, there is no room for democracy."[114] According to Erzberger, William was also so indiscreet as to say that Helfferich's insertion of the word *Ausgleich* (compensation) in Michaelis's speech of the day before made it compatible with annexations. He even suggested one or two such possibilities.[115] Many of William's hearers could hardly regard such statements as anything but deliberate insults, although they were doubtless prompted more by frivolous thoughtlessness than by malice. Almost worse than such remarks was the way William monopolized the discussion, if indeed what was essentially a monologue deserves to be called a discussion. It was a poor way to establish contact with the deputies, and that was the purpose of the gathering. Helfferich later thought his idea a mistake, but whether the onus for failure should fall on him for inadequately briefing the Kaiser or on the latter's personal shortcomings is not clear. William himself thought the evening a "great success," and the affair doubtless reinforced his high regard for Helfferich.

In the meantime, the problem of Helfferich's future employment had been solved, although, as soon became apparent, only temporarily. While Helfferich had agreed on 13 July to remain in office until his successor had been chosen, he properly submitted his written resignation the next day.[116] His first ground for resigning was that, since the Interior Office was to be divided, his departure would provide Michaelis with an "open road" to do what he wished. Second, he thought that Michaelis would burden

[114] As translated in Hans W. Gatzke, *Germany's Drive to the West (Drang nach Westen): A Study of Germany's Western War Aims During the First World War* (Baltimore, 1950), 202.

[115] Erzberger later said that the Kaiser's statement was what convinced him that Helfferich had to be driven from office at all costs; *Prozess*, 71-72. During this soirée at least one deputy began to have some inkling of Bethmann's problems; David, *Kriegstagebuch*, 249, entry of 20 July 1917.

[116] *Weltkrieg*, III, 155-56; Braun, *Von Ostpreussen*, 116, entry of 14 July 1917.

himself unnecessarily by keeping someone in his government who had been through "thick and thin" with Bethmann and was in any case unpopular with the majority parties. It would hardly be going too far to say that Helfferich's incumbency was one of the aspects of the Bethmann government to which the majority parties objected most. Helfferich was not the only one to whom that consideration occurred. Furthermore, Arndt von Holtzendorff believed that the personalities of Helfferich and Michaelis were too different to permit fruitful cooperation.[117] Michaelis had a reputation for being unreceptive to advice, and there was little point in Helfferich's remaining in the government if he was not to give the new Chancellor the benefit of his experience. Nor was Helfferich a man who would refrain very gladly from giving advice or take it in good part if it were not followed. There were excellent reasons for Helfferich to resign.

Nevertheless, the Kaiser refused to accept his resignation, and Michaelis once again asked him to stay on. Helfferich's position became even more solid when on 16 July the Supreme Command asked that past differences be forgotten and that they work together in the future. Although Admiral von Müller accepted Helfferich's gratified report that hostilities were over with a cynical "until next time," the rapprochement proved to be a lasting one.[118] Since several witnesses testify that the generals continued well on into July to regard Helfferich as the "evil genius" of the Bethmann government, their change of opinion is at first glance surprising.[119] The clue is perhaps Hindenburg's rueful comment to Helfferich: "Now I understand what you meant when you said, 'Better in the trenches than here in Berlin.' "[120] The Supreme Command's personal dealings with the deputies

[117] "Bericht" 679, 15 July 1917, "HB."

[118] Görlitz, *Müller*, 307, entry of 17 July 1917; Kurt von Raumer, "Helfferich," in Kurt von Raumer and Kurt Baumann (eds.), *Deutscher Westen—Deutsches Reich: Bd. I: Saarpfälzische Lebensbilder* (Kaiserslautern, 1938), 212-13.

[119] On the hostility of the Supreme Command toward Helfferich during the crisis, see, among others, Max von Baden, *Erinnerungen und Dokumente* (Stuttgart, 1927), 109.

[120] Haussmann, *Schlaglichter*, 140.

235

during the crisis had created a new sympathy for the difficulties which the civilian leaders faced. Once such sympathy had been aroused, Helfferich's clear, forceful manner and obvious ability probably did the rest.

Michaelis first considered appointing Helfferich as Zimmermann's successor in the Foreign Office and offered him the post on 16 July.[121] Although he perhaps thought that Helfferich's knowledge of foreign affairs would supplement his own considerable shortcomings, other considerations seem to have been uppermost in his mind. He thought Helfferich the ideal man to form a commission within the Foreign Office for the preparation of peace terms and also believed that as an outsider Helfferich was the ideal person to rid the office of its *Nulpen*, the nonentities with which it was supposedly infested.[122] William confidently assured Admiral von Müller that Helfferich would accept the position, and the latter was greatly tempted.[123] But there were good reasons for refusing. Erzberger, who heard of the appointment on the day it was tendered, wrote indignantly to Colonel Bauer that for Helfferich to hold three offices in two and a half years was a sign of the "jitters" and a "public confession of the dearth of able men."[124] His other arguments against Helfferich were more convincing. First, he said that Helfferich "enjoyed no sympathy or authority whatsoever in the Reichstag," and, second, he said that Helfferich's previous utterances had disqualified him from negotiating with either the English or the Russians at the peace table. At another of Bethmann's farewell dinners, Zimmermann reported that several deputies had asked him to remain in office "to prevent Helfferich from coming."[125] And as von Braun predicted, the press raised a great cry against the appointment as soon as they got wind of it. By 18 July, Lerchenfeld was able to report to Munich that because of hostile press opinion there

---

[121] Braun, *Von Ostpreussen*, 117-18, entry of 15 July 1917; *Weltkrieg*, III, 156-57.

[122] *IFA*, I, 105.

[123] Görlitz, *Müller*, 306, entry of 16 July 1917.

[124] Erzberger to Bauer, 16 July 1917, Bauer "Nachlass"; Erzberger, *Erlebnisse*, 288.

[125] Görlitz, *Müller*, 307, entry of 17 July 1917.

was little likelihood that Helfferich would accept the appointment, and on the following day Helfferich told von Braun that he was "determined" not to take the post.[126]

After strengthening Helfferich in his decision to refuse the Foreign Office, von Braun suggested that he would make the perfect ambassador to Constantinople. "I would accept that at once and go there gladly," was Helfferich's reply. There was much to be said for this proposal, for, as von Braun said, Helfferich knew the Near East "like no other." Because neither the Kaiser nor Michaelis wished Helfferich to leave Berlin, however, to Helfferich's evident regret the idea was abandoned. Although Helfferich was determined not to return to his old post in the Treasury or to remain in his present office (as some suggested), it struck him that he might instead retain the Deputy Chancellorship and at the same time become a minister without portfolio in the Prussian Ministry.[127] He could then manage an *ad hoc* commission for the preparation of peace negotiations. His scheme upset an earlier plan to make Roedern Secretary of the Interior, since Roedern refused to accept the office unless it carried with it the Deputy Chancellorship. There was some delay in implementing Helfferich's idea because William departed on 21 July for two weeks on the eastern front, and the Chancellor left for south Germany and elsewhere; but on the day after William's return, 5 August, the preliminary arrangements were completed. The Interior Office, which Max Wallraf was to receive, was to lose many of its administrative functions to a new agency, the Reich Economic Office (Reichswirtschaftsamt), with its own Staatssekretär, Rudolf Schwander. In addition, the Secretary of the Interior was to lose his duties as "deputy of the Chancellor" to Helfferich, who was to become Vice-Chancellor. Until the Reichstag granted the necessary salary money in the fall session for the two new posts (Vice-Chancellor and Secretary of the Economic Office), Helfferich was to remain Secretary of the Interior, with Wallraf and Schwander serving under him as undersecre-

---

[126] Lerchenfeld to Lössl, "Bericht" 579, 18 July 1917, GStA, "PA"; Braun, *Von Ostpreussen*, 118-19, entry of 19 July 1917.

[127] *Ibid.*, 119, entry of 20 July 1917; "Bericht" 683, 19 July 1917, "HB."

taries. The vacancy in the Foreign Office was filled by the appointment of Richard von Kühlmann, at the time of his appointment ambassador to Constantinople.

Since Helfferich was easily the most unpopular man in the Reich government at the outbreak of the July Crisis, his survival was rather remarkable. The explanation seems to be that, as the crisis developed, the anti-Bethmann forces seized the initiative from the left-wing parties, which had originally begun the attack against the government. Had this not occurred, Helfferich would surely have fallen, because the Left was against him almost to a man. As it was, the anti-Bethmann forces concentrated their fire on the Chancellor and made no particular effort to dislodge Helfferich. Once Michaelis was appointed Chancellor, however, Helfferich became temporarily indispensable. Both Michaelis and the Supreme Command depended upon him for advice. When the Supreme Command came to appreciate something of the realities of the political situation in Berlin, his survival was virtually assured. Another of Helfferich's strengths was the regard in which he was held by the Kaiser. Yet like nearly everything else connected with the resolution of the July Crisis, the arrangements made for Helfferich's political future were fundamentally unsound. The Reichstag adjourned in July with the Peace Resolution majority feeling vaguely frustrated, aware that it had failed to achieve what it set out to, but unable to put its finger exactly on where its failure lay. But it suspected that it had been hoodwinked, with the predictable result that when its suspicions were confirmed,[128] it would vent its fury on Helfferich, the man whose continued presence in office symbolized the unsatisfactory outcome of the crisis and mocked its pretensions to political power.

[128] See, for example, the numerous evidences that the Left did not trust the government to carry through Prussian electoral reform in Patemann, *Wahlreform*, 97-102.

VII. THE INSIDER BECOMES
AN OUTSIDER

Chancellor Crisis Again

Except for his unpopularity in the Reichstag and in the press, Helfferich had to all appearances emerged from the July Crisis stronger than ever. Secure in the affections of the Kaiser and on good terms with the Supreme Command, he might logically have expected to wield great influence as mentor of the inexperienced Michaelis. The events soon gave the lie to such expectations. Yet since Helfferich's influence declined only very gradually, it is difficult, lacking precise evidence, to date the stages of its decline. Kühlmann's appointment as Foreign Secretary probably represents the point at which Helfferich's metamorphosis from an insider to an outsider began.[1] Kühlmann, a professional diplomat and a personality more congenial to Michaelis than Helfferich, soon replaced the latter as the Chancellor's principal adviser on foreign-policy questions. As Helfferich's relations with Kühlmann never went beyond a formal correctness, Kühlmann neither discussed matters with Helfferich informally as Zimmermann had nor did Helfferich feel free to offer his opinion in the old way.[2]

Moreover, not only the extent but also the character of Helfferich's influence changed. Helfferich had first established his right to be heard in foreign-policy questions through his disquisi-

---

[1] It may have begun even earlier; the usually well-informed Viktor Naumann, *Profile: 30 Porträt-Skizzen aus den Jahren des Weltkrieges nach persönlichen Begegnungen* (Munich and Leipzig, 1925), 59, 62, states that Wilhelm von Stumm was Michaelis's principal foreign-policy adviser before the appointment of Kühlmann; and Kühlmann and Stumm were closely related. See also Ritter, *Staatskunst*, IV, 45, and for Kühlmann's policies, 43-66.

[2] Helfferich later testified before the Untersuchungsausschuss on 19 Dec. 1921 that his knowledge of the day-to-day conduct of Germany's foreign affairs depended on his close personal relationship with Bethmann and Zimmermann. (He had started off with Zimmermann in the Foreign Office in 1901); "Untersuchungsausschuss," 2112H/1124/457523-24.

tion on the economic aspects of submarine warfare and had by degrees extended his influence to foreign-policy questions in which economic considerations were at best secondary. Now he once again confined himself—or was confined—to opinions on the economic aspects of such questions. His role in determining the response to the Papal Peace Note of 1 August 1917 strikingly illustrates how rapidly he was reverting to his original role of economic expert. The note, essentially a call to all belligerents for a peace without annexations and indemnities, represented the most important effort of the entire war to reach a negotiated peace.[3] As such, it was the subject of much discussion within the German government. Considering that Helfferich was Vice-Chancellor, he did not participate very much in these discussions. He seems to have taken part in only one of the preliminary conferences called to prepare for a Crown Council, in which the line to be taken toward the Pope, particularly on the troublesome question of Belgium, was to be determined. In the one such session that he did attend, a meeting of the Prussian Ministry on 4 September, he confined himself to a long review of past thinking on the sort of economic and political guarantees to be demanded of Belgium. On the following day, he actually began a vacation (his first of the war) at Ralswiek, the estate of his friend Count Angus Douglas on the isle of Rügen. From there, he submitted a memorandum (dated 7 September) detailing how German objectives in Belgium might be achieved if it proved necessary to promise a complete restoration of Belgian sovereignty.[4] He thus had to be hurriedly recalled when the Crown Council finally convened on 11 September. Although no formal record of these deliberations was kept, Helfferich later recalled that he had "not been asked to speak"; he was no longer the indispensable man of July.

Too much should not be made of the foregoing example. Helfferich had talked to Kühlmann and Michaelis before the meeting,

<hr>

[3] Steglich, *Friedenspolitik*, I, Ch. 3, provides an exhaustive account of the note. See also Gatzke, *Germany's Drive*, 219-32; Fischer, *Griff*, 539-54; Ritter, *Staatskunst*, IV, Ch. 1.

[4] Prussian Ministry Protocol, 4 Sept. 1917, "Preussen" 11, 3169/1613/-675237-65; Fischer, *Griff*, 545-47. For a fuller discussion of Helfferich's views on Belgian and other war-aims questions, see below, pp. 256-69.

and it may be that, as Michaelis later stated, he was merely being thoughtful in not wishing to interfere more in Helfferich's vacation when he seemed "so exhausted."[5] But there are other signs of his growing isolation. He became noticeably reserved in the meetings of the Prussian Ministry. Even on questions about which he had earlier shown a burning interest, such as the reform of the Prussian electoral law, he left most of the talking to others. Characteristically, the only occasions upon which he spoke with his old vigor were when the economic aspects of war-aims questions were under consideration.[6] By the end of September, Helfferich's isolation was so noticeable that Arndt von Holtzendorff reported to Ballin that there appeared to be three centers of power in the government; first, the "triumvirate" Kühlmann-Roedern-Solf; second, Michaelis, who acted as a kind of "middleman" between Berlin and the Supreme Command; and third, Helfferich, "who seems . . . to stand somewhat aloof."[7]

The Reichstag, however, continued to set as high an estimate on Helfferich's influence as ever. Eduard David, a right-wing Socialist, voiced the opinion of most Socialists of both factions when he said that Helfferich was the "evil genius" of the domestic policy and "very dangerous" in foreign policy. Even Helfferich's supporters, among whom Stresemann, Gothein, Payer, and Naumann were the most important, had given up trying to gloss over his Reichstag manners and merely insisted that he would be indispensable in the peace negotiations.[8] Before the Main Committee session of 22 August 1917, in which Michaelis gave a disastrous explanation of his phrase, "as I interpret it," Helfferich had

[5] Testimony of Helfferich and Michaelis, 19 Dec. 1921, "Untersuchungsausschuss," 2112H/1124/457529, 457536. Helfferich did not find out all of the important details about what happened in September after the Crown Council until 1919; ibid., 457533.

[6] Prussian Ministry Protocols, 7 and 16-17 Aug., 14 and 21 Sept., 3 and 27 Oct. 1917, "Preussen" 11, 3169/1613/675129-72, 675181-230, 675266-85. See also Prussian Ministry Protocol, 1 Oct. 1917, "Geheime Akten betreffend Innere Angelegenheiten: Elsass-Lothringen," Bd. 4, 3169/1613/675571-93, in which Helfferich spoke at length on the future of Alsace; Prussian Ministry Protocol, 4 Nov. 1917, "Weltkrieg 20 geheim: Die Zukunft der besetzen Gebiete Polens," Bd. 19, 3169/1613/675539-50.

[7] "Notizen," 27 Sept. 1917, "HB."

[8] IFA, I, 133-35. See also ibid., 130n12.

rather obtusely denied that he was unpopular. After the committee session, his and the Chancellor's unpopularity were all too apparent, and Helfferich began to fear an explosion in the fall Reichstag session.[9] Some sharp questioning in the Budget Committee on the 24th about Groener's recent dismissal and rumored changes in the Auxiliary Service Law undoubtedly heightened his fears.[10] On 20 September, about a week before the session, Helfferich told Holtzendorff that he was "completely clear" about the amount of ill-feeling against him. He feared that this hostility might be expressed as a refusal to vote the necessary moneys for his salary as Vice-Chancellor. He imagined that Erzberger was the leader of the intrigues against him, although Erzberger, possibly only maintaining party discipline, later regretfully voted in favor of money for his post.[11] Perhaps Helfferich was just imagining what he would have done in Erzberger's place; von Braun noted in his diary on 22 September that legal actions were being readied against Erzberger because of his alleged "betrayal of military secrets" and "tax evasion."[12] It is hard to believe that Helfferich had no part in these actions, neither of which came to anything. As it happened, Helfferich's fears that his post might be voted down proved unfounded, although the outcome remained in doubt on into the first week of October.[13]

Understandably enough, Helfferich was loath to accept the idea that this new demonstration of his unpopularity could in any way be attributed to his personal shortcomings. He alleged that every Interior Secretary was necessarily unpopular if he did his job. "One must tread on so many people's toes," he told Holtzendorff. He said that he had never attempted to pass the blame along to someone else, even when this was justified. He asserted that he was unaware that "he had ever been unfriendly or discourteous to the Reichstag," but he admitted that it was always

[9] "Berichte" 691 and 698, 16 and 23 Aug. 1917, "HB." See also David, *Kriegstagebuch*, 251, entry of 22 Aug. 1917.

[10] Feldman, *Army, Industry, and Labor*, 412-13.

[11] "Bericht" 718, 20 Sept. 1917, "HB." See also *IFA*, I, 342.

[12] Braun, *Von Ostpreussen*, 126-27, 144, entries of 20 and 22 Sept. 1917.

[13] Ballin and Stresemann did what they could behind the scenes; "Notizen," 24 Sept. 1917, "HB." See also "Notizen," 2 and 4 Oct. 1917, *ibid*.

his aim to be "very brief" and "objective." He did not intend "to put up with simply everything."[14]

On 6 October, Otto Landsberg of the Majority Socialists opened the day's debates in the Reichstag with a well-documented interpellation attacking the government's apparent connivance in spreading the propaganda of the Vaterlandspartei (Patriots' Party), an extreme annexationist organization founded expressly to combat the Peace Resolution of 19 July 1917.[15] Landsberg's catalog of abuses ranged from instances in which civil officials and Army officers had pressured subordinates into joining the Vaterlandspartei to the instructions of the Supreme Command for supposedly nonpartisan political briefings. At one point in the Army instructions, prospective speakers were advised to "compare the state with the body, which is not moved by the majority decision of the limbs, but by the single will of the head." The real issue was whether Michaelis intended to stand behind the Peace Resolution, and the evidence indicated that he did not. Landsberg concluded with an appeal to Michaelis to explain his views about the Vaterlandspartei.

General von Stein, the War Minister, spoke first for the government. He dismissed Landsberg's detailed case as a "few insignificant examples," but, letting the cat out of the bag, he admitted that the troops were being indoctrinated on the "consequences of a lost war"—or, in other words, on what war aims equaled victory. Stein's reply was frivolous and quite insufficient. The President of the Reichstag had to call the House to order no less than eight times during the general's short speech. Next, Helfferich spoke in behalf of the absent Michaelis. He later claimed that he had "leapt into the breach" because of the Chancellor's failure to appear.[16] That would explain why his speech was badly prepared

[14] "Notizen," 4 Oct. 1917, *ibid.*

[15] Landsberg spoke in support of two Socialist interpellations, "Interpellation . . . betreffend Agitation durch Vorgesetzten im Heere zugunsten alldeutscher Politik," and "Interpellation . . . betreffend Handhabung des Vereins- und Versammlungsrechts durch die stellvertretenden Generalkommandos"; *RTV*, Vol. 310, 6 Oct. 1917, 3714-23.

[16] *Ibid.*, 3723-25 (Stein); 3725-27 (Helfferich). There was later much dispute over whether Michaelis had been summoned and failed to appear, or

and virtually without content. He attempted to refute only one
of Landsberg's numerous detailed charges, and that with mis-
information, as Landsberg later established.[17] Yet, since Landsberg's interpellation, which was necessarily known to the government in advance, presented incidents that had already appeared
in detail in the *Berliner Tageblatt*, the deputies not unreasonably
expected a carefully prepared defense from the government.
Thus, although Helfferich's failure to present such a defense perhaps only indicated inexcusably poor coordination between
Michaelis and himself, it looked to the deputies as if Helfferich
did not consider them worth the trouble of a careful answer. The
remainder of Helfferich's speech strengthened this impression.
After berating the House for its bad manners, Helfferich replied
to Landsberg's request that Michaelis speak. He loftily informed
the house that the matters at hand hardly required the busy
Michaelis's presence: a great political debate was not on the
agenda, and "for what is on the agenda—I believe I dare make
such a claim—I am man enough . . . to give the [Chancellor's]
answer." His speech concluded with the following burst of
temper:

> Gentlemen, I believe that what I have said should reassure
> you—(Denial from the left.)
> Gentlemen, if you do not trust the men that stand at the head
> of the Reich government and the army administration to make
> good their word—(Shout from the left: "No!")—then there is
> no purpose in my speaking to you.

As it happened, this was to be Helfferich's last speech in the
Imperial Reichstag.

From this point on, the situation of the Michaelis government,
never good, rapidly worsened. The following day (7 October),
the Majority Socialists announced in the Interparty Committee
that the behavior of Helfferich and Stein had been "so provocative" that for either to remain in office was out of the question. So
poor an impression had Helfferich made that his former sup-

---

whether he had been advised to stay away. Helfferich claimed that he sent
twice for Michaelis; "Bericht" 742, 2 Nov. 1917, "HB."

[17] *RTV*, Vol. 310, 6 Oct. 1917, 3755.

porters abandoned him, and general agreement with the Socialists' verdict was expressed.[18] Speaking in the Main Committee on the 8th, Michaelis attempted to repair matters, without success. When the public debates recommenced on 9 October, tempers were hotter than ever. Wilhelm Dittmann of the Independent Socialists began with some remarks about the "spirit of Zabern" so blatantly expressed in the speeches of Helfferich and Stein. He went on to criticize the manner in which the Navy authorities had handled the recent "mutinous" disturbances at Kiel. Speaking after Dittmann, Michaelis made even less effort to maintain the proprieties than had Stein or Helfferich. The only part of the Chancellor's speech that anyone remembered later was his statement that, although he viewed with total objectivity all parties loyal to the state, "so far as I am concerned, the Independent Socialists stand on the other side of that line." Even more surprising things followed. In rebuttal to Dittmann, Admiral von Capelle, the Secretary of the Navy, accused three Independent Socialist deputies, Dittmann, Haase, and Vogtherr, of proven complicity in the Navy disturbances.[19] There was some substance to Capelle's charge, but not enough to support a prosecution of the deputies. Since Capelle knew that when he spoke (having been so advised by his legal experts), he was foolish to make such an outrageous charge in the Reichstag.[20] Michaelis later claimed that Capelle had departed from his prepared text.[21] After Capelle's statement, which Michaelis made no attempt to repudiate, it was only a question of the precise manner in which the bankrupt Michaelis government was to be liquidated.

Nevertheless, events developed more slowly than might have

[18] *IFA*, I, 216. Stein's speech was merely the last of a series of provocative acts, as far as the left-wing parties were concerned; Feldman, *Army, Industry, and Labor*, 413, 425-35.

[19] *RTV*, Vol. 310, 9 Oct. 1917, 3765-73 (Dittmann); 3773-75 (Michaelis and Capelle).

[20] Helfferich had earlier wished to take legal action against the Independent Socialists but could see no way to do so, "since the material [against them] is now weaker than before"; *UA*, x (1), 86. See, however, Feldman, *Army, Industry, and Labor*, 428.

[21] *IFA*, I, 321n5, 585-86. Although Michaelis was probably telling the truth, his attempt to dump the entire responsibility for the affair in Capelle's lap was not very creditable.

been expected, for the simple reason that the man with the power of ultimate decision, the Kaiser, was traveling in the Balkans. In discussing the situation with Conrad Haussmann on 12 October, Helfferich said that it was still not clear to Michaelis how serious the crisis was.[22] The Chancellor even talked of journeying to Courland in order to have some time to collect his thoughts. They agreed that Michaelis would have to resign, but Helfferich was less explicit about his own future. Thinking aloud, Helfferich said that he had often wondered whether he should not have insisted on resigning when Bethmann did. Haussmann answered that, had he done so, "everyone would be calling for you now, Parliament and Kaiser [alike]. . . ." Helfferich also agreed with Haussmann that the present relationship between the Kaiser and the Reichstag could not continue; indeed, it was in hopes of creating a better relationship that he had suggested the Kaiser's ill-fated meeting with the deputies of the previous July. They then discussed the possible replacements for Michaelis and finally concluded that there was no manifestly superior candidate. From this, Haussmann deduced that the only satisfactory solution would be for the new Chancellor to accept before assuming office a program and a cabinet agreeable to the Reichstag. This was the solution finally adopted, though the results can hardly have been what the Reichstag intended.

While Helfferich was talking to Haussmann, Albert Südekum, representing the Majority Socialists, was imparting some "home truths" to Michaelis. The latter's remarks, revealing a naïve optimism quite unjustified by the situation, are mainly of interest as the first indication that Michaelis meant to save himself by claiming that he was the indispensable man for carrying through the Prussian electoral reform. Südekum offered the Chancellor no encouragement in this or his other proposals and, when asked his opinion of Helfferich, said he thought that the question came "awfully late"; he could "hardly picture as salutory collaboration with Helfferich." He warned Michaelis that any attempt of the latter to save himself by jettisoning Helfferich and Capelle would scarcely "touch upon the essential question," namely, the resigna-

[22] *Ibid.*, 221-23.

tion of the Chancellor himself. The same evening, Michaelis had a similar conversation with the Center Party leader Karl Trimborn.[23] Shortly thereafter, nothing daunted, he departed on his planned trip to the east.

Helfferich had also heard rumors that, in order to remain Chancellor, Michaelis intended to sacrifice him to the Reichstag and had indeed already offered the Vice-Chancellorship to Friedrich von Payer, leader of the Progressive Party. When Helfferich put the matter to Payer directly, the latter scotched the rumor, but the fact that Helfferich thought the question worth asking is another indication of the poor relationship between Helfferich and Michaelis.[24] Helfferich evidently considered his isolation virtually complete; he told Holtzendorff on 18 October that he had had no warning of the content of Michaelis's disastrous speech. When the discussion with Holtzendorff turned to the question of Michaelis's successor, Helfferich said that he was against Kühlmann because of the difficulties that a Bavarian would encounter with the Prussian electoral reform. Since he had earlier expressed entirely different objections to Kühlmann, it is difficult to suppress the suspicion that his real objections, conscious or unconscious, were personal. Although Helfferich thought that Roedern's chances were good, his personal choice was Johann H. Bernstorff, then ambassador in Constantinople. This choice was "not wholly unselfish," he admitted, since Bernstorff's elevation would free the Constantinople embassy for himself. Perhaps he was not entirely serious, but Ballin saw in the statement evidence of "how quickly politics ruins the character."[25]

Although Helfferich's remarks indicated that he thought Michaelis's departure was settled, he changed his mind the very next day. After listing Helfferich's varying estimates of the political situation, Lerchenfeld added a postscript to a letter of 19 October in which Helfferich was reported to favor Michaelis's remaining long enough to attempt the Prussian electoral reform. Then if he failed, as Helfferich thought likely, he at least would not have fallen to the Socialists. Furthermore, after Michaelis's

---

[23] *Ibid.*, 224-26 (Südekum); 230-31 (Trimborn).   [24] *Ibid.*, 227n8.
[25] "Bericht" 728, 19 Oct. 1917; Ballin to Holtzendorff, 21 Oct. 1917, "HB."

failure, the government would have ample excuse for postponing electoral reform until after the war.[26]

After the Kaiser returned to Berlin on 21 October, the pace of events quickened. William was determined to retain Michaelis and Capelle in office, and the Interparty Committee was equally determined that they, and Helfferich, resign.[27] By this time, Helfferich's views on the situation had undergone further refinement. As he put it to Holtzendorff, the parties were really more at fault than the government in the Michaelis-Capelle fiasco, because instead of censuring the Independent Socialists, they had turned against the government.[28] The discussion then turned to what Helfferich characterized as "the unheard of" efforts of Bülow in behalf of his own candidacy and to rumors that Stresemann meant to carry the suit for Bülow directly to William himself. Helfferich thought that William ought to receive not only Stresemann but the leaders of all parties, hear them out, and then announce that he, the Kaiser, meant to choose the new Chancellor and that he thought that the parties had shown a lack of skill in the Michaelis matter that belied their political pretensions: "instead of pulling the car from the mud [you have] shoved it in even deeper." Otherwise, Helfferich's views differed little from those he had imparted to Lerchenfeld on the 19th.

When Helfferich took up the matter once again with Lerchenfeld on 25 October, he particularly emphasized the desirability of retaining Michaelis until the fate of the Prussian electoral reform was settled. If it was defeated, another crisis was inevitable within a month.[29] Lerchenfeld gently reminded him that such considerations were entirely irrelevant to the existing crisis. Lerchenfeld's appraisal was undoubtedly correct. Helfferich's sudden ardor for Michaelis is, in fact, a little difficult to explain. He may merely have been trying out an idea on Lerchenfeld

[26] Lerchenfeld to Hertling, 19 Oct. 1917, GStA, "Briefwechsel." See also Görlitz, Müller, 326, entry of 22 Oct. 1917.

[27] Ibid., entry of 21 Oct. 1917; IFA, I, 246-47, session of 22 October.

[28] "Bericht" 731, 22 Oct. 1917, "HB."

[29] Lerchenfeld to Hertling, 25 Oct. 1917, GStA, "Briefwechsel." Helfferich made similar statements to Admiral von Müller and Conrad Haussman; Görlitz, Müller, 327, entry of 25 Oct. 1917; IFA, I, 312-14, 317.

(and others) in which he did not have much confidence himself. Alternatively, he may genuinely have believed that it was still possible to save Michaelis as Chancellor, though it is hard to believe he was so naïve.

The day following Helfferich's conversation with Lerchenfeld, the Kaiser met with Helfferich and other trusted advisers to decide Michaelis's fate. By this time even Michaelis could see that it would be impossible for him to remain Chancellor. Shortly before the meeting, however, he hit upon the idea of turning the Chancellorship over to Hertling while retaining the Prussian Minister-Presidency himself. Because Michaelis was not invited, he asked Helfferich to present his proposal. Helfferich readily agreed. Hertling had earlier been his choice to succeed Bethmann, and Michaelis's proposal offered a means of freeing Hertling from the odium of the failure of Prussian electoral reform.[30] It may also have occurred to Helfferich that, with the historic unity of the Chancellorship and the Prussian Minister-Presidency divided, his own position as Vice-Chancellor would be relatively more important. Michaelis, on the other hand, doubtless hoped to revive his political fortunes by carrying out the electoral reform. At any rate, William fell in with the proposal, and Lerchenfeld therefore summoned Hertling to Berlin late on 26 October.

Although Hertling arrived in Berlin only on 28 October, he soon made known that he was willing to accept the now diminished Chancellorship. Evidently following Helfferich's suggestion, however, Hertling did inform William that he would not accept unless he could reach agreement with the parties on a program.[31] The principal obstacle to such agreement, Erzberger gave Hertling to understand that same evening, was the separation of the offices of Chancellor and Prussian Minister-President. On the following day in the Interparty Committee, it was generally agreed that the precedents for even a temporary separation of offices were overwhelmingly unfavorable and that in any case

[30] *Ibid.*, 322n4; *Weltkrieg*, III, 208-10. Hertling was evidently the choice of most people in the government, and he himself had overcome the objections to serving that he had had earlier; Naumann, *Profile*, 25-27.
[31] *Weltkrieg*, III, 211.

Michaelis's departure was a *sine qua non* for resolution of the crisis. Opinion also ran strongly against Hertling, and even more strongly against Helfferich.[32]

The latter's influence was believed to be more pernicious than it actually was. Less than a week before, a rumor had sprung up that Helfferich had promised the Kaiser he could split the existing majority when new credits were voted (in December), create a new majority, and drive the Socialists into opposition. When Conrad Haussmann, acting in the name of the Interparty Committee, questioned Helfferich about the rumor, the latter denied harboring any idea of the kind.[33] Now Erzberger saw in Helfferich the "evil genius" who had fathered the "separation [of offices] idea," and David asserted that Hertling would move toward the Right and "under Helfferich's influence dissolve the Left."[34] These statements reveal more about the fevered political atmosphere which two political crises in quick succession had created than they do about the state of Helfferich's intentions. Despite his poor relations with the Socialists in the Reichstag, he realized in his less excitable moments that they had to be held behind the government at almost any cost.

Further meetings between Hertling and the deputies on 29 and 30 October revealed that the parties would not permit the offices to be separated. Particularly disheartened by the poor reception that Stresemann had given him at the last of these meetings, Hertling told Helfferich at noon on the 30th that he saw his mission as "a failure." Helfferich pointed out that Stresemann favored Bülow for Chancellor, as did Erzberger, the only Center representative with whom Hertling had spoken. He asked that Hertling wait at least until Trimborn returned to speak officially for the Center Party before making his final decision. Hertling agreed.[35] Reporting to the Prussian Ministry later in the afternoon on the past days' events, Helfferich said that he considered it assured that the Center would back Hertling, but he was uncertain whether Hertling would swallow his objections to assum-

[32] *IFA*, I, 326-32, 334-58.
[33] *Ibid.*, 304-305, 308, 312-14, 317. In his conversation with Haussmann, Helfferich revealed that he had learned of a number of important events only recently, among them Südekum's visit to the Chancellor on 12 October.
[34] *Ibid.*, 341-44. [35] *Weltkrieg*, III, 214-15.

ing both offices.[36] For some reason, Hertling decided that evening that his weak constitution might after all sustain the burdens of both offices. Thus, when Trimborn told Hertling the next day that the separation of offices was impossible, he was preaching to a convert, and when he assured Hertling that the Center would back him, the issue was as good as decided. Hertling for his part agreed to the Interparty Committee's program, insisting only that his choice of associates be unrestricted.[37] The Michaelis crisis was over.

With Michaelis out, the great problem still unsolved was what to do with Helfferich. This turned out to be a much more worrisome problem than anyone anticipated. Both on 28 October, when Hertling first announced his willingness to accept the Chancellorship, and on the 31st, when he finally accepted it, Helfferich offered in writing to resign, but he did not actually submit a formal letter of resignation. According to Helfferich, Hertling told him on the latter occasion that there could be no question of his resigning. Moreover, the Kaiser let Helfferich know that Hertling was possible as Chancellor only if he remained Vice-Chancellor.[38] The parties, however, continuing to regard Helfferich with implacable hostility, demanded that the office of Vice-Chancellor be filled by a Progressive in order to prevent a "march to the right."[39] Hertling heard this demand without comment when informed of it by a delegation of majority representatives on 1 November. The following day, Helfferich reported to Holtzendorff a scheme whereby Roedern was to become Vice-President of the Prussian Ministry and he was to return to the Treasury Office. Since Helfferich conspicuously failed to mention who was to be Vice-Chancellor, it may be that Hertling was trying to conciliate the Kaiser (and Helfferich) by keeping Helfferich in the cabinet, while simultaneously opening the way for the appointment of a Progressive as Vice-Chancellor. But Helfferich would have none of it; he meant to leave, "first for a vacation, and then for the front."[40] That was evidently his firm

---

[36] *IFA*, I, 374-80.
[37] *Ibid.*, 385-86, 405, 476; *Weltkrieg*, III, 217.
[38] *Weltkrieg*, III, 211-14, 217-18.
[39] *IFA*, 385-426, and esp. 398, 411, sessions of 31 Oct. and 1 Nov. 1917.
[40] "Bericht" 742, 2 Nov. 1917, "HB."

intention at the time, for he told Erzberger the same day that he was resigning and leaving government service.[41] He still had not submitted a formal letter of resignation, but apparently anticipated that Hertling would soon ask for such a letter.

That afternoon, the Interparty Committee received with satisfaction Erzberger's apparently authoritative report of Helfferich's resignation. The following day, the truth was revealed. In the Interparty Committee, there was much indignation about Hertling's "passive resistance" in the Helfferich affair, and Eugen Schiffer and Paul von Krause, now members of the Reich government, were reported to say that it was "doubtful" whether Helfferich's resignation (which had been offered but not submitted) would be accepted. On the 4th, the committee once again dispatched Haussmann to discover from Helfferich himself just what the situation was. Helfferich professed, doubtless truthfully, to be in the dark about Hertling's intentions, but Haussmann noted that Helfferich "cherishes silent hopes of his indispensability for 'objective' reasons."[42] The following day, Helfferich told William that he did not wish to remain in the government, but that if he did stay, he insisted on remaining Vice-Chancellor, and with "undiminished authority."[43] On his side, Hertling told Erzberger and Stresemann that Helfferich would remain, at least temporarily, to run the government until he returned on 15 November from Munich. In the course of the conversation, Erzberger suggested that Helfferich be made the president of a "private commission for the discussion of economic questions connected with the peace." Hertling was quick to recognize the golden bridge which Erzberger had built him; he said that the proposal was "sympathetic" and would achieve the main purpose for which Helfferich was being retained. He suggested that the Reichstag create the necessary secretaryship.[44]

On 6 and 7 November, the "Helfferich question" was again much discussed in the Interparty Committee. Most criticized were the attempts being made to save Helfferich on "objective"

[41] *IFA*, I, 428-29. [42] *Ibid.*, 439, 454-55.
[43] *Weltkrieg*, III, 221; "Bericht" 745, 5 Nov. 1917, "HB"; Görlitz, *Müller*, 330, entry of 6 Nov. 1917.
[44] *IFA*, I, 478-79.

grounds, after everyone had conceded that his parliamentary personality was impossible. Kühlmann and Roedern, who only a few days before had been at best lukewarm supporters of Helfferich,[45] were in fact arguing that in the last days their colleague had shown "altogether extraordinary ability." That Helfferich had revealed these unsuspected talents in the discussions on eastern war aims over which he was then presiding was itself a source of indignation to the deputies, who were mightily incensed at his failure to consult them. As it was reluctantly agreed that "completely sawing off Helfferich" was perhaps impossible, the deputies readily fell in with the idea of making Helfferich "Secretary for the Occupied Areas." Erzberger pointed out that the salary for the post could be paid from war funds without a special appropriation. David ironically commented that "if possible" Helfferich's offices should be located not in Berlin but in Warsaw.

Immediately after the interparty discussions of the 7th, Haussmann informed Helfferich of the outcome. In so doing, he indirectly forced the solution of the "Helfferich question." The upshot of their conversation was that Helfferich went straight to Hertling to demand that his uncertain situation be clarified. This was obviously necessary and was the key to the whole Helfferich situation. Helfferich said that his personal wish was to resign. He apparently also made it clear, however, that he thought that parliamentarianism had gone far enough, and that it would be a mistake to give way to the parties in the "Helfferich question." Nevertheless, whatever the decision, it had to come soon. Helfferich said that not only was he tired of being portrayed "three times a day" in the press as a "tiresome *Kleber*" ("clinger"—to office), but that the continuing crisis was bound to diminish the authority of both the Crown and the Chancellor. Hertling agreed that things could not continue as they were and left both Helfferich and Valentini with the "impression" that he would remain "firm" in support of Helfferich. Hertling also instructed Roedern

[45] See, for example, the record of the Kühlmann-Erzberger conversation of 30 Oct. 1917, in which Kühlmann is reported to have characterized a program which included the dismissal of Helfferich as "excellent"; *ibid.*, 380-84. On the conferences of the 6th and 7th, see *ibid.*, 480-509, 517-45.

to tell the deputies who were to meet him that evening that the final decision would come the next day.[46]

What happened after Roedern's meeting with the deputies was the subject of contradictory reports. According to Helfferich, when Roedern saw Hertling after the meeting the latter informed him that Helfferich would remain in office. Valentini confirms this much of Helfferich's account but not what follows: Roedern then allegedly "urgently requested" Helfferich not to submit his resignation. On the basis of information of uncertain origin, Stresemann later claimed, however, that Kühlmann, Roedern, and Breitenbach joined forces to urge upon an exceedingly reluctant Helfferich his immediate resignation.[47] Helfferich is said to have resisted on the grounds that his resignation would signify the "surrender of the Crown" to parliamentary pretensions. Although Helfferich is usually a reliable witness, Stresemann's account cannot be dismissed. Not only had Roedern made virtually no effort to defend Helfferich in the meeting with the deputies, but Helfferich had earlier linked his remaining in office with the interests of the Crown and was to do so again: Stresemann's account rings true.

In the event, Hertling apparently had another of his overnight changes of heart (if change it really was). On the morning of 8 November, he asked Helfferich to submit his letter of resignation. Even then Admiral von Müller confidently assured Helfferich that the Kaiser would never accept it. Helfferich disagreed, "as mistaken as he considered the step, just at the very moment when the deputies were beginning to fear [the consequences of] their own hunger for power." He was correct. William tried to soften the blow by sending Helfferich "an unusually cordial handwritten letter" of appreciation for his services.[48] Since Helfferich refused to accept a lesser post in the cabinet, he found himself, for the first time since his student days, a man without a job.

Helfferich's downfall reveals much about the transitional con-

---

[46] *Weltkrieg*, III, 222-23; Schwertfeger, *Valentini*, 182; *IFA*, I, 546-48.

[47] *Weltkrieg*, III, 224; Schwertfeger, *Valentini*, 182; *IFA*, I, 550, 582 (Stresemann). The entire matter is most confusing. Roedern followed Hertling's instructions when he conferred with the deputies on the evening of 7 November; *ibid.*, 547-49.

[48] Görlitz, *Müller*, 331, entry of 8 Nov. 1917; *Weltkrieg*, III, 224-27.

stitutional character of the period. Helfferich may perhaps have been concealing his motives when he linked his remaining in office with the best interests of the Crown, but in the main he was undoubtedly sincere. His conception of office was bureaucratic. As long as he administered his office properly and retained the confidence of the Kaiser, he believed it his duty to remain in office, however miserable the Reichstag made his existence. But by the fall of 1917 the power of the Reichstag had so increased that Helfferich's interpretation of the constitution was no longer tenable. The Kaiser's power had in fact become largely negative: he could still prevent the naming of anyone who, like Bülow, was particularly objectionable to him. Since the Reichstag was able to force Helfferich's resignation and von Payer's appointment in his place, the deputies probably had the power to name the new Chancellor had they been able to agree on a candidate. To be sure, the Reichstag carefully avoided infringing on the Kaiser's prerogative of naming the Chancellor, but this reluctance appears suspiciously like a rationalization for its unwillingness to exercise the power that had devolved upon it. Helfferich himself naturally did not accept very philosophically the constitutional changes that his downfall symbolized. Far from viewing the increased power of the Reichstag as progress, he was inclined to see it as a sign of decay. At the age of forty-five, at the height of his physical and intellectual powers, he considered that he had been set aside simply because the Reichstag would not get along with him.

War Aims and Other Matters

Helfferich at first refused to accept any further responsibility for the economic preparations for peace. He announced to the King of Bavaria his willingness to go to the front, rented an apartment in Berlin, and departed for another vacation with the Douglases at Ralswiek. Returning to Berlin the last week of November, he proudly told Holtzendorff that Bonn University had offered him a professorship in economics. He had regretfully refused the offer, because the Kaiser had asked him to remain available. By this time Helfferich had abandoned his reluctance to coordinate economic peace terms. On 4 December, an Imperial Proclamation duly proclaimed him head of what came to be known as the "Büro Helfferich." Explaining to Holtzendorff that the first job of his new office would be to work on Russian peace terms, Helfferich noted that his *Atelier* would be small, since it would do nothing but coordinate the efforts of others. He anticipated that everything would go smoothly "since [I] stand well with the individual department heads." Ballin's comment was: "Helfferich is the most unsuitable personality imaginable for treating with the Russians."[49]

Ballin's strictures notwithstanding, Helfferich was in many ways ideally qualified for his new post. He had participated in most of the important war-aims discussions since the beginning of the war, and his practical knowledge of continental economic and financial matters was enormous. As compared with his former chief, Bethmann Hollweg, whose position on war aims Fritz Fischer has developed at such length, Helfferich's views were similar to Bethmann's though more extreme. While Fischer exaggerated in picturing Bethmann as a hard-line annexationist, he was much closer to the truth when he pictured Helfferich as one.[50] Although Helfferich was never so immoderate and crass as the soldiers and could probably have been persuaded to accept a *status quo* peace, he was much more influenced by purely economic considerations than Bethmann. Since his political judgment was also less acute, he was therefore more inclined to insist on extreme aims.

Stimulated by German conquests first in Belgium and later in the east, Helfferich worked out his own war-aims program early in the war. Essentially indifferent to territorial aggrandisement per se, he mainly wanted to secure Germany against "an economic war after the war." Since he thought that the object of this war would be to cut Germany off from its former overseas markets, he proposed to counter this threat by binding the lesser

[49] "Berichte" 761 and 768, 29 Nov. and 6 Dec. 1917; and Ballin to Holtzendorff, 14 Dec. 1917, "HB." See also *Weltkrieg*, III, 252-54; Fischer, *Griff*, 571-72. Although Helfferich was not appointed on 9 November as Fischer says, it is possible that some tentative arrangement was made then. The full title of the Büro Helfferich was: Kriegsstelle zur Vorbereitung der Wirtschaftsfragen für die Friedensverhandlungen (Spezialbüro Dr. Helfferich).

[50] Fischer, *Griff*, Ch. 3, esp. 113; 533.

continental states to Germany.[51] Because economic and financial ties would bind effectively and inconspicuously, he held that direct annexation or other political ties with the other states of this new "Continental System" were for the most part unnecessary. What Helfferich was proposing was a system of continental economic satellites, and he meant to impose it by the same methods which he had earlier recommended for tying the German colonies to the mother country.

Helfferich's Belgian program is the earliest illustration of how this continental system was to be imposed. Building upon his initial recommendations (in August and September 1914) for maximizing Belgian war contributions, he had elaborated by mid-1915 all of the essential measures for the economic penetration of Belgium. In the early fall of 1917, however, when the Papal Peace Note confronted the Germans with the possibility of peace at the price of promising to restore Belgian sovereignty, the Germans were forced to reappraise the entire Belgian program. On 4 September, Michaelis summoned the Prussian Ministers and announced that he intended to promise a conditional restoration of Belgian sovereignty.[52] In amplification, Helfferich said: "The more the political and military aims . . . are reduced, the more far-reaching the economic aims must be, and the more tenaciously they must be followed." The first such aim, he said, was control of the Belgian transportation system. He and Breitenbach, the Prussian Railway Minister, had earlier agreed that German-Belgian companies should run both the Belgian railways and Antwerp harbor, which according to Breitenbach was the "first and the dominant harbor of *Mitteleuropa*." Since Germany had borne most of the burdens of the war, Helfferich quaintly deduced that "it was only fair" that Germany receive the majority of the stock in these companies. Second, Helfferich noted that it had earlier been planned "to infiltrate Belgian industry and com-

---

[51] Such views were widespread. For an excellent discussion of the way in which they influenced thinking on war aims, see Egmont Zechlin, "Deutschland zwischen Kabinettskrieg und Wirtschaftskrieg: Politik und Kriegführung in den ersten Monaten des Weltkrieges 1914," *HZ*, 199 (1964), 394-405, 419-22.

[52] See protocol cited in n.4 above. For Helfferich's earlier views, see Fischer, *Griff*, 324-29.

merce" by charging Belgium a war indemnity payable in stocks and bonds. The third aim, which Helfferich considered the keystone of the entire system, was a customs, currency, and banking union. The customs union was not only to level the German-Belgian customs frontier and set common external duties, but was also to unify German and Belgian social and monopoly-control legislation and even equalize some taxes. The currency and banking measures were equally far-reaching. "It must be demanded," Helfferich insisted, "that Belgium leave the Latin Currency Union and tie itself to Germany in currency and banking matters." Karl von Lumm, Director of the Banking Division of the Belgian civil government, had already taken important steps in this direction. Following Helfferich's advice, he had suppressed the issue powers of the Belgian central bank, replaced the bank with a German-controlled central bank, and stabilized the mark/franc ratio at a level that insured the ultimate disappearance of the franc.[53] In the course of the session, Helfferich also explained a series of more modest alternatives for accomplishing the same ends, should the Chancellor find it necessary to promise a complete restoration of Belgian sovereignty. But he also warned that since "the enemy still means to force us to our knees, . . . the question of conditions is therefore secondary." "Setting up a minimum program" and the "proclamation of Belgian integrity" would probably not bring peace. Helfferich continued to insist on this same extensive program well into the spring of 1918.[54]

Political considerations prevented Helfferich from recommending such drastic interference in the affairs of Germany's allies, but the ultimate purpose of the measures that he did recommend was much the same: to secure Germany an unassailable postwar economic position in those countries. Proposals for tying Germany economically to the most important of its allies, Austria-Hungary, had been made even before the war, which made such projects seem more timely than ever. In 1915, the most famous of the economic unification proposals, Friedrich Naumann's *Mitteleuropa*, appeared. Although Helfferich disagreed with some of Naumann's more extreme recommendations, such

[53] Lumm, *Helfferich*, 50-53.   [54] Fischer, *Griff*, 332-33, 796-97.

as unifying German and Austrian steelmakers' associations, he agreed with Naumann's basic aim, the gradual economic unification of both empires.[55] He thought that the best way to start unification would be to adopt a series of preferential duties, which he hoped would eventually lead to a customs union. As he explained one evening in April 1915 at a party at Bethmann's, "Austria must be economically strengthened as much as possible, mainly because the political collapse of Austria is inevitable, whether in the short run or the long." Nearly everyone present, including Bethmann, Jagow, and Helfferich himself, admitted the economic disadvantages for Germany of a closer union, but Helfferich nevertheless asserted: "If Austria-Hungary collapses our enemies will doubtless slice the hunks that suit them off the cadaver and will do everything to prevent the strengthening of Germany economically. The whole business will be a repetition of what happened in Turkey." Apparently impressed, Bethmann commented that Helfferich's remarks were "extraordinarily important," indeed, "decisive."[56] Helfferich's interest in closer economic ties with Austria was motivated, in short, by a desire to achieve a commanding position within the unstable old empire before the final debacle.

The negotiations with Austria over economic unification ran into so many obstacles, however, that the original design had to be altered greatly. On 23 August 1917, Helfferich told the Main Committee of the Reichstag that, since Germany's trade with Austria constituted only about 10 per cent of Germany's total foreign trade, preferential duties ran counter to German interests. The Austrians, on the other hand, feared that anything as far-reaching as a customs union would reduce them to hopeless dependence on Germany. The Germans were therefore trying new approaches:

> We are seeking new forms for a rather close economic connection with the Danube Monarchy. We want to conclude a wide-

[55] "Notizen," 17 May 1915, and "Bericht" 477, 5 Sept. 1916, "HB." See also Henry C. Meyer, *Mitteleuropa in German Thought and Action, 1815-1945* (The Hague, 1955), 155; Redlich, *Tagebuch*, II, 94, entry of 16 Jan. 1916.

[56] "Notizen," 11 April 1915, "HB." See also "Berichte" 140-41, 18 and 23 April 1915, *ibid.*

ranging series of separate economic agreements in the areas of domiciliary rights, commercial law, and transportation, as well as in customs policy per se. We hope thus to reach a considerable degree of economic unity.[57]

Was it only regard for a faithful ally that led Helfferich to advocate such modest measures? Perhaps, but he was more likely motivated by the same considerations which led him in 1915 to deny the wisdom of dividing up Turkey. He thought it sufficient to implement the prewar Turkish agreements with England and France; "the greater intelligence, industry, and honesty of our people will do the rest."[58] He also expressly repudiated the idea of settling Germans in Turkey after the war as some, among them Albert Ballin, proposed. In general, he thought that the views of the more extreme proponents of German-Turkish friendship, and especially those of Ernst Jäckh, were "rather rose-colored."[59] Since Germany's allies were also likely to be victims of an "economic war after the war" and were agricultural producers, their postwar interests would naturally coincide with Germany's own interests. Moreover, Helfferich perhaps anticipated that the debts which Germany's allies owed it would, when combined with even the most modest measures of economic unification, give Germany all the leverage needed to secure the desired economic concessions. Whether these speculations accurately reflect Helfferich's thinking or not, there was certainly no sentiment in his approach to Austria or Turkey. In 1916 Helfferich had contemplated securing peace with Russia by forcing the Turks to give up the Straits, and in the spring of 1918 he reckoned that under certain circumstances Germany itself might have "to deliver the death stroke to Austria."[60]

But as the war dragged on, the stalemate in the West and the difficulties in reaching a satisfactory economic settlement with Austria turned German attention east, where the prospects of

[57] Hans von Schoen to Munich, "Bericht" 678, 23 Aug. 1917, GStA, "PA."
[58] "Notizen," 29 March 1915, "HB."
[59] Ibid., and "Bericht" 367, 4 March 1916, ibid.
[60] "Bericht" 868, 6 May 1918, ibid. Helfferich made the remark after hearing that Austria had allegedly undertaken negotiations for a separate peace. Although he was an abstemious man, perhaps not all of Helfferich's after-dinner remarks are to be taken too seriously.

realizing the most fantastic kind of war aims improved almost daily. Yet even here there were problems, the most troublesome being the future of Poland. Poland's future was not only the great question in German-Austrian relations but was the source of much agitated discussion within the German camp. Helfferich could see no good solution to the problem, merely a choice of evils. Although it never occurred to him to recommend abandoning any of German Poland, he was dead set against annexing any more of Russian Poland than was absolutely necessary for military reasons.[61] He at first favored the "German-Polish solution," or the creation of a nominally independent buffer state bound to Germany with the familiar economic ties. But, "seeing the entire affair from the standpoint of a *Handelspolitiker*," Helfferich was willing enough to abandon the "German-Polish solution" in the interests of high policy.[62] By the fall of 1917, he had become a warm advocate of the "Austro-Polish solution," or the creation of a quasi-independent Polish monarchy ruled by a Habsburg prince and joined loosely to Austria-Hungary. Helfferich was not being altruistic, but was as usual guided by very practical motives. First, this new "Austro-Poland" was still to remain within the German economic sphere. Second, Helfferich hoped to trade German support for the "Austro-Polish solution" for closer economic ties between Germany and Austria. And last, reversing the German offer of May 1917 to exchange Rumania for Poland, Helfferich intended to force Poland on Austria so that Germany could exploit the far more valuable Rumania.[63] The Germans threshed out the whole Polish question among themselves in a series of meetings on 3, 4, and 5 November 1917. On the 5th, the Kaiser pronounced in favor of the "Austro-Polish solution," which had been most vigorously represented by Kühlmann, Roedern, and Helfferich. In the ensuing conferences with the Austrians, however, no real agreement was reached.[64]

[61] Görlitz, *Müller*, 284, entry of 7 May 1917; Fischer, *Griff*, 586-88.

[62] Conze, *Polnische Nation*, 298-99. The epithet *Handelspolitiker* was that of General Hans von Beseler, Governor-General of Warsaw.

[63] *Ibid.*, 291-92, 325.

[64] See the Prussian Ministry Protocol, 4 Nov. 1917, cited in n.5 above; the excerpts from the protocols of the Prussian Ministry meetings and the Crown Council of 4 and 5 November printed in Leo Stern (ed.), *Die Aus-*

The policy to be followed in the Baltic was also discussed in the November meetings. The problem here was merely to refine plans which had already been drawn up in considerable detail. Late in 1916 Helfferich had told Holtzendorff: "We must create a protective barrier against Russia by setting up an independent Poland and by occupying the Baltic provinces."[65] Only after the March revolution, however, did the government examine Baltic questions in any detail. In one of the many conferences (on 21 April 1917) which the revolution occasioned, the creation of a series of "autonomous" Baltic states was proposed. Although autonomy implied independence, the ingenious Helfferich had little difficulty in refashioning this apparently innocuous concept into an engine of economic penetration. Instead of occupying the Baltic states, he suggested demilitarizing them (of Russian forces), tying them to Germany economically, and settling sparsely inhabited areas with Germans.[66] (In the wonderland of German war aims, some words meant whatever the Germans chose them to mean.) Over the summer these ideas were further refined. Plans were made to ensure that the Baltic states "voluntarily" allied with Germany. In the November meetings, a series of treaties for binding Lithuania and Courland closely to Germany were proposed. Helfferich recommended haste in preparing these treaties, in order to get all of the necessary formalities out of the way before the opening of negotiations with Russia, expected to begin any day. A *"fait accompli"* would thus be created which would greatly strengthen Germany's position in the peace negotiations. This advice came none too soon. The great Bolshevik revolution began three days later on 7 November. On the following day, the Bolsheviks broadcast their famous proclamation "to all" for a peace of "no annexations and no indemnities," and, after

---

wirkungen der grossen Sozialistischen Oktoberrevolution auf Deutschland (4 vols., Berlin, 1959ff.), IV, 154-63; and the record of one of the conferences on 6 November with the Austrians, *Ursachen und Folgen*, I, 414-18. See also Fischer, *Griff*, 572-75, 593-95; Ritter, *Staatskunst*, IV, 194-97.

[65] "Bericht" 534, 3 Dec. 1916, "HB."

[66] The following is based largely on Fischer, *Griff*, 532-35, 596-600. For the negotiations preparatory to armistice talks with Russia, see also Steglich, *Friedenspolitik*, I, 236-48.

some rather complicated negotiations, armistice talks between the Central Powers and Russia began on 3 December.

Since peace negotiations were to begin immediately after conclusion of the armistice, the Germans had little time to draft detailed plans. Although Helfferich himself did not participate in any of the preparatory conferences of early December, he was generally satisfied with the results.[67] He had good reason to be, for the civilians and the soldiers had agreed to use the principle of national self-determination to pry loose Russia's western provinces. Once these areas were detached from Russia, it would be simple to attach them to Germany with economic and other less covert ties. But Kühlmann had not been a week in Brest-Litovsk, the site of the negotiations, when Helfferich began to criticize his conduct of affairs; Kühlmann had asked neither Helfferich himself nor his right-hand man, Geheimrat Albert, to handle the economic negotiations. On 27 December 1917, Helfferich complained bitterly to Ernst Jäckh's son Hans and others about the folly of sending "mediocrities" like Johannes Kriege and Hermann Johannes to handle the legal and economic side of the negotiations.[68] He was unhappy that Kühlmann had gone to Brest at all, especially since the Russians had sent only their "second string." "But Kühlmann will take orders only from a strong Chancellor, and we don't have one," Helfferich lamented. He also complained that Czernin had "completely wrested the leadership from Kühlmann." He concluded his jeremiad by condemning Kühlmann and Czernin for accepting as the basis for negotiations the Russian program of no annexations and no indemnities, and national self-determination by plebiscite—the so-called "Six Points" of 22 December. When one of those present criticized one of the points, Helfferich burst out, "All six are unacceptable, all six!" Hans Jäckh later noted: "He revealed himself a wholehearted Imperialist and a man who really does not (or better: definitely does not) feel and think like a democrat."[69]

[67] "Bericht" 770, 8 Dec. 1917, "HB."

[68] His judgments of Kriege, a very able jurist, were not always so harsh; *Weltkrieg*, III, 450. On Kriege, see also Winfried Baumgart, *Deutsche Ostpolitik 1918: von Brest-Litowsk bis zum Ende des Ersten Weltkrieges* (Vienna and Munich, 1966), 275.

[69] Jäckh, *Pflug*, 475-76; "Bericht" 788, 27 Dec. 1917, "HB." Since Czernin

Kühlmann and his subordinates probably could have done little that would have satisfied Helfferich, since the quarrel between them was as much a personality conflict as a disagreement over substantive issues. On New Year's Eve, Ernst Jäckh commented on "the strong personal antagonism between them" and their tendency to speak of each other in tones "which go beyond mere criticism to passion and, yes, even to hatefulness."[70] Shortly afterward, Baron Hans-Karl von Stein, Secretary of the Reich Economic Office, mentioned to Holtzendorff the difficulties of Helfferich's position. Not only did his new office have a quite undefined constitutional position, but Helfferich himself also encountered much "silent opposition" from Kühlmann. Holtzendorff reflected: "The rivalry between those two will have unfortunate consequences yet."[71] The most perceptive analysis of Helfferich's *malaise* came from Hans Jäckh:

> He gives the impression of a man discontented and at odds with himself, a man who, ambitious as he is, has been forced from office, laid on the shelf, in the best years of his life. What best characterizes this state of discontent and thwarted ambition is the inscription on the picture he gave my father: "The deed is everything, fame nothing."[72]

Helfferich's difficulties in adapting to his decline in fortune are hardly surprising. It was, after all, the first important setback in a career previously characterized by rapid ascent. Such a setback was bound to affect Helfferich, who was in any case hardly a contemplative or philosophical person. Emil Helfferich holds that the years 1917-1918 represent a time of severe personal crisis for his brother, a crisis all the more severe because it came comparatively late in life.[73]

The substantive differences between Helfferich's Russian

---

and Kühlmann in reality only seemed to accept the Six Points, Helfferich's strictures were unjustified; Steglich, *Friedenspolitik*, I, 300-305. For the German side of the negotiations, see also Ritter, *Staatskunst*, IV, 109-50.

[70] Jäckh, *Pflug*, 384-85. See also the patronizing estimate of Helfferich in Richard Kühlmann, *Erinnerungen* (Heidelberg, 1948) 474-75.

[71] "Bericht" 796, 4 Jan. 1918, "HB."

[72] Jäckh, *Pflug*, 475-76.

[73] Interview with Emil Helfferich, 19 March 1962.

policy and Kühlmann's were also considerable. Although Kühlmann in the end had enormous client states thrust upon him by the Supreme Command, he clearly would have preferred a moderate peace with Russia which would have allowed Germany to concentrate all her strength in the West. Helfferich's own views were enough more extreme to explain why Kühlmann largely ignored them in the drafting of the Treaty of Brest-Litovsk.[74] In discussing the future of Russo-German relations with Bethmann on New Year's Eve of 1917, for example, Helfferich denied Bethmann's contention that detaching the border provinces would irreparably compromise future relations between Russia and Germany. He asserted that "an absolute antagonism" existed between the "foreign peoples" and "Great Russia, and especially Great Russian Communism." He also denied that being cut off from the Baltic was necessarily such a hardship for the Russians, since Russo-German agreements could be drafted to provide Russia with the needed rail corridors and Baltic harbor facilities.[75] Although he apparently did not discuss the point with Bethmann, he did not foresee Russia itself as a part of *Mitteleuropa*. He did, however, intend to bring Russia firmly within the German sphere of economic influence and at different times suggested various ways of accomplishing this aim.[76]

But the Foreign Office showed little interest in Helfferich's views. Finally unable to stand being ignored any longer, on 26 February 1918 Helfferich wrote an aggrieved letter to Hertling.[77] The immediate occasion for the letter was the German "ultimatum" to the Russians of 21 February 1918, which informed the Russians of the peace terms that they had to accept. Although the

[74] *Weltkrieg*, III, 309; "Notizen," 15 March 1918, "HB." Accustomed to playing a larger role, Helfferich probably underestimated his influence somewhat. It is very difficult to tell just what the influence of the Büro Helfferich on the drafting of the peace terms was, at least with material available in the West. Fischer, *Griff*, 571, says that Helfferich's office was "highly influential," but does not commit himself on Helfferich's personal influence. My own view is that Helfferich's office is best described as "potentially important" or possibly "historically significant" rather than "highly influential."

[75] Jäckh, *Pflug*, 384-85.

[76] See, for example, Fischer, *Griff*, 633-35, 643; letter, Helfferich to Kühlmann, 2 Jan. 1918, in Stern, *Auswirkungen*, IV, 883-85.

[77] Helfferich to Hertling, 26 Feb. 1918, "Büro Helfferich," No. 19,286, Bl. 170.

ultimatum was harsh, Helfferich believed that in some respects the demands for legal and commercial privileges did not go far enough, being "set forth in such a way that subsequent extensions and alterations in our favor appear practically out of the question." He then listed seven specific demands agreed on by the Reich economic agencies and himself which the Foreign Office had quite failed to consider: 1) prohibition of "any economic warfare whatsoever"; 2) equality with Russian citizens in the acquisition of real property; 3) withdrawal of all privileges and concessions made to the Entente during the war; 4) railway settlements favorable to Germany; 5) most-favored treatment of Germans by state monopolies; 6) licensing of German worker-recruiting organizations; and 7) settlement of private damage claims by an impartial board of some kind. According to this conception, which was hardly compatible with the sort of socialist state Lenin was creating, Russia was to become a source of laborers and raw material. It was not to be formally a part of *Mitteleuropa* but was to enjoy a status more like that of pre-World War I Turkey or China, with the difference that the "open door" was to admit mainly Germans.

In his letter to Hertling, Helfferich also pointed out that his "lack of participation in formulating the economic peace terms" not only made his official efforts as coordinator "practically worthless," but also saddled him with collegial responsibility for decisions over which he had had no influence. He implied that unless he played a more important part in future policy decisions he would resign. On 1 March, two days before the Treaty of Brest-Litovsk was initialed, he wired directly to Brest demanding that a provision be included in the treaty for the compensation of any German citizen who had suffered losses as a result of Soviet nationalization of private property.[78] Hertling and Kühlmann hardly dared entirely ignore Helfferich's demands even if they wanted to. Kühlmann was coming under steadily heavier attacks from the right-wing parties in the Reichstag and from the Supreme Command, and Helfferich in any case spoke for very

[78] Albert Norden, *Zwischen Berlin und Moskau: zur Geschichte der deutsch-sowietischen Beziehungen* (Berlin, 1954), 124-26; Günther Rosenfeld, *Sowjetrussland und Deutschland 1917-1922* (Berlin, 1960), 89-90.

powerful interests in the government and in the economy. His resignation was not likely to strengthen the position of either the Chancellor or his Foreign Secretary. Perhaps for these reasons, a provision was hastily inserted in the final draft of the Russian treaty which stated that economic and legal matters were to be definitively settled by a supplementary treaty. This action mollified Helfferich, although he continued to request that the economic agencies and the Foreign Office cooperate more closely.[79]

Helfferich was equally unhappy about his lack of influence over the economic arrangements being made with the border states and Rumania, all of which were to be incorporated into *Mitteleuropa.* Alleging that he was "only a 'clearing house,' " he asserted that the dominant influences were Kühlmann, Roedern, and Baron Stein.[80] Helfferich was exaggerating a little, but the settlements with the border states undoubtedly fell short of his expectations, principally because the Foreign Office once again showed too little interest in asserting the right of German citizens to compensation for war damages.[81] On the question of more positive measures of economic penetration and exploitation, Helfferich was often closer to the diplomats than he admitted. In the case of the Ukraine, the most important of the so-called border states, the Foreign Office apparently had no quarrel with Helfferich's short-run aim, expressed in a conference on 19 January 1918, of "getting out of the Ukraine what there is to be gotten" by reestablishing trade relations as soon as possible. His long-range aims, however, were again more extreme. In a conference on 5 March 1918, he held that Germany should attempt to secure control over railways and natural resources, particularly the valuable iron deposits of the Krivoi Rog and the Ukrainian grain surpluses. The narrowing of the Ukrainian railways from the broad Russian gauge (6 feet) to the standard gauge (4 feet 8½

[79] Helfferich to Hertling, 30 March 1918, "Büro Helfferich," No. 19,286, Bl. 188.

[80] "Notizen," 15 March 1918, "HB."

[81] The Foreign Office feared that setting precedents for the right of civilians to damages would in the long run work to Germany's disfavor because of the damage done by German armies in the west. See Wilhelm von Stumm's comments on the matter in: Protocol of Büro Helfferich session, 8 Feb. 1918, "Büro Helfferich," No. 19,286, Bl. 166Rff.

inches) agreed upon in the same conference shows how far the proposed measures of economic control actually went.[82]

The situation in Rumania was more complicated, but Helfferich's general program remained the same. According to Fritz Fischer, all influential Germans, from Helfferich and the Supreme Command to Kühlmann and the Chancellor, agreed that control of Rumanian oil, grain surpluses, and the transportation system were the essentials to be secured in the peace treaty. As soon as the Austrians got wind of the drastic measures of expropriation which the Germans had planned, however, they objected violently to them. Once again proving equal to the occasion, Helfferich proposed late in February 1918 "another form" for achieving German ends.[83] A complicated network of rental contracts for state oil lands and a trade monopoly were to be substituted for crude expropriation. Only Entente and American oil properties were to be expropriated, and even here Helfferich planned to justify the measure as retaliation for similar measures taken by Germany's enemies. With his eye mainly on German property in the United States, Helfferich planned that the expropriation would take a form whereby after the war Germany and the United States could exchange the property they had seized.[84] The trade monopoly was patterned after earlier proposals for the international ownership of the Bagdad Railway, with Germany owning a 56 per cent, Austria a 24 per cent, and Rumania a 20 per cent interest in the monopoly. Although a 56 per cent interest would seem to have safeguarded German interests sufficiently, the German government was also to control the Rumanian interest through a series of complicated arrangements with the great German banks. The Deutsche Bank and the Diskontogesellschaft, both of which had very large interests in

---

[82] Protocol of Büro Helfferich session, 19 Jan. 1918, *ibid.*, 153Rff.; Fischer, *Griff*, 661-62, 713. For what actually was secured, see Baumgart, *Ostpolitik*, 132-36, 146-51; Ritter, *Staatskunst*, IV, 227-28.

[83] Fischer, *Griff*, 682, 685-87. Kühlmann's later difficulties, caused in part by his failure to pursue these economic aims actively enough, may indicate that he was never so wholehearted a supporter of them as Fischer maintains. Helfferich's intentions toward Rumania, on the other hand, were not so harmless as he makes them appear in his memoirs; *Weltkrieg*, III, 308-309.

[84] "Notizen," 15 March 1918, and "Bericht" 887, 3 June 1918, "HB."

Rumania, would presumably have been the beneficiaries of this arrangement. The entire scheme was to be justified as compensation for German help in rebuilding the Rumanian economy.

The peace negotiations with Rumania went very slowly, however, first because Rumania was unwilling to cede the Dobruja to Bulgaria and then because German economic demands were so extreme. Irritated by these delays and by the alleged failure to safeguard private economic interests, the Supreme Command launched another attack against Kühlmann toward the end of March 1918. The wildest tales of Kühlmann's sexual revels in Bucharest went the rounds in Berlin, and on 20 March Ludendorff asked Payer, the Vice-Chancellor, about the possibility of replacing Kühlmann with Helfferich.[85] Although Helfferich also was unhappy about Kühlmann's sacrifice of private economic interests, he did little to encourage the intrigues against Kühlmann. Earlier, in January, he had indirectly helped Kühlmann stave off the onslaughts of the Supreme Command by explaining to the Crown Prince the folly of abandoning Kühlmann in the middle of the negotiations with Russia.[86] Now he refused the request of the industrial baron Hugo Stinnes that he mention Kühlmann's "misconduct" to the Chancellor. He did, however, refer Stinnes to Payer, who had evidently become a clearing house for complaints about the Foreign Secretary.[87] Stinnes and Kühlmann's other enemies nevertheless continued to campaign for Helfferich as Foreign Secretary, and Helfferich began to receive tips on how to handle the Reichstag in case he should receive Kühlmann's post. Payer even expressed the surprising view that it might be possible to reconcile Helfferich with the Reichstag.[88] Speculation reached a high point on 8 April when Helfferich departed for Supreme Headquarters. There was talk of a Helf-

[85] On Kühlmann's revels, see, for example, the undated memorandum in the Stresemann "Nachlass," 6914/3079/136606; and on Ludendorff's soundings, "Bericht" 850, 20 March 1918, "HB." By this time, Ludendorff and Kühlmann were personally on about the worst possible terms; Baumgart, *Ostpolitik*, 71.

[86] Herre, *Kronprinz*, 131-32; *Weltkrieg*, III, 279-80.

[87] "Bericht" 850 and 852, 20 and 22 March 1918, "HB." Payer, incidentally, was against dropping Kühlmann.

[88] "Bericht" 856, 26 March 1918, and "Notizen," 6 and 9 April 1918, *ibid.*

ferich-Bülow Foreign Secretaryship, with Helfferich handling
the business end and Bülow the personal side of the secretary's
duties. Since Helfferich and Bülow had been at odds for some
time, such talk was absurd, but it does illustrate what fanciful
rumors were circulating. A day later, the usually well-informed
Lerchenfeld reported to Munich that Hertling believed it "questionable" whether Kühlmann could be saved. Lerchenfeld
thought that the Supreme Command's candidate was Westarp,
although all other sources indicate Helfferich.[89]

What went on between Helfferich and Ludendorff at Supreme
Headquarters has never come out, but it seems likely that Helfferich refused to accept Kühlmann's post and may even have interceded for him. At any rate, the furor against Kühlmann temporarily died down, and Helfferich later defended Kühlmann
against charges of social misconduct.[90] Having no illusions about
his own unpopularity with the Reichstag, Helfferich had little
wish to fill the thankless and difficult office of Foreign Secretary,
however much he objected to Kühlmann's handling of the economic side of the various peace negotiations. With Helfferich's
refusal to succeed Kühlmann (if indeed Ludendorff tried to
persuade him to do so), the generals were obliged for the moment to abandon their campaign against the Foreign Secretary
since they had no other candidate for the post. But Kühlmann's
days were numbered.

Moscow and After

Even before the end of the negotiations with Rumania, Helfferich found himself with so little to do that in early May he
took another vacation. He returned to Berlin only on 21 May, the

[89] Lerchenfeld to Otto Ritter von Dandl, Bavarian Minister-President,
"Bericht" 337, 9 April 1918, GStA, "PA." For evidence that Helfferich was
the Supreme Command's candidate, see Görlitz, *Müller*, 367, 370, entries of
29 March and 8 April 1918; *IFA*, ii, 349-50n20; Max von Baden, *Erinnerungen*, 266; Karl von Hertling, *Ein Jahr in der Reichskanzlei: Erinnerungen an
die Kanzlerschaft meines Vaters* (Freiburg, 1919), 92.

[90] "Notizen," 14 April 1918, "HB." Helfferich seems on the whole to have
behaved more honorably toward Kühlmann than the latter did toward him.
For an account of this affair, see Ritter, *Staatskunst*, iv, 229-35.

day before the Treaty of Bucharest was signed.[91] Although he was still in charge of coordinating the work on economic peace terms, the only important business remaining was negotiating the supplementary treaty with Russia which was to settle the still outstanding legal and economic questions. On the basis of past experience, however, Helfferich must have judged it unlikely that he would materially influence the outcome of these negotiations. He did not resign from his position but did begin working on his war memoirs.[92] Because the Supreme Command and the Right were more dissatisfied with Kühlmann than ever, Helfferich continued to receive discreet inquiries about his readiness to assume the Foreign Office.[93] Finally, on 24 June 1918, Kühlmann made the tactical blunder of stating in the Reichstag what the Supreme Command privately admitted: that Germany might after all have to settle for a "compromise peace." Although even that estimate of the situation was highly optimistic, the outraged Supreme Command and its right-wing Reichstag allies demanded Kühlmann's head, and Ballin predicted a "Helfferich-Bülow era."[94] Ballin was mistaken, but in the end Hertling was unable to save Kühlmann.

His replacement was Paul von Hintze, a former naval officer turned diplomat, who was at this time minister to Norway. He had originally earned the Kaiser's favor while attached from 1903 to 1911 to the St. Petersburg embassy as naval attaché (until 1908) and as Militärbevollmächtigter (Military Plenipotentiary). The first week in July, he had been summoned to Headquarters at Spa for consultations with the Kaiser and Hertling about the

[91] "Bericht" 876, 21 May 1918, "HB."

[92] Interview with Ulrich Ehrhardt, 6 Jan. 1962. Ehrhardt, a former student of Professor Kurt von Raumer of Münster University, once intended to write a study about Helfferich and kindly told me of what he had learned from Frau Helfferich and others.

[93] Colonel Hans von Haeften, Ludendorff's liaison officer with Hertling, suggested Helfferich to Ludendorff as late as 30 June 1918; Baumgart, Ostpolitik, 90-91n92.

[94] "Notizen," 25 June 1918, "HB." Helfferich thought Kühlmann's speech a blunder, but even a week later, when Kühlmann's fall was sure, he refused to consider accepting the Foreign Office, although he could suggest no one else for the post; Görlitz, Müller, 390, entry of 2 July 1918.

possibility of his replacing the "Bolshevized" minister to Moscow, Count Wilhelm von Mirbach-Harff.[95] On 6 July, before the unfortunate Mirbach could be recalled, he was assassinated in the drawing room of his own legation. On hearing the news, Kühlmann, who was in Berlin at the time, telegraphed the Kaiser suggesting that Hintze be appointed to replace Mirbach. William naturally agreed. But on the following day, he was apparently brought around to naming Hintze as the replacement, not for the slain minister, but for Kühlmann himself. Hintze was reluctant to take on the Foreign Office. He was ideally qualified for the Moscow post, for one thing, and for another Kühlmann's fate was hardly encouraging. He also had something of a reputation as a reactionary. Because the Reichstag had not been consulted in his appointment, the news of it, which became generally known on the 9th, struck the majority parties, as Helfferich put it, "like a bombshell."

That reopened the question of who was to become minister to Moscow. The Supreme Command evidently preferred an officer, and at the Kaiser's request Ludendorff had suggested one for the post.[96] Hintze himself is said to have favored Gerhard von Mutius, the chief of the political section of the Polish civil government and a cousin of Bethmann Hollweg's.[97] Before anything could be decided, Helfferich astonishingly offered—sometime before 14 July—to take the post himself.[98] Ludendorff welcomed Helfferich's offer, and, as neither Hertling nor Hintze was at the time in a very solid position politically, they swallowed whatever objections they may have felt toward Helfferich and accepted his

---

[95] "Bolshevized" was the Kaiser's expression; Baumgart, *Ostpolitik*, 223. For Hintze's appointment, see *ibid.*, 88-92, 223-25, and for Mirbach's brief Moscow career, *ibid.*, 208-24.

[96] Ludendorff to Hintze, 24 July 1918, "Deutschland" 131, Bd. 44.

[97] Lerchenfeld to Ludwig, "Bericht" 774/XCI, 16 Aug. 1918, GStA, "PA."

[98] "Bericht" 897, 21 July 1918, "HB." See also *Weltkrieg*, III, 448-49; Kurt von Raumer, "Das Ende von Helfferichs Moskauer Mission 1918," in *Srbik Festschrift: Gesamtdeutsche Vergangenheit: Festschrift für Heinrich Ritter von Srbik zum 60. Geburtstag am 10. November 1938* (Munich, 1939), 393. Von Raumer had access to Helfferich materials since lost, but his piece, though a good estimate of Helfferich as minister (not ambassador, as is usually asserted), contains little specific information not now available in the documents or Baumgart, *Ostpolitik*, 233-57.

offer. His appointment, announced on 23 July, caused another sensation.

In Moscow, the Bolsheviks correctly interpreted the appointment of a man of Helfferich's importance as a sign that the Germans had given up the idea of breaking with them over Mirbach's assassination and were on the contrary seeking closer economic ties. The German military personnel in Moscow, drawing much the same conclusions, hoped that Helfferich might actually succeed in seizing control of the economic negotiations then in progress in Berlin.[99] Helfferich may have had something of the kind in mind, although he gave different reasons for accepting the appointment. First, he wanted to see for himself what was actually happening in Russia. Second, he hoped to implement a policy that would secure for Germany the long desired but as yet unharvested economic fruits of her eastern victory, and, last, he wished to free himself from his frustrating position as coordinator of the economic peace terms.[100] There is no reason to doubt his explanation, but there was understandably much speculation in Berlin about his motives for accepting such an unpromising post. None of Helfferich's friends thought the experience likely to profit him politically. Lerchenfeld chose to think that Helfferich merely wished to reach the Constantinople embassy by way of Moscow, but that idea seems farfetched.[101] At any rate, Helfferich departed for his new post on 26 July 1918.

Because the Bolsheviks dared not risk the assassination of another German minister, Helfferich's arrival in Moscow took place in great secrecy. At the request of the Russians themselves, he got off the train forty kilometers from Moscow and was driven the rest of the way by his staff and the multifarious Karl Radek, earlier a member of the Russian delegation to Brest-Litovsk. The same extreme security precautions prevailed after his arrival. He and Kurt Riezler, the German chargé d'affaires, visited Georgi

---

[99] Karl von Bothmer, *Mit Graf Mirbach in Moskau: Tagebuch-Aufzeichnungen und Aktenstücke vom 19. April bis 24. August 1918* (Tübingen, 1922), 105, 111, entries of 22 and 26 July 1918. See, however, Baumgart, *Ostpolitik*, 209n6, who points out that the published diary differs from the original in important respects.

[100] *Weltkrieg*, III, 448-49.

[101] "Bericht" 898, 22 July 1918, "HB"; n.98 above.

Chicherin, the new Commissar for Foreign Affairs, only once during Helfferich's stay, and Helfferich's only other foray from the legation consisted of a short walk in the immediate neighborhood. After that Chicherin placed him under what one of the Germans called "house arrest" and would not allow him to drive to the Kremlin to present his credentials. Chicherin assured Helfferich that he would pick up the credentials at the German legation himself, but never did so. Helfferich naturally chafed at these restrictions and thought his position "undignified and impossible."[102] So it was, but Chicherin was not merely imagining the danger of assassination, as the shooting on 31 July of Field Marshal Hermann von Eichhorn, the German commander in the Ukraine, made abundantly clear. Helfferich's incarceration in the German legation unfortunately left him almost entirely dependent upon his staff for his picture of the local political situation. The Bolsheviks' professed inability to guarantee his security led him to accept the most pessimistic conclusions about their future. It looked bleak indeed, but what the Germans in Moscow could perhaps not be expected to see was how weak, disunified, and politically bankrupt the anti-Bolshevik forces were.

Helfferich's Russian policy appears to have sprung full grown from the head of his chargé, Riezler, whom one of the latter's friends aptly called a "pessimist."[103] Riezler and the rest of the legation staff were not long in convincing Helfferich that the Bolsheviks would not last much longer and that the Germans thus should take steps to tie the Bolsheviks' successors to Germany.[104] Helfferich began almost at once bombarding the Foreign Office with recommendations about what Germany's Russian policy should be. On 1 August, he advised attempting to unite all anti-Bolshevik forces by means of a three-point program which comprised a "demonstrative disavowal" of the Bolsheviks,

---

[102] *Weltkrieg*, III, 460-64, 484; Bothmer, *Moskau*, 120-21, entry of 5 Aug. 1918. The expression "house arrest" is Bothmer's.

[103] Harry K. U. Graf von Kessler, *Tagebücher 1918-1937* (Frankfurt a. M., 1961), 107.

[104] For Riezler's views, see Riezler to Hertling, Dispatch 252, 19 July 1918, "Deutschland" 131, Bd. 44. See also Baumgart, *Ostpolitik*, 216-21, 237, from which it is clear how exactly Helfferich's views resembled those of the embassy staff and his murdered predecessor.

modification of the territorial provisions of the Treaty of Brest-Litovsk—"at least as far as the Ukraine is concerned"—and "effective military support of the anti-Bolshevik forces."[105] He thought that a "disavowal" of the Bolsheviks would probably in itself be enough to unseat them, since "at the moment the Bolsheviks' strongest support is the impression generally prevailing here that we are backing them." He explained that only by moving the legation from Moscow to "Petersburg" could the necessary impression of disavowal be created. Moreover, in Petrograd it would be easier to make contacts with anti-Bolshevik forces than it would be in Moscow. On the question of military support, Helfferich emphasized that, although such support would "considerably improve" Germany's position with the "new regime," a "demonstration" against Petrograd and "amnesty for the [Bolsheviks'] Latvian [troops]" would suffice. Helfferich was obliged to play down the need for German military action, since he had been told before his departure that Germany had no forces to spare for Russian ventures.[106] "Immediate action may be necessary at any moment," he concluded dramatically.

In the days that followed, Helfferich stepped up his campaign to get his policy accepted. Although the tone of his telegrams sharpens—one on the 5th began: "In the expectation that my task here is not the blind execution of instructions"—his arguments hardly varied.[107] The only novelty was the recommendation which he attached to a proposal from Chicherin on 2 August that the Germans and the Russians act together to block the English advance south from Archangel and Murmansk.[108] Helfferich advised that the Germans should "seemingly" accept this proposal, make the necessary military preparations, and then "at the last minute" join the "Cossack leaders" to overthrow the Bolsheviks. In addition to these lucubrations about the Russian policy,

[105] Helfferich to FO, No. 616, 1 Aug. 1918, "Deutschland" 131, Bd. 44.

[106] For Helfferich's predeparture briefing, see "Bericht" 900, 24 July 1918, "HB."

[107] The two most important telegrams were Helfferich to FO, Nos. 636, 653, 3 and 5 Aug. 1918, "Deutschland" 131, Bde. 44a, 45.

[108] Helfferich to FO, No. 622, 2 Aug. 1918, *ibid.*, Bd. 44a. For the full story about the Russian démarche and the later history of the proposed expedition against the English, see Baumgart, *Ostpolitik*, 106-17.

Helfferich peppered the Foreign Office with alarming little tele-grams about plots in Moscow to overthrow the Bolsheviks "next week," assaults planned against the German legation, new evi-dences of Bolshevik military disintegration, and rumors of secret goings-on in the Bolshevik inner councils which strengthened his allegations about how much the Bolsheviks depended on German recognition and friendship.[109]

In a series of replies aimed as much at the Kaiser and Luden-dorff as at Helfferich, Hintze patiently but thoroughly annihi-lated Helfferich's arguments. "The expectation that the Bolshevik government will soon give way to another may well prove true," he admitted.[110] He denied that the Germans could do much to in-fluence a new government in their favor, since any new govern-ment would necessarily be committed to overthrowing the Treaty of Brest-Litovsk. It was important to hold fast to the Bol-sheviks and the Brest Treaty and if possible "nail down" the obligations of the treaty by concluding the supplementary treaty. If the Bolsheviks fell, the new government would still be bound in international law by the treaties, an advantage not to be un-derestimated. He also asserted that, given the existing political situation in Russia, "unification of several [political] groups for concerted action is impossible, and . . . beginning military sup-port will soon obligate us for forces that the Supreme Command can by no means spare." As a concession to his nervous repre-sentative, however, he said that Helfferich might move the lega-tion out of Moscow if it really was in danger. But he also pointed out that unless such a move followed some immediate provoca-tion, it was tantamount to severing diplomatic relations.

Hintze's major effort in persuasion was not directed at Helf-ferich, however, but at Ludendorff. Helfferich's reports had con-firmed what Ludendorff already believed: that the Germans should overthrow the Bolsheviks. The general was particularly taken with Helfferich's proposal of 2 August to exploit Chiche-rin's call for assistance against the English to overthrow the

[109] Helfferich to FO, Nos. 624, 635, 637, 651, 2-4 Aug. 1918, "Deutschland" 131, Bde. 44a, 45.

[110] Hintze to Helfferich, No. 691, 2 Aug. 1918, *ibid.*, Bd. 44a. See also Hintze to Helfferich, No. 700, 4 Aug. 1918, *ibid.*, Bd. 45.

Bolsheviks themselves. Ludendorff eagerly telegraphed Hintze that he could support such a venture with "several divisions," which he thought would suffice to "support a government with the people behind it." Hintze, well aware how rapidly Ludendorff's military resources were diminishing, noted drily on the bottom of Ludendorff's wire: "If any new government had the people with it, the Bolsheviks would [already] have fallen." Expanding this comment into an astute analysis of Germany's eastern policy in his reply to Ludendorff, Hintze explained why the present policy of upholding the Bolsheviks was in Germany's best interests.[111] As Hintze's logic was irrefutable, Ludendorff allowed himself to be convinced, at least for the moment.[112] Hintze understood very well, however, that he had not removed Ludendorff's basic doubts about the wisdom of supporting the Bolsheviks.

He therefore combined his efforts at persuasion with an effective move to secure his policy against further interference from Helfferich, who could claim with each passing day to speak with more authority about what the confused situation in Russia really was. Taking his cue from the Kaiser's comment on 4 August that Helfferich was too valuable a personage to lose, Hintze ordered Helfferich on the 5th to report to Berlin for personal consultations.[113] Helfferich's last official act before leaving Moscow on the 6th was to order the transfer of the legation to Petrograd.[114] Since Hintze believed Petrograd actually more dangerous than Moscow, he in turn ordered (on 10 August) the legation to withdraw to Pskov behind the German lines. Helfferich's homeward journey can only be described as bizarre and slow.[115] He arrived in Berlin on 10 August.

In the meantime, Hintze had continued to strengthen his posi-

---

[111] Ludendorff to Hintze, No. 1843, 5 Aug. 1918, *ibid.*; Hintze to Lersner (for Ludendorff), No. 1866, 6 Aug. 1918, *ibid.* Hintze's telegram is printed in entirety in Baumgart, *Ostpolitik*, 392-94. Baumgart misdates Ludendorff's telegram as 6 August.

[112] Ludendorff to Hintze, 7 Aug. 1918, "Deutschland" 131, Bd. 45.

[113] Kurt von Grünau (Foreign Office representative at Supreme Headquarters) to FO, No. 398, 4 Aug. 1918, *ibid.*, Bd. 44a, reporting the Kaiser's views on Helfferich; Hintze to Helfferich, No. 715, 5 Aug. 1918, *ibid.*, Bd. 45.

[114] Helfferich to FO, No. 667, 6 Aug. 1918, *ibid.*

[115] *Weltkrieg*, III, 487; Jäckh, *Pflug*, 387-88.

tion and quietly to undermine Helfferich's. He not only secured the express support of the Kaiser and Ludendorff for his policy, but also took care to point out to the latter that Helfferich was in no sense a reliable witness on Russian conditions: "Even a genius, if plucked out of his milieu and set down in Moscow, could hardly master a situation completely foreign to him inside of ten days from the enforced seclusion of his own house and with this 'orientation' expect to reverse . . . the policy of a great empire."[116] Hintze avoided seeing Helfferich on the 10th on the pretext of sickness. Helfferich therefore had no chance to express his opinion of the supplementary treaty with Russia which was signed the same day.[117] Although Hintze did see Helfferich on the 11th, he was very reluctant to allow Helfferich to attend the major foreign-policy conference scheduled for 14 and 15 August at Supreme Headquarters.[118] According to Alfred Niemann, an officer attached to the Kaiser's entourage, Hintze represented Helfferich's departure from Moscow to the Kaiser as a "kind of flight from the colors," which naturally left William "out of sorts" with Helfferich. As a result, Helfferich's efforts to justify his policy got nowhere.[119] Since Hintze represented Helfferich's departure as flight on at least three other occasions, Niemann's account is probably true.[120] Whatever may be said of Hintze's methods, Helfferich's policy was by this time irrelevant, because it assumed military resources which Germany simply did not have. Isolated in Moscow and cut off from the sources of infor-

[116] Hintze to Ludendorff, No. 1893, 9 Aug. 1918, "Deutschland" 131, Bd. 45.

[117] *Weltkrieg*, III, 488-89. This was a source of some astonishment in Reichstag circles; *IFA*, II, 504-505.

[118] Lerchenfeld to von Lössl, 11 Aug. 1918, GStA, "PA"; Hintze to Supreme Headquarters (Hertling), No. 1867, 13 Aug. 1918, "Deutschland" 131, Bd. 45.

[119] Alfred Niemann, *Kaiser und Revolution: die entscheidenden Ereignisse im Grossen Hauptquartier* (Berlin, 1922), 62. See also the report of another eyewitness, Chef des Zivilkabinetts Friedrich von Berg; Baumgart, *Ostpolitik*, 251n90, 252-53.

[120] See, for example, Gustav Hilger and Alfred G. Meyer, *The Incompatible Allies: A Memoir-History of German-Soviet Relations 1918-1941* (New York, 1953), 10. The legend is still appearing in the works of reputable historians; Zeman, *Germany and the Revolution in Russia*, 137n2. For a correct account, see Baumgart, *Ostpolitik*, 246-47.

mation formerly at his disposal, he perhaps did not realize how fast Germany's military position was deteriorating.[121] After the conference Helfferich returned disgruntled to Berlin, determined to submit a detailed memorandum of his views on the Russian policy.

Helfferich's memorandum, which he asked Hertling to submit to the Kaiser, is not so important for what it says as for the curious fate it suffered. Founded on a gross overestimation of German military strength and freedom of action, it is essentially a more detailed and more carefully written version of the views he had expressed from Moscow.[122] The only thing new is Helfferich's appraisal of the supplementary treaty initialed on 10 August. Although he found most of the treaty "excellent," he objected to the provisions whereby Russia was to pay Germany a flat sum, 6 billion gold rubles, for all expropriated property. Given his firm views on the sanctity of private property, his arguments against the provision were predictable: he stated that the arrangement would "act as a direct provocation" to total expropriation, which was the same as the "total sabotage of the economic and financial foundations" of Russia. Although Hertling realized that the time had passed for worrying about such matters, he was still concerned about William's reaction to the memorandum. He therefore asked Hintze to write a countermemorandum for submission along with Helfferich's. Hertling did not receive Hintze's memorandum until 30 August, but by then it was out of date. The same day, evidently irritated by the lack of reaction to his memorandum of 20 August, Helfferich submitted his resignation. One last time he outlined his views on the Russian policy. He also criticized at length Hintze's removal of the legation from Petrograd to Pskov, because he thought it impossible in Pskov to "prepare the foundations from which the hoped-for fruits of the eastern peace might yet be secured." The removal

---

[121] Since General Max Hoffmann, the German commander in the East, also did not realize how rapidly the military situation in the West was worsening, it seems unlikely that Helfferich, a civilian, would have; Nowak, *Hoffman*, II, 228.

[122] Helfferich to Hertling (for presentation to the Kaiser), 20 Aug. 1918, "Deutschland" 131, Bd. 46. For the complete text, see Baumgart, *Ostpolitik*, 394-400.

of the legation was one of the formal grounds for his resignation, the other being his manifest disagreement with Hertling and Hintze on the Russian policy.[123]

On 5 September, Hertling asked Helfferich if the latter would resume his duties as head of the Büro Helfferich.[124] The question implied that Helfferich's resignation would be accepted momentarily, but Hertling actually did not send Helfferich's resignation (along with the memorandum of 20 August and Hintze's rebuttal) to the Kaiser until 17 September.[125] Another five days elapsed before the resignation was accepted. Placing the worst possible construction on Hertling's motives, Helfferich attributed the delay to Hertling's desire to silence him as long as possible.[126] By the end of September, Helfferich was very bitter about the way he had been treated, but he had probably judged Hertling's motives correctly. The Chancellor was coming under increasing attack from the parties and doubtless had little wish to add Helfferich to his critics. It is also possible that Hertling, faced with the accelerating collapse of Germany's military position in the west and suffering from rapidly deteriorating health, simply had more urgent matters on his mind than Helfferich's resignation. Yet for whatever reason, Helfferich was unquestionably rather shabbily treated.

Despite his frequent threats to enter the lists against the government, Helfferich did allow Hertling to persuade him to return to his post as head of the Büro Helfferich.[127] By this time neither could have had many illusions about the significance of the office; Helfferich told Holtzendorff that Geheimrat Albert, his principal collaborator, would be released to the Treasury Office.[128] Helfferich confined his public utterances to speeches in support of the

[123] Hertling to Hintze, 22 Aug. 1918, "Deutschland" 131, Bd. 46; Hintze memorandum, 30 Aug. 1918, *ibid.*, Bd. 47; Helfferich to Hertling, 30 Aug. 1918, *ibid.*, Bd. 50. See also Baumgart, *Ostpolitik*, 292-94.

[124] Görlitz, *Müller*, 409, entry of 5 Sept. 1918.

[125] Hertling to Kaiser, 17 Sept. 1918, "Deutschland" 131, Bd. 50.

[126] *Weltkrieg*, III, 492.

[127] As early as 23 August, Jäckh wrote Paul Weitz of Helfferich's intention of speaking out in opposition to the government's eastern policy; Jäckh, *Pflug*, 389.

[128] "Bericht" 937, 23 Sept. 1918, "HB."

ninth and last war-loan drive. In one of these speeches, given in October 1918, Helfferich implicitly expressed what were probably his motives for remaining in the government. Speaking after the exchange of notes with President Wilson over armistice conditions had already begun, Helfferich asserted that the German people had to show by extensive participation in the loan drive that "we are not broken, not ripe for just any [peace] terms, but are determined and are able, if it must be, to fight to the last man for our honor and existence." He went on to assure his hearers that the debt, though enormous, could be and would be repaid. As so often in the past, he painted a glowing picture of the postwar advantages that bond ownership would confer. He concluded with a ringing peroration to stand by the fatherland: "We are fighting not for a constitutional or a parliamentary Germany but simply for the fatherland itself. No one may stand aside. Everyone must turn to and do his utmost for the fatherland in its hour of direst need."[129]

In private, Helfferich criticized the new government of Prince Max von Baden, who had succeeded Hertling on 4 October 1918, very savagely indeed: "dilettantes" and "lackluster windbags," he called them.[130] Since Ludendorff had shortly before (on 29 September) demanded an immediate armistice in order to save the German armies from total collapse, Prince Max's most pressing task was to end the war on whatever basis he could. Nothing he did suited Helfferich. At a Holtzendorff Abend on 12 October, Helfferich expounded at some length on the initial note exchange between Prince Max and President Wilson. Challenging the source of the German armistice offer, Ludendorff's estimate of the military situation, Helfferich insisted that the other senior commanders should have been heard before such a fateful step was taken. The magic of Ludendorff's name was still so great, however, that Helfferich's statement encountered lively opposi-

---

[129] Helfferich, *Rede über die deutsche Volkskraft: gehalten am 11. Oktober 1918 vor den Vertretern der Kriegsanleihe-Werbeorganisationen* (Berlin, 1918).

[130] Annette Helfferich to Kuno Graf von Westarp, 24 Oct. 1924, Westarp "Nachlass." The letter cited refers to the quoted expression, "Dilettanten und schimmerlose Schwätzer," which Frau Helfferich wished to strike from a letter published in *Reichstagsreden 1922-1924*.

tion, although in fact collapse was not so near as Ludendorff supposed. Referring to Prince Max's offer to negotiate on the basis of Wilson's "Fourteen Points" of 8 January 1918 and to evacuate all occupied areas, Helfferich sarcastically demanded: "Why did [he] have to give up all the trumps at once?" He considered such sweeping offers at the very beginning of the negotiations the height of folly; one was left nothing to bargain with. He thought that the minimum result of the government's diplomatic clumsiness would be the loss of Alsace-Lorraine and that the abdication of the Emperor and the Crown Prince was "inescapable." Both Holtzendorff and Ernst Jäckh commented on Helfferich's "high temper" and the "passion" with which he made his remarks.[131]

In Helfferich's eyes, Prince Max's conduct of the armistice negotiations went from bad to worse. Personally favoring direct contacts with the English and the French, Helfferich had from the beginning been against calling on Wilson. He believed that the American President was prejudiced against Germany and a hypocrite as well. A *Realpolitiker* himself, Helfferich never fathomed the nature of Wilson's idealism, and Wilson was in truth about as different from Helfferich as anyone could have been. Helfferich thought that Prince Max's policy of appeasing Wilson on one hand merely encouraged the latter to make more and more excessive demands and, on the other hand, prevented the exploitation of the natural feelings of outrage of the German people at such demands.[132] He did not think that Germany could hold out forever, but he did believe that if the enemy were threatened with a *levée en masse* they might well offer Germany better terms. Helfferich tried to see Prince Max and Wilhelm Solf, the new Foreign Secretary, in order to present his views, but, his attempts failing, he sent Solf a draft note (dated 21 October) which was intended as the basis for a reply to Wilson's second note of 14 October.[133] Helfferich's draft was very brusque and could only have alienated Wilson to no purpose, had Solf sent it. Finally, at dinner parties on 25 and 26 October, Helfferich

[131] "Bericht" 946, 13 Oct. 1918, "HB"; Jäckh, *Pflug*, 437.
[132] *Weltkrieg*, III, 535-36, 540, 560-61.
[133] Helfferich draft note, 21 Oct. 1918, Solf "Nachlass."

had a chance to propound his views to Solf in person.[134] Neither Solf nor the other guests—Bethmann Hollweg, Arndt von Holtzendorff, Ernst Jäckh, and Lerchenfeld, among others—thought Helfferich's policy at all practicable. Everyone agreed that an armistice was vital, and better soon than late, while German armies and Germany itself were still intact and before the country fell victim to "Bolshevism." Solf also correctly pointed out that enemy forces were building up rapidly, whereas German forces were as rapidly diminishing. Helfferich's idea of a *levée en masse* was a fantastic scheme, and though that remarkable man, Walther Rathenau, also suggested it, the idea did little credit to the political judgment of either. Holtzendorff supposed that Helfferich's great "inner bitterness" caused by his rapid decline in fortunes had spoiled his judgment, "otherwise so clear." He also supported Solf's contention that, as with Rathenau, "wounded vanity" contributed "heavily" to the same effect.

Helfferich had in the meanwhile been trying to shed his (as he put it) "honorary office" as coordinator of the economic peace terms. But Prince Max wished to keep him on, and since Helfferich had no chance to discuss his resignation with Max as the latter requested, the matter was evidently still outstanding at least as late as the end of October. Once free, Helfferich intended to join the troops at the front, perhaps to follow his own counsel (at dinner on the 25th) that "every German should allow himself to be shot dead before we surrender." "Better that my Pfälzer homeland also go up in flames," he added. Despite these desperate words, Helfferich was so much the civilian that even in the fifth year of war Holtzendorff felt obliged to add Helfferich's reserve rank (major) when relating the matter to Ballin.[135] The closest Helfferich got to the front was apparently Neustadt, where he went at the end of October.[136] Returning to Berlin on

[134] Görlitz, *Müller*, 438, entry of 26 Oct. 1918; Jäckh, *Pflug*, 441-42, 444-48; "Bericht" 958, 25 Oct. 1918, "HB."

[135] Jäckh, *Pflug*, 441-42; "Bericht" 949, 16 Oct. 1918, "HB." Helfferich had been trying to shed the Büro Helfferich since at least as early as 3 October; Görlitz, *Müller*, 425.

[136] According to Scheffbuch (*Helfferich*, 63), Helfferich went to Neustadt to make a speech, but I have been unable to locate it.

6 November, he made one last desperate effort to help avert at least domestic catastrophe by appearing in uniform at the offices of the Berlin district commander. Along with a great many other officers, he was sent home. He reappeared on the following days only to be sent away again, his last efforts to help save his beloved *Kaiserreich* frustrated.[137] On 9 November, the day of his last appearance, William abdicated, and a Socialist government replaced that of Max von Baden. In a Socialist government, Helfferich clearly had no place, not even as the holder of an "honorary office." His metamorphosis from an insider to an outsider was complete.

Helfferich confirms how "shaken" he was by the collapse of the empire. On 29 October he wrote:

> We must all accustom ourselves to the idea that in the future we will live in an entirely different world than before. Everyone must look to himself to find his own way and build himself a new life. What sustains me . . . is the belief that a people like ours can indeed be humiliated and vilified, but it cannot perish. For the present generation, however, I foresee that the most it can do is prepare the way for a new ascent by hard and humble work; it will itself experience no new golden age.[138]

Exactly a month later, he again revealed his thoughts, and once again it seems best to let him speak at length for himself:

> So great a change, a plunge into the depths such as no people in history has experienced in such a short time! I perhaps feel it more than most others, since my entire life, all my work, all my wishes and aspirations (*Sinn und Trachten*) for as long as I can remember have been totally centered on the great causes

---

[137] Görlitz, *Müller*, 448, entry of 9 Nov. 1918; Max von Baden, *Erinnerungen*, 622.

[138] Letter, 29 Oct. 1918, in *Reichstagsreden 1922-1924*, 18-19. In the letter to Westarp cited n.130 above, Frau Helfferich refers to this letter and the one cited immediately below, but whether the letters were originally addressed to her or to someone else is not clear. Since Helfferich ordinarily wrote his correspondence in longhand and did not keep copies, it is very likely that Frau Helfferich was the recipient. At this time she was a war widow and did not actually marry Helfferich until December 1920. They had, however, known each other for a good many years; she was Georg von Siemens's daughter.

which are now in ruins. And as if it were really a political necessity! How little was lacking for things to have turned out differently. Avoidable mistakes, easily avoidable errors and stupidities, and in the decisive last year a lack of political leadership . . . are what finally tipped the scales against us. I really think that if they had listened to me even as late as August [1918] when we were already at the abyss, the worst could have been avoided. Now we must drink the cup to the lees, for only a fool can hope for mercy.[139]

Helfferich had clearly wasted no time in constructing a very flattering version of the last days of the empire. Already recovered from the worst of the shock, he had begun to think of the future. But he was well aware that he was too closely associated with the old regime to play much of a public role in the immediate future. As he put it in the same letter, "Too many people are afraid of compromising their virginal republican-revolutionary convictions through association with someone as notorious as me." Since Helfferich was of no mind to remain permanently on the sidelines, his next task was to rehabilitate himself politically.

The Past and the Future

The collapse of the German Empire on 9 November 1918 was the great turning point in Helfferich's career. Before 9 November, all of Helfferich's varied activities had served essentially the same end: German economic expansion. Sincerely convinced that economic expansion was the best way, indeed the only way, to provide the German people with a rising standard of living, he was equally convinced that Germany's safety and its place in the world ultimately depended on the strength of its economy. As a young man supporting the government against the attacks of the bimetallists, Helfferich appeared liberal because he advocated political reform as a means of combatting the bimetallists' Junker followers. But these reforms were not an end in themselves. As the industrial and financial community came to carry more weight in the councils of state, he lost his former interest in political reform. By 1914, Helfferich, who was now heard in the

[139] *Ibid.,* 19.

very highest circles, was satisfied with the *status quo*. Most of the dangers that had earlier worried him seemed past, and he looked with pride on the powerful, dynamic Germany that he and his fellows had done so much to build.

During the war, Helfferich's appointment as Treasury Secretary and Interior Secretary must have confirmed his judgment about the basic soundness of the German political edifice. His rapid rise was proof that talent did not go unnoticed and unrewarded. Regardless of his personal outlook, however, as Interior Secretary Helfferich was confronted with the problem of satisfying the demands of the people for political reform. He viewed such demands with misgivings, although he sincerely believed that the tremendous wartime sacrifices of the German people in some sense justified those demands for reform. He also recognized that standing pat against reform would in the long run probably lead to revolution. He hoped that if minor reforms were granted early, it might be possible to avert major reforms, or worse, later. On the great question of the day, electoral reform in Prussia, he therefore advocated the introduction of the Reichstag suffrage. Since at first he stood nearly alone in the Prussian Ministry in favoring such a "radical" measure, he took on a very democratic hue. But Helfferich only looked like a democrat because his opponents in the ministry justified their stand against the Reichstag suffrage with such reactionary arguments.

As his relations with the Reichstag show, Helfferich was no democrat. Even as a young assistant in the Colonial Division, he believed that government ought to be left to experts like himself. He regarded the Reichstag's every interference in his own areas of competence as ignorant, time-consuming meddling. He thought that the Reichstag's refusal to back Bethmann and himself on the submarine warfare issue in the fall of 1916 was merely the first of many occasions when the Reichstag, through sheer blindness to the consequences of its acts, had prepared the way for total disaster. He thought, moreover, that the Reichstag was all too willing to sacrifice the best interests of Germany to increase its own power. In the case of the Auxiliary Service Law, for example, Helfferich strongly condemned the Reichstag for seizing the opportunity to increase its power, when the result of

286

such self-aggrandizement was to make the Auxiliary Service Law virtually worthless. Even worse in Helfferich's eyes was the cynical way in which the Reichstag majority first acquiesced in Bethmann's overthrow in July 1917—after he had secured for it the promise of the long-sought Reichstag suffrage for Prussia— and then undermined the morale of the country and blasted hopes for a victorious peace with its futile Peace Resolution of 19 July. His own fall three months later merely confirmed his belief that the growing power of the Reichstag had to be curbed: an able man had been dismissed for no better cause than a trivial clash of personalities.

After his fall in November 1917, Helfferich continued to hope that he might yet play a decisive role in the peace settlements. But this hope, too, remained unfulfilled, for whatever Helfferich's influence may still have been, it clearly disappointed his expectations. His ten days in Moscow capped the frustrations of a bitterly frustrating year. Yet he remained silent, not an easy thing for Helfferich, mainly because of loyalty to the fatherland in time of need, but also because he recognized that the government, for all its weaknesses and faults, was made up of men such as he. What followed would probably be worse. Nevertheless, standing on the sidelines in the last year of war had some advantages. Helfferich was easily able to persuade himself that he was a prophet without honor, and that consequently none of the blame for the collapse was his. The Reichstag, and to a lesser extent Hertling, Prince Max, and the Supreme Command, were responsible for the defeat, but not he. This way of looking at things freed Helfferich from any inhibitions that he might later have felt about reentering public life after the war.

VIII. HELFFERICH RETURNS
TO POLITICS

Once Germany had become a republic, Helfferich's opportunities for political activity were naturally very much restricted. That would have been true even if he had had a more fortunate political past. Although the center of the political establishment was far to the left of where it formerly had been, Helfferich remained loyal to the old order. As a result, he had no place in the political establishment; for the first time he was an outsider, and necessarily a critic. But for Helfferich the role of opposition critic —although not the role of controversialist—was unwelcome and uncomfortable. He liked to feel that he was helping to make the wheels turn, and, as a member of the opposition, his influence on policy was at best limited. Nevertheless he believed that he had to do what he could. The danger to the German economy was no longer from the Right but from the Left. He feared that the republic, through ignorance or malice or weakness, was quite likely to destroy the foundations of the economy: Helfferich had seen in Russia a drastic example of what happened to a country that strayed too far from sound economic principles. Moreover, until the economy was rebuilt, Germany could hardly expect to win back her "rightful" political place in the world. Thus, quite aside from his need to vindicate himself personally, Helfferich had ample motive for reentering public life and had a great many targets for his accumulated venom.

Preparations

As Helfferich soon discovered, returning to politics was not easy. The refusal of any party to accept him as a candidate for the forthcoming elections (of January 1919) to the National Assembly merely underlined how difficult his task would be.[1] He

[1] The National Assembly was a constituent assembly which was to meet

288

had been such a tenacious opponent of the Reichstag's wartime attempts to increase its power that he could not hope to find much favor among professed democrats. Conservatives, on the other hand, could not yet forgive him his steadfast support of Bethmann Hollweg, the man whom they considered mainly responsible for Germany's defeat. Politically, Helfferich was a virtual pariah. Yet despite his dubious prospects, within a year he was once again playing an important role in German politics. This was a remarkable achievement, a measure of Helfferich's energy, determination, and the skill with which he transformed himself from a monarchical bureaucrat into a republican politician.

At first, Helfferich had to limit himself to rather unimportant activities. Although addressing a "whole series of assemblies" on his own initiative, neither of the principal right-wing parties, the Nationalists (Deutschnationale Volkspartei, or DNVP) and Stresemann's People's Party (DVP), allowed him to do more for them than stump the hinterland.[2] He spoke mainly in conservative, sparsely settled Mecklenburg and Pomerania. It seems clear that the party chieftains were only willing to allow Helfferich a forum in areas where they did not feel very much was at stake.[3]

Otherwise, Helfferich lived quietly in Berlin, working on his war memoirs and covertly supporting right-wing political ventures such as Eduard Stadtler's "Anti-Bolshevik Movement." Stadtler, an ex-officer who had been attached to the Moscow legation while Helfferich was minister, had been very disturbed by what he had seen of communism in Russia. As he explained his aims to Helfferich in November 1918, he wanted to save Germany from such follies by mounting a large-scale propaganda movement against the extreme Left. Helfferich refused to sup-

---

early in 1919 to reorder German political life along democratic and parliamentary lines. It continued to govern Germany until May 1920.

[2] *RTV*, Vol. 345, 4 Nov. 1920, 948. Helfferich's activities in this period are somewhat obscure. His son confirms that he made a practice of addressing political assemblies and rallies during this period; Friedrich Helfferich, notes on MSS, February 1970. His activities were not reported in the principal Berlin dailies. For more on his party affiliations, see Ch. 9 below.

[3] Gustav Stresemann, *Vermächtnis: der Nachlass in drei Bänden*, ed. Henry Bernhard (Berlin, 1932-1933), II, 458.

port Stadtler openly, saying his support would only compromise the movement. But he did put Stadtler in touch with Friedrich Naumann, now one of the leaders of the Democratic Party, and Paul Mankiewitz, a director of the Deutsche Bank. With the 8,000 marks that Naumann and Mankiewitz provided, Stadtler was able to organize his movement. Stadtler soon used up the money, however, and had to turn again to Helfferich for assistance. Early in January 1919, Helfferich once more telephoned Mankiewitz, and together they drafted a telegram to be sent to some fifty industrialists and bankers. The summons, to a meeting which Stadtler was to address, was unequivocal: "Appear in person, send no stand-ins," it ordered. According to Stadtler, "the entire *haute volée* of industry, banking, and commerce appeared." Stadtler's harangue was a success, and the financial drought ended. Stadtler could now mount a massive anti-left propaganda campaign which soon covered most of north Germany. The campaign owed its inception at least in part to Helfferich's indispensable mediation between Stadtler and the business community.[4]

The last recorded encounter between Helfferich and Stadtler occurred on 25 June 1919, shortly after the National Assembly had voted to ratify the Treaty of Versailles. Although Helfferich had not anticipated an easy peace, the treaty apparently exceeded his worst expectations, and he had hoped to the last that the National Assembly might reject it.[5] "*Finis Germaniae!* The end of Germany!" he gloomily predicted. Stadtler attempted, not unsuccessfully, to put some heart into Helfferich and pointed out what the latter had to do: "The struggle must be taken up against Erzberger, the most vital personality of the new system."[6] In

---

[4] Eduard Stadtler, *Als Antibolschewist 1918-1919* (Düsseldorf, 1935), 12-13, 43-46. Stadtler is the only source for these events. For Stadtler's role in the right-wing movements of the day, see Klemens von Klemperer, *Germany's New Conservatism: Its History and Dilemma in the Twentieth Century* (Princeton, 1957), 102-11.

[5] Helfferich had already begun to speak out against the treaty; *Die Friedensbedingungen: Vortrag gehalten am 23. Mai 1919 in der Mitgliederversammlung des Verbandes Berliner Grosshändler und Fabrikanten für Nährungs- und Genussmittel e. V.* (Berlin, 1919). The content of this speech is summarized in "Helfferichs Unannehmbar," *VZ*, No. 261, 24 May 1919.

[6] Stadtler, *Antibolschewist*, 188. See also Ernst Troeltsch's interesting

fact, Helfferich had decided quite some time before to stake his own return to politics upon destroying Erzberger. Helfferich later asserted that as early as July 1917 he had come to see Erzberger as "the nemesis of the fatherland" and had at that time resolved upon "war to the knife" against him.[7] Although there is little reason to doubt Helfferich's statement, it is all but certain that Helfferich began to lay the groundwork for his anti-Erzberger campaign in the fall of 1918 at the latest. When Stadtler talked to Helfferich in June 1919, the latter's preparations for his campaign against Erzberger were nearly complete.

The Campaign Against Erzberger

Erzberger was a natural target for Helfferich. Since their dispute over colonial matters in 1905 and 1906 their relationship had been stormy, and they had had a series of bitter wartime encounters. Erzberger was also unpopular with a great many others besides Helfferich. His recent political activities had made him the most hated of all the new men. In the deepening crisis of the last days of the Hertling government, Erzberger had been a leader in the movement for democratization. A place in the short-lived cabinet of Prince Max of Baden was his reward. Shortly thereafter the post of Armistice Commissioner was thrust upon him. Aware that the post was likely to become a political liability, he accepted it unwillingly and only as a service to his country. He was to hold the post until late June 1919. He probably obtained as many concessions in the armistice talks as could reasonably have been expected. The final terms were very hard, however, and his name was indissolubly bound to them. In the revolutionary atmosphere of the winter of 1918-1919, large sections of the population were easily persuaded that Erzberger had treacherously abandoned German rights and had, indeed, cheerfully granted all that the French demanded.[8]

---

comments on Erzberger's dominant position; *Spektator-Briefe*, 72-73, entry of 8 July 1919.

[7] *Prozess*, 318-19.

[8] It was widely assumed that Erzberger was in the pay of the French or the English; Bachem, *Zentrumspartei*, ix, 401; Epstein, *Erzberger*, 393. For

His continuing role in the execution of the armistice terms during the winter and spring of 1919 only confirmed his critics in their hostile opinions of him. His overly optimistic arrangements to "surrender" the German merchant fleet in return for much needed food imports were particularly held against him. Although not a member of the German delegation to Versailles, Erzberger worked informally with the allies to secure better terms. His techniques were rather questionable, and in the end unsuccessful.[9] Had his diplomacy been irreproachable, however, the mere fact that he was one of the leaders in the Reichstag for ratification would have sufficed to condemn him in many circles. Finally, as if he were not already unpopular enough, Erzberger accepted the post of Finance Minister in the government formed by the Majority Socialist Gustav Bauer on 21 June 1919.

Erzberger was extremely vulnerable to attack, and Helfferich had planned his campaign with typical thoroughness. In outline, the campaign was strikingly similar to his earlier one against the bimetallists. Where Arendt had once stood for the sins of the bimetallists, Erzberger was now pictured as the archetype of the corrupt politician who was ruining Germany in the name of democracy and peace. The general pattern of the literary campaign was also the same, with Helfferich's writings and speeches falling into three general classes. The first group included pamphlets, speeches, and interviews which dealt with the principal issues that the war and the treaty had raised, matters such as war guilt and the economic background of the war. The tone of most of these writings was moderate, the appeal of the arguments was to reason rather than to the emotions, and they were comparatively free from personal vituperation.[10] Helfferich may perhaps

---

accounts of Erzberger's activities during this period, see *ibid.*, Chs. 11-12; Morsey, *Zentrumspartei*, 182-88.

[9] For the sorts of comments about Erzberger going the rounds, see Kessler, *Tagebücher*, 122-23, entries of 8 and 9 Feb. 1919. For hostile criticisms from the other side, see John M. Keynes, *Essays and Sketches in Biography, Including the Complete Text of Essays in Biography and Two Memoirs* (New York, 1956), 202, 234.

[10] Works in this category include: *Die Friedensbedingungen: ein Wort an das deutsche Volk* (Berlin, 1919); *Die Friedensbemühungen im Weltkrieg: Vortrag gehalten in der deutschen Gesellschaft 1919 am 1. September 1919*

have written some of these pieces without much thought of his campaign against Erzberger, but they nevertheless served to buttress his case, either by justifying the actions of the old regime or by undermining some position taken by the new. Second was a series of highly personal attacks on Erzberger himself, written with a cutting verve reminiscent of Helfferich's best invective against Arendt.[11] Last, Helfferich's war memoirs play the same role in the campaign against Erzberger that his two-volume *Reform des deutschen Geldwesens* had played in the campaign against Arendt: it was the intellectual foundation upon which all of his shorter pieces rested. It was also the reading of history against which all subsequent events and assertions were to be judged, and once its premises were accepted, its conclusions were difficult to avoid.

When Helfferich talked to Stadtler late in June, his memoirs were nearly finished. The first two volumes had already appeared, and the final volume was in press. In the "Foreword" to Volume I, which introduces the entire work, Helfferich explained that he had "some not altogether unimportant things" which he "must say" about the history of the war. "The world thirsts for enlightenment," he asserted: "it wants to know how things could have happened as they did, and whether it all was inevitable." His intention, he stated, was to do more than "enrich the memoir literature." He intended to place the events in "their larger context." Ultimately, the impulse which led him to set down the events he had witnessed was the "will to [discover] the truth." The truth he in turn hoped would "contribute to the healing of the German spirit and body politic and to creating tolerable relations between nations."[12]

These were praiseworthy aims, and Helfferich came closer to

(Berlin, 1919); *Der wirtschaftliche Hintergrund des Weltkrieges: Vortrag gehalten in der Gehe-Stiftung zu Dresden am 18. Oktober 1919* (Leipzig, 1919); "Dr. Helfferich über die Entschädigungen," interview, *DAZ*, No. 54, 2 Feb. 1919; *Das Reichsnotopfer* (Berlin, 1919); and the speech cited in n.5 above.

[11] Most notably *Der Friede von Versailles: Rede an die akademische Jugend gehalten am 26. Juni 1919 im Auditorium Maximum der Berliner Universität* (Berlin, 1919), and *Fort mit Erzberger!* (Berlin, 1919).

[12] *Weltkrieg*, I, 9-10.

fulfilling them than a great many memorialists. He did, in fact, throw a great deal of light on the workings of the German wartime government, and his account was all the more valuable because he was the only leading civilian to leave a detailed record. He had begun collecting the material for his work after resigning as Vice-Chancellor in November 1917. He seems mostly to have drawn upon his excellent memory to reconstruct the various events in which he had participated, but he also used documentary sources.[13] Wherever he got his information, his facts were astonishingly accurate. His worst errors, if such they should be called, were omissions: on occasion he simply did not mention important questions about which he must have been very well informed. Still, even in the matter of omissions, he compared favorably with other memoir writers. He was remarkably candid even about matters which reflect no particular credit upon himself, although this was doubtless partly because he did not see that the episodes in question show him in an unfavorable light. Finally, he wrote with his usual literary flair and pace, which make the memoirs eminently readable.

Yet, despite these virtues, the general tendency of the memoirs was misleading. In the first volume, *Die Vorgeschichte des Weltkrieges* (The Antecedents of the World War), he first discussed some of the "driving forces" behind the diplomatic crises which preceded the assassination of Archduke Ferdinand in June of 1914. During the interval since early 1915, when he had first written about the origins of the war, his stated views had changed somewhat. He now ascribed the key role in the outbreak of the war to England instead of Russia. The Germans failed only in that they lacked the diplomatic skill to exploit all the opportunities to shake "French ideas of *revanche*," or to dissipate the tension between the Central Powers and Russia which was "created by the Pan-Slav pressure in the southeast." When in this situation England acted to strengthen the Triple Entente after the collapse of Anglo-German negotiations aimed at a détente, "thus giving the warlike tendencies among its allies new encouragement, the judgment for war or peace had really fallen." With

[13] He began making memoranda as soon as he resigned; *Prozess*, 315-16; interview with Annette Helfferich, 11 July 1962.

the assassination of the Archduke and the Ultimatum to Serbia, Russia had the excuse it sought for war. In his discussion of the final critical month, Helfferich took considerable pains to prove that the German government wanted peace and had taken all possible steps to preserve it. Even after the Ultimatum had been presented, he concluded, "the decision lay in the hands of the English," who opted for war by refusing to restrain their allies.[14]

In the final two volumes, which constituted the main body of the memoirs and dealt with the war itself, Helfferich propounded the thesis which was implicit in his view of the origins of the war, and which we have already encountered in his letter of 29 October 1918. In essence, Helfferich's thesis was that Germany's leaders had not only fought a defensive war but had also made a number of peace overtures, which the Entente had scornfully rejected. In this situation, according to Helfferich, Germany had no choice but to wage all-out war. So successful were its efforts, however, that by the summer of 1917, Russia was virtually out of the war, and England, the *Hauptfeind*, had been brought to the verge of disaster by unrestricted submarine warfare. Unfortunately, Erzberger and the Reichstag majority foolishly nullified Germany's military successes with the abortive Peace Resolution of July 1917, which created the impression in the enemy camp that Germany had reached the end of its rope. After July 1917, the decline in Germany's military fortunes kept pace with the advance of democratization.

Although few historians today would accept Helfferich's version of events, many of Helfferich's countrymen did. His thesis naturally appeared more plausible when embedded within his smooth, accurate, and detailed narrative than it does here in bare outline. Moreover, although Helfferich did not hesitate to criticize both men and policies, he usually did not descend to personalities. This objectivity, which is quite in contrast to the polemics aimed directly at Erzberger, contributed to the book's air of reliability. The speed with which Helfferich was able to complete his memoirs doubtless strengthened their impact, for they were among the first war memoirs to appear. Neither Erzberger nor Helfferich's other political opponents had the time in 1919 to

14 *Weltkrieg*, I, 166, 200.

write memoirs, occupied as they were with the grave responsibilities of governing a defeated country. Helfferich's version of the
past temporarily enjoyed a virtual monopoly. The memoirs were
quite capable of sustaining their function as the intellectual
foundation and historical justification for the campaign against
Erzberger.

Helfferich publicly launched his campaign in a speech delivered on 26 June 1919 to the students of Berlin University.[15] The
speech, ostensibly about the peace treaty, began with a provocative portrayal of the final ceremonies at Versailles, where the
Germans "were forced to sign, surrounded by the representatives
of thirty-three states—from Great Britain, France, and America
down to the nigger-republics of Haiti and Liberia. . . ." He discussed the peace terms in the same vein, asserting that, although
they allegedly embodied the ideals of "humanity and justice,"
they reflected the hostile "spirits of Louis XIV and Edward VII."
And why did Germany have to accept this "devil's work of Versailles"? He did not leave his hearers long in doubt: "In the unparalleled panic and bewilderment [at Weimar, when the peace
terms first became known], one man seized the helm, the man
who was Germany's greatest nemesis in this war, greater even
than Lloyd George, Clemenceau, and Wilson rolled into one: the
Reichsverderber ('debaucher of the Reich') Matthias Erzberger.
With black and red flag flying, he brought the ship of peace into
the harbor of dishonor." Hard words, but words equally hard
were to follow.

Erzberger was not only made responsible for the acceptance
of the treaty, he was also held responsible in large measure for
the state of "moral collapse" that made such an act possible. Helfferich traced the beginnings of the collapse directly to the Peace
Resolution of July 1917, which helped to "inoculate" the masses
with several fateful "delusions." The most important of these
were that German "imperialism" was responsible for the war,
that "the lust for conquest" and "militarism" were prolonging it,
and that if the old regime were overthrown, Germany could

---

[15] All quotations in the following two paragraphs are from *Der Friede
von Versailles*, cited in n.11 above. The audience was so large that the
largest lecture hall of the university was required; *VZ*, No. 322, 27 June
1919.

make peace on honorable terms. As a result of these misapprehensions, Helfferich said, "the trust of the people and the Army in our good and just cause, in the rectitude of our civilian and military leaders, and in the Kaiser's sincerity and love of peace, was shaken. Our sharp sword was blunted." Although Helfferich also included others besides Erzberger among the *Reichsverderber*—most notably the liberal journalist Maximilian Harden—he went on to discuss Erzberger's activities during the armistice in a way which made quite clear just how ruinous the latter's activities were. "You need only recall," he reminded his hearers, "how he delivered up the merchant fleet for a mess of potage!" Having thus laden Erzberger with most of the responsibility for the disasters which had befallen Germany since mid-1917, Helfferich concluded with a ringing call for national unity: "Above all, we must bring the honor that is due it to the great truth that . . . the individual, both the individual person and the individual class, is nothing outside the community of his people and his state."

This version of the history of the past two years only wanted a few refinements to turn it into a full-blown *Dolchstoss-Legende*. Helfferich had indeed not actually called Erzberger a traitor, but the overall import of his charges was hardly less, especially since he had also damned Erzberger with the responsibility for the armistice and the peace treaty. Nevertheless, had Helfferich made his charges only once, Erzberger would probably have ignored them, serious though they were. He was already under heavy attack from the Right, both in the press and in the National Assembly. He was, in addition, about to undertake extensive reforms of the German tax laws and revenue service which were to have the effect of burdening the propertied classes much more heavily. To engage in public debate with Helfferich at such a time was hardly to Erzberger's advantage if he could avoid it. But Helfferich's Berlin University speech was only the beginning. Less than a week later, on 1 July 1919, he repeated the substance of his earlier charges about the fatal influence of the Peace Resolution in a series of slashing articles in the conservative *Kreuzzeitung*, which the old Conservative, Count Westarp, had thrown open to him "without restriction."[16]

[16] Lewis Hertzman, "The German National People's Party (*DNVP*)

Erzberger was finally obliged to answer these attacks. Helfferich, a former minister and a major figure in his own right, was too important, and the charges were too devastating, to ignore.[17]

On the following day (2 July 1919), Erzberger replied to Helfferich's first *Kreuzzeitung* article in the semi-official *Deutsche Allgemeine Zeitung*, and for the remainder of the week the two enemies disputed various aspects of Erzberger's role in the July Crisis of 1917. Because the details of the crisis have already been discussed, it is sufficient to note that in rhetorical violence Erzberger by no means stood second to Helfferich. Indeed, he carried the quarrel from the press into the National Assembly, where on 8 July 1919 in the course of defending his fiscal reforms he called Helfferich "the most frivolous of all finance ministers." This epithet, a trifle unfair but no more outrageous than some of the labels Helfferich had pinned on Erzberger, was one of those memorable phrases destined to haunt Helfferich in the years to come.

In the short run, however, Helfferich was able to turn Erzberger's attack in the National Assembly to his own advantage. First, he accused Erzberger (on 9 July 1919) of failing to answer his last set of charges about the July Crisis and of slandering him from behind the screen of parliamentary immunity. Actually, the charges which Erzberger had supposedly failed to answer had already been thoroughly aired, and to imply as Helfferich did that Erzberger failed to reply because no adequate reply was possible was extremely misleading. It was also a trifle bizarre for Helfferich to assume the mantle of injured innocence because Erzberger had assailed him from within the halls of parliament. Helfferich nonetheless insisted thereafter that he was merely defending his honor against Erzberger's assaults.

Erzberger's attack also provided Helfferich with a welcome opportunity to shift the ground of the conflict and to open the second phase of his campaign. His article of 9 July 1919 was en-

---

1918-1924" (Doctoral dissertation, Harvard University, 1954), 300. The entire polemic in the press, including both Helfferich's attacks and Erzberger's replies, is reprinted in *Fort mit Erzberger!*

[17] On 23 July 1919, *BT*, No. 355, commented, "Herr Erzberger cannot let such a serious charge go unanswered. Gentlemanly silence will not do for a minister."

titled "The Question of Financial Guilt." In it he compared the monthly outlays of his own fiscal stewardship with the larger ones of the postwar period.[18] Because of the inflation which had occurred in the meantime, it was not altogether fair to ask, as he did, "Where does the 'frivolity' *really* lie, then?" Although postwar fiscal policy left much to be desired, to ask such a question was to ignore both the deleterious effects of his own financial policy and the frightful (and expensive) problems which the postwar governments faced.

But what was really new about this phase of the campaign was the manner in which Helfferich began to attack Erzberger's character as well as his policies. Admitting that experience had shown that wartime taxes probably should have been higher than they were, Helfferich said that such statements came with bad grace from Erzberger, who at the time (1916) had opposed any new taxes whatever. Moreover, in order to block the wartime tax program by rallying the Center against it, Erzberger deliberately misrepresented some of Bethmann's actions toward him. "So much," Helfferich scornfully deduced, "for the *creditability* of the man who is supposed to set the *credit of the Reich* to rights again." After another exchange in the press, in which Erzberger mistakenly said that Helfferich "had turned down cold" all tax legislation—enabling Helfferich to remark that his opponent had once again "consciously told the opposite of the truth"—the matter was for a time allowed to rest.

Erzberger's allegation that Helfferich had refused to bring in any tax legislation during the war illustrated another of the difficulties under which Erzberger labored. He was so busy with his pressing official responsibilities that he could do no more than mark out the main lines of his defense against Helfferich's charges, while leaving the details to his press representatives, Otto Driesen and Heinrich Hemmer. They were often careless in checking their facts, and Helfferich was thus able to score points that Erzberger himself might not have allowed.[19] He not only

[18] He made many of the same points about the financial situation and Erzberger's unsuitability for his post in a speech at the Nationalist Party Day on 13 July; *DAZ*, No. 331, 13 July 1919. See also his comments at the Nationalist Party Day in Stettin in late October; *BT*, No. 505, 25 Oct. 1919.

[19] *Prozess*, 238-58; Epstein, *Erzberger*, 352.

made Erzberger look foolish by exposing his errors but used them as proof that his opponent was a thoroughly mendacious man. Helfferich, on the other hand, could devote his full time to the press quarrel and was at his best in matters which required mastery of masses of detail. He also had the assistance of Max Alsberg, one of the finest attorneys of his day; his charges were very carefully framed, so much so that one of the state attorneys in his later libel trial with Erzberger commented that a great many of Helfferich's epithets, though insulting, were not legally libelous.[20] Finally, Helfferich was very skillful at introducing new material bit by bit, so that no sooner had the maximum effect been squeezed from one item than another was ready. This technique also had the advantage of keeping Erzberger off balance. Altogether, the circumstances surrounding the quarrel were to Helfferich's advantage.

On 21 July, Helfferich returned to the attack in the *Kreuzzeitung*, exploiting one of Erzberger's new tax laws, the *Reichsnotopfer*, to mount his assault. He claimed that the *Notopfer*, a nonrecurring capital levy, gave the Finance Minister a kind of power to interfere in the affairs of the individual which could only be entrusted to a man of impeccable antecedents and irreproachable honesty.[21] To prove that Erzberger was no such man, Helfferich dredged up incidents from Erzberger's past dating back to the colonial scandals of 1905 and 1906. This long list of offenses took in everything from instances of untruthfulness to cases of alleged conflict of interests. For example, Erzberger had become a director of a construction company, Julius Berger Tiefbau, shortly after having acted (in 1917) as an arbitrator in a dispute between Berger and the Reich Canal Office. Although Erzberger's action was improper (he had conditionally accepted the position while the case was still pending), in retrospect it does not seem to have been an indication of moral turpitude so much as of naïveté: he failed to foresee the view that would inevitably be taken of his action, which was apparently innocent enough. Helfferich thought otherwise: "From the standpoint of social and political propriety this man is, for me, finished." He

[20] *Prozess*, 807.
[21] See also his *Reichsnotopfer*, cited in n.10 above.

300

concluded with the Cato-like refrain, repeated with variations in the following days, "Shall the German nation and the German people be brought to ruin by the cancer Erzberger?"[22]

In response to this bitter attack, Erzberger made a scorching reply, accusing Helfferich of "grossly irresponsible demagoguery, of a kind one ought not to have to expect from a man who calls himself Staatsminister." He also replied to the other charges and carried the war to his enemy's camp with the accusation that it was mainly such things as the wartime plans that heavy industry had developed under Helfferich's aegis for exploiting Belgium which had brought Germany to its present lamentable situation. "A dirty lie" and a "low-down denunciation of my person [as a war criminal] to the Entente," was how Helfferich characterized Erzberger's counterattack.[23] He dared Erzberger to sue him for libel and asked with a flourish, "Does Erzberger really believe that he can simply sweep all these facts aside with cavalier gestures and cheap invective?" Although Erzberger dropped the press quarrel at this point, he once again attacked the old regime in the National Assembly, charging it with having failed properly to exploit the opportunity offered by the Papal Peace Note of August 1917. The quarrel had thus returned to its starting point, the July Crisis and the events surrounding it. It is hardly necessary to consider Helfferich's remaining *Kreuzzeitung* articles, the content of which is adequately conveyed by a few of the titles: "Erzberger's Self-Exoneration Offensive," "Erzberger's Betrayal of the People," and "The truth is on the March."

Early in August 1919, Helfferich compiled all of his articles, Erzberger's replies, and some other materials damaging to Erzberger in a long pamphlet entitled *Fort mit Erzberger!* (Away with Erzberger!). In grouping his material together in this way, Helfferich was employing the same technique which he had successfully used earlier against Arendt, and for the same purpose: "In order to throw light on the truth, I have carried on my fight against the *Reichsverderber* Erzberger with an acerbity that is otherwise contrary to my nature, merely for the purpose of forc-

---

[22] *Fort mit Erzberger!*, 32.
[23] *Ibid.*, 36-40. Helfferich was on none of the lists of war criminals. With few exceptions only military men achieved this dubious distinction.

ing a legal action against me. . . ." His conclusion, a masterpiece of polemical writing, reiterated the long list of charges against Erzberger and ended with the demand: "There is but one salvation for the German people. With irresistible force the cry must resound throughout the land: Away with Erzberger!"

Helfferich had placed Erzberger in a very difficult position. It was not only, as Helfferich said, that "he [knew] how to suffer without complaining!" To sue Helfferich promised to be a ticklish proceeding, for, as will be shown, German libel laws placed the plaintiff under unusually severe handicaps. Yet Helfferich's articles and the pamphlet *Fort mit Erzberger!* had attracted so much attention that for Erzberger to drop the quarrel at this point was impossible. Too many people would assume that he refused to sue because Helfferich's charges were true. Besides, Erzberger was a fighter. On 16 August, the Bauer cabinet at his request decided to have the Justice Ministry determine whether a suit against Helfferich might succeed.[24] On the following day, Helfferich himself wrote to President Friedrich Ebert demanding that suit be brought against him or that Erzberger be forced to resign. When nothing (apparently) happened, Helfferich wrote another letter to Ebert (on 5 September 1919) repeating his demands and threatening to start things going in the press again if nothing was done.[25] This was unnecessary, the cabinet having agreed less than a week before that Erzberger should bring suit. During the fall of 1919 the details were arranged.[26]

Helfferich, Hindenburg, and the Dolchstoss-Legende

Even before the trial began, Helfferich inflicted another crushing blow upon the republic. Late in August 1919, the National Assembly voted to set up a series of investigating committees to discover the truth about the origins of the war and the reasons

[24] "Kabinett-Protokolle," 16 Aug. 1919, 3438/1667/742977.

[25] Friedrich von Oertzen, *In Namen der Geschichte! Politische Prozesse der Nachkriegszeit* (Hamburg, 1934), 13-14.

[26] "Kabinett-Protokolle," 1 Sept. 1919, 3438/1667/743005. Even arranging the details was a matter of acrimony. Helfferich and his attorney Max Alsberg later asserted that Erzberger and his lawyers had done everything they could to delay the trial, a charge which Erzberger denied; *Prozess*, 25-26; *DAZ*, Nos. 613, 615, 13-14 Dec. 1919.

why all wartime peace moves had failed.[27] Although all parties were to be represented on the committees, the left-wing parties clearly hoped to strengthen democracy and the republic by discrediting Germany's former Imperial governors. Ultimately, the committees did uncover much valuable historical material, some of which reflected little credit upon the Imperial government. The initial hearings of October and November 1919 were nevertheless a disaster for the republic, largely because the democrats on the committee failed to foresee the opportunities which the hearing might provide a determined anti-republican such as Helfferich.

When the hearings opened on 21 October, chairman Adolf Wermuth announced that his Second Committee would study wartime peace moves, not with the aim of making judgments, but to establish the facts. But he added, rather ominously, that if a Supreme Court (Staatsgerichtshof) were later established, the evidence uncovered might form the basis for prosecutions—presumably for treason. Because the first peace move to be considered was Wilson's attempt of 1916 to mediate between the belligerents, Germany's wartime ambassador to the United States, Johann Bernstorff, was the first witness to testify. Helfferich and Bethmann Hollweg sat together in attendance, awaiting their turn. The relatively small hearing room, soon abandoned for a larger one, was jammed. The press had turned out in force and so had the public. The matters at hand were highly controversial and had already been the subject of much publicity.[28] The first days passed smoothly enough, but the fireworks soon began.

The committee soon fell under the domination of the Majority Socialist Hugo Sinzheimer and the Independent Socialist Oskar Cohn. According to Moritz Bonn, who was serving the committee as an independent expert, Sinzheimer, a first-rate jurist, was the "driving force" behind the committee. Regretably, while cross-

[27] On the genesis of the committees, see "Die Untersuchung der Kriegsschuld," in *DAZ*, No. 503, 14 Oct. 1919. A reading of the Berlin press during the summer of 1919 makes it appear probable that the public controversy over the events of the summer and fall of 1917 strongly influenced the decision to establish the investigating committees.

[28] *DAZ*, No. 516, 21 Oct. 1919. The hearings received excellent press coverage, with the public proceedings being reported nearly verbatim.

examining witnesses, he combined "oily pathos with caustic interjections," an "unfortunate habit" which drove witnesses into a fury. Such a manner was indeed hardly calculated to bring out the best in former chancellors, ambassadors, admirals, and other dignitaries. Bonn characterized Cohn, on the other hand, as essentially a "harmless dreamer."[29] Both men meant to score as many points against the old regime as they could, and the subjects under discussion offered them ample opportunity to do so. In the course of reviewing the factors which influenced Wilson's German policy in the fall of 1916, for example, Bethmann and Zimmermann found themselves hard put to defend the civilian government's policy toward the deportation of Belgian workers.[30] By the time Helfferich's turn on the witness stand came, the hearings already had a short but stormy past.

Though sworn in on 6 November, Helfferich did not actually take the stand as the principal witness until the 12th. For him, the hearings had come at a fortunate time. The press campaign against Erzberger was over, and the libel trial was not due to begin until January. The hearings provided him with a means of keeping himself in the public eye and a platform from which to continue his fight against the republic. At first glance, however, the subject on which he was to testify, unrestricted submarine warfare and his own shifting position toward it, seemed more calculated to embarrass him than the republic. But he was a past master at exploiting the most unpromising situations, and he was to do so in this case.

Before he began to testify, he called attention to the "juristic abnormality" of the proceedings and challenged the right of the committee to force a witness to answer each and every question put to him. He did so on the ground that, although the committee was not a court of law, the witness was obliged to testify under oath. His answers might therefore (as Wermuth had indeed pointed out) be used as the basis for a later prosecution. Although Helfferich promised to answer all questions put to him,

[29] Bonn, *So macht man Geschichte*, 234. Although Bonn describes Sinzheimer as a "radical," the epithet seems of questionable accuracy since he was later a leading union lawyer and professor of jurisprudence.
[30] *DAZ*, Nos. 542-43, 4-5 Nov. 1919.

he had served notice that he regarded the committee as the enemy. It was, he clearly implied, a body of dubious legal standing, a kangaroo court, the main purpose of which was to condemn members of the old wartime government. The tension, already high, increased noticeably.

After this initial flurry, Helfferich settled down to give an account of his views on submarine warfare. Bonn correctly describes this rendition as "somewhat colored," and it differs little from that in Helfferich's memoirs.[31] Helfferich's next day on the stand was eventful enough—Wermuth repeatedly called him to order for the sharpness of his utterances—but the real excitement did not come until the third day, 15 November.[32] Cohn started things off by asking Helfferich a rather tendentious question "to determine the methodology of [his] testimony," or, in other words, to reveal how slanted Helfferich's account was. Helfferich refused point-blank to answer the question, claiming, first, that if he were in a court he would have the right to refuse Cohn as a judge, and, second, that he also had "personal grounds" for not answering Cohn's question.[33] Wermuth attempted to smooth things over by conceding that the committee did share many of the attributes of a court. But he pointed out that even if the committee were in every way similar to a court, Helfferich would still be obliged to answer all questions that did not in some way incriminate him. Would Helfferich, he asked in an attempt to save face all around, answer "certain" questions from Cohn? The answer was a resounding no. The committee, Helfferich said, was a "curious mixture of parliamentary commission and court of law and I myself am a curious mixture of witness and defendant." Since Cohn had earlier said that the purpose of the committee was to expose the "crimes" of the Imperial government, he intended to answer no more of Cohn's questions.

[31] Bonn, *So macht man Geschichte*, 237.

[32] *DAZ*, Nos. 561-64, 14-16 Nov. 1919.

[33] No less a historian than the ex-lawyer Erich Eyck has pointed out how flimsy Helfferich's legal reasoning was; Eyck, *Weimarer Republik*, I, 187. See also Eduard Heilfron, "Die Rechtsstellung des Untersuchungsausschusses," *DAZ*, No. 633, 24 Dec. 1919. Actually the question of the legal rights and safeguards for witnesses testifying before parliamentary committees is not a simple one, as the difficulties of witnesses testifying before Congressional committees in this country amply illustrate.

This was all quite unprecedented. The committee retired in confusion to deliberate in secret about what to do next. According to eyewitnesses, by the time it returned, "tension had increased to the breaking-point." Wermuth first announced that the committee was ready to declare explicitly that it was in no way a court, nor were its proceedings to form the basis for later court action. Although this was a partial victory for Helfferich, what followed was not. Wermuth next announced that the committee had voted four to two (with Cohn abstaining) that "personal considerations" were not adequate grounds for refusing to answer questions, and that a witness could not refuse to answer questions put by an individual committee member. Helfferich, nothing daunted, still refused to answer Cohn's questions, whereupon Wermuth said that the committee had anticipated such an eventuality and had voted (again four to two) to fine Helfferich 300 marks, the maximum penalty for contempt. "At this," a reporter noted, "part of the audience broke into derisive laughter." Well they might, for such a paltry sum was little enough to pay for the banner headlines and the political capital that Helfferich's act of defiance had earned him. The impression which Helfferich had made was heightened when Wermuth resigned the chairmanship of the committee and thus apparently aligned himself with Helfferich.[34] The public also greeted this announcement with great merriment. It did not know that the climax was yet to come.

The first act of the new chairman, Georg Gothein (a member of the Democratic Party), was to press Helfferich to reveal the "personal considerations" which prevented him from answering Cohn. Helfferich, after strongly protesting the fine, was more than ready to oblige. First, he said that, although the committee was supposed to be investigating the causes of Germany's col-

[34] Although Helfferich and Wermuth were both Nationalists, Wermuth was apparently not influenced by partisan considerations. An experienced jurist, Wermuth held that an investigating committee was an *"Unding"* unless it was to recommend either legislation or legal action against some individual. Wermuth accordingly considered that Helfferich had ample grounds for refusing to answer questions. For a good discussion of this and related questions, see Peter Rassow, "Der Untersuchungsausschuss," *DAZ*, No. 327, 9 July 1920. In Rassow's opinion the committees were "legally an unfinished edifice."

lapse, Cohn himself "was very directly connected" with this collapse. What came next turned out to be the real surprise: "In a time when the fatherland was waging its desperate struggle against a stronger enemy," Helfferich thundered, "Dr. Cohn had [Adolf] Joffe [then Soviet Minister] place moneys of the Soviet government at his disposal so that he could revolutionize Germany." Therefore, he avowed, "no power in all the world can force me to answer to Dr. Cohn for anything."

Cohn, goaded to fury, fell into Helfferich's trap. Instead of ignoring Helfferich's charges, which revealed nothing new and had nothing to do with the matters at hand, he attempted to refute them. Although he alleged extenuating circumstances and said that he had long ago explained how he had come to receive the Soviet gold, his explanation carried little conviction.[35] He had had to admit once again that some of the money *had* been for the purpose of fomenting revolution, and the fact that he had received it only on 6 November 1918, or too late to affect the outcome of the war, did not alter the fact that the intent was still there. Cohn completed his disastrous recital by referring to Helfferich's earlier remarks that he felt himself to be a mixture of witness and accused: "To that I can only say what I consider his position to be, namely, that I do look upon Dr. Helfferich as the accused in these investigative proceedings." So the truth was finally out in the open: Cohn had confirmed that, for himself at least, the committee was just what Helfferich said it was, a machine for smashing the men of the old Imperial government.

Cohn did not improve the bad impression which he had made when he subsequently fell to arguing with Gothein about some of the expressions he had used. How long this absurd dialogue would have continued had Helfferich not interrupted with a question cannot be said. Gothein admonished Helfferich sharply that his function was to answer questions, not to ask them. The hearings abruptly concluded with the following exchange:

Helfferich: "But I can refuse to testify; I will simply leave." (Agitation.)
Gothein: "Well, we know what to do about *that*."

[35] Cohn had admitted more on some occasions than on others; Baumgart, *Ostpolitik*, 365-67, esp. n.141.

Helfferich: "If the discussion is to continue in this vein, I'm leaving." ([He] gets up, collects his papers together, and steps back from his place a few paces.)

Cohn: "Since Dr. Helfferich for the moment still honors us with his presence, I must say to him once again: I am indeed not responsible for the collapse, but for the outbreak and conduct of the war, one man is guilty: Dr. Helfferich." (Great agitation.)

Gothein: "For this expression I call Dr. Cohn most emphatically to order. —Hearing adjourned. I will set the time for the next meeting later."

The reporter who wrote, "Today's session of the investigating committee was, as a result of several onslaughts by Helfferich, 'exploded,'" hit the mark.[36] Helfferich had made a shambles of the hearings. His last day on the stand, 17 November, was thus something of an anti-climax. Both sides more or less pretended that the events of the 15th had not occurred, although Helfferich once again refused to answer Cohn's questions and was fined another 300 marks.[37] But the public's attention was already elsewhere: it was waiting for Hindenburg and Ludendorff to appear.

Although the committee had originally requested only Ludendorff to testify, the general had requested that he appear together with his wartime chief, Hindenburg, and the committee had agreed. Early on the 11th, a week before he was to take the stand, Hindenburg journeyed to Berlin from his home in Hanover. He was greeted at the station in Berlin by Helfferich, Ludendorff, Colonel Reinhard, and numerous officers of the old Supreme Command. The Reinhard Brigade was drawn up in review, and a pretty girl presented the Field Marshal with flowers as he stepped off the train. When the delegation stepped outside the station, the large crowd broke into "Deutschland, Deutsch-

---

[36] *DAZ*, No. 563, 15 Nov. 1919. For similar expressions see "Helfferich-Skandal im Untersuchungsausschuss," *VZ*, No. 584, 15 Nov. 1919; "Helfferichs Überfrechheit," and "Der Feind steht rechts," *Vorwärts*, No. 586, 15 Nov. 1919; and "Revolte gegen die Wahrheit," *Vorwärts*, No. 587, 16 Nov. 1919.

[37] *DAZ*, Nos. 566-67, 17-18 Nov. 1919.

land, über alles!" The Right was already revealing a sense of theater that their democratic opponents lacked.[38]

Hindenburg had originally planned to stay with General Walther von Lüttwitz, later the military leader of the Kapp *Putsch*, when in Berlin. But Lüttwitz's house was full and, as a result of obscure arrangements, Hindenburg became Helfferich's guest.[39] After Hindenburg's arrival, the Reichswehr showed him great deference, posting an honor guard at Helfferich's door. To prevent the area from becoming the scene of demonstrations and possible violence, the police cordoned off Helfferich's house and the surrounding streets. That did not, however, prevent the Freikorps Lützow from holding an impromptu and unauthorized review (in battle dress) for the Field Marshal before Helfferich's house. Indeed, whenever Hindenburg set foot outside the house there were nationalistic demonstrations of some kind.[40]

After Helfferich had "exploded" the hearings on the 15th, Hindenburg told Helfferich that he warmly admired his conduct and would also like to discomfit the committee when he testified. According to Annette Helfferich, the only source for this exchange, Helfferich pointed out that this would not be easy. The committee members were skilled cross-examiners, and nothing in Hindenburg's background had prepared him to cope with such adversaries. Helfferich was correct, and he must have given Hindenburg pause.[41] Unfortunately, Annette Helfferich's account breaks off at this point but, in view of what actually happened when Hindenburg took the stand, what occurred next seems

[38] *VZ*, No. 581, 14 Nov. 1919.

[39] Walther von Lüttwitz, *Im Kampf gegen die Novemberrevolution* (Berlin, 1934), 107. Helfferich was hardly the most obvious second choice as host for Hindenburg. According to Walter Hubatsch, who has examined the Hindenburg "Nachlass," there is no Helfferich-Hindenburg correspondence from this period; interview with Walter Hubatsch, 11 Feb. 1962. See also Andreas Dorpalen, *Hindenburg and the Weimar Republic* (Princeton, 1964), 49-52.

[40] *DAZ*, Nos. 566-67, 17-18 Nov. 1919. These demonstrations were a source of considerable alarm in some circles; "Die Deutschnationalen auf der Strasse," *BT*, No. 544, 15 Nov. 1919.

[41] Interview with Annette Helfferich, 11 July 1962. There is no way to confirm Frau Helfferich's account, but it seems inherently plausible.

clear enough: Helfferich must have carefully coached the old man on what he was to say. As Helfferich's friend and associate, Count Westarp, later dryly remarked: "Through his adroit interference he prevented the cross-examination of Hindenburg and Ludendorff from turning into an all too distressing and undignified spectacle."[42]

On the day of the hearings, Hindenburg rode to the Reichstag with Ludendorff in one car, while Helfferich and other high-ranking officers followed in a second. When the party arrived, crowds of right-wing demonstrators sang patriotic songs and greeted it with cries of: "Long live Hindenburg!"; "Down with the Jew-Republic!"; and "Down with the Investigating Committee." Bands of Leftists shouted "Down with Ludendorff!" and "Long live Cohn!" in reply, and the police were unable to prevent the rival demonstrators from scuffling. Hindenburg himself was ushered before the committee with great deference. To the Reichstag staff he was still the "demigod" of old. On the table before him lay a bouquet of chrysanthemums tied up with a ribbon in the old Imperial colors, black, white, red. The ribbon and the other preliminaries set the tone for what followed.[43]

Hindenburg was merely supposed to answer questions about the unrestricted submarine warfare decision. First, however, he insisted on reading a statement about the condition of the nation in 1916, when he and Ludendorff first assumed the Supreme Command. Alluding to the unsatisfactory Auxiliary Service Law as a symbol of their failure to pull the country together, Hindenburg said: "From that moment on, the homeland no longer supported us. . . . After that, the clandestine subversion of the army and the fleet also began." Gothein attempted to cut this disastrous recital short, quite without success. The old man courteously heard Gothein out but then went majestically on as before.[44]

[42] *Reichstagsreden 1922-1924*, 20.

[43] *Vorwärts*, No. 591, 18 Nov. 1919; *DAZ*, Nos. 568-69, 18-19 Nov. 1919. Ludendorff, for example, said they would both testify with the same legal reservations that Helfferich had announced on 12 November. See also Walter Görlitz, *Hindenburg: ein Lebensbild* (Bonn, 1953), 231-33; Bonn, *So macht man Geschichte*, 239-40.

[44] John W. Wheeler-Bennett, *Hindenburg, The Wooden Titan* (London, 1936), 234-37, asserts that the general "did not read well," but Bonn states

Such was his prestige that none cared to oppose him. He capped his recital by stating: "An English general [Frederick Maurice or possibly Neill Malcolm] has with justice said that the German Army was stabbed in the back. Where the guilt lies requires no proof." That virtually ended the proceedings. The stunned committee feebly cross-examined both generals and then adjourned *sine die*. "With all the puppet strings in Helfferich's hands," as one shaken member of the government wryly noted, the Wooden Titan had completed Helfferich's work.[45]

Lacking final proof, we cannot say with absolute assurance that Hindenburg did not write the statement himself. The skill with which the account exploited the Auxiliary Service Law in order to shift the discussion from submarine warfare (where Hindenburg could hardly have made a creditable showing) to the final collapse in 1918 suggests that a more practiced advocate than he had a hand in writing it. Under the circumstances this can hardly have been anyone but Helfferich.[46] This appears all the more likely because the statement reflects Helfferich's known opinions about the questions upon which it touched. There were manifest advantages to having Hindenburg state these opinions, because he lent them a veracity which Helfferich himself could never have given them.

In addition to helping propagate the *Dolchstoss-Legende*, Helfferich's earlier disruption of the investigating committee's activities exposed how awkwardly the defenders of the new order employed the instruments of power. It hardly required extraordinary foresight to see that the men of the old regime could not be expected to testify gladly about why they had been unable to end the war sooner or about such blunders as they might have

---

that both generals were "well prepared, if not to say drilled," and the newspaper accounts do not mention any particular awkwardness on Hindenburg's part.

[45] Johannes Erger, *Der Kapp-Lüttwitz Putsch: ein Beitrag zur deutschen Innenpolitik 1919/20* (Düsseldorf, 1967), 71-72.

[46] Görlitz, *Hindenburg*, 232, asserts without citing evidence that Hindenburg and Ludendorff wrote the statement together. Since Ludendorff had been spreading his own version of the *Dolchstoss-Legende* for some months, it is reasonable to assume that he had a hand in writing the statement. The particular character of the argument, however, suggests Helfferich as the dominant influence.

committed. It was therefore incumbent upon the National Assembly to define precisely the committee's competence and the purposes for which its testimony was being taken. This was not done. Possibly lulled into a false sense of security by the cooperation of the first witnesses, the committee was caught completely off guard when Helfferich's refusal to answer Cohn exposed the anomalies of its position. There was no legal substance to his defiance of Cohn, but there was substance to his charge that the functions of the committee were inadequately defined, as Wermuth's resignation signified. The committee as a whole revealed its inner doubts about its standing by taking so long to set a penalty for Helfferich's act of contempt; and these doubts, if such they were, turned out to be quite justified when the courts later determined that the committee had no power to impose such penalties.[47] When the committee ultimately resumed its investigations, it relied less on outside testimony and more on its own research. It also limited its questioning to more purely factual matters, chose its witnesses more carefully, and specifically disavowed any intention to use its findings for later judicial proceedings. But by then, the damage had been done, and it cannot be said that the committee ever fulfilled the hopes of its more extreme anti-capitalist proponents.[48]

The Erzberger Trial

After routing the Investigating Committee, Helfferich dropped momentarily from the public eye. Although his activities during this period are somewhat obscure, he presumably was completing his defense against Erzberger's charges of libel. On 19 January 1920, in the Moabit district of Berlin (Strafkammer des

[47] "Geldstrafe gegen Helfferich nicht vollstreckbar," *VZ*, No. 39, 22 Jan. 1920.

[48] For the committee's efforts to avoid a repetition of the Helfferich-Hindenburg fiasco, see *DAZ*, Nos. 575, 587, 607, and 611, 22 and 29 Nov. and 10 and 12 Dec. 1919. For the later history of the committee, see Eugen Fischer-Baling, "Der Untersuchungsausschuss für die Schuldfragen des ersten Weltkrieges," in Alfred Herrmann (ed.), *Aus Geschichte und Politik: Festschrift zum 70. Geburtstag von Ludwig Bergstraesser* (Düsseldorf, 1954), 119-28.

Landgerichts I Berlin), the trial began.[49] It was the final battle in Helfferich's campaign to drive Erzberger from public life. Helfferich intended that the trial should establish beyond doubt that the charges he had leveled at Erzberger were accurate and that the latter was indeed as corrupt and unsuited to high public office as he had long asserted.

For the seven-odd weeks that the trial lasted (until 12 March 1920), the proceedings created "a regular sensation." Helfferich and Erzberger were both striking personalities who could be counted on to provide excitement, and the outward circumstances of the trial also assured that the press would cover it in detail. A fascinated public was titillated by the minutest details of Erzberger's private life ("how much [I] paid for dinner," as Erzberger himself said); Bethmann Hollweg and other notables of the old empire testified about such controversial matters as the July Crisis of 1917; and the *kugelrund aber nicht kugelsicher* (bullet-round but not bullet-proof) Erzberger was wounded by pistol shots early in the trial by a fanatical ex-cadet hardly out of his teens.[50] Finally, the nature of the trial itself guaranteed that the attention of the public would remain focused upon it, for it was to be a judicial proceeding of a most unusual kind.

The singular character of the trial became apparent almost immediately. After a day devoted to legal technicalities, Helfferich began the proceedings with a statement in which he first recounted his difficulties in forcing Erzberger to sue—"he had to fight for months"—and then presented a detailed and highly colored indictment of his opponent. It included most of his previous examples of Erzberger's "sins" plus quite a number not

[49] The best account of the trial is Epstein, *Erzberger*, Ch. 14. For other pro-Erzberger accounts, see Siegfried Löwenstein, *Der Prozess Erzberger-Helfferich: ein Rechtsgutachten* (Ulm, 1921); Ludwig Quessel, "Ein Rückblick auf den Prozess Helfferich-Erzberger," *Sozialistische Monatshefte* (April 1920), 241-48. For pro-Helfferich accounts, see "A" [Adolf Stein], *Gerichtstage über Erzberger* (Berlin, 1920); and Oertzen, *Politische Prozesse*, 9-34. For useful background material on the German legal system, see Howard N. Stern, "Political crime and justice in the Weimar Republic" (Doctoral dissertation, The Johns Hopkins University, 1966), 1-22.

[50] "How much . . . ," *Prozess*, 40; "Kugelrund . . . ," Troeltsch, *Spektator-Briefe*, 105, entry of 6 Feb. 1920.

previously disclosed. Although the statement took "over two hours" to deliver, it was to appear the very next day as a widely distributed Nationalist Party propaganda pamphlet, a further indication of the nature of its contents.[51] Helfferich had at the very beginning effectively obscured who was on trial by forcing Erzberger onto the defensive. He was to remain there for the remainder of the trial. In part, that was because, as Landgerichtsdirektor Baumbach, the presiding judge, put it: "In every trial of this kind, the co-plaintiff [Erzberger—the state was the other co-plaintiff] appears more or less as the accused; that is so in every trial for slander."[52] At one point, this confusion about who actually was on trial became so great that a witness asked in bewilderment, "Who is the accused?"[53] It was a fair question. Legally, Helfferich was the accused, but everyone understood that the man really on trial was Erzberger.[54]

Besides revealing some of the legal pitfalls in Erzberger's path, Helfferich's speech exposed the bias of the court. Practically everyone, from Judge Baumbach to the lowliest court flunkey and most of the audience, favored Helfferich. Occasionally this prejudice expressed itself in very petty ways, as on the day when there were flowers at the places of Helfferich and Baumbach but not of Erzberger.[55] The rotund Finance Minister could doubtless have borne such trivial insults, but for Baumbach to permit what Erzberger's attorneys rightly protested as a "political speech" was a far more serious matter. Baumbach did offer Erzberger a chance to reply, but when the latter did so he merely gave Helfferich's charges all the more publicity and thus played into his

---

[51] *VZ*, No. 36, 20 Jan. 1920. The speech was reprinted as: *Gegen Erzberger: Rede vor der Strafkammer in Moabit, 20. Januar 1920* (Berlin, 1920). *Vorwärts* reprinted on 20 January a Nationalist Party notice dated 17 January, which notified party members that the speech would be available as *Flugschrift* 49; *Vorwärts*, No. 36, 20 Jan. 1920.

[52] *Prozess*, 446. See also the complaints of Richard von Kühlmann about the difficult position of the plaintiff in libel suits; Kühlmann, *Erinnerungen*, 564. Helfferich, be it noted, won when *he* sued for slander; see, for example, "Ein neuer Helfferich-Prozess," *DAZ*, No. 612, 14 Dec. 1920; *Prozess*, 238-58.

[53] *Ibid.*, 835.

[54] See for example Georg Bernhard, "Politische Moral," *VZ*, No. 46, 26 Jan. 1920.

[55] *Vorwärts*, No. 79, 12 Feb. 1920.

opponent's hands. In the days that followed, Helfferich usually introduced whatever new material was to be considered with similar (though shorter) speeches. These speeches, which would be inconceivable in an American court, were aimed as much out the window at the press as at the court. Once on the record, such speeches, in which Helfferich used expressions such as "the acme of corruption," and "profiteering schemes" to characterize things Erzberger had said or done, were no longer actionable for libel and could be reprinted in the press without penalty.[56] Helfferich was usually able to time his speeches so that they made the evening papers, whereas the rest of the day's proceedings often had to wait for the morning editions. This technique enabled Helfferich constantly to refocus attention on Erzberger's "turpitude."[57] Baumbach should never have permitted such behavior, for political harangues were no more usual in German courts than in our own.[58]

Although Baumbach may have been prejudiced against Erzberger, the trial testimony suggests that this is not the entire explanation for his conduct.[59] Apparently rather too impressed by Helfferich's opening remarks about the unusual features of the case—a minister suing an ex-minister, for instance—Baumbach allowed Helfferich to persuade him that ordinary courtroom norms did not fully apply in this unprecedented situation. Baumbach was not the man to master such a situation (which was partly of his own making), and his efforts to do so are best characterized as well-meaning but futile. He repeatedly threatened to clear the court, for example, when the audience (mainly elegant society women and other Nationalist ladies and gentlemen with nothing to do)[60] applauded Helfferich or booed Erzberger, yet never once did he do so. In this "Homeric struggle," as Baumbach himself described it, his role was not so much to preside as

[56] *Prozess*, 635, 623-24. In an American court such utterances would never have been allowed in the record in the first place.

[57] Helfferich was apparently very skillful in his handling of the press, providing reporters with advance copies of his speeches and otherwise keeping his case before them; Epstein, *Erzberger*, 356.

[58] Erich Eyck, "Das Erzberger Urteil," *VZ*, No. 131, 13 March 1920. Such political speeches were to become, unfortunately, all too common.

[59] See, however, Epstein, *Erzberger*, 372-73n9.

[60] *Ibid.*, 355.

to comment on events after the manner of a chorus in a Greek tragedy.[61] In short, the usual procedural safeguards broke down completely. Toward the end of the trial, Baumbach, who clearly had the feeling that he had taken the wrong turn somewhere, plaintively remarked to Helfferich: "The public is gradually acquiring the impression that I am allowing Your Excellency too much leeway, and in the long run this will [adversely] influence the feeling of impartiality [of the court]."[62] This was a belated awakening indeed, coming as it did the day before the concluding arguments were to begin.

Helfferich's speeches indirectly revealed a number of additional hurdles before Erzberger. The greatest of these was the extreme latitude which German libel law allowed the defendant to establish his case.[63] In the press campaign, Helfferich had alleged that Erzberger was guilty of three main categories of offenses, "conflict of interest," "habitual untruthfulness," and "offenses against the proprieties." He had produced relatively few concrete examples to substantiate these vague charges, however. In most countries (to oversimplify somewhat the legal situation) Helfferich's defense would necessarily have rested on the truth of these examples. In Germany it was perfectly permissible to introduce new material, as Helfferich did in his opening speech, if it bore on the original charges. This explains the trial's length. Helfferich ultimately offered sixty examples to substantiate his major charges.[64] This quirk in the law placed Erzberger in an extremely difficult position, for instead of having to refute Helfferich only on the matters for which he had originally brought suit, he found himself continually confronted with new material. With little chance to review his personal records, consult friends, or otherwise refresh his memory, he was forced to testify under oath on business and political matters in which he had been involved, usually quite a number of years earlier. In

---

[61] *Prozess*, 619. [62] *Ibid.*, 770.

[63] Löwenstein, *Prozess*, 101-107, contains an excellent discussion of the legal technicalities, comparing German with foreign libel law and making suggestions for reform.

[64] These cases are too numerous and complex to discuss here. For the details on the most important ones, see Epstein, *Erzberger*, 109-11, 360-64, 413-19, 422-30.

part, to be sure, this situation was of Erzberger's own making, because, in order to clear his name, he specifically agreed that all cases in which he supposedly had acted improperly might be considered.

The need to testify on short notice on every conceivable action in his past worked greatly to Erzberger's disadvantage. On one occasion, Helfferich asked Erzberger a question to which the latter was forced to reply, "I can no longer remember all the details." Helfferich then posed a hypothetical situation related to the previous question and asked Erzberger what he would have done in such a situation. When Erzberger failed to answer, Helfferich triumphantly announced: "Then I will not embarrass the witness [Erzberger]. I will forego an answer and leave the decision on the question to the judgment of the court."[65] Contrary to the implications of this statement, later testimony revealed that in the affair in question Erzberger's conduct was in no way reprehensible. Had he been able to remember "the details," he could have established that he had nothing to hide.

The second example explains in part why Erzberger was reluctant to commit himself under oath about matters far in the past. In the press campaign, Helfferich had maintained that Erzberger's formal business relations with the steel baron, August Thyssen, went back at least to early 1914. During the trial, Erzberger stated on a number of occasions that his formal connection with Thyssen began only in 1915, when he had become a Thyssen director. Toward the end of the trial it developed that their formal business relations went back to 1913, when Erzberger had taken money from Thyssen to invest in a new blasting process in which he had an interest and which was supposed to reduce the danger from fire-damp explosions in the mines. The court held that this evidence substantiated Helfferich's allegation (although at the time he made it, the evidence was unknown to him) and that Erzberger, if not actually untruthful, was extremely careless in his testimony, although it also admitted that the remoteness of the affair somewhat excused such carelessness. Such was the dilemma facing Erzberger: if he failed to testify, he allowed Helfferich to make cheap debating points by imply-

[65] *Prozess*, 103.

ing that he knew the answer but did not wish to incriminate himself,[66] and if he did answer, and was so unfortunate as to suffer a lapse in memory, he was likely to find himself labeled a perjurer.[67]

Another factor which favored Helfferich was the disorganized way in which the business of the trial was conducted. Sometimes several questions were discussed on the same day, and sometimes one question was discussed on several different and widely separated days. Because the witnesses on a given question were not always available at the same time, this state of affairs was not always avoidable. In practice, however, it enabled Helfferich to keep hammering away at a question until the maximum propaganda benefit had been extracted from it. It also allowed him to pique the curiosity of the public about dramatic future revelations. On the fourth day of the trial (24 January 1920), for example, some preliminary technicalities having to do with Erzberger's connection with a construction company, Julius Berger Tiefbau, were first discussed (later treated on 10 and 12 February). Then Helfferich's attorney, Max Alsberg, asked Erzberger just what sort of business activities he thought permissible for a deputy; would Erzberger care to explain how he had come to purchase stock in the HAPAG steamship company early in 1919 (later treated on 23 February)? After Erzberger had begun his explanation—and to speak with effect he needed to acquire a certain momentum[68]—Alsberg interrupted with an irrelevant question. Erzberger and his attorneys immediately protested the interruption, but it did them no good. Alsberg continued to interrupt Erzberger whenever he wished to break into the latter's train of thought or destroy the impact of his words. In the present instance, Helfferich commented irrelevantly about *his* conduct as a minister in private business mat-

[66] One of Erzberger's attorneys pointed out in his final summation Helfferich's use of this technique; *ibid.*, 939.

[67] To establish that he was not a perjurer, Erzberger later asked that suit for perjury be brought against him, but the court which heard the matter decided after investigation that the evidence to prosecute was lacking. This may cast some doubt on some of the original judgments; Epstein, *Erzberger*, 372; Bachem, *Zentrumspartei*, IX, 416.

[68] Oertzen, *Politische Prozesse*, 19.

ters. Alsberg then asked Erzberger if he thought it proper for a minister to own stock in a company whose principal customer was the government; what did Erzberger have to say about his stock holdings in the Firma Richter, which supplied the state railways (later treated on 17 February)? Since this was the first occasion on which this particular question had been mentioned, Erzberger's attorneys again protested, and Alsberg dropped the matter. Only then did discussion turn to the main item on the agenda, namely, Erzberger's business relations with August Thyssen.[69]

This is only a small sampling of the ways in which Helfferich and Alsberg exploited the bias of the court and every chink in the law to conduct what has correctly been termed a "campaign of character assassination." The material they uncovered and served up to the public, though disappointing in some respects, was damaging enough in others. In his opening speech, Helfferich had charged his opponent with "amassing a very considerable fortune" by peddling his great political influence in return for business favors. Neither in the courtroom nor elsewhere was Helfferich ever able to uncover this "fortune." Indeed, it developed that Erzberger had earned from his business activities only about 135,000 marks (three-quarters of which was salary from Thyssen) during the entire nine-year period before 1920.[70] Although he interceded on numerous occasions with government agencies for his business associates (the conflict-of-interest issues will be discussed below), the testimony revealed that this intercession had not been much help to the companies in which he had invested. He had cheerfully speculated in everything from a whooping-cough nostrum called Pnigodin to railway switching devices and the aforementioned blasting process. It was apparently as much the naïve hope of reducing human misery and loss of life as the desire to make his fortune that induced Erzberger to sink his money in such dubious enterprises. Still, finance ministers are supposed to be hard-headed, calculating men, and to be made a laughing-stock in these questions hurt Erzberger almost as much as the revelation of huge ill-gotten gains would have done. It also hurt Erzberger, who liked to picture himself as a

[69] *Prozess*, 104-12.   [70] *Ibid.*, 932.

champion of the little man, to be revealed as a man who hob-nobbed with the barons of industry.

In some cases, Erzberger proved to have had no better judg-ment about the persons he assisted than about the firms he in-vested in. One man whom he helped during the war, a malt-factory owner named Eugen Angele, was arrested about six months later for misconduct while a local representative of the Reich Barley Office (Reichsgerstenstelle). Although Erzberger could hardly have known of Angele's illegal activities at the time he assisted him, the impression was created that he consorted with criminals. Even worse, it came out that Angele had regu-larly sent Frau Erzberger food in defiance of wartime rationing regulations. She had accepted the food (for which she had paid) in order to make her husband, among other things, his *Lieblings-gericht* (favorite dish) of Spaetzle. This picture of Erzberger fattening on Spaetzle—and here his roly-poly form worked against him—at a time when most Germans were on very short rations was most unflattering. He appeared as the petty bour-geois at his worst, as a man who would go to any lengths to keep his stomach full. It was the raking over of such trivia as this that led one observer to note that what the trial was really uncovering was "what a very common man Erzberger was."[71]

These were minor matters. Far more important were Erzberg-er's business relations with August Thyssen and Julius Berger. To outline the externals of his connection with Thyssen: after some years of consulting Erzberger informally on political matters, Thyssen asked him in 1915 to accept compensation for his serv-ices in the form of a directorship at the sizable annual salary of 40,000 marks. Erzberger accepted, and on a number of subse-quent occasions interceded on Thyssen's behalf with various gov-ernment agencies. In the late summer of 1917, after Erzberger's political views had shifted to the left, he resigned. Principally at issue was, first, whether his intercession for Thyssen had been guided by selfish motives and, second, whether he had resigned voluntarily or whether Thyssen had fired him. In retrospect, it does not appear—the judgment of Helfferich and the court to the contrary—in either his relations with Thyssen or Berger or in the

[71] Troeltsch, *Spektator-Briefe*, 105.

320

numerous other conflict-of-interest cases that Erzberger allowed his pocketbook to influence his actions either as a deputy or as an arbitrator.

Nevertheless, Erzberger's conduct in these cases was intrinsically improper, however justified his individual acts to assist his various business friends may have been. One of the most useful functions of an elected representative is to help constituents and others who deserve assistance to cut the bureaucratic red tape that all too often is a part of the modern state. Bureaucrats usually resent such pressure, as they did from Erzberger, but in practice it often serves the useful function of making the administration work more efficiently and justly. Erzberger had begun his political career with an assault on the bureaucrats, when he had helped to expose and to correct the abuses in the colonial administration. To intercede for a company of which one is a director is quite a different matter, however, and this was apparently what Erzberger failed to see. His motives were probably honorable, but in interceding for Thyssen he could no longer be considered nothing more than a simple Reichstag deputy seeking the welfare of his country. In the Berger case, the circumstances under which he had accepted the position were bound to lead to questions about whether he really had been an impartial arbitrator. Thyssen and Berger both employed him at least in part because of his political position—although there were other important reasons—and that was the essential weakness of his situation. It was simply impossible to separate Erzberger the director from Erzberger the deputy: the conflict of interest was implicit in the very situation itself.

Nor can the argument that Erzberger's position was no different than that of Gustav Stresemann, Eugen Schiffer, and other deputies who sat on the boards of various companies be accepted without important qualification. These men (and the numerous landlords who sat in the Reichstag) had come from the business world, and everyone knew in advance for whom they spoke. Erzberger, on the other hand, who had made his parliamentary reputation as a tribune of the people and was a newspaper editor by profession, could hardly make such a claim.[72]

[72] Or such was the opinion of Georg Bernhard, himself an editor; *VZ*,

Still, it is possible to argue that this is hair-splitting. If other deputies could without criticism serve as directors, knowing where to draw the line was in practice difficult, but not impossible. It was not a determination which a court, made up of men who were by training bureaucrats rather than politicians, was especially well qualified to make. At stake were moral issues, for in none of the 42 conflict-of-interest cases which Helfferich produced was Erzberger guilty of any violation of the law. In this country, a legislator charged with such offenses would probably be judged by the legislature in which he sat. If it judged him guilty of unsuitable conduct it might conceivably unseat him even if he had committed no formal violation of the law. Such a procedure would probably have been the most appropriate way to handle Erzberger's case,[73] although Helfferich had made it difficult to ask for a trial before a Reichstag court of honor. Had such a court cleared Erzberger, Helfferich would probably have charged it with whitewashing a fellow deputy. As it was, the court was to judge that Helfferich had established 7 of his 42 cases of conflict of interest.

A tribunal of men without parliamentary experience was even less well equipped to judge the other two categories of offenses. Most of the cases of "habitual untruthfulness," for example, involved things which Erzberger had said in connection with the so-called Pöplau Case (an affair connected with the Colonial Scandals of 1905 and 1906), the budget debates of early 1916, or the July Crisis of 1917. It appears that in all of these cases what was mainly at issue was misunderstandings or honest differences of opinion about what had been said (or what was meant), although Erzberger's conduct during the July Crisis was equivocal enough (see Ch. 6 above). Nevertheless, much of what was revealed was new to the public, and the revelations could not have come at a worse time for Erzberger.[74] It did not help him when

---

No. 46, 26 Jan. 1919. At the time Erzberger took the Thyssen position, Arndt von Holtzendorff speculated that it was "not a very smart move," because his political independence would suffer for it; "Bericht" 203, 11 July 1915, "HB."

[73] Löwenstein, *Prozess*, 106-107.

[74] The day Bethmann was to testify, several hundred people were waiting

Bethmann Hollweg, a man whose integrity no one seriously questioned, testified toward the end of the trial that he was "completely surprised" by Erzberger's attack on 6 July 1917, an attack which Erzberger himself claimed he had warned the government might be coming.[75] Perhaps even more damaging was the testimony of Peter Spahn, one of the elder statesmen of Erzberger's own Center Party, who claimed that the party was "in the dark" about Erzberger's intended attack.[76] These statements did much to establish Helfferich's contention that Erzberger was an unprincipled man who was not even above deceiving his fellow party members if he found it expedient. The court was to judge that Helfferich had established six of the thirteen cases of "untruthfulness" and three of his cases of "offenses against the proprieties."

On 2 March 1920, Chief State's Attorney (Oberstaatsanwalt) Krause, one of the two state attorneys, began the concluding arguments. Discussing only the conflict-of-interest cases, he held against Erzberger in one case after another. Because it was virtually unheard of for a state attorney to side with the accused (the state and Erzberger were, after all, co-plaintiffs), Krause's words made a tremendous impression on the public.[77] The effect on Erzberger, hoping to the last for vindication, can only be imagined. What Krause had begun, First State's Attorney (Erster Staatsanwalt) Clausewitz, who discussed the remaining charges, finished. After Helfferich's and Erzberger's attorneys had given their summations, Erzberger, instead of simply defending himself, carried the war for the first time to Helfferich by attacking his wartime policies and exposing some of the motives for his at-

---

to enter the courtroom before the doors opened. On the next day of the trial, the crowds were even larger. "At the beginning of the trial over two hundred persons had to be turned away, some of whom were demanding entry in a rather tumultuous way"; *DAZ*, Nos. 105 and 112, 26 Feb. and 3 March 1920.

[75] *Prozess*, 712.

[76] *Ibid.*, 711. Johann Giesberts, a party colleague, later testified that Spahn was mistaken. As Spahn suffered a stroke shortly afterward and was much occupied with other matters during the party meeting in question, it seems likely that his memory may not have been altogether reliable about these events; *ibid.*, 757-58.

[77] Eyck points out what a liability for Erzberger this was; see n.58 above.

tacks. This last-ditch effort to salvage something of his reputation came too late. He antagonized the court without convincing either it or the public.[78]

After the prosecuting attorneys had come down so decisively on the side of Helfferich, there was little doubt about what Baumbach's judgment would have to be. "For the most part," he announced on 12 March "[Helfferich] has succeeded in proving the truth [of his major charges]."[79] Holding that Helfferich had not established all of his examples, however, and was hence formally guilty of libel, Baumbach fined him the purely nominal sum of 300 marks. Helfferich was also charged with all costs, which observers estimated at the very considerable sum of "well over a hundred thousand marks."[80] It was not a high price to pay for driving Erzberger from public life; the discredited Finance Minister resigned that very day. So complete was Helfferich's triumph over his hated opponent that not even *Vorwärts*, the organ of Erzberger's Socialist political allies, was willing to defend him. "One can indeed point out that despite the Marconi Scandal Lloyd George is still in charge in England . . .," the paper warned its readers, "but for us republicans in particular, who have the greatest interests in maintaining the purity of the Republic, that is no [satisfactory] precedent."[81] For the moment, even the Socialists were apparently willing to accept Helfferich's case at face value.

By destroying Erzberger politically, Helfferich had made himself a widely popular figure. To many Germans, Erzberger per-

---

[78] See for example Clausewitz's indignant rebuttal of some of Erzberger's statements; *Prozess*, 977.

[79] *Ibid.*, 989.

[80] *VZ*, No. 133, 12 March 1920; "A," *Erzberger*, 76. According to Friedrich Helfferich, his father received a great many donations and offers to pay the costs of the trial, none of which he accepted. Both Helfferich's punctiliousness in money matters and ordinary political prudence would have dictated such a course. Since Alsberg represented Helfferich from personal conviction, the latter's costs were at least reduced by what would presumably have been a sizable fee; Friedrich Helfferich, notes on MSS, February 1970.

[81] *Vorwärts*, No. 133, 12 March 1920. Far from considering Baumbach prejudiced against Erzberger, the paper considered the judgment less favorable to Helfferich than expected, given the opinions of the two state attorneys. Erzberger also received little support from the leadership of his own party; Morsey, *Zentrumspartei*, 297-302.

sonified the failures of the republic, the inadequacies of democratic government, and all of the humiliations which Germany
had suffered since 1918. That so many Germans considered acceptable the means by which Helfferich had achieved his ends
says much about the existing standards of conduct in German
political life. Nevertheless, it would appear that, to achieve his
stated purpose of cleaning up public life by driving the "corrupt"
Erzberger into retirement, Helfferich had used methods and language that were bound to have the opposite effect.[82] He hardly
improved the tone of politics by calling his opponent a *Reichsverderber* and his *Stammtisch* the "grave of virtue." It also did
not help to browbeat witnesses so violently that even the tolerant
Baumbach felt constrained to remark, "Yes, in this trial every-
body's feet get stepped on, even the witnesses'."[83] The same
objections can be raised about Helfferich's press campaign and
some of the techniques he used during the trial. A practical demonstration that such methods were likely to miscarry came early
in the trial, when the unsuccessful attempt to assassinate Erzberger occurred. At his own trial, the would-be assassin testified
that reading *Fort mit Erzberger!* had convinced him that the
only way to save the fatherland was to shoot Erzberger. He had
the concluding pages of the pamphlet placed in the record to explain his motives.[84] That certainly put the moral onus for the
deed where it rightfully belonged, squarely on Helfferich's
shoulders. Whatever he might (and did) say in condemnation
of the deed, he could no more abjure responsibility for it than—
to borrow Justice Holmes' simile—the man who falsely shouts
"Fire!" in a crowded theater can escape the consequences of his
act.

But while Helfferich's methods for cleaning up public life
hardly seem calculated to do so, they are readily explained by
the underlying motives for his attack that were subsumed in his
stated aim. These motives came out clearly in his final summary
to the court. He admitted his "righteous hatred" of Erzberger, a
man who (as he had said earlier) saw "a 'preordained harmony'
between the common good, [his] convictions of the moment, and

[82] He made the statement in his concluding summation; *Prozess*, 979.
[83] *Ibid.*, 7, 469, 531.　　　　[84] Epstein, *Erzberger*, 358.

[his] own advantage." Although he had first come to see Erzberger in this light during their quarrels over colonial affairs in 1905 and 1906, his own wartime political career had given him a particular stake in destroying Erzberger that he had not had earlier. As he put it in asking the court for clemency:

> My tenure in office . . . with all of its sorrows and struggles, with its disappointments and suffering, is a piece of my personal life, of my very being . . . of the name that I shall carry beyond my mortal existence into history. Was it not in the defense of legitimate interests that I proceeded with all possible vigor against a man who helped to destroy all that I was trying to save, and who, I am sure, if allowed to continue as minister and politician, will destroy what yet remains to us?[85]

Herein Helfferich summed up the earlier political indictment in *Fort mit Erzberger!*: that Erzberger was the principal author of the July Crisis of 1917, which marked the beginning of the end for Germany; that Erzberger had made disastrous concessions to the victors during the armistice and peace negotiations; and that as Finance Minister Erzberger was likely to ruin the German economy.

Helfferich also revealed in his summary the depths of his frustration and hatred, passions which he was only too glad to discharge against Erzberger and which he could not suppress during the trial. He frequently lost his temper; as Baumbach put it, "Your Excellency cannot even say two sentences without getting personal."[86] And not only his disposition suffered, but also his critical faculties. He suspected any act, no matter how trivial or outwardly innocent, if Erzberger had committed it. The reverse was also true: if some unspeakable thing had occurred, then Erzberger was undoubtedly at the bottom of it. This way of looking at things led Helfferich to attribute some far-fetched and Machievellian motives to Erzberger. If the latter had been as calculating as Helfferich assumed, however, he would never had left so many openings for attack in the first place. Erzberger was often extremely indiscreet and was none too scrupulous in money matters. But when he said of Helfferich, "The accused exaggerates

[85] *Prozess*, 984, 391, 987.   [86] *Ibid.*, 624.

immoderately," he was speaking no more than the truth.[87] As the trial wore on, Helfferich's tendency to see Erzberger behind everything became so notorious that one of the state attorneys commented adversely on it.[88] It is possible that Helfferich did not take seriously all of the charges he leveled at Erzberger and was merely following the well-known principle of throwing the maximum amount of mud in the hope that as much as possible would stick. For the most part, however, Helfferich undoubtedly believed his charges to be true. Temperamentally incapable of separating issues from personalities, he had come to regard his opponent as evil incarnate.

Epilogue

Helfferich did not harvest the benefits in publicity that he might reasonably have expected from the verdict. The day after the trial was over, the Kapp *Putsch* (which began on 13 March) completely superseded it as a topic of political conversation.[89] An ill-considered attempt to overthrow the republic, the *Putsch* was engineered by Wolfgang Kapp, one of the founders of the Vaterlandspartei, and General Walther von Lüttwitz, who has been aptly described as "technically a Bonaparte and psychologically a Captain from Köpenick."[90] Lüttwitz, the driving force behind the *Putsch*, called the trial a "ray of light in a dark time," and several observers agreed that Helfferich had done a great deal to create the proper atmosphere for the *Putsch*.[91] According to the well-informed journalist, Adolf Stein, and Major Pabst, one of the participants in the *Putsch*, the Kappists offered Helfferich a cabinet post, which he refused.[92] Too shrewd to become involved

---

[87] *Ibid.*, 973.

[88] *Ibid.*, 860. See also "A," *Erzberger*, 38, 60.

[89] See Hertzman, "German National People's Party," 301-302. For a full account of the *Putsch*, see Erger, *Kapp-Lüttwitz Putsch*.

[90] The description of Lüttwitz was that of the Democrat Erich Koch-Weser; Karl Brammer (ed.), *Fünf Tage Militärdiktatur: Dokumente zur Gegenrevolution* (Berlin, 1920), 8.

[91] Lüttwitz, *Im Kampf*, 111. See among others the estimate of Staatskommissar für öffentliche Ordnung Ritter und Edler von Berger that "the outcome of the trial against Helfferich has severely shaken the prestige of the present government"; *Ursachen und Folgen*, IV, 85.

[92] "A" [Adolf Stein], *Sieben-Tage-Buch: Kappregierung und Generalstreik*

with such hopeless dilettantes as Kapp and Lüttwitz, Helfferich was actually rather exasperated with the Kappists for nullifying the political effects of his triumph over Erzberger.[93] Even worse, by seeming to encourage such absurd ventures, Helfferich's campaign against Erzberger inevitably lost some of its luster.

Less than two months after the end of the trial, Erzberger himself survived another assassination attempt—someone threw a grenade into a hall where he was speaking—to embark upon his own campaign of political rehabilitation.[94] The campaign had certain parallels with Helfferich's. He too wrote his memoirs and discussed in a variety of writings matters such as Germany's future foreign policy and the failure of both the capitalist and socialist systems. He also undertook successful actions to clear his name of charges of perjury and tax evasion. By the summer of 1921, his campaign of rehabilitation had progressed so far that he planned to resume his Reichstag duties in the fall. With his characteristic optimism, he even thought that before too long he would be Chancellor. He was never to find out. On the evening of 25 August two young ex-officers, both members of the notorious Organisation Consul, riddled Erzberger with bullets.[95] Hit eight times, their victim mercifully died almost immediately. The *Frankfurter Zeitung* justly commented: "He was a sacrifice to the poisoned atmosphere which was created by the people who have engaged in such unprincipled and brutal rabble-rousing."[96] Among the foremost of such persons had been Helfferich.[97]

(Berlin, 1920), 18; Erger, *Kapp-Lüttwitz Putsch*, 230n4. See also Ludwig Schemann, *Wolfgang Kapp und das Märzunternehmen vom Jahre 1920: ein Wort der Sühne* (Munich, 1937), 192-93.

[93] Lewis Hertzman, *DNVP: Right-wing Opposition in the Weimar Republic, 1918-1924* (Lincoln, Neb., 1963), 100.

[94] On the assassination attempt, see *VZ*, No. 248, 16 May 1920. For Erzberger's rehabilitation campaign, see Epstein, *Erzberger*, Ch. 15, from which the following summary is taken.

[95] On the Organisation Consul and political murder, see Stern's fine study, "Political Crime and Justice in the Weimar Republic," esp. Ch. 7.

[96] As quoted in Bachem, *Zentrumspartei*, IX, 447.

[97] Helfferich was often mentioned by name. See, for example, the obituary article about Erzberger in Conrad Haussmann, *Aus Conrad Haussmanns politischer Arbeit*, ed. by friends (Frankfurt a. M., 1923), 108. See also the

Nevertheless, he certainly had never wished to see Erzberger murdered. The crime appalled him, and in addition it turned Erzberger from the ridiculous figure of the trial into something like a martyr, and Helfferich from a savior of the people into something like an assassin.

---

later testimony of one of the murderers, Heinrich Schulz; "Aus den Akten der Prozesse gegen die Erzberger-Mörder," *VfZ*, 10 (1962), 449.

IX. OPPOSITION CRITIC

Recalling an earlier remark, a contemporary aptly noted that the Kapp *Putsch* was "more than a crime, it was a mistake."[1] Helfferich shared this view, but the *Putsch* brought him one solid gain. It encouraged the Socialist-led government of Hermann Müller to advance the Reichstag elections from the fall of 1920 to early June. In contrast to the situation before the elections to the National Assembly, the Nationalists now clamored for Helfferich's services as a candidate. Placed on the party lists in a number of districts, he headed the lists in three, Hesse-Nassau, Hanover-South, and Hamburg. After election from all three, he chose to represent Hesse-Nassau in west central Germany because it was the largest of the districts.[2] He was at the beginning of his last career, that of Reichstag deputy. Before considering this career, however, something should be said of Helfferich's pre-1920 relations with the Nationalist Party.

Helfferich and the Nationalists: 1919 to 1920

Before the elections to the National Assembly, Helfferich had apparently hoped to join the People's Party. Although willing to accept him, Stresemann could not break down the resistance of the local organization in the Berlin district from which Helfferich was to run; they said that he stood "too far to the Left."[3] Perhaps because he still cherished hopes of forming a great party which combined elements of all parties to the right of the Socialists, Helfferich campaigned for both the People's Party and the Na-

[1] Quoted in Troeltsch, *Spektator-Briefe*, 189.

[2] Kuno von Westarp, "Helfferich," in Georg von Below and Hans von Arnim (eds.), *Deutscher Aufstieg: Bilder aus der Vergangenheit und Gegenwart der rechtsstehenden Parteien* (Berlin, 1925), 376; Hans-Erdmann von Lindeiner-Wildau, "Nachruf," in anon. (ed.) [Annette Helfferich?], *Karl Helfferich zum Gedächtnis* (n.p., n.d. [1924?]), 92.

[3] "Helfferichs Wandlungen," *Vorwärts*, No. 204, 1 May 1924.

tionalist Party before the National Assembly elections.[4] He probably also wished to keep doors open into both camps. Given the character of the parties at the time, his action was understandable. Although the Nationalists stood farther to the Right, the parties hardly differed ideologically. Both stood for constitutional monarchy, a strong state, capitalism, and the Imperial heritage, and both repudiated the revolution. The differences in tone and nuance which were later to distinguish them had not yet become especially apparent. Stresemann, who dominated the People's Party, was not yet the *Vernunftrepublikaner* he was later to become, nor were the leading Nationalists as immoderate as they later became. The more reactionary and racist Nationalists—and the two groups were not altogether synonymous—were still overshadowed by the moderates. Together the parties formed a small but usually united right-wing opposition in the National Assembly. For all these reasons, and also because the People's Party was so small (22 seats out of 423) that many of its members despaired of its independent future, influential men from both parties negotiated persistently throughout early 1919 toward fusion. These efforts, which came the closest to success in June 1919, all failed because Stresemann steadfastly opposed them. Fear of losing personal power was his main objection to merger, but his hope of later attracting disillusioned Democrats and his antipathy toward some of the more reactionary Nationalists also weighed heavily in his considerations.[5]

As Helfferich undoubtedly shared many of Stresemann's antipathies, his eventual choice of the Nationalist Party (if the choice was indeed his) is something of a puzzle. To solve it, one is reduced to speculation. The most important difference in the political viewpoints of the two men was on the issue of parliamentary versus bureaucratic government. If at first no true re-

---

[4] Stresemann "Nachlass," 3068/6891/133906. See above, p. 289.

[5] The best guides to the People's and Nationalist parties during this period are Henry A. Turner, *Stresemann and the Politics of the Weimar Republic* (Princeton, 1963), Ch. 2, and on the question of fusion, esp. 32-34, 44-46; Hertzman, *DNVP*, Chs. 2-3. On the question of fusion, see also Wolfgang Hartenstein, *Die Anfänge der deutschen Volkspartei 1918-1920* (Düsseldorf, 1962), 132-42.

publican, Stresemann had at least been convinced by his wartime experiences of the need for parliamentary government.[6] Helfferich, on the other hand, was equally convinced that the wartime increase of the Reichstag's power was a major cause of Germany's defeat. He accepted democratic, parliamentary government as one of the realities of the postwar situation but was still inwardly unreconciled to it. Stresemann characteristically found the idea of working with the Socialists much easier to accept than Helfferich did. The Socialists were much more ready to accept Stresemann than Helfferich, to whom they remained irreconcilably opposed. Still, in 1919 these abstract considerations were perhaps less important than personal considerations. After the elections to the National Assembly, Stresemann perhaps had second thoughts about taking Helfferich into his party. He had not fought off all attempts to merge his party with the Nationalists only to accept a man who might eventually be expected to challenge his leadership and who was almost sure to frighten away the Democrats whom Stresemann counted on attracting. For his part, Helfferich doubtless envisaged playing a much larger role in the Nationalist Party than he could ever expect to do in the People's Party. Besides being larger, the Nationalist Party could boast no one of Stresemann's stature. Helfferich may have hoped from the beginning to make the party his own, and he nearly succeeded.

In early 1919, however, the days when Helfferich was to dominate the party were still to come. In the beginning he had to make his way in the face of the hostility of many members, although others were ready enough to welcome him. Unlike the relatively homogeneous People's Party, which was basically the old National Liberal Party stripped of its right and left wings, the Nationalist Party was a very diverse agglomeration indeed. Under its banners rallied "Conservatives, Free Conservatives, Racists, Christian Socialists, Pan-Germans, and other assorted agrarians and 'patriots.' "[7] What held this motley band together

[6] Turner, *Stresemann*, 8-10, 41-43; Marvin L. Edwards, *Stresemann and the Greater Germany 1914-1918* (New York, 1963), Ch. 8.

[7] Hertzman, *DNVP*, 34. See also Werner Liebe, *Die Deutschnationale Volkspartei 1918-1924* (Düsseldorf, 1956), 12-39. The latter is particularly strong on organizational questions.

was not a common ideology but the certain knowledge that only if unified could it have any political influence in the republic. Thus, although the party sheltered many of Helfferich's bitterest right-wing foes of the past (or the groups that they represented), the tendency immediately after the war was to bury old quarrels in the interest of survival. Furthermore, those groups within the party which were most opposed to Helfferich—the more extreme Conservatives, Racists, agrarians, and Pan-Germans—were as much under a cloud right after the war as Helfferich. In many cases they had succeeded no better than he in securing districts from which to run for the National Assembly.

There were a number of developments in 1919 which leveled some of the obstacles to Helfferich's full participation in party activities. The more moderate and progressive elements in the party, which sought to create a broad national right-wing movement, were rather successful in the elections to the National Assembly. Although the old Conservative Party had provided the organizational nucleus around which the Nationalist Party had been organized, the new party moved into many areas where Conservatives seldom or never had been elected. Moreover, the old Conservatives were defeated, in many cases, even in their former East Elbian strongholds. After the election, the titular head of the party, Oskar Hergt, managed to create a national organization which represented the party as a whole and was not merely a forum for the groups which had joined to form it. Pruning Conservative influence sharply, Hergt shared his leadership with the moderate left wing of the party, the old Free Conservatives and Christian Socialists. This meant that at the national level the party was in the hands of former bureaucrats. Hergt himself had been the last Prussian Finance Minister before the revolution. The leader of the National Assembly delegation, Count Arthur von Posadowsky-Wehner, was a former Imperial Interior Secretary and a noted *Sozialpolitiker*. He was ably supported by another ex-Interior Secretary, Helfferich's former patron and colleague, Clemens von Delbrück. These men could not conceivably view Helfferich's past career as the old Conservatives did. Whereas the latter sharply condemned Helfferich's wartime loyalty to Bethmann Hollweg, Posadowsky and Delbrück could only approve of it. Whatever their disagreements with Helfferich on substantive questions may have been, he had at least behaved according to a code which they understood; like themselves, he was a bureaucrat.

With such men in control of the party at the national level, it is hardly surprising that Helfferich was one of the principal exponents of party views on economic and fiscal policy at the first great party congress of July 1919.[8] Although all party congresses were to be important occasions, this congress was especially so. Seeing each other in many cases for the first time, the delegates acquired a sense of solidarity that they had hitherto lacked. They also hammered out solutions to many important organizational and doctrinal questions. For Helfferich to speak on such an important occasion meant that he had been accepted, at least at the national level.

By this time Helfferich had also acquired another powerful ally within the party, the foremost of the old Conservatives, Count Kuno von Westarp. Although a man of resolutely conservative political outlook, Westarp was not a doctrinaire. His strength as political leader, which lay in his ability to work out compromises between dissident factions of the party, was in large measure responsible for the Nationalists' cohesion. He did not hold Helfferich's support of Bethmann against him. Westarp became one of Helfferich's most enthusiastic advocates, and, although two such independent-minded men could hardly be expected to agree on all questions (nor did they), they became good friends as well.[9]

Yet in all this there was still something missing, for however popular Helfferich was with the party bosses, the rank and file continued to regard him with suspicion. This distrust was important, for while Hergt had created a national organization which effectively represented the party as a whole, he was not strong enough to dictate in all matters to the financially dominant

[8] Helfferich's speech was an attack on Erzberger's fiscal policy; *DAZ*, No. 331, 13 July 1919. He also spoke at a Party Congress in Stettin in October; *BT*, No. 505, 25 Oct. 1919.

[9] *Reichstagsreden 1922-1924*, 7-8. One issue, among others, on which they differed sharply was the Racist issue discussed below, Ch. 10.

district and regional organizations.[10] As late as the fall of 1919 none of the districts could be forced to accept Helfferich as a prospective Reichstag candidate.[11] When it was proposed to run him from Pomerania, the Conservatives who controlled that organization attempted, unsuccessfully, to persuade Westarp to run instead. Helfferich's prewar forays against the agrarians and his wartime career were still too much for these reactionary gentlemen to swallow. Not his assaults on Erzberger, nor his brilliant performance against the republic before the Investigating Committee, nor even his close association with Hindenburg were enough to overcome their distaste for him. Helfferich was also meeting opposition in other quarters. In the district of Potsdam II, in Berlin, the local anti-Semites were making much of his former connections with Jewish finance capital, and the ladies, who had great influence in this organization, wanted a place on the list for a woman if Helfferich were to be a candidate. Although the latter condition did not constitute an outright rejection of Helfferich, since no such condition was set for anyone else it did not indicate much enthusiasm for him.

The outcome of the Erzberger trial changed everything. No longer merely accepted on sufferance, Helfferich became a much sought after speaker at party rallies before the June 1920 elections. On one such occasion, when he was to speak in the Charlottenburg suburb of Berlin, such a throng wished to hear him that the doors had to be closed an hour before the program began.[12] His Bremen speech of early May is a fair sample of his campaign oratory, which varied little from one engagement to the next.[13] The government parties (the Majority Socialists, the Center, and the Democrats) were campaigning on the slogan, *Der Feind steht rechts* (the enemy stands on the Right). Because the ties between the Nationalists and the Kappists were extremely compromising, Helfferich found himself hard put to defend his

[10] Liebe, *DNVP*, 32-34.   [11] Hertzman, *DNVP*, 111-12.

[12] "Helfferich-Versammlung in Charlottenburg," *VZ*, No. 270, 29 May 1920.

[13] Helfferich, *Vortrag in Bremen am 6. Mai 1920* (Bremen, 1920). See also the accounts of the speech he made on 21 April in Hanover; "Helfferichs Kandidatenrede," *VZ*, No. 207, 23 April 1920; "Helfferich auf hohem Pferde," *Vorwärts*, No. 207, 23 April 1920.

party against the charge. He claimed that the Kappists had merely been defending the constitution against a government which was illegally prolonging the National Assembly long after its work of constitution-making had been finished. He deplored the violence which had accompanied the *Putsch*, but he also asserted, "We must nevertheless concede that the leaders acted out of wholly decent motives." (Most political assassins would say the same thing, of course.) He also implied that the credit for ending the *Putsch* was due the Nationalists, who had persuaded the Kappists to give up their absurd venture, rather than to the "Godlessly proclaimed general strike" of the Socialists. Helfferich notwithstanding, it clearly was the general strike that brought home to the Kappists (or at least their fellow travellers) how fantastic and dangerous their undertaking truly was.

After presenting this tendentious interpretation of recent events, Helfferich proceeded to criticize the government and the government parties. Much of what he said was merely a repetition of his case against Erzberger, whom he continued to bludgeon unmercifully. Otherwise, his speeches took their tone from remarks such as those he made about Bolshevism and the "yellow peril." Exercising considerable ingenuity, Helfferich managed to present the two as a combined threat. "It is an indication of the enormity of the danger . . . ," he warned, "that from the beginning the Chinese were the elite troops of the Bolshevik armies, and today they are not so very far from the borders of East Prussia." When Helfferich had been minister in Moscow, he had claimed that the elite troops were Latvians; he evidently had little regard for the fighting qualities of the Russians themselves. "Today," he continued, "the great Asiatic peril, together with Bolshevism, knocks at the German gate, as in the days of the barbarian invasions." He then asked his countrymen if they could once again save Western culture as they had so often in the past. Having already noted that the German sword "lay broken on the ground," he presumably thought the answer was no. It is difficult to say how much of what he said he took seriously. Although he was genuinely convinced of the dangers of Bolshevism and believed in white superiority, it seems a little unlikely that he really worried very much about the "yellow peril."

In general, his campaign speeches were on about the same level as his earlier diatribes against Erzberger. He was demonstrating the effectiveness of an appeal which exploited the fears and doubts of the middle classes. Their confidence badly shaken by defeat and revolution, these people were ready to accept incredible explanations for the incredible events of the recent past. Unable to grasp what had happened, afraid that all they had achieved with so much hard work was jeopardized, they were already fairly well convinced that what the conservative middle-class critics of the new order were saying was true.

"In the Sharpest, But Not in Fruitless, Opposition"

Although the Nationalists claimed that the Kapp *Putsch* had cost them ten seats that they would otherwise have won, they nonetheless gained a respectable two dozen seats.[14] Sixty-two Nationalists sat in the new Reichstag, which now totaled 466 members. They were not the only party to benefit from the polarization of political sentiment against the Weimar majority, for the People's Party and the Independent Socialists gained even more heavily. The old majority, which had hoped to benefit from the popular indignation against the Kappists and their right-wing fellow travelers, found that it had seriously miscalculated. The principal losers were the Majority Socialists and the Democrats. The Independent Socialists went so far as to say that, because of the shift to the Right, a "Stresemann-Helfferich government" would have to come. Although *Vorwärts*, the Majority Socialist daily, greeted this suggestion with scorn and sarcasm, the Majority Socialists were not eager to join the new government.[15] The loss of some 50 seats to the Independents had hit them very hard; they concluded that political safety lay in opposition. As a consequence, it was almost three weeks after the elections before the aged Center Party leader, Konstantin Fehrenbach, was able to form a government. Only the Democrats, the Center, and the

---

[14] Walther Graef-Anklam, "Der Werdegang der DNVP," in Max Weiss (ed.), *Der nationale Wille: Werden und Wirken der Deutschnationalen Volkspartei 1918-1928* (Essen, 1928), 41.

[15] "Reichskanzler Helfferich: zum Vorschlag der 'Freiheit,'" and "Die U.S.P. will Helfferich!" *Vorwärts*, Nos. 290, 296, 9 and 12 June 1920.

People's Party were represented in the cabinet, which could hence not command a parliamentary majority. To survive, it had to rely on the benevolent neutrality of the Majority Socialists.

Helfferich was very disappointed that his party had not been included in the cabinet. "We are *Realpolitiker* enough . . . ," he said in his first address as deputy, "to subordinate our constitutional desires [for some form of monarchy] to practical collaboration in the rebuilding of Germany."[16] Although this was the first such statement Helfferich had made, it was not to be his last, for to his sorrow the Nationalists were never to enter a cabinet during his lifetime.[17] His interest in joining in the "positive work" of government did not reflect any fundamental changes in his political attitudes. His sardonic comment about the income-tax discussions of 1921 summed up his opinion of parliamentary government—"it is difficult not to write satire about parliamentary government in Germany"[18]—and he was inclined to ascribe Germany's foreign-policy difficulties to the weaknesses of the republican form of government.[19] "The feared and respected German Empire, . . . the Eden of our past and the Nirvana of our future," as he described it in a saccharine moment, remained his ideal.[20] He was an energetic defender of the exiled Kaiser and visited him in Doorn in May 1923.[21] Still, if his almost total fail-

---

[16] *RTV*, Vol. 345, 2 July 1920, 132.

[17] See, for example, his remarks of 16 March 1922; *ibid.*, Vol. 353, 6309.

[18] Helfferich, "Die Neugestaltung der Reichseinkommensteuer," *Bank-Archiv*, 20 (1921), 190. At the time of the *Ermächtigungsgesetz* debates of 9 Oct. 1923, he backed up Westarp's remarks that the Nationalists "were in no way adherents of the parliamentary system" and were not inclined to save it from its own followers "in this crisis"; *RTV*, Vol. 361, 12,068.

[19] Helfferich, "Die Note der Reparationskommission: Entmündigung und Zwangsvollstreckung," *Wirtschaftliche Nachrichten aus dem Ruhrbezirk*, 2 (4 April 1920), 622.

[20] *RTV*, Vol. 355, 23 June 1922, 7988. See also his remarks of 27 April 1921; *ibid.*, Vol. 349, 3433.

[21] *Ibid.*, Vol. 345, 4 Nov. 1920, 944, and for the visit to Doorn, see Sigurd von Ilsemann, *Amerongen und Doorn: Aufzeichnungen des letzten Flügeladjutanten Kaiser Wilhelms II.*, ed. Harald von Koeningswald (2 vols., Munich, 1967), I, 279-80, entry of 27 May 1923. Helfferich was evidently the first deputy to visit the Kaiser. Although Ilsemann did not state the purpose of the visit, he provides other information suggesting that Helfferich sought to dissuade the Kaiser from hopes of returning to Germany in the near future.

ure to comment elsewhere on constitutional questions is any indication, they were in practice a matter of almost complete indifference to him. On the few occasions when he did express himself on such matters, it was usually to say that for the moment they were not important. When the French marched into the Ruhr in January 1923, for example, he stated: "Today there are no second- and third-rank questions, and also no question of monarchy [versus] republic. We [Nationalists] defend the fatherland as it is."[22]

Failing a monarchy, what Helfferich sought was a *bürgerlich* bloc of all the non-Socialist parties. He believed, both in 1920 and later, that only such a government promised to be strong enough to guide successfully the work of rebuilding. For the moment, he blamed the Democrats for the failure to form a *bürgerlich* bloc: allowing "partisan fastidiousness" to get the better of their judgment, they had refused "to sit at the same table with the 'evil German Nationalists.' "[23] Actually, most of the fault lay on the Nationalist side. Both Stresemann and Carl Petersen, a leading Democrat, pointed out that the kind of electioneering demagoguery in which Helfferich and the other Nationalists had indulged made it difficult to collaborate with them. In addition, Stresemann noted, their extreme views would make the Nationalists an impossible foreign-policy liability for any government.[24] In order to hold the disparate elements of the Nationalist Party together, the party leaders had set such a high price on their inclusion in any government that it was practically impossible for other parties to accept their terms.[25] These same considerations were to thwart all future Nationalist attempts to collaborate in the formation of governments for the duration of the Reichstag session (which ended in May 1924).

With the Nationalists thus thrown more or less permanently into the opposition, the question for the party was deciding what the parliamentary role of an anti-republican party was to be. An extreme minority believed in consistent obstruction in order to

[22] *RTV*, Vol. 358, 26 Jan. 1923, 9516.

[23] *Ibid.*, Vol. 344, 2 July 1920, 134.

[24] *Ibid.*, 168-71 (Petersen); *ibid.*, 28 June 1920, 61 (Stresemann).

[25] In October of 1923, for example, the Nationalists refused to join any cabinet in which Stresemann was Chancellor; Turner, *Stresemann*, 121-23.

bring down the republic.[26] Helfferich did not have much patience with this view. He held that such intransigence was futile and would only dissipate whatever influence the party might otherwise have. It was far better to work, particularly in committee, to make the laws as good as possible.[27] The party had followed essentially this policy on domestic questions in the National Assembly, and in the new Reichstag, Helfferich became one of its most effective practitioners. His activities in the tax and budget committees in good part justified his claim that his party stood "in the sharpest, but not in fruitless, opposition."[28] At times even Wilhelm Keil, the Majority Socialist tax expert, was willing to concede the justice of Helfferich's viewpoint on some questions.[29] Other committee members were downright fulsome in their praise of his committee work,[30] although on occasion it was claimed that his committee activities were less disinterested and more obstructive than Helfferich alleged them to be.[31] Within a year, in fact, Keil was complaining that Helfferich "had . . . already emerged as the leader of the *bürgerlich* parties on tax questions."[32]

Helfferich's importance as a deputy did not end with his committee work. Indeed, it was his position within the Nationalist Party which assured that he would be on the committees in the first place.[33] At the beginning of the session, the Nationalists were not an experienced delegation. Over two-thirds of them, including Helfferich, had never sat in the Reichstag before. Most of these new men could not draw on parliamentary skills gained as ministers or in other legislatures to supplement their lack of

[26] For a sample of such opinion, see Axel Frhr. von Freytag-Loringhoven, *Deutschnationale Volkspartei* (Berlin, 1931), 13-21. See also Hertzman, *DNVP*, 77-79, 147, and Ch. 6.

[27] *RTV*, Vol. 347, 1 March 1921, 2571; *ibid.*, Vol. 353, 20 March 1922, 6381.

[28] *Ibid.*, Vol. 344, 2 July 1920, 135.

[29] *Ibid.*, Vol. 348, 19 March 1921, 3268-69.

[30] *Ibid.*, Vol. 353, 17 March 1922, 6325 (Johann Becker, DVP); 6345 (Hermann Fischer, DDP).

[31] See, for example, *ibid.*, Vol. 357, 14 Dec. 1922, 9324 (Paul Hertz, SPD).

[32] *Ibid.*, Vol. 347, 22 Feb. 1921, 2018.

[33] For Helfferich's role in the party during these years, see Hertzman, *DNVP*, 165-72; Westarp, "Helfferich," *Deutscher Aufstieg*, 377.

Reichstag experience. Helfferich, on the other hand, could look back over fifteen years to his first appearance as a young Legationsrat in the Budget Committee. Both experience and ability assured Helfferich a place as a Nationalist representative on the most important and influential committees, Budget, Taxes, and Foreign Affairs. Furthermore, because the elections had greatly weakened the Free Conservative elements within the party, Hergt turned increasingly to Helfferich for support. Representing the moderate wing of the party, Hergt and Helfferich thought alike on most important questions. They developed an excellent working relationship, with Hergt handling internal party matters and Helfferich determining the broad outlines of the party's position on domestic financial policy and Western foreign policy.[34] Helfferich's ability to express himself trenchantly made him ideally suited to such a role, and he eventually came to overshadow not only Hergt but also everyone else in the party. There were other able men in the party, but as its history after Helfferich's death reveals, no first-rank political personalities. Most party members are said to have regarded him with considerable awe. Even Alfred Hugenberg, who later led the party into Hitler's camp, was content to remain in the background as long as Helfferich lived.[35] That was perhaps all the more noteworthy because in the National Assembly Hugenberg had led the Nationalists in the fight against Erzberger's fiscal reforms.

As the leading Nationalist speaker on fiscal and foreign policy, Helfferich was necessarily one of the leading right-wing critics of the majority's policy in these areas. The content of his addresses assured him a packed and attentive house when he spoke. He was all the more effective because his audience knew that influential business and bureaucratic circles paid close attention to his words.[36] Finally, he spoke with the authority of a professional

[34] Otto Hoetzsch, "Die Aussenpolitik der DNVP," in Weiss, *Nationaler Wille*, 91-92.

[35] Reinhold G. Quaatz, "Zur Geschichte der Wirtschaftspolitik der DNVP," in *ibid.*, 244-47. Hugenberg preferred the shadows anyhow.

[36] See the complaints of the Socialist Paul Hertz; *RTV*, Vol. 358, 15 March 1923, 10,153. See also Constantino Bresciani-Turroni, *The Economics of Inflation: A Study of Currency Depreciation in Postwar Germany 1914-1923* (London, 1937), Ch. 2, esp. 42-47. But if Helfferich had the ear of business,

economist and financier at a time when the great political questions were also economic questions. Helfferich has also been described as the "best hated man" in the Reichstag during these years.[37] Although this hatred reflected in part upon his personality and political methods, it was also a measure of his influence and importance. While given to extreme language, he could never be dismissed solely as a rabble-rouser like some of his party colleagues; he was hated precisely because so much of what he had to say had to be taken seriously.

The hatred for Helfferich was greatest on the Left. He was regularly assailed for his wartime past and for economic policies and political views which were anathema to the Socialists; he was a symbol of all that they disliked about the Right. The Majority Socialist Rudolf Breitscheid once summed up this view: "I must say, to my regret, that the presence of Dr. Helfferich is extraordinarily welcome to me; because to see here such a classic example of unrepentant reaction is extraordinarily bracing and stimulating for every left-wing politician."[38] It certainly was, to judge from how often Breitscheid's colleagues interrupted Helfferich with catcalls. The house was often reduced to such turmoil when Helfferich spoke that the presiding officer had to intervene frequently to restore sufficient order for him to finish. Shouts of "the accused," "the political well-poisoner," "Pharisee," "war criminal," "he belongs before the bar of justice," and the like were the usual accompaniment of his speeches. Helfferich, it must be admitted, invariably returned this vituperation in kind.

Probably no one, however, took Helfferich's Reichstag activities more seriously than he. As a minister he had been sure that the deputies were wasting a great deal of his time in pointless debating. His unconcealed exasperation with this state of affairs was one of the things which had made him so unpopular with the

---

it also had his. Among his closest Reichstag associates were men like Jacob Reichert, business manager of the Verein deutscher Eisen- und Stahlindustrieller, and Johann Becker of the Rhenische Stahlwerke. While Helfferich had severed all business connections upon becoming minister in 1915, the Left was correct in regarding him as a spokesman for big business.

[37] Raumer, "Helfferich," 220.

[38] *RTV*, Vol. 347, 24 Jan. 1921, 2076.

Reichstag. As a deputy he soon came to see things differently. When he spoke on financial questions, he expected the Finance Minister to be in the Reichstag, not off somewhere else. On one occasion when the latter was called away before debate ended, Helfferich tartly commented: "Unfortunately, the Finance Minister is conspicuous by his absence, this time physical."[39] Helfferich himself could never be reproached with irregular attendance. He spoke frequently (his collected speeches from July 1920 to March 1924 make up two fair-sized volumes), was an omnipresent heckler, and seldom missed a roll-call vote. In contrast to many members, he only once requested an official leave-of-absence, and that was in the fall of 1923 when his health forced him to retire for a time to Switzerland.

The year 1920 also marked a profound change in Helfferich's personal life. At the age of forty-eight, when most men who have never married can be counted as confirmed bachelors, Helfferich wed an old acquaintance, Annette von Siemens. He had first encountered his future wife, who was Georg von Siemens's fourth daughter, twenty years before, in 1900. She was only about fourteen at the time, but the connection between Helfferich and the Siemens family survived the death of the elder Siemens in 1901. Siemens's wife, Elise, was mainly responsible because of the biography of her husband that she asked him to write. Because of the pressure of other responsibilities, however, he did not finish even the first volume until the summer of 1921. Annette had in the meantime married Hans von Müffling, a Bavarian. Müffling, a Legationsrat in the Foreign Office, was mobilized at the outbreak of hostilities in 1914 and was killed in France in the October campaigns of that year.[40]

A highly intelligent woman, Annette was an ideal wife for Helfferich. She shared his intellectual interests and followed his political career with great enthusiasm. At times this zeal even endangered her health; she insisted on sitting through long

---

[39] *Ibid.*, Vol. 345, 4 Nov. 1920, 967-68. See also *ibid.*, Vol. 353, 20 March 1922, 6384; *ibid.*, Vol. 361, 9 Oct. 1923, 12,068. To supervise the execution of the *Ermächtigungsgesetz* of 1923, he also favored the establishment of a Reichstag watchdog committee; *ibid.*, 12,073. As minister, he had violently opposed a similar committee during the *Hilfsdienstgesetz* debates of 1916.

[40] Helfferich, *Siemens*, III, 252n.

Reichstag sessions early in 1922 when her pregnancy was well advanced. As a result, she suffered a relapse of an illness which had troubled her earlier. Later in the year, however, she bore Helfferich a healthy son, whom they named Friedrich after his paternal grandfather. Helfferich enjoyed his new family immensely. Within it, he revealed a warmth and a tenderness that one hardly associates with Helfferich the public man. We find him writing to his brother August to send watercolors and other odds and ends forgotten when the family departed too hastily on vacation.[41] One of his last pictures, taken shortly before his death, shows him carrying his infant son Friedrich on his shoulders. In the picture Helfferich looks rather sheepish but at the same time extremely pleased.[42]

Against Fehrenbach and Wirth, June 1920 to November 1922

The domestic and foreign-policy problems facing the Reichstag when it convened in late June 1920 would have daunted any legislature. Unfortunately, the Reichstag did not represent a united nation, but embodied in microcosm the deep divisions within the German people. About the most that can be said of the Weimar Republic of 1920 was that, like the French Third Republic in an earlier day, it was the form of government which divided Germans the least. Aside from some important political changes, the revolution and the new constitution had altered the nation's basic institutions very little. Most important, Germany was still a capitalist country. Despite general dissatisfaction with existing political and economic arrangements, they were accepted because major changes no longer seemed worth the struggle or even possible. Pressing domestic and foreign problems also called urgently for solution. The parties tried to solve these problems in ways which would bring them closer to long-range goals that they had failed to obtain in the National Assembly or earlier. For the Left, that meant defending or extending earlier

---

[41] Postcard, Karl Helfferich (Sils-Maria) to August Helfferich (Neustadt), 28 Aug. 1923, "Kleine Erwerbungen," 45.4.
[42] Scheffbuch, *Helfferich*, facing 96.

political and economic gains, and for the Right, undoing some of what had been done since 1918.

The principal foreign and domestic problems, the continuing budget deficits and fulfillment of the Versailles Treaty obligations, were intimately connected. The budgetary problem was simple enough. Revenues had lagged far behind expenditures since 1914 and showed no signs of catching up. The debt, only 5.5 billion gold marks at the outbreak of the war, had reached the astonishing sum of 220 billion paper marks by mid-1920. When one considers that the far poorer England of 1815 had borne a debt that in real terms was much heavier per capita, the Germans were not so impossibly burdened as it seemed to them at the time.[43] The difficulty was that the deficit continued to increase very rapidly, even though peace had come a year and a half earlier. Part of the problem was that heavy expenditures of wartime origin did not end in 1918. Pensions had to be paid, holders of foreign and other assets seized by the Allies had to be compensated, and interim reparations and Allied occupation costs had to be met. In addition, the Reich had assumed increased welfare obligations and many government responsibilities formerly left to state and municipal authorities.

German foreign-policy problems were equally simple to apprehend and equally difficult to resolve. Here the question was what to do about the obligations imposed by the Treaty of Versailles. Nearly all Germans agreed that the treaty was a horrid document which burdened the German people with impossible and humiliating obligations. A National Assembly majority had ratified it in 1919 because there had seemed no reasonable alternative. While Helfferich thought that "if the German government had shown the necessary firmness . . . we would have gotten a better peace," to many it seemed more likely that the French and English would have marched in, and "Chancellor Helfferich would have made peace in Berlin."[44] Once the treaty was signed, however, Helfferich and many others who originally opposed it assumed that Germany was honor-bound to fulfill it if possible.

[43] Lloyd George also pointed this out; *VZ*, No. 107, 5 March 1921.
[44] *RTV*, Vol. 344, 2 July 1920, 147; *ibid.*, Vol. 351, 3 Nov. 1921, 4830 (Adolf Braun-Franken).

Others, putting the issue in less moralistic terms, assumed that, since only the victors had the power to alter the treaty, they had to be convinced that the more onerous terms of the treaty were impossible to fulfill or unnecessary. Republican Germany, in short, had to create the conviction in the West that it was no longer the bad, militaristic Germany of the "mailed fist" and that it regarded treaties as something more than "scraps of paper." This could only be done if an honest attempt was made to fulfill the terms of the treaty to the letter. By whatever line of logic they chose, then, most responsible Germans agreed that the proper stance toward the treaty was fulfillment rather than defiance, and nominally, at least, it became the policy of every republican government before 1930.

In practice, this agreement on fulfillment meant very little, because of the violent differences of opinion which developed over the question of reparations. It was accordingly possible for Helfferich to become one of the bitterest critics of fulfillment as the Reichstag majority interpreted it. The battle over fulfillment did not, however, reach its most acute stage until the Allies presented their reparations bill, the so-called London Ultimatum, on 5 May 1921. Reparations made the treaty a domestic problem by adding enormous fiscal burdens to the existing large deficit. It thus exacerbated already violent conflicts over the fiscal question. Since, however, the fiscal crisis became acute before the reparations question, it seems appropriate to treat Helfferich's views on budgetary matters before his views on foreign policy.

From March 1920 until November 1922, the man who dominated the government's fiscal policy was Joseph Wirth.[45] He had assumed both the Finance Ministry and leadership of the left wing of the Center Party from Erzberger when the latter resigned. He became Chancellor when the London Ultimatum revealed the bankruptcy of Fehrenbach's foreign policy and forced the resignation of his government. Although Andreas Hermes replaced Wirth as Finance Minister when the Wirth government was reorganized in the fall of 1921, finance policy did not change

---

[45] For a full account of Wirth's political assumptions and policies, see Ernst Laubach, *Die Politik der Kabinette Wirth 1921/22* (Lübeck and Hamburg, 1968), stronger on foreign policy than on budgetary questions.

markedly.[46] The challenge facing Helfferich as an opposition leader thus remained roughly the same until Wirth resigned in November 1922.

Wirth inherited from his rotund predecessor a financial machinery greatly strengthened since Helfferich's day. Erzberger had provided the Reich with its own financial administration and made it the supreme tax authority. He had also provided the Reich with a comprehensive series of very heavy property and income taxes and capital levies.[47] Such extensive administrative changes and revisions in the tax structure had, however, created many problems which Erzberger himself had not had time to resolve. Wirth unfortunately was no match for Erzberger in technical fiscal knowledge, a deficiency which ultimately ruined his foreign as well as domestic policy. The British ambassador, Viscount D'Abernon, went so far as to say, "Directly one discusses the details of the German budget with him, his attention flags and he seems unable to follow even my most lucid developments."[48] A reading of Wirth's speeches confirms this unfavorable impression. He leaves one with the feeling that he regarded his fiscal problems as hopeless. His successor, Andreas Hermes, was no improvement. In the Reichstag, Wirth depended heavily on his Socialist allies, particularly Wilhelm Keil, to find arguments to sustain his positions.[49] Wirth was not the man to set German finances in order.

The Left saw Erzberger's taxes as more than a means for bal-

[46] Wirth disliked Hermes, but as far as policy went he differed from him mainly on foreign, not fiscal, policy; Morsey, *Zentrumspartei*, 452-53, 485, 500n8. For why Hermes replaced Wirth as Finance Minister, see Laubach, *Wirth*, 106.

[47] The best general treatment of the reform is Epstein, *Erzberger*, Ch. 8. See also Paul Beusch, *Die Neuordnung des deutschen Finanzwesens: drei Vorträge* (M. Gladbach, 1919). For a more technical treatment, see Erwin Respondek, *Die Reichsfinanzen auf Grund der Reform von 1919-20* (Berlin, 1921). All of these accounts suffer from proceeding on rather old-fashioned economic assumptions. An up-to-date financial history of the Weimar Republic is badly needed.

[48] Viscount Edgar D'Abernon, *An Ambassador of Peace* (3 vols., London, 1929-1930), I, 230, entry of 24 Nov. 1921. See also the judgment of Otto Braun, *Von Weimar zu Hitler* (New York, 1940), 120, and the recent estimate in Morsey, *Zentrumspartei*, 386-92.

[49] Keil, *Erlebnisse*, II, 221-23.

ancing the budget. They were intended to effect a sharp redistribution of income. Erzberger and the left-wing majority of the National Assembly thought it monstrous that industrialists and others who had made so much money during the war, a time of misery and sacrifice, should be allowed to retain their gains in peacetime. Many also considered that in a defeated and impoverished Germany great wealth, from whatever source, was intolerable. Finally, the Socialists were quite open about expressing their wishes to use taxes as a means for expropriating the capitalists whom they believed had dragged Germany into the war for the sake of selfish gain. (Cohn's bitter charge in the Investigating Committee that Helfferich was one of the instigators of the war is a good example of this sentiment.) There was admittedly a decided element of frustration in the Socialist demand that the rich had to pay. It reflected their unwilling abandonment of their long-cherished plans to nationalize German industry. It had been difficult for them to give up these plans—and they never openly admitted doing so—especially since the revolution had brought them relatively little in the way of social welfare legislation beyond the eight-hour day. Once reached, the promised land was not quite as the Socialists had envisioned it.

Helfferich's analysis of the state's fiscal woes proceeded from rather different assumptions. "We consume more than we produce, that is the root of the evil," he said in his first Reichstag address.[50] This had happened because so many Germans had been blinded by Marxist doctrines that they could not see how poor the war had left Germany.[51] Too little had been done "to awaken the German people to an understanding of our frightful situation." Socialist welfare measures had encouraged a most unhealthy euphoria. Helfferich particularly wanted to abolish the eight-hour day. He thought it absurd to reduce working hours

[50] Except where otherwise noted, the Helfferich quotations from this and the following paragraph are from his speech of 2 July 1920; *RTV*, Vol. 344, 141-43.

[51] In 1922, when Helfferich made his most detailed estimate of war losses, he concluded that national weath had been reduced from the 310 billion gold marks that he had estimated for 1913 to about 200 billion gold marks, or roughly the level he had estimated for 1890; *Politik der Erfüllung*, 16-19.

when production was needed more than ever.[52] He emphasized that he was not in principle against welfare legislation, "but it can cost only what the community can bear." He also sharply criticized excessive wages in many industries, public and private, especially for the unskilled. No rise in productivity justified these wages, only the Socialists' improved political position and the rise in living costs. Since productivity had fallen, wages actually should have been cut, and real wages had in fact declined. "And why?" asked Helfferich. "Because real wages cannot, in any country or under any system, in the long run exceed productivity."[53] If they did, the "necessary result" would be the shutting down of the works in question, whether privately or publicly owned. Finally, although he recognized that worn-out plant was partly responsible for the fall in productivity, he also believed that the workers were less energetic than formerly. For this, too, he blamed the Socialists: "The workers have been told too often that once you were in power, everyone could work less and would live better."

Getting more out of the worker was only part of Helfferich's prescription for raising productivity. He also demanded that state controls be removed as rapidly as possible. This measure would encourage "the spirit of enterprise," which alone could get the economy working "normally" again. He delighted in regaling the Reichstag with examples of ignorant bureaucratic interference. He also considered it urgently necessary to improve German industrial technology and to rationalize the organization of the German economy, in order to cut costs of production and distribution. He thought such modernization most likely to occur if the German entrepreneurs who had created one "great age," as he once termed prewar days, were given free rein. He was accordingly violently opposed to the ultimate Socialist remedy for German economic ills, nationalization of industry. He held that

[52] For a contemporary defense of the eight-hour day, which held that it was not the main cause for the decline in output, see Paul Hertz and Richard Seidel, *Arbeitszeit, Arbeitslohn und Arbeitsleistung: Tatsachen über die sozialpolitische Bedeutung des Achtstundentages in Deutschland und im Auslande* (Berlin, 1923).

[53] *RTV*, Vol. 347, 22 Jan. 1921, 2022.

they did not really take it seriously themselves, it being "mainly a desperate expedient for holding the party together."[54] Rather than preaching class war and nationalization of industry, Helfferich urged the Socialists to proselytize for "social reconciliation" and national unity.

Helfferich was under no illusions about the difficulties of achieving such a reconciliation. He conceded that the rapidly advancing welfare and social legislation of the Wilhelmine Reich had failed to prevent a "gulf" from dividing the German people. The cause, he believed, was that in the great industries "the inner identity between the worker and his work" had been "increasingly destroyed." He thought it necessary to recreate this identity by "creating new forms of collaboration between capital and labor." Stock-purchase schemes, profit sharing, and *Mitbestimmungsrecht* (participation in management decisions) were among the devices he suggested.[55] It cannot be said, however, that Helfferich did much to encourage the social reconciliation he sought. He never gave any sign that he was willing to regard the leaders of the Socialist masses as political equals. Calling on them to meet him halfway on the road to reconciliation at one moment, at the next he harangued them for showing a "total inability to do anything positive while in office" and for "creating machines which work with the greatest possible expenditure to achieve the least possible effect."[56] No wonder the Socialists suspected that it was they who were to make the most of the concessions and found it difficult to take his advice.

If Helfferich had followed the precept *fortitur in re, sauviter in modo*, the Left would still have found his fiscal proposals unpalatable. In addition to calling for more work and fewer con-

---

[54] *Ibid.*, Vol. 345, 4 Nov. 1920, 956.

[55] *Ibid.*, 958. All of these devices have been tried since Helfferich's day, and none has been very successful. On the *Mitbestimmungsrecht* in postwar Germany, see Henry C. Wallich, *Mainsprings of the German Revival* (New Haven, 1955), 306-10, 313; Werner Mangold, "Literatur über das deutsche Gewerkschaftswesen: III, Soziologische Werke zur Praxis der Mitbestimmung," *Politische Vierteljahreshefte*, 4 (1963), 101-11. The *Betriebsträte* introduced in many industries in 1919 were supposed to provide workers with a substantial role in management decisions but in practice never amounted to much more than the usual sort of works committees.

[56] *RTV*, Vol. 353, 16 March 1922, 6316; *ibid.*, Vol. 361, 9 Oct. 1923, 12,069.

trols, Helfferich also sought a simplified tax structure with lower rates and a sharp reduction in government expenditures. Only then would the entrepreneurial classes be left with sufficient funds to finance vitally needed capital improvements.

"An unimaginative hodge-podge of all possible and impossible direct and indirect taxes," was how Helfferich characterized one set of revenue measures.[57] But it was not indirect taxes on consumption that he objected to; these he thought should have been higher. What disturbed him was the level of direct taxes on income and property. This category of taxes, to which capital levies should be added, was large and rates were high. Ordinary income and inheritances were taxed at sharply progressive rates. Substantial taxes were levied against property and a variety of financial transactions. A series of capital levies was imposed on anyone worth more than a certain figure. By the fall of 1921, when work on a major tax reform was begun, things had reached the point that some fifteen separate laws came up for reconsideration by the Reichstag. Helfferich argued that, taken together, even the annual taxes in some cases approached or exceeded the taxpayer's income.[58] "Whoever sees in private property the basis for every social order with a potential for growth can only view this socialization by means of taxes with the greatest possible concern," he lamented.[59]

The Socialists, with Paul Hertz and Wilhelm Keil in the vanguard, claimed that despite Helfferich's plaints the capitalist classes were getting off very lightly because inflation continually reduced what appeared to be very large tax bills to what in practice were rather small ones. It was true. It was not true, however, that the Socialist remedy of raising tax rates was necessarily the appropriate one. The difficulty was that, as rates were increased,

[57] Helfferich, *Die Lage der deutschen Finanzen: Rede am 3. September 1921 auf dem 3. deutschnationalen Parteitag in München* (Berlin, 1921), 8-9.

[58] It is difficult to assess the validity of this charge, because the tax laws were all so complicated that a whole series of cases would have to be examined before one could make a definitive judgment about how burdensome taxes were in practice. As Staatssekretär Zapf of the Finance Ministry said: "The study of our tax-system is . . . no simple matter for the foreigner, especially in times that are so unsettled that even here in Germany opinions are extraordinarily divergent"; *RTV*, Vol. 358, 8 March 1923, 10,022.

[59] *Ibid.*, Vol. 345, 4 Nov. 1920, 951.

an increasing number of exemptions and special considerations had to be allowed for in the laws in the name of justice. As Helfferich put it, "Thousands of considerations that may be individually justified are taken into account, but when an attempt is made to consider every isolated case, the law simply cannot be administered." And the result? "Napoleon, who is supposed to have understood something of government, once said, 'any government that works (*qui marche*) is good'. . . . Our fiscal legislation does not 'work,' ergo it is bad."[60] When assessments ran a year late and more, when taxes had to be abandoned because they could not be administered, when the tax officials themselves could hardly hack their way through the regulations, it would seem that the system did fall short of the ideal. Helfferich thought lower rates would make possible simpler laws and would reduce the premium for tax evasion.[61] He considered that existing rates did not "catch the dishonorable man, but [struck] the honorable man dead"; they were encouraging a "splendid vintage of profiteers."[62] Finally, Helfferich thought that lower, simpler taxes would actually increase revenues by encouraging investment and hence creating a larger tax base. Like modern tax cutters, Helfferich suspected that the longest way around was sometimes the shortest way home.[63]

On the liabilities side of the budget, Helfferich admitted that he had no radical proposals for reducing expenses. He did, however, suggest sharp cuts in the civil service and more efficient management of the great state enterprises, the railways and the post. Appraising the growth of the bureaucracy, Helfferich commented: "Although the Reich has grown smaller and poorer, the civil service has grown as if we had not lost the war but had conquered the entire world."[64] He took as an example the rise of the

[60] *Ibid.*, Vol. 351, 3 Nov. 1921, 4795-96.

[61] *Ibid.*, 7 Nov. 1921, 4853. A striking commentary on how complicated the life of the taxpayer had become was the appearance of regular columns such as Max Lion's "Praktische Steuerfragen" in the *BT*.

[62] *RTV*, Vol. 351, 7 Nov. 1921, 4853; *ibid.*, Vol. 353, 16 March 1922, 6314. He went on to say: "The profiteer is gaining control over the economy and, I fear, will ultimately gain control over the state too."

[63] *Ibid.*, Vol. 348, 19 March 1921, 3261. Helfferich was not, however, what one could call a Keynesian.

[64] *Ibid.*, Vol. 351, 7 Nov. 1921, 4849.

Economics Ministry from the forty officials of his day to over a thousand: "I cannot imagine how it could be possible for [it] to acquire so much water on the brain."[65] The example sounds like a grotesque parable on Parkinson's Law. It was not. When stabilization of the mark was seriously undertaken in the fall of 1923, it was clear that it would fail unless the budget were balanced. One of the first steps taken was to dismiss some 300,000 government employees and to sharply reduce the salaries of the rest.[66]

Helfferich's complaints of waste, mismanagement, and overstaffing in government agencies and businesses were echoed by a series of Allied experts between 1921 and 1924. A sizable postwar increase in personnel was undoubtedly necessary because of the new duties the Reich had assumed. Too much of the increase, however, represented compassionate hiring of the unemployed and bureaucratic empire-building.[67] Wirth himself took far too passive an attitude toward his problems. In presenting the first of the supplementary budgets for 1921, he commented helplessly: "I certainly cannot envisage presenting to you today tax plans which embody the possibility of covering even the greatest part of the extraordinary budget."[68] In other words, deficits were accepted as inevitable. The problem was seen primarily as one of producing more revenues, mainly by raising tax rates, rather than as one of reducing expenditures. Things did not improve when Wirth brought Andreas Hermes into the cabinet as Finance Minister in November 1921.

[65] *Ibid.*, Vol. 344, 2 July 1920, 141.

[66] The continuing promises of the government to reduce the size of the bureaucracy and its continuing failure to execute them were a source of much unfavorable comment in the press. See, for example, Max Paehler, "Der Abbau der Behörden," *VZ*, No. 606, 23 Dec. 1922. For figures on the increase and some of the causes, see Ernst Schulze, *Not und Verschwendung: Untersuchungen über das deutsche Wirtschaftsschicksal* (Leipzig, 1923), 437-44. For details on the later reductions, see Karl-Bernhard Netzband and Hans P. Widmaier, *Währungs- und Finanzpolitik der Ära Luther 1923 bis 1925* (Tübingen, 1964), 43-50, 121-29.

[67] Wirth at first had trouble preventing his colleagues from spending money for which they had no budgetary authorization. Only by threatening to resign (in late 1920) was he able to obtain powers to stop such practices; Respondek, *Finanzen*, 31-33; Laubach, *Wirth*, 28. See also Helfferich's indignant complaints; *RTV*, Vol. 345, 4 Nov. 1920, 955.

[68] *Ibid.*, Vol. 350, 6 July 1921, 4768.

The alleged deleterious effects of the inflation, moreover, do not excuse the rapidly rising budget deficit. The inflation did admittedly complicate enormously the work of drawing budgets and collecting taxes. But it was not true, as Wirth stated, that "every fiscal policy, every tax policy, is reduced to absurdity so long as the mark continues to plummet into the abyss." Wirth saw only that the inflation was reducing the real value of revenues and not that it was having the same effect on most expenditures. In fiscal 1920, when the foreign exchange value of the mark remained fairly constant, the deficit was smallest in the months when the exchange value of the mark fell the most rapidly. Not until the summer of 1922 did the inflation begin to have the effects that Wirth had attributed to it earlier.[69]

Wirth's fiscal problems thus reflected his failings as an economist. These failings might still not have been so serious if his government had not been so weak politically. A strong left-wing government would presumably have paid for expensive government programs and reparations—though balance-of-payment problems complicate the reparations question—with heavy but uncomplicated taxes which it could easily administer. Or it might simply have expropriated the capitalists outright, as the Bolsheviks had done in Russia. A strong right-wing government, on the other hand, would have cut and simplified taxes and balanced the budget by reducing government expenditures. As it was, weak early Weimar governments were unable to resist left-wing pressures for high levels of spending and high taxes. They were increasingly unable to resist efforts of the Right to safeguard its economic position by making the necessary alterations in the tax laws in the name of practicality and justice. Everyone had his way. Money was spent, taxes were not effectively collected. The government financed its enormous deficits with the tax on cash balances known as inflation.

Helfferich's own fiscal proposals, of course, represented those of the strong right-wing government in the model suggested above. He proceeded from orthodox and conservative economic assumptions. Since he favored many of the measures later responsible for the post-1948 *Wirtschaftswunder*—a balanced

<hr />

[69] *Ibid.*, 4469; Bresciani-Turroni, *Economics of Inflation*, 54-67.

budget, relatively few market controls, and a tax structure designed to encourage investment and production for export rather than consumption—one must ask whether such policies had much chance for success in the early twenties.[70] After both world wars, fundamental changes in the structure of the world economy faced government and business with the problems of adapting to a new economic environment. But that problem was not clearly seen after 1918. A legacy of prewar and wartime hatreds, moreover, made it impossible in the twenties for the Left to see Helfferich's emphasis on the virtues of capitalism and the need to rebuild as anything more than a gambit to save the rich from taxes. The Right, on the other hand, fearful of expropriation and suspicious of democracy, exacerbated the hostile feelings of the Left by its provocative behavior, by the sort of "cheeky arrogance" in manner that one Socialist attributed to Helfferich.[71]

After World War II the situation was quite different. Partly because of the development of the conceptual tools of Keynesian economics and partly because of the experiences of the interwar years, the necessary adaptions to a new economic environment were made everywhere much more smoothly. The Adenauer government was more competent "to plan not to plan," as it were, than any government in the twenties, and German businessmen were able to operate more intelligently, and in a better world economic setting, than were Helfferich's contemporaries. Also, the bitter experiences of the Third Reich and the years of suspended animation after 1945 chastened both labor and capital: capitalists were reconciled to democracy and workers to capitalism. Thus Helfferich's fiscal proposals must be awarded a Scotch verdict, for however successful they might in modified form prove after 1948, they clearly depended on presuppositions not wholly obtaining in the twenties, as the equivocal prosperity of the years after 1925 was to reveal.

To return to more immediate matters, the genuine merits of Helfferich's views on fiscal questions convinced an increasingly large Reichstag audience as time passed. More and more often, he was able to point to some breakdown in Wirth's policy and

[70] Wallich, *German Revival*, 13-21, *et passim*.
[71] *RTV*, Vol. 350, 6 July 1921, 4493 (Artur Crispien).

say, in effect, "I told you so." But he still found himself in a minority on tax questions, because on decisive issues such as the *Zwangsanleihe* (forced loan), the key measure of the "tax compromise" of 1922, a party's vote was largely determined by its stand on foreign policy. Helfferich accused the People's Party of supporting the "Socialists' " *Zwangsanleihe*, despite its agreement with his criticisms of the law, simply because to reject the law was to reject Wirth's foreign policy.[72] It was true: agreement on fiscal questions was not enough to hold a *bürgerlich* bloc together. Everyone complimented Helfferich on his work in the tax committee, but too few deputies trusted his ideas about foreign policy. In a sense, Helfferich the Nationalist foreign-policy expert was the greatest single hindrance to acceptance of the program of Helfferich the Nationalist fiscal-policy expert.

As has been mentioned, the battle over fulfillment did not reach its most acute stage until after the presentation of the London Ultimatum, the terms of which Wirth committed himself to fulfill when he formed his government.[73] In accepting the Ultimatum, Wirth did not suppose the government could long support its burdens. He hoped that if the government established its good will by making the initial payments, the diplomatic atmosphere might clear sufficiently to permit a more favorable settlement. Given the other disputes then contributing to bad relations between Germany and the West, such as the dispute over Upper Silesia, Wirth's estimate now seems excessively optimistic. Wirth also seems to have underestimated the difficulties of making even

---

[72] *Ibid.*, Vol. 353, 20 March 1922, 6376-83, esp. 6379. The *Vossische Zeitung*, not a paper normally favorable to Helfferich, agreed with his criticisms of *Zwangsanleihe* and expressed its irritation that its defenders were not attempting to refute the critics on objective grounds but simply accused them of making trouble; Erwin Steinitzer, "Zwangsanleihe und Koalition," *VZ*, No. 113, 8 March 1922; "Helfferich und Wirth," *VZ*, No. 129, 17 March 1922; Georg Bernhard, "Die Zwangsanleihe," *VZ*, No. 289, 21 June 1922. Bernhard also had some unkind things to say about Helfferich's *Zwangsanleihe* proposals, however. See also Laubach, *Wirth*, 145-48, 157-59; Helfferich, *Die Zwangsanleihe* (Berlin, 1922).

[73] The most useful accounts of the reparations negotiations are Laubach, *Wirth*; Carl Bergmann, *Der Weg der Reparationen: von Versailles über Dawes Plan zum Ziel* (Frankfurt a. M., 1926); and for the early period, Keynes's witty and entertaining *Revision*.

the initial reparations payments. The first, one billion marks in gold, was due on 1 August 1921 and the second, the first regular payment under the London schedule of 500 million marks, was due 1 November. With the budget already badly out of balance, to pay these sums was going to require more money in a hurry. Because Wirth never found the money, or even the money to balance the budget when reparations payments were subtracted, his statements to the Allies about German fiscal capability came increasingly to lack credibility. How could one trust the statements of a man who, though clearly filled with good will toward the West, was so obviously failing to master the domestic fiscal crisis?[74] Wirth's inadequate fiscal policies thus helped to rob his country of the gains which his sensible foreign policy might otherwise have brought it.

Helfferich lost no time in pinpointing the economic shortcomings of Wirth's version of fulfillment. Three articles written in May 1921 were the opening cannonades of his campaign. Their titles accurately reflect the rhetoric in which he stated his case: *Germany in the Chains of the Ultimatum,* "The German Government as the Bailiff of the Entente," and "The Way into the Darkness."[75] The titles accurately reflect the character of Helfferich's rhetoric against fulfillment, the violence of which increased with time. Stripped of their demagogic trappings, however, many of his economic arguments against fulfillment were eminently sensible. They added up to reasons why Germany could not pay reparations.

Helfferich's economic case against reparations payments started with the impact of such payments on the budget deficit, already great even before the new burdens were added. Essentially, however, his case rested on the impossibility of paying

[74] Bergmann, *Reparationen,* 137, noted that informed American circles believed that the mark was being deliberately ruined in order to enable Germany to escape reparations payments. See also the remarks of Secretary of the Treasury David F. Houston of 1 March 1920; Harold G. Moulton and Leo Pasvolsky, *War Debts and World Prosperity* (New York, 1932), 63; and Laubach, *Wirth,* 260-61 on Poincaré's similar views.

[75] *Deutschland in den Ketten des Ultimatums* (Berlin, 1921); "Die Reichsregierung als Exekutor der Entente," *Deutsche Tageszeitung,* 31 May 1921; "Der Weg ins Dunkle," *Die Woche,* 23 (28 May 1921).

reparations in cash when the German balance of payments was heavily unfavorable. In a speech on 6 July 1921, he calculated this payments deficit at 112 billion paper marks, or 7.5 billion gold marks.[76] He asked, "Where is the magic wand that is going to turn all this paper, which is all you can get out of Germany no matter how tight you turn the tax screws, into gold?" He concluded that under the circumstances Germany could only make reparations in kind. He calculated that to satisfy such claims in kind extremely large amounts of goods were needed, and pointed out that the victors mainly wanted goods which Germany could not supply such as cotton and copper. The problem was that "deliveries in kind are not only dependent on our good will but also on the good will of others." On the deliveries in kind that Walther Rathenau, newly appointed Minister for Reconstruction, was trying to arrange with the French, Helfferich said that "even if an angel came down from Heaven to help," Rathenau would be unable to arrange deliveries of the size required. Nor in the event did he.[77]

Helfferich also advanced other lines of economic argument which reveal why reparations was such an explosive domestic issue. What he feared was *Überfremdung*, or the transfer of German assets to foreigners. Because the high taxes required to pay reparations could not be met out of current income but only by liquidating assets, Germany would become a nation of sellers.

[76] *RTV*, Vol. 350, 6 July 1921, 4473-80. This figure is probably too high; according to Bresciani-Turroni, *Economics of Inflation*, 86-87, German imports were to a considerable extent paid for by the expropriation through inflation of foreign speculators in marks. Ellis also notes: "To command as great an excess of imports as possible, Germany sacrificed everything salable at disastrously low values"; *German Monetary Theory*, 284.

[77] For Helfferich's opinion of the Wiesbaden agreements which Rathenau concluded with the French on deliveries in kind, see his speech of 7 Nov. 1921; *RTV*, Vol. 351, 4847-63. For a more detailed exposition of his views on deliveries in kind, see his "Die Beteiligung der deutschen Industrie an dem Wiederaufbau Nordfrankreichs," *Industrie Kurier*, 6 (17 and 24 June 1921), 386-88, 425-28. D'Abernon, no friend of Helfferich's, called the Wiesbaden agreements a "fallacy based on a swindle"; *Ambassador*, 1, 214, entry of 7 Oct. 1921. See also Keynes, *Revision*, 94-96; Laubach, *Wirth*, 73-79. According to Bergmann, in 1922, total deliveries in kind (aside from ships, dye, and coal) came to only 220 million gold marks, of which Yugoslavia took 116 million; *Reparationen*, 126-27.

Foreigners would be able to buy up German productive facilities for less than the value of a *"Butterbrot,* for a crust of bread in fact."[78] It is hard to say how seriously Helfferich took this danger, which because of inflation was not very great.[79] In less impassioned moments, he admitted that only limited *Überfremdung* could occur because most German property was not the sort foreigners were interested in.[80] But he did reveal, nonetheless, what actually underlay his fears of *Überfremdung.* "I often have the impression," he said, ". . . from statements coming from the Left that there are men in those circles who would take a certain malicious pleasure in seeing this monstrous fate [of *Überfremdung*] overtake us, who would say, 'Now we've got the clamps on the owners of real assets, and this is how we shall dispossess them.' " The danger from fulfillment was not so much *Überfremdung* as it was plain, old-fashioned expropriation of the capitalists.

The socialists took little trouble to conceal that such an outcome was just what they sought. Artur Crispien of the Independent Socialists called for the "seizure of gold values" and admitted that he hoped the measure would be a "further step on the way to socialization."[81] The working classes could see no reason why those they considered to have frivolously led Germany to war in 1914 should not suffer the consequences of defeat. If Germany was as much poorer as Helfferich claimed, then those who could best afford the losses ought rightfully to bear them. In the fall of 1921, the Majority Socialist Adolf Braun called more firmly than ever for the *Erfassung der Sachwerte,* or seizure of real values.[82]

[78] See n. 76 above.

[79] At other times, Helfferich claimed that inflation would have the same effect and to some extent it undoubtedly did; see n. 76 above. Otherwise, the inflation, by reducing the real value of taxes, made it possible to bear what would otherwise have been prohibitive taxes and thus worked to prevent sales. Those who owned productive assets were naturally the ones least endangered by the inflation and high taxes.

[80] Helfferich, *Ketten,* 16-17. As Helfferich himself elsewhere pointed out, the more important companies assured that control would not fall into the "wrong" hands by issuing stock with special voting rights which was closely held by insiders.

[81] *RTV,* Vol. 350, 6 July 1921, 4495.

[82] *Ibid.,* Vol. 351, 7 Nov. 1921, 4826-32.

A number of plans were then in circulation detailing how to do it.[83] One proposal envisaged mortgaging all business property in favor of the state. A second scheme proposed turning over a portion of the shares of the more important industrial concerns to the state. The intent of such measures was to permit the state to share directly in the profits of business and to provide it with negotiable paper which it could pledge for international reparations loans.

Speaking after Braun in the tax and foreign-policy debates, Helfferich lost no time in countering the demand for *Erfassung der Sachwerte*.[84] He alluded in particular to an industry proposal to provide the Reich with foreign exchange for reparations in return for domestic concessions, the most notorious of which was the demand that the state railways be returned to private ownership.[85] He claimed that the industry proposal proved that it stood ready to assist the government, but warned against "compulsory mortgage organizations," such as the *Sachwerte* proposals foresaw: "you would build our enemies an artificial pumping station . . . which they could use to pump the last drop of blood from the body of the German people."

Helfferich's specific recommendations, made on a number of occasions, for solving the reparations problem were entirely sensible. The first step was to bring about some sort of international settlement. In Helfferich's metaphor, "the entire world is bound in a golden chain, one end of which is wrapped around the neck of the German people, and the other end of which lies in the hands of the American people." If anyone was to be saved, the chain had to be loosened. The second step, if the victors were to obtain anything from Germany, was to bring the German economy "back to health." That meant the end of gold payments

[83] Helfferich describes most of them in his *Politik der Erfüllung*, 55-71. See also Bresciani-Turroni, *Economics of Inflation*, 56-57; Bergmann, *Reparationen*, 132; Laubach, *Wirth*, 84-86, 120-22.

[84] See *RTV*, Vol. 351, 7 Nov. 1921, 4847-63, for quotations in this and the following paragraph.

[85] For an important analysis which relates this proposal to the politics of the day, see Lothar Albertin, "Die Verantwortung der liberalen Parteien für das Scheitern der Grossen Koalition im Herbst 1921: ökonomische und ideologische Einflüsse auf die Funktionsfähigkeit der parteienstaatlichen Demokratie," *HZ*, 203 (1968), 566-627.

for some years to come. He emphasized, indeed, Germany's need for credits. Otherwise, Germany could provide at most goods. Last, the government had to take a firm stand on the question of reparations: "So long as [the French] see a possibility of squeezing millions in gold out of us, so long as we have a government that again and again assures, 'we will pay and pay again,' the French will not stir a finger, nor indeed can any French government do so." Although these were excellent precepts, they were easier to give than to follow.

The entire aim of fulfillment was to bring about just such a solution as Helfferich had recommended. His advice was supererogatory. Wirth's government was failing to obtain these hoped for benefits from fulfillment in part because it was also conspicuously failing to solve its domestic fiscal problems. The victors were, after all, long accustomed to thinking of Germany as a very tough competitor in export markets. Germany had also put on a very impressive economic performance during the recent war. It was thus difficult for the victors, suffering from a mild trade depression themselves, to see why the government could not squeeze reparations out of a country as apparently prosperous as Germany appeared to be in 1921 and 1922.

As time went on and Wirth proved unable to harvest the fruits of fulfillment, Helfferich's criticisms had an increasing domestic impact. By the spring of 1922, after looking back on the disasters that marked the course of Wirth's foreign policy, Helfferich noted in vitriolic superiority: "The fantastic illusion . . . that reparations could be paid out of current income has completely broken down."[86] As the future was to show, this assessment was correct. But, though Helfferich could warn that the policy of al-

---

[86] *RTV*, Vol. 353, 16 March 1922, 6312-19. Helfferich had nothing to say about the one foreign-policy coup of the Wirth government during these months, the Treaty of Rapallo with Soviet Russia. Indeed, Helfferich said very little about Russia during these years, which is surprising given his early involvement with the Bolsheviks. Although Otto Hoetzsch, the DNVP foreign-policy expert on Russia, said "conditions in the East were less familiar to him" than those in the West, one may speculate that the main reason for Helfferich's silence was that in foreign-policy terms he was a "Westerner" in a party where "Easterners" were numerous and influential and that he accordingly kept silent for the sake of peace in the party; Hoetzsch, "Aussenpolitik," 91.

ways accepting the "lesser evil" was only leading the German people deeper into the morass, his words did not persuade the majority of his hearers. The difficulty was that, however sensible some of his arguments, he never offered an alternative that seemed likely to have any appeal to the Allies.[87] It was very well to say that Germany could pay nothing, but such a statement did not offer a starting point for negotiations. The tragedy was that subjective expectations were so far from objective realities. Any practicable German foreign policy had to take account of this situation. Time was required to bring Allied expectations into line with German realities, and fulfillment, even though undermined by Wirth's lack of fiscal credibility, was a way to buy this time. Helfferich's policy, on the other hand, seemed likely to lead to disaster. Moreover, his tendency to clothe a sensible economic analysis in sensational rhetoric undermined his credibility in the way that Wirth's fiscal policy undermined his. It was too easy abroad to write Helfferich off as an unrepentent hard-liner, a man of the "mailed fist," who sought nothing more than to prepare his people for a war of *revanche*.

Helfferich's tendency toward increasingly extreme utterances in foreign-policy matters is nowhere better illustrated than in his violent rebuttal of a Rathenau speech of 21 June 1922. Rathenau, who in the meantime had become Foreign Minister, was himself making more extreme statements than either he or Wirth had earlier. Their continual rebuffs at the hands of the French and their failure to obtain a more satisfactory reparations settlement or an international loan at any of the international conferences of the spring and early summer of 1922 were probably the causes. Rathenau's speech of the 21st was thus extreme enough, one would suppose, to satisfy the most ardent nationalist.[88] He spoke of the French government of the Saar as providing the "typical picture of foreign domination" and noted approvingly that the "population . . . had united all the more firmly to protect

[87] There was no lack of critics to point this out at the time; see especially, *RTV*, Vol. 351, 7 Nov. 1921, 4830 (Otto Braun); *ibid.*, Vol. 353, 17 March 1922, 6334 (Karl Herold, Center); *ibid.*, Vol. 355, 22 June 1922, 7949 (Friedrich Stampfer, SPD).

[88] *Ibid.*, 21 June 1922, 7945.

what they consider to be their supreme good: their Germanic character."

"Trembling with excitement," Helfferich began his speech of rebuttal on 23 June by characterizing the agenda as a "grave documentation of Germany's afflictions."[89] Referring to the various bills and interpellations under discussion, he said: "One accusation follows another, each more urgent than the last, accusations against those who have used national self-determination, democracy, and international reconciliation as a hypocritical means of deception and with these grand phrases have deluded and confounded countless Germans about those who are now revealing to the German people nothing more than unlimited despotism, brutal tyranny, scorn, hatred, the will to annihilation, and the furor of destruction." He did not stop at generalities, but took Rathenau specifically to task for speaking so calmly of the matters on the agenda. He cautioned that "there is nothing personal in what I say" and claimed to recognize that a Foreign Minister had to weigh his words carefully. But he rather destroyed the effect of these caveats when he read a sentence from Rathenau's speech with the comment: "By God, what stale lemonade!" The Saarlanders, he added, felt "betrayed and sold down the river."

These inflammatory remarks were only the prelude to a detailed indictment of fulfillment which brought up events as comparatively remote as the Treaty of Versailles. Some of what Helfferich had to say about the government's more recent efforts to achieve a satisfactory reparations settlement was comparatively mild. But the general tendency of his remarks was sensational enough. He called one measure that the government had accepted "flaming madness, no more than that, a crime." He implied that in accepting certain obligations, the government had exceeded its constitutional powers because it had not informed the Reichstag as completely as it should have. He also made much of textual differences between the French and the German versions of certain of the German government's notes. Although the government later asserted that the German version obtained,

---

[89] The characterization is Erich Dombrowski's; "Eine stürmische Reichstagsitzung: Helfferichs Katastrophen-Politik . . . ," *BT*, No. 293, 24 June 1922. For the speech, see *RTV*, Vol. 355, 23 June 1922, 7988-8001.

the French version was admittedly somewhat more extreme in its statement of German obligations. In pointing out these textual discrepancies, Helfferich was not so unreasonable as some critics have asserted, but when he implied that they were part of a deliberate conspiracy to hoodwink the Reichstag—"they cannot be a matter of chance"—he was grasping at straws, or worse. He concluded this portion of his speech by saying: "A German government which gives up important attributes of sovereignty . . . [to the Reparations Commission] belongs on trial for treason."

His speech otherwise consisted largely of ideas he had developed earlier, although he presented them in a particularly acrid form. He complained about occupation costs, which were scandalously high; whether it helped to call the occupation "administration by satraps" may be doubted. He called for an end to such high costs, insisted that the "blemish of the war-guilt lie" be removed, and demanded that reparations be set at a reasonable level. Basically he thought that the government misapprehended the motives behind French policy. They were not primarily interested in money but in political domination or, as he had earlier put it, the "*Drang nach dem Rhein* and beyond."[90] They had learned, however, in the days of Louis XIV and Napoleon that Germany could not be held with bayonets. They had therefore substituted a "system of financial strangulation." In dealing with such people it was folly to suppose that a show of good will would induce moderation in return: "that was, and is, your great error." The time had come to stand firm, to show the other side that "they were dealing with men!" By the time Helfferich had finished, the Reichstag had been reduced to such turmoil that one observer could say, "one would have believed himself to be in bedlam."[91]

[90] *RTV*, Vol. 349, 27 April 1921, 3441. The alleged continuity of French policy was a favorite theme of nationalist speakers during the twenties; see the remarks of Chancellor Wilhelm Cuno at the time of the Ruhr invasion, *ibid.*, Vol. 357, 13 Jan. 1923, 9422, which repeated Helfferich's words almost verbatim. See also Werner von Rheinbaben, *Von Versailles zur Freiheit: Weg und Ziel der deutschen Aussenpolitik* (Hamburg, 1927), 16, 22; Erich Koch-Weser, *Deutschlands Aussenpolitik in der Nachkriegzeit 1919 bis 1929* (Berlin, 1929), 73.

[91] Dombrowski, "Eine stürmische Reichstagsitzung."

X. ERFINDER DER
RENTENMARK

The Rathenau Crisis

During the March budget debates, the Socialist Hermann Kahmann speculated with some misgiving about whether the campaign against Wirth and fulfillment would take the same fatal
course as the earlier campaign against Erzberger.[1] Kahmann
might well have wondered. It turned out that he had not mistaken the campaign's effects, only the name of the victim. On the
morning after Helfferich's speech, Rathenau was machine-
gunned while riding in his open car on the way to the Foreign
Office. The assassins were members of the Organisation Consul,
the same secret band which the previous summer had murdered
Erzberger. Helfferich was at a Tax Committee hearing when
news of the deed arrived at the Reichstag. Eduard Bernstein and
Josef Hartlieb, both Socialists, immediately jumped up and flung
in Helfferich's face the judgment, "You're the murderer! That is
the effect of your speech yesterday."[2] That indeed was the almost
universal opinion. Because Rathenau was the second of Helfferich's opponents to fall victim to assassins in less than a year,
many people naturally saw Helfferich's speech as a kind of death
sentence, or at very least as intellectual justification for what was
about to occur.[3] Actually, the timing of Helfferich's speech and
the murder were entirely fortuitous, however improbable such
a coincidence seemed at first.

When the deputies gathered early in the afternoon for the
main session, the Reichstag became a scene of unparalleled disorder and confusion. A group of Nationalist students had placed
a bouquet at Helfferich's seat bearing the inscription, "To the

[1] *RTV*, Vol. 353, 20 March 1922, 6391-92.

[2] "Stürmische Szenen in den Parlamenten," *BT*, No. 294, 24 June 1922.

[3] For a sample of this sentiment, see Georg Bernhard, "Wer schützt die
Republik?" *VZ*, No. 296, 24 June 1922.

defender of German honor," an act which increased the tumult. Although the students had acted before the murder was generally known, under the circumstances a more tactless deed could hardly be imagined.[4] The President of the Reichstag, Paul Löbe, advised Helfferich to stay away from the session for his own safety, but the latter demanded that Löbe do his duty and provide the necessary protection. "Even as he appeared . . . ," Löbe later recalled, "he was enveloped in a torrent of angry cries, from which the word 'murderer' repeatedly rang out." Left-wing deputies shouted at Helfferich, "You're next!" Löbe managed to quiet things momentarily, but "as the situation began to get dangerous again because left-wing deputies were pushing in on Helfferich, old granny [Margarete] Behm placed herself in their path in front of him. [Only] reluctance to assault an old lady or to push her aside restrained these furious men from violence." After this ignominious rescue by his female colleague, Helfferich discreetly remained away from the evening session.

Actually, Helfferich had shown considerable courage in appearing in the Reichstag at all, although he would greatly have increased the risk of being charged with either complicity or cowardice had he not done so. To appear cannot have been easy for him, because in the conventional sense of the word he was not a brave man. He had none of that careless disregard for physical danger that was later to enable Ludendorff to saunter through the hail of police bullets which ended Hitler's *Putsch* at the Feldherrnhalle in 1923. After the Erzberger murder, Stresemann commented that Helfferich made a "downright anomalous" impression because threatening letters from Erzberger partisans had made him so "nervous."[5] An unsuccessful attempt to seize Helfferich shortly after the Erzberger murder doubtless contributed to his uneasiness.[6] Yet he had refused police protection

---

[4] The following paragraph is based on material cited in n. 2 above and Paul Löbe, *Der Weg war lang: Lebenserinnerungen* (2nd edn., Berlin, 1954), 102-104.

[5] Kessler, *Tagebücher*, 282, entry of 28 March 1922.

[6] Some workers from Darmstadt had tried to seize Helfferich when he was staying at the Schloss Heiligenberg at Jungenheim a. d. Bergstrasse, but he had already departed for Munich for the annual Party Congress; *RTV*, Vol. 351, 30 Sept. 1921, 4656-59 (Wirth); 4665-67 (Helfferich). A similar incident

—though he was not above bragging about it[7]—because he apparently thought that accepting it was politically the wrong thing to do. In short, while he behaved as his intellect told him a man in his position ought to behave, the Rathenau murder and its aftermath left him thoroughly shaken. Unburdening himself to a Swiss acquaintance in August 1922 he said:

> The last six weeks have been particularly difficult for me and my wife on account of the idiotic agitation which seeks to make me responsible for the murder of Rathenau and [thus] to sacrifice me to the mob. This senseless crime has taken the only clear head from the cabinet, the only man who understood something of the art of international negotiations. I was not in agreement with his policy and had to charge him with proceeding from assumptions that were far too optimistic. Nevertheless, on the basis of long personal acquaintance, I have always had the highest regard for him as a man of ideas and great conceptions....[8]

In more revealing moments, Helfferich was willing to admit a moral responsibility of sorts for the assassination. When party colleagues attempted to persuade him that he had no moral responsibility for the act, he is alleged to have replied that he had brought all of his friends misfortune, against his will, to be sure, but through his own acts.[9] But Helfferich's recognition of the effects of his words on the politically unsophisticated (if recognition it truly was) was as belated as it was fleeting. His utterances were to be as immoderate in the future as they had been in the past. Since he lacked great sympathetic insight, it is possible that he underestimated the effect of his words. Alternatively, he may have gauged them correctly—and he certainly was a calculating man—but have failed to consider that a law-abiding and "correct" people like the Germans might go beyond registering its

---

occurred after Rathenau's murder, when a number of left-wing toughs broke into the Neustadt house of his brother Philipp under the mistaken impression that it was his; *Rheinpfälzer*, 6 Dec. 1923. According to Helfferich's son, there were other attempts; Friedrich Helfferich, notes on MSS, February 1970.

[7] *RTV*, Vol. 351, 4667.   [8] Scheffbuch, *Helfferich*, 87n1.
[9] Fischer, *Helfferich*, 94.

indignation at the ballot box. He wished to drive his opponents from office; it was obviously not in his interest to see them murdered.

Helfferich was not the only Nationalist to come under fire as a result of Rathenau's murder. Indignation ran equally high against the Racist wing of the party. The Racists had seized upon Rathenau as the archetype of the Jew who was ruining Germany and had carried on a campaign of scurrility against him which exceeded in virulence even the earlier campaigns against Erzberger. One such article, a piece written by the Nationalist deputy Wilhelm Henning, drew from Wirth the rebuke that if the Nationalists did not purge Henning they stood condemned of complicity in the Rathenau murder. Wirth was not the first to make such demands, which had also come from within the party itself. The Rathenau murder was, after all, the third infamous deed to be linked to the Nationalists within two years. It was clear that they could ignore the demands for a purge only at the peril of renouncing all claims to being a moderate, middle-class, *koalitionsfähig* opposition. Hergt, Helfferich, and the other moderates were by no means prepared to abandon all hope of ever entering the government. On their side, the Racists of the Nationalist Reichstag delegation (Henning, Albrecht von Graefe, and Reinhold Wulle) also had a number of grievances, some recent, some of long standing. The Rathenau murder thus precipitated a struggle between the moderates and the Racists in which a number of fundamental questions about the party's future course were resolved.[10]

There had been trouble between the Racists and the rest of the party from the beginning, although not because the majority were opposed to anti-Semitism as a matter of principle. Even Helfferich, who was no anti-Semite, opposed excluding Jews from the party in 1919 only on the tactical ground that it would

[10] The following account of the difficulties which the Racist issue caused within the Nationalist Party follows Hertzmann, *DNVP*, Ch. 5. For additional background on racism in the party, see George L. Mosse, *The Crisis of German Ideology: Intellectual Origins of the Third Reich* (New York, 1964), Chs. 12, 13; and his "Die deutsche Rechte und die Juden," in Werner E. Mosse (ed.), *Entscheidungsjahr 1932: zur Judenfrage in der Endphase der Weimarer Republik: ein Sammelband* (Tübingen, 1965), esp. 227-36.

give the party a bad odor in respectable circles. He was not above accepting the aid of the anti-Semites who campaigned for him in Hesse-Nassau in the elections of 1920. When taken to task about their efforts after the election, he is reported to have said: "At six-o'clock today anti-Semitism has ceased to exist in the Nationalist Party."[11] (This was equivocal behavior, perhaps, for a man who set such high standards for his opponents in matters of political principle.) He was speaking prematurely, for anti-Semitism was still very much alive. The truth was that scarcely anyone in the party was adverse to exploiting the agitational appeal of anti-Semitism.[12] The Racists differed from everyone else in that for them anti-Semitism was the only part of the party platform that really mattered. The majority was content to let the party remain vaguely anti-Semitic so long as nothing concrete was done, such as imposing membership restrictions, to implement this anti-Semitism and so long as it remained subordinate to the rest of the party platform.

The difficulty was that the Racists, being zealots, were never content with a subordinate role, either for their ideas or for themselves. They were rightist revolutionaries, and they expected to gain their ends by force. Clashes between the Racists and the majority of the party were inevitable. The first major contest occurred in the summer and fall of 1921. At the Munich Party Congress of that year it had been necessary to sidetrack Racist demands that Jews be formally excluded from membership by referring the question to a special study committee. The committee, on which Helfferich sat, was also to consider whether the Racists were to be allowed to form a separate, fiscally autonomous organization within the party. The committee sessions were bitter. According to one account, the Racists were defeated only by a single vote. Helfferich, Hergt, Hugenberg, and the Party Whip, Georg Schultz-Bromberg, threatened to leave the party if the Racists had their way. In November 1921, when the entire matter came before a gathering which included the party

[11] Wahrmund, *Helfferich*, 169.

[12] In 1919 even so moderate a man as Hergt was able to say that the "wave of anti-Semitism will facilitate in an extraordinary manner the electioneering of the DNVP"; quoted in Mosse, *German Ideology*, 243.

executive and district representatives for final decision, Helfferich introduced a motion to leave the party statutes unchanged. It carried 103 to 81.

But that was not the end of the matter. Even before Rathenau's murder, the party, worried about Henning's increasingly questionable right-radical associations, had undertaken an investigation of his activities. Although he was cleared of the charges against him, a reexamination of his conduct after the Rathenau murder resulted in his expulsion from the Nationalist Reichstag delegation. From then on, it was merely a question of how much damage the departing Racists—and it was clear that Graefe and Wulle would join Henning—could do the party. Hergt and Helfferich took the position that what was at stake was not a question of principle but of party discipline. Helfferich took a particularly intransigent line toward the Racists, introducing in the Executive (on 17 October 1922) a very sharply worded resolution requiring the total submission of the Racists to the dictates of the Party Executive.[13] Although the defeat of the Racists was never in much doubt, the question remained of how much support the Hergt-Helfferich leadership had in the party as a whole. The question was answered at the annual Party Congress (26-28 October 1922) in Görlitz, during which the leaders received the general support of the party.

Shortly after Görlitz, the Racists left the party to form a racist party of their own, the Deutschvölkische Arbeitsgemeinschaft. Once they were definitely out of the party much of their previous support fell away. They contributed to this result by their increasingly immoderate words and actions; they revealed themselves for what they had always been, the lunatic fringe of the party. Hergt and Helfferich emerged from the struggle decisively in control of the party. They had made the party potentially more *koalitionsfähig* and saved it from the odium of being associated with Hitler's disastrous Munich adventure in 1923. Their triumph represented the victory of the ideal of a conservative middle-class party committed to reaching office legally and not by force. It was not a victory of moral principle, however, for the

---

[13] This was one notable question on which Helfferich, absolutely refusing to hear of compromise, broke with Westarp; Liebe, *DNVP*, 68.

party remained as committed to anti-Semitism (however vague) as ever.

Like many of his political actions in the twenties, Helfferich's role in the Racist controversy is ambiguous and hard to assess. On the basis of the available evidence, his attitude toward the Racists does not seem to have been very much influenced by Rathenau's murder. Both before and after the murder he was very hostile to the Racists, mainly because they threatened the cohesion of the party and its chances to participate in the government. One may also speculate that he found them wild and unpredictable, and thus personally antipathetic. These were adequate grounds for fighting the Racists, and in a party where anti-Semitism was so pervasive, it was probably not practical to choose any other. There was no place in the Nationalist Party for someone who publicly opposed anti-Semitism as a matter of principle. Although it is certainly possible to argue that Helfferich, as a man who did not hold with anti-Semitism, once again sacrificed conviction for power, it is also possible to argue that he performed the greater service by remaining in the party and driving the Racists out. After the Racists were gone, the Nationalist Party had an excellent chance to become the broad conservative movement that Helfferich had always hoped for, and in any case it was more difficult to see the road to Auschwitz in 1922 than it is now.[14] Helfferich probably underestimated the appeal of anti-Semitism, especially for the young. To someone brought up in the orderly world of the nineteenth-century German bourgeois, it must have seemed that there was really no place for anti-Semitism to go.

Rathenau's murder had repercussions which reached far beyond the internal affairs of the Nationalist Party. It is hardly an exaggeration to say that his death marked the beginning of a national crisis which lasted until the end of 1923. Although Nationalist politicians later asserted that only by successfully exploiting Rathenau's murder to cover up the failure of fulfillment

[14] See in this connection the interesting remarks of Rudolf Heberle, in *From Democracy to Nazism: A Regional Case Study on Political Parties in Germany* (Baton Rouge, 1945), 61, who notes the success of the party in appealing to the farm vote in the elections of 1924 and estimates that "the DNVP had a fair chance of becoming a popular conservative party."

was Wirth able to save his government, just the opposite seems to have been true. Rathenau, to be sure, accomplished very little during his brief tenure as Foreign Minister. He was nevertheless the first republican Foreign Minister who had about him an aura of greatness, who men believed might yet avert the disaster foretold by steadily worsening Franco-German relations.[15] It is doubtful whether Rathenau could have fulfilled these hopes, but at the time he seemed to have the best chance of anyone. It was, moreover, difficult to hold very much hope for the future of a nation which seemed bent upon destroying its best men, for Rathenau's murder was merely the most notorious of a long series of political murders. Under the circumstances, Wirth's "Law for the Protection of the Republic," rushed through the Reichstag in the summer of 1922 to prevent future outrages, had the look of too little and too late.

Without Rathenau, the Wirth cabinet was a girdled tree, left standing because there was no axman with an alternative policy. Its demise was inevitable. Early in September 1922, Georg Munch, a financial columnist with the *Vossische Zeitung*, noted: "Now as earlier the dollar rules our entire business life. Wherever one looks or listens, one feels its truly 'almighty influence.' "[16] After Rathenau's assassination, the mark, which had recently been fairly stable (though its changes in value were on the balance downward) at about 340 to the dollar, climbed to 2,000 by 25 August and reached the astonishing figure of 7,000 early in November 1922.[17] In the face of this momentous fall in

[15] Lloyd George believed that Rathenau had been slain because he was attempting to recreate good relations between Germany and the rest of Europe and the general opinion of the French and English press was that his murder was of "European significance"; *BT*, No. 296, 26 June 1922. For a far less hopeful estimate of Rathenau's future as Foreign Minister, however, see Bergmann, *Reparationen*, 176.

[16] *VZ*, No. 417, 3 Sept. 1922.

[17] Both Helfferich and Bergmann attribute the decline to the failure of the Paris loan conference earlier in June; *RTV*, Vol. 358, 26 Jan. 1923, 9510; *Money*, 600, 618; Bergmann, *Reparationen*, 176. See also "Morus" [Richard Lewinsohn], *Die Umschichtung der europäischen Vermögen* (Berlin, 1925), 19. Although the failure of the Paris conference was undoubtedly a factor of great importance in the decline of the mark, the daily dollar quotations in the press indicate that Rathenau's murder was a more important cause of the catastrophic fall of the mark, which began late in June

the value of the mark, with all that it signified for his policies, it is little wonder that Wirth allowed himself to be driven from office because of a defeat on a minor issue in late November 1922.

Cuno and the Ruhr Imbroglio

Wirth's successor was Wilhelm Cuno, head of the Hamburg-America Line. A man without conspicuous party ties, Cuno was chosen precisely because he had no record as a politician and an excellent record as a senior bureaucrat and businessman.[18] The thinking was that a businessman heading a "cabinet of experts"—which Helfferich, among others, had long demanded—might master the problems which had so long defeated the politicians. Although Cuno kept on many Wirth appointees (among them, Hermes), his arrival was nevertheless a windfall for Helfferich and his political friends. Cuno, who had been a wartime subordinate of Helfferich's in the Treasury Office, thought highly of his former chief and respected his opinions. Friedrich von Rosenberg, a professional diplomat who was another of Helfferich's old cronies, became the new Foreign Minister. Their original acquaintance probably dated from Helfferich's days as a Vortragender Rat in the Foreign Office and had undoubtedly been strengthened by their close cooperation during the Bagdad settlements. They had remained close friends ever since.[19] The last new cabinet member with whom Helfferich had ties was Johann Becker-Hessen, the Minister of Economics. Becker, who was

---

1922. See especially the following: "Die Börse und die Ermordung Rathenaus: Dollar bis über 353—grosse Nervosität," *BT*, No. 294, 24 June 1922, in which it was noted that for the first time the record of 348 set in March 1922 had been exceeded. See also "Der Sturz der Mark," *ibid.*, No. 304, 12 July 1922, which attributed the sharp fall of the mark (which had already reached the level of 550 to the dollar) to the political crisis following the murder which had shown how "little consolidated the domestic situation of the republic is." See also Bresciani-Turroni, *Economics of Inflation*, 268; Karsten Laursen and Jørgen Pedersen, *The German Inflation* (Amsterdam, 1964), 20; Widmaier and Netzband, *Ära Luther*, 10.

[18] For other grounds which made Cuno appear a good choice, especially his American connections, see Eyck, *Weimarer Republik*, I, 305-306; Friedrich Stampfer, *Die ersten 14 Jahre der Deutschen Republik* (2nd edn., Offenbach a. M., 1947), 309-10.

[19] "Bericht" 457, 25 July 1916, "HB."

from the right wing of the People's Party, had views that were indistinguishable from Helfferich's on most economic questions. He had in the past been one of the latter's ablest—and most uncritical—supporters in the debates.

It is not surprising that Helfferich soon acquired a sinister reputation as an insider, enjoying power without responsibility. It was reported that he visited the Chancellery almost daily,[20] that Rosenberg's foreign policy was really Helfferich's,[21] and that Becker, under Helfferich's malign influence, had forced Hermes completely into the background on economic and fiscal matters.[22] For his part, Helfferich denied that his influence reached very far. Still, he was very disappointed (for reasons to be discussed) when, contrary to his advice, Cuno decided to resign in mid-August 1923.[23] Everything suggests that Helfferich had more influence than he admitted to, if not as much as he might have wished. Although he clearly had no trouble obtaining a hearing for his views, given the available evidence it is all but impossible to document specific instances where they were actually followed.

What gave substance to the talk about Helfferich's influence was that Cuno followed foreign policies similar to those which Helfferich had so long recommended. He clothed them, moreover, in the same rhetoric. His policy was ostensibly fulfillment,

[20] Stampfer, *14 Jahre*, 309-10; Stresemann, *Vermächtnis*, II, 68. See also the comments in Kurt Geyer, *Drei Verderber Deutschlands: ein Beitrag zur Geschichte Deutschlands und der Reparationsfrage von 1920 bis 1924* (Berlin, 1924), 152, and Raphael Gaston, *Hugo Stinnes: der Mensch: sein Werk: sein Wirken* (Berlin, 1925), 146, on a dinner at Helfferich's in December 1922, which was attended by Cuno, Becker-Hessen, Stinnes, and Hergt.

[21] Stresemann, *Vermächtnis*, II, 170-71; D'Abernon, *Ambassador*, II, 219. Helfferich had recommended Rosenberg as a possible choice to replace Simons in the spring of 1921; Stresemann "Nachlass," 3089/6927/138625. See also the complaints of Harry Kessler, who believed that Helfferich had seen to it that his usual sources of Foreign Ministry information were cut off; *Tagebücher*, 365, entry of 11 March 1923.

[22] S. William Halperin, *Germany Tried Democracy* (New York, 1946), 245.

[23] *Reichstagsreden 1922-1924*, 29. Left-wing circles believed that the reason why the Nationalists under Helfferich's leadership supported Cuno so actively in August 1923 was to keep him in office; Geyer, *Drei Verderber*, 193-94; Keil, *Erlebnisse*, II, 273-74.

but it soon became apparent that fulfillment meant something quite different to Cuno and Rosenberg than it had to Wirth and Rathenau. With Poincaré determined to try accounts with the Germans, a clash was unavoidable. After the Reparations Commission had determined late in December 1922 and early in January 1923 that the Germans had fallen behind on the delivery of telegraph poles and other items, the French marched into the Ruhr. The long expected, oft deferred, had finally happened. Cuno replied by stopping reparations payments in kind, by prohibiting the sale of coal to France and Belgium (which meant that the mines were soon idle), and by forbidding state employees (including railway workers) to carry out the orders of French occupation officials. These acts constituted the so-called "passive resistance." Although Cuno's action was tremendously popular and had the almost united support of the country, he had certainly carried passive resistance too far. First, he played into Poincaré's hands by providing the latter with pretexts to take increasingly severe measures in the occupied areas, and, second, he assumed financial liabilities—mainly for the support of the unemployed populace of the Ruhr—which the state could not bear.[24]

Helfferich had nothing but enthusiasm for these extreme measures, which he criticized only because they were not more drastic. In a speech on 26 January 1923, he called maintaining diplomatic relations with "such a state" as France an "impossibility."[25] He recommended, though not in so many words, throwing out the remaining Allied control commissioners, beginning with General Nollet of the Disarmament Commission. He held that the actions of Poincaré had placed the observance of the entire Versailles Treaty in jeopardy. He demanded that the German government explicitly refuse to negotiate until the French had departed from the "zone of occupation" in the Ruhr. Once the talks had begun, the entire treaty would have to be "brought into line with the most elementary dictates of justice and humanity."

---

[24] Eyck, *Weimarer Republik*, I, 314-16; Bergmann, *Reparationen*, 226ff.

[25] *RTV*, Vol. 358, 9515-16. See also his "Dies Irae . . ." and "Um Leben und Tod," *Der deutsche Führer: nationale Blätter für Politik und Kultur*, 2 (January 1923), 33-36, and (February 1923), 63-65.

This was surely a bold and a forthright program, but also one with some fundamental flaws. To take only two of Helfferich's proposals as examples, expelling Nollet would have been insane since it would have occasioned yet more drastic measures from Poincaré and would probably have alienated the growing pro-German sentiment in England and the United States. But even where Helfferich's views coincided with those of the government, as on the refusal to negotiate with the French until they had departed from the Ruhr, his advice was a counsel of despair. Apparently neither he nor Cuno saw that time worked not for them but for Poincaré. Although passive resistance might be uncomfortable for the French, it was ruinous for Germany; and who was to force Poincaré to leave until he was ready?

Helfferich's views on the passive resistance did not soften with time. During the April 1923 foreign-policy debates, when he made one of his few concrete suggestions about what should be done, he insisted that the government demand an international settlement, and not one with France alone. Such an agreement had to be contingent upon the evacuation of both the Ruhr and the Rhineland, for only if Germany were freed of all occupation costs could it pay any reparations. Evidently not recognizing that the road to Locarno lay through Paris and once again vastly overestimating the inherent strength of Germany's position, he repudiated the Socialists' demands—which were to be seconded on 20 April by Lord Curzon, the English Foreign Secretary—that Germany make a new reparations offer. Such an offer would in his opinion merely destroy the united front at home and give the impression abroad that Germany could not hold out much longer; Poincaré's answer would be "scorn, and another kick."[26] Although that was quite possibly true, Breitscheid and Ledebour had earlier criticized Helfferich's remarks for being just the sort of thing Poincaré needed to keep his nationalist following stirred

[26] *Ibid.*, Vol. 359, 18 April 1923, 10,607-15, esp. 10,613-15. That was also the view of Cuno and Rosenberg, if the note of 26 April in D'Abernon's diary is any indication: "Cuno and Rosenberg have got a phrase into their heads which will go far to wreck the chance of agreement about reparations. It is this: 'Germany will not make any offer she is not certain to be able to carry out' "; *Ambassador*, II, 203. For the entirely insufficient offer finally made on 2 May, see Bergmann, *Reparationen*, 238.

up against Germany. On this occasion, Ledebour also pointed out that such remarks only postponed the day of reconciliation between the two countries and, given the fact of German disarmament, were "saber rattling with a cardboard saber."[27]

Even in July 1923, when the end of the passive resistance was clearly only a matter of time, Helfferich's sole regret was that it had not been adopted immediately upon the receipt of the London Ultimatum.[28] Had French demands been refused then, he believed that Germany would have been in a much more favorable position to resist than it was in 1923. He was not alone in making such assertions, but the burden of proof rests on those who make them.[29] Although the Ruhr imbroglio ultimately had the effect of clearing the air, to have provoked the French to such measures can only be justified by the same kind of logic used to justify preventive war. As a result of the Ruhr adventure, the French learned the limitations of force in extracting reparations, and the Germans learned, or many more of them did, that there was really no alternative to fulfillment. In the end, the Dawes Plan agreement of 1924 provided the French with the productive pledges and the Germans with the manageable reparations settlement that each wanted, and the Locarno Agreements of 1925, by guaranteeing the Rhine frontier, safeguarded the Germans from another Ruhr invasion. Could all these beneficial ends have been reached as early as 1921 or 1922, as Helfferich believed? Had the Germans refused the London Ultimatum, it seems likely that the English would have cooperated with the French in occupying the Ruhr, as they did not do in 1923. Lloyd George would doubtless have taken such action reluctantly, but he would have taken it; it was, after all, the London, not the Paris, Ultimatum. It is also highly doubtful that most people in England, France, and Germany saw the essential realities of the situation as clearly in 1921 as they did even two years later in 1923. To raise such doubts is to question whether the Ruhr adventure

[27] *RTV*, Vol. 358, 26 Jan. 1923, 9522-26 (Ledebour), 9526-30 (Breitscheid); *ibid.*, Vol. 359, 18 April 1923, 10,615-17.

[28] Helfferich, "Vortrag von 4. Juli 1923 vor dem Verein Eisen- und Stahlindustrieller," in *Reichstagsreden 1922-1924*, 288-320.

[29] According to Stampfer, *14 Jahre*, 313, "rightist and heavy industrial circles reckoned with the occupation as something inevitable. . . ."

would have been the catharsis in 1921 that it proved to be in 1923. In any event, given the hardships which the Ruhr occupation imposed on the German people, it is hard to see how any conscientious German statesman could have asked his people to assume such a burden as long as there was any chance of negotiating a more reasonable reparations settlement. That was not appeasement, as Helfferich considered it to be, but the only sensible course of action.

While Cuno sat and waited for the passive resistance to soften up Poincaré, the inflation relentlessly melted away German power to continue the resistance. The inflation would have been a serious enough problem without the Ruhr invasion. It had already begun to assume pathological proportions after Rathenau's assassination.[30] Even before the beginning of the Ruhr adventure, the tax problem was increasingly seen as one of altering existing tax laws in a manner which would provide the additional revenues needed to keep pace with the inflation. Whether it was because the *bürgerlich* "tax-robber bloc," as one Socialist styled the majority that under Cuno wrote most tax law, refused to accept any real solution to this problem, or because the problem was not to be solved in this way, it never was solved.[31]

The tax debates during Cuno's Chancellorship began in December 1922 and continued intermittently until July 1923. They reveal by their very duration the complexity of adapting the tax laws to the inflation. With accelerating inflation rapidly destroying the purchasing power of the mark, the old problems of delayed assessment and collection of taxes were causing more animosity than ever. In general, the Socialists believed that the propertied classes were successfully petitioning for all sorts of favors when the inflation worked to their disadvantage, while simultaneously exploiting the inflation ruthlessly when it worked in their favor. Speaking in mid-December 1922, Paul Hertz called the rise of the relative contribution of the wage and salary with-

[30] For an introduction to the theoretical problems of such inflations, see Philip Cagan, "The Monetary Dynamics of Hyperinflation," in Milton Friedman (ed.), *Studies in the Quantity Theory of Money* (Chicago, 1956), 25-26.

[31] *RTV*, Vol. 358, 14 March 1923, 10,148 (Wilhelm Koenen).

holding deduction (a flat 10 per cent taken at the source) from 20 per cent of the income tax in 1920 to 72 per cent in October 1922 a clear indication that the working classes bore a disproportionate share of the burdens of the state.[32] "The ostentatious edifices," the great amounts being invested in new equipment, and the fever pace at which the economy was working also seemed to the Socialists (and to foreign observers) to belie Helfferich's lamentations about the straits to which the capitalist classes were supposedly being reduced.[33]

Although Helfferich accepted many of the Socialists' facts, he disagreed with most of their conclusions. The most he would concede was that the practice of paying taxes late in order to take advantage of the continuing depreciation of the currency was too widespread to be tolerated. He was quoted as saying in the December 1922 committee hearings, "we must fix it so that the ones who pay on time are not the 'squares'"; and he helped to pass laws which inflicted severe penalties on the tardy.[34] He believed, however, that the Socialists greatly exaggerated the significance of tardy tax payments and of the profiteers' wealth symbolized by the "ostentatious edifices."

The real causes for the rise in the relative share of the wage and salary withholding deduction, both as a percentage of the income tax and of revenues as a whole, were far more complex. As Helfferich put it, the central cause was "that the share from the yield from capital . . . has declined in an absolutely horrifying way."[35] Bond yields were infinitesimal, rental property brought in next to nothing (because of rent controls which stated maximum rents in fixed numbers of marks), and stock yields were not much better, as the sharp fall in the yield from the *Kapitalertragssteuer* proved.[36] Many who had formerly lived in modest re-

---

[32] *Ibid.,* Vol. 357, 14 Dec. 1922, 9308-10.

[33] "Edifices"; *ibid.,* 9316 (Hermann Kahmann). The Socialists were very indignant about capital investment, much of which they believed occurred simply because it could be written off on taxes; *ibid.,* Vol. 358, 10,041-42 (Paul Hertz). Poincaré was in substantial agreement with the Socialists. See his note of 29 June 1923 to the English; Bergmann, *Reparationen,* 245-46.

[34] *RTV,* Vol. 357, 14 Dec. 1922, 9327 (Hertz).

[35] *Ibid.,* 9311.

[36] His most complete expositions of this view are *ibid.,* Vol. 358, 26 Jan. 1923, 9513-14; *ibid.,* 9 March 1923, 10,046-49; *ibid.,* 15 March 1923, 10,168-71

tirement had been forced back into the labor market in order to survive. Helfferich also emphasized the plight of the professional and scholarly middle classes, whose incomes were so reduced that they, too, were unable to contribute their normal share in taxes.[37] Last, Helfferich called attention to the great decline in consumption-tax revenues, once among the "pillars of Reich finance." With the important exception of the coal, wine, and turnover taxes, which were percentages of the selling price, these taxes cost several times their own value to collect.[38] He therefore accused the Socialists, as anxious as ever to seize the *Sachwerte*, of being blind to the needs of the state when it came to raising taxes on beer and sugar. For the most part, however, Helfferich emphasized in his tax arguments the decline in the yield from capital rather than the decline in indirect tax revenues.

By 1923 there was not really much chance that the Reichstag would accept *Erfassung der Sachwerte* as the solution to the state's fiscal difficulties. The parties agreed that the most satisfactory solution to the problem of raising more revenue would be to valorize taxes by stating the taxpayer's obligation in something other than paper marks. If directors' salaries could be stated in terms of coal, why not taxes? Despite the plausibility of such schemes, the technical difficulties standing in the way of their widespread adoption were all but insuperable.[39] In practice, the parties disagreed so violently over the impact of the inflation on various social groups and categories of goods that discussion never advanced far enough to make serious consideration of the technical problems of valorizing taxes worthwhile. Failing any political agreement on the essentials of fundamental reform, the Reichstag relied on a series of palliatives to keep revenues coming in. The most important was to incorporate into existing laws multipliers which increased rates by the amount the mark had

---

For his detailed analysis of the impact of the "tax reform" of March 1923, see *Das neue Steuergesetz (Gesetz über die Berücksichtigung der Geldentwertung in den Steuergesetzen vom 20. März 1923)* (Berlin, 1923).

[37] His fullest exposition of his views on this problem is in *Money*, 578-83.

[38] *RTV*, Vol. 360, 6 July 1923, 11,665-69.

[39] For a discussion of some of the difficulties, see Walther Lotz, *Valutafragen und öffentliche Finanzen in Deutschland* (Leipzig, 1923), 84.

fallen in value since the law was last amended. Drastic penalties were also enacted for late payment, and provision was made for ever larger advance payments. At a time when the inflation was entering its last and most serious stage, such measures could hardly have been more futile, and the wrangling between Helfferich and the Socialists over all these matters seems in retrospect somewhat beside the point.

To a degree, Helfferich and the Socialists were both correct in their assessments of those who had suffered most from the inflation. The workers, the middle classes, the *Kleinrentner*, and the great fund-holders all made heavy weather of it. Where Helfferich and the Socialists differed was in their assessment of the fate of producers, who were also mostly debtors. To the Socialists, the Stinneses, the Herzfelds, and the other great inflation profiteers were the prime realities. Looking upon such men, it was easy for them to believe that inflation did not destroy wealth so much as redistribute it to the most asocial kinds of men. What creditors and little men lost, debtors and big men gained. In part, the rationale which underlay the desire to seize the *Sachwerte* was that, by enjoying the profits of the producers, the state was to reform the inequitable distribution of wealth. Helfferich admitted that wealth was being redistributed but also held that in a very real sense it was being destroyed. Although the "fanciful figures" he sometimes used to make this point were nothing more than demagoguery,[40] he was probably correct in emphasizing the economic waste which the inflation caused. Much of the economic activity during this period was by normal standards irrational and useless. To protect themselves from the consequences of the falling value of the mark, consumers bought goods which they neither needed nor wanted, industrialists built plants which later had to be torn down, and farmers bought machinery far beyond any foreseeable future need. Helfferich also believed that the inflation had blinded many businessmen to their real situations; the "ostentatious edifices" were real enough, but the appar-

---

[40] Lewinsohn, *Umschichtung*, 208. Helfferich occasionally used the decline in stock prices in terms of gold to prove that wealth had actually diminished, a line of reasoning which was also commented upon adversely by his Reichstag opponents; *RTV*, Vol. 358, 26 Jan. 1923, 9517 (Paul Frölich, Communist Party).

ent profits which paid for them were all too often really losses concealed by failure to make the proper bookkeeping allowance for inflation.[41]

Helfferich was sincerely alarmed about the effects of the inflation, which he probably appreciated better than the majority of his critics. In one of his more passionate utterances, he said: "At the beginning of this accursed development, in which we are accelerating ever faster downward, a Finance Minister [Erzberger] once stated that the inflation was the best means of socialization. Today I should rather say that the inflation was the worst kind of proletarization."[42] In the last revision of his book, *Money*, which he completed in 1923, he warned more explicitly of some of the dangers which attended expropriation by means of inflation:

> These classes [of bond-holding capitalists] . . . had largely accumulated their wealth as a result of productive activity, and used it both as an insurance for old age and more especially for bringing up their children to be useful members of society, or for the service of the state. These classes . . . at the same time handed on the torch of economic and intellectual progress. How far the catastrophic destruction of these classes is affecting and will affect the further development of Germany cannot be estimated.[43]

The forebodings about the future expressed in this statement proved in the event to be all too justified. Once the inflation was over, the professional and official middle classes recovered, to be sure, much of their old position. The recovery was one of earning power rather than of savings and did not much profit either the great fund-holders or the *Kleinrentner*. Nevertheless, by destroying the results of years, of decades, of hard labor, by destroying these results in a way which was incomprehensible to most of the

---

[41] *Money*, 610-11; Bresciani-Turroni, *Economics of Inflation*, Ch. 5, esp. 201-203; 388-90. For an opposed interpretation, see Laursen and Pedersen, *Inflation*, Chs. 6-8.

[42] *RTV*, Vol. 358, 26 Jan. 1923, 9513.

[43] *Money*, 606. This was not merely wisdom after the fact. He had warned of the consequences of the inflation in 1920; *RTV*, Vol. 345, 4 Nov. 1920, 949.

victims, and by so greatly profiting a few asocial men, the inflation probably led to sharper questioning of the dominant moral and social imperatives than even the war and the revolution had done.

Erfinder der Rentenmark: Helfferich's Explanation of the Inflation and his Stabilization Plan

Helfferich thought that the inflation had originally begun after the war because the workers had exploited their new political strength to achieve wage gains which bore no relation to worker productivity.[44] The result had been a "race between wages and prices," and an increase in the demand for money to which the German monetary system offered little or no resistance. The most he would concede was that possibility of unlimited increase in the note issue "provided the necessary condition for unlimited increases in prices and wages." Money had lost value, but there was no inflation in the sense that more notes had been issued than were needed to meet the demands of the economy. Even so, had Germany not been saddled with huge reparations obligations, it might still have been possible to cope with the situation. In the last edition of *Money*, Helfferich carefully traced the effects of the London Ultimatum, the loss of Upper Silesia, other important foreign-policy reverses, and arrived at the following explanation for the later stages of the "inflation":

> First came the depreciation of the German currency by the overburdening of Germany with international liabilities and by the French policy of violence. Thence followed a rise in the prices of all imported commodities. This led to a general rise in prices and wages, which in turn led to a greater demand for currency by the public and by the financial authorities of the Reich; and finally, the greater calls upon the Reichsbank . . . led to an increase in the note issue.

Helfferich bolstered this line of reasoning by comparing the multiples of the increase in the dollar rate (335), the imported-goods index (435), the "home-products" index (353), and the

[44] Unless otherwise noted, the quotations and the argument of the following paragraphs are from *Money*, 597-604.

note circulation of the Reichsbank (70) between May 1921 and March 1923. To Helfferich, these figures confirmed that, far from being the cause in the loss of value of the mark, the increased note issue had followed the rise in prices only "slowly and at some distance of time." In terms of gold, the note issue was worth in the summer of 1923 only about 5 per cent of the prewar mark circulation. As transactions had hardly declined by a like amount, the inevitable result was "an acute shortage of money."[45] He thought that even the relative success of this "small" issue in meeting the needs of the economy could "only be explained by the feverish increase in the speed of circulation, which . . . was a consequence of the panic fear of further depreciation."[46] All of these facts proved that the ordinary quantity-theory explanations of the mark's loss in purchasing power were incorrect; it was not true that inflation of the note issue had raised domestic prices, with the effect that the terms of trade and hence the dollar rate had turned against the mark.[47] He also warned against accepting the remedy of the quantity theorists, which, as he stated it, was to stop the presses. Such an act would bring the "entire communal and economic life" of the country to a "standstill" because the "indispensable" medium of exchange would be lacking.

From the monetary theorist's point of view, Helfferich was correct in objecting to many contemporary quantity-theory explana-

[45] Both in *Money* and in the hearings on the failure of mark-support action undertaken by the Reichsbank in the spring of 1923, Helfferich maintained that the rise in interest rates was as much a reflection of the shortage of money as of the desire of the bankers to protect their principal; *ibid.*, 599-600. The *Vossische Zeitung* went so far as to say that Helfferich and Bernhard Dernberg were deliberately attempting to conceal the fact that some men (Stinnes was the name most often mentioned) were exploiting the low Reichsbank rates to make huge profits with borrowed money; *VZ*, No. 268, 8 June 1923. Such profiteering had in fact occurred and Helfferich may have been guilty as charged, but his assertions can also be explained by reference to his known views on how the value of money was determined.

[46] Helfferich, "German Currency and Finance," *Statist*, 23 Feb. 1924, 261. This article, which continues in six more installments through the 12 April issue, is of considerable interest as the fullest consideration Helfferich ever gave to the monetary phenomena of the last days of inflation and the initial phases of stabilization.

[47] He admitted that examples of this kind of inflation had occurred in the past, most notably with the "Continentals" and the *assignats*; *Money*, 66-70, 599.

tions of the inflation, because the equation of exchange as it was then mechanistically interpreted hardly allowed for the subjective feeling of the individual about the value of his money.[48] Yet, although Helfferich clearly recognized the importance of psychological imponderables in determining the purchasing power of the mark, he also allowed such imponderables too little scope in his own interpretation of the inflation. He mistakenly assumed that, because the exchanges advanced before internal prices advanced, the former necessarily *caused* the latter. We have already encountered the reasoning by which Helfferich connected changes in the exchange rate through a series of commodity price increases to increases in the note issue. In reality, matters were far more simple. Foreign doubts about the future of the mark occasioned by the continual floods of new money coming off the presses and Germany's dubious political future were translated directly, especially from the summer of 1922 on, into lower mark quotations with each new political reverse which Germany suffered.[49] There was no inherent connection through a chain of changing commodity-value relationships between the exchange rate and the internal value of the mark. Indeed, as Helfferich himself pointed out, by mid-1923, when the German public had become more sophisticated about the effects of the inflation, changes in the dollar rate were directly reflected in immediate changes in domestic retail prices. Had new money not continually rolled off the presses, however, real price differentials between Germany and abroad would have prevented the mark exchanges from falling by more than a certain amount.

Theoretical merits or shortcomings aside, the practical effects of Helfferich's interpretation of the inflation were disastrous. We have already seen that his interpretation blinded him to the inflationary effects of his own war finance policies. "His" interpretation, which had the support of a great many academic econo-

---

[48] For technical discussions of Helfferich's explanation of the inflation, see Ellis, *German Monetary Theory*, Ch. 14, esp. 253-56, 289-95; Cagan, "Hyperinflation," 90-91. See also Milton Friedman, *Quantity Theory of Money*, 20-21, who attributes the ill repute into which the quantity theory fell during the twenties and thirties to the rigid insistence of some of its adherents that velocity (and frequently transactions) was a constant.

[49] See, for example, Keynes, *Revision*, 103.

mists and much of the financial press, similarly blinded his republican successors.[50] It was a very flattering interpretation, because it placed the principal blame for the ruin of the mark on the victors. Of all of Helfferich's successors in the Finance Ministry, Hermes probably expressed this view most forcefully with his remark: "The French policy of force bears the sole responsibility for our [financial] ruin."[51] Even Wirth, who disagreed with Helfferich about nearly everything else, agreed with him about the causes of the inflation, though not about when it began.[52] Although great obstacles admittedly stood in the path of any government which attempted to follow sound monetary policies during this period, the failure of all governments before Stresemann's, which came to power 13 August 1923, to undertake the steps necessary to end the inflation must in good part be attributed to the mistaken monetary views of those in the key policy-making positions.[53]

Having helped to begin the inflation with his wartime policy of finance through loans, it was perhaps fitting that Helfferich should have been the one to contrive the basic plan by which the mark was stabilized and the inflation ended. He worked out the details of his plan late in July 1923 while on vacation in Switzerland—"up there in the hills is where the good ideas come to one."[54] When he returned, he had a draft law all ready to present to Cuno and his cabinet. He was evidently counting on playing

[50] Bresciani-Turroni, *Economics of Inflation*, 42-47; Ellis, *German Monetary Theory*, Ch. 14.

[51] *RTV*, Vol. 357, 25 Jan. 1923, 9494.

[52] See "Der Reichskanzler über die Wirtschaftslage," *BT*, No. 450, 23 Oct. 1922, in which Wirth is quoted as saying: ". . . the huge issue of notes is not the cause, but the unavoidable consequence, of the fall in value of the mark."

[53] Another key figure who accepted the Helfferich explanation was Reichsbank President Havenstein. In the spring and summer of 1923, he actually apologized for raising the bank rate from 12 to 18 and finally to 36 per cent and also took the position that in the face of enormous difficulties the Reichsbank was heroically supplying the economy with the money it needed to carry on; *BT*, Nos. 191, 262, 363, 24 April, 6 June, and 4 Aug. 1923. See also Bergmann, *Reparationen*, 140.

[54] Lumm, *Helfferich*, 102-109. See also Cuno's account, *ibid.*, 152-53, Helfferich's own account, *RTV*, Vol. 361, 9 Oct. 1923, 12,070-73, and Otto von Glasenapp, "Helfferich, der Schöpfer der Rentenmark," an unpublished article Friedrich Helfferich kindly sent me.

a major part in the execution of his plan, a hope which may belie his protestations that he had little influence on the Cuno government.[55] To his great disappointment, Cuno was forced from office before anything could be done about the stabilization plan. Refusing to accept this reverse, Helfferich immediately (on 15 August 1923) brought in a resolution in the Reichstag calling upon the new Stresemann government to present currency reform proposals. Although the resolution was overwhelmingly defeated, Hans Luther, the energetic Minister for Food and a carry-over from the Cuno cabinet, had already brought Helfferich's plan to Stresemann's attention.[56] In the days to come, Luther was to be the plan's most persistent advocate within the cabinet, largely because, with the growing refusal of the farmers to trade their grain for worthless marks, he saw the plan as the most promising way to get food supplies moving into the cities again. On the day following the defeat of Helfferich's resolution, Hans von Raumer, the new Economics Minister, wrote to Helfferich asking him to present his plan to the cabinet and promising that certain conditions which Helfferich had attached to the use of his plan would be met. On 18 August, Helfferich, accompanied by his colleague Jacob Reichert, presented his plan to Stresemann, von Raumer, Luther, and Rudolf Hilferding, the Finance Minister. Thus began the high-level discussions from which the final stabilization decree emerged almost two months later, on 15 October 1923.

In devising his stabilization plan, Helfferich reasoned roughly as follows.[57] By 1923 he had reluctantly decided that Germany would have to stabilize its currency without the help of any such

[55] According to Lumm, Helfferich was to have headed a small commission to work out the details of the plan; Lumm, *Helfferich*, 106-107. See also Stresemann, *Vermächtnis*, III, 81-82.

[56] Hans Luther, *Politiker ohne Partei: Erinnerungen* (Stuttgart, 1960), 113-14. See also material cited in n.54 above. In later years, Werner von Rheinbaben also claimed credit for bringing Helfferich's plan before the Stresemann cabinet; *Viermal Deutschland: aus dem Erleben eines Seemanns, Diplomaten, Politikers 1895-1954* (Berlin, 1954), 143-44.

[57] Helfferich's thoughts are most easily followed in the *Statist* article cited in n.46 above. The most detailed account of Helfferich's stabilization plan and of the others which were also proposed is Paul Beusch, *Währungszerfall und Währungsstabilisierung*, ed. G. Briefs and C. A. Fischer (Berlin, 1928), which also provides copies of the various draft proposals.

foreign stabilization loan as had recently been granted to Austria. Yet the state clearly would require large advances to tide it over the period of stabilization until it could set its own finances in order. A paper currency, though "in another form," was therefore still necessary. Somebody other than the state had to issue it, however, if it were not to be instantly repudiated, because popular confidence in state money was completely gone. A new private bank, backed by the various economic associations, would instead issue the new money. The backing for the new money was to be a first mortgage equal to 5 per cent of the *Wehrbeitrag* assessment on the landed and industrial property of Germany. As Helfferich saw it, the problem at this point became one of preventing the new notes, issued against the backing of Germany's productive assets, from suffering the same fate as the *assignats*. He believed that the *assignats* had declined because, although issued against land as security, they were not convertible into it. (Actually, overissue was the main reason for their depreciation.) His solution to the "problem" of convertibility was what constituted the real novelty of his scheme.

The value of the mortgages was not to be stated in terms of gold but in terms of rye or, in the case of industrial undertakings, some other commodity. These commodities supposedly supplied the cover for the issues of the new "currency bank." The new notes themselves, *Roggenmark* (rye marks) as they were to be called, were not convertible directly into the hard goods which provided the cover for the notes but into *Rentenbriefe*, or certificates bearing an interest rate of 5 per cent, the exact gold value of which was determined by the gold price of rye at the time of the interest payment. Many of Helfferich's critics, both then and later, have asserted that these provisions would have subjected the value of the currency to the same fluctuations as the price of rye, but it is certainly possible to doubt it.[58] Beginning in 1922, the Oldenburg *Land* government began issuing *Roggenrentenbriefe*, the value of which did not follow changes in the price of rye but rather the fluctuations in the mark rate on

[58] For the opinion of another doubter, see Kurt Singer, *Staat und Wirtschaft seit dem Waffenstillstand* (Jena, 1924), 217-22.

the New York money market.[59] Nevertheless, the final stabilization plan, which followed Helfferich's plan in all important theoretical particulars, did state the value of the *Rentenbriefe* and thus the notes issued against them in terms of gold rather than rye. This change did not prevent a momentary fall in the exchanges after January 1924, which occurred because the Reichsbank granted excessively large credits to business and thus permitted excessive purchases of foreign exchange by those who once again had come to doubt the future of the currency. Finally, at a time when the actual market rates were between 12 and 18 per cent on valorized short-term commercial loans, the 5 per cent interest which the *Rentenbriefe* paid was too low to prevent the latter from falling sharply if the public once began to doubt the value of the new notes and to demand their conversion into *Rentenbriefe*.[60] In other words, the so-called convertibility features of the new currency were largely spurious. The *Rentenmark* was as much a paper mark as the old mark had been, and it is hard to see why the same factors which actually determined its value would not have prevailed in the case of Helfferich's original *Roggenmark*. It is also worth noting that Helfferich himself acquiesced in the change from rye to gold after only token opposition, which would seem to show, considering all the publicity he secured for the alleged rye basis of his original *Roggenmark* plan, that he did not consider the question of gold versus rye to be very important.

During the month of September, the obstacles blocking the acceptance of Helfferich's plan fell one by one.[61] The principal stumbling block was the new Finance Minister, Rudolf Hilferding. As a Socialist, Hilferding was hardly inclined to accept monetary salvation from his party's worst enemy. Besides, he was

---

[59] Beusch, *Währungszerfall*, 33-35, 127. Helfferich was familiar with the Oldenburg *Rentenbriefe*; see *Money*, 509-10, which also describes expedients in use elsewhere.

[60] Bresciani-Turroni, *Economics of Inflation*, 350-61. Ch. 9 *passim*.

[61] Luther, *Politiker*, 114-18, Beusch, *Währungszerfall*, 47-61, and Widmaier and Netzband, *Ära Luther*, Ch. 2, provide the best accounts of the behind-the-scenes discussions of the various currency plans. See also Stresemann, *Vermächtnis*, I, 115-21.

probably the most important socialist monetary theorist of his day, and he had a plan of his own. Unfortunately, he followed Karl Marx in the erroneous view that money took its value from the labor required to produce it. Hence he believed that for a paper currency to circulate without depreciating, it had to be convertible into gold (or some other substance having "intrinsic value"); he was a very old-fashioned metallist.[62] Considering Helfferich's plan to be a theoretical monstrosity, he planned to create a gold-note bank which, because gold was in such short supply, could issue notes to the very limited amount of 360 million gold marks. Luther, by now (mid-September) more alarmed than ever about the food situation, rightly pointed out that, if the prewar circulation of 5 billion gold marks was any precedent, Hilferding's wee issue could not provide the necessary advances to the government, nor could it meet the needs of domestic trade. Helfferich himself tried to hurry things along by publishing his original plan in the papers and by writing directly to Hilferding.[63] In the face of all this pressure, Hilferding gave way. In a series of conferences between 15 and 19 September, Luther and his advisers modified Helfferich's original plan in ways that overcame most of the original objections to it. Gold, not rye, was made the measure of value, the division of the new Rentenbank's profits was altered in favor of the state, the Rentenbank was not allowed to grant private credits, and the preliminary advances to the state were sharply reduced from Helfferich's original 2 billion gold marks to 1.2 billion.[64]

[62] Ellis, *German Monetary Theory*, 93-101, lays bare the shortcomings in Hilferding's monetary theory, which almost predestined him to fail as a currency reformer.

[63] Stampfer, *14 Jahre*, 369-70; Hans Luther, "Die Stabilisierung der deutschen Währung: aus persönlichen Erinnerungen erzählt," in Hermann Müller (ed.), *Zehn Jahre deutsche Geschichte* (Berlin, 1928), 168.

[64] There is a tendency to mistake the essential nature of these alterations, which did not affect the fundamental character of Helfferich's arrangements so much as they did the details of how profits of issue were to be divided and of other matters of essentially political import. Schacht more or less admitted that some changes were made solely to prevent the Nationalists from gaining all the credit for the stabilization; Hjalmar H. G. Schacht, *Die Stabilisierung der Mark* (Stuttgart, 1927), 60-61. Whether it was a good idea to cut the credits to be offered the state so sharply has been dis-

Although the draft stabilization law was presented to the Reichstag on 1 October, it was never formally debated. Stresemann had already called for emergency constitutional powers to enable him to combat the threatening internal disorders and to carry out the necessary economic stabilization measures. The fall of his government on 3 October hardly delayed things, for he had soon reconstituted his cabinet with nearly the same personnel. Significantly, however, the vacillating Hilferding gave way to Luther as Finance Minister.[65] Helfferich's first chance to speak on the currency stabilization bill thus came during the enabling-act debates of 9 October. Although he had been consulted periodically about the details of his plan, he now asserted that Hilferding had "denatured" it.[66] The conditions under which he had first offered his proposal had not been kept. Formally, this was correct. He had first demanded that property be freed from the *Betriebsabgabe* of 11 August 1923, because it would have to bear the burdens of stabilization. His second demand had been that his proposal be accepted without major alteration, so that it might succeed in "staving off the catastrophe [and not] merely accelerate it." Although Helfferich was later eager to take credit for the scheme when it succeeded, he was prudently providing himself avenues of retreat in case it failed.[67]

Once the enabling act was passed, Luther moved quickly to complete the remaining measures necessary to carry out the stabilization. It was decided to wait until 15 November, however,

---

puted. For an opinion in favor, see Luther, *Politiker*, 117. For an opinion against, see Beusch, *Währungszerfall*, 53.

[65] Hilferding was generally agreed to have been insufficient, even by some Socialists; Noske, *Erlebtes*, 248; Braun, *Weimar*, 126-27. See also Luther, *Politiker*, 119. For defenses of Hilferding, see Hildemarie Dieckmann, *Johannes Popitz: Entwicklung und Wirksamkeit in der Zeit der Weimarer Republik bis 1933* (Berlin, 1960), 34; Georg Bernhard, *Die deutsche Tragödie: der Selbstmord einer Republik* (Prague, 1933), 173; Stampfer, *14 Jahre*, 367-71.

[66] *RTV*, Vol. 361, 9 Oct. 1923, 12,072.

[67] In "Dr. Helfferich und die Rentenbank," *Frankfurter Zeitung*, No. 79, 30 Jan. 1924, the paper commented ironically that it was interesting to compare Helfferich's utterances before and after the plan was successfully executed. See also "Dr. Helfferich über die Vorgeschichte der Rentenbank," *ibid.*, No. 85, 1 Feb. 1924, commenting on Helfferich's "Zur Geschichte der neuen Währung," *Deutsche Tageszeitung*, 31 Jan. 1924.

before putting the new currency into circulation, in order to permit as complete as possible a liquidation of the passive resistance and thus to reduce the strain on the budget. In the interim, a president for the new Rentenbank had to be chosen. Helfferich was in some ways the obvious choice, but he allegedly refused to consider the post, saying that he was so unpopular in some circles that he was likely to discredit the new bank and the *Rentenmark* along with it.[68] Perhaps he was hoping for a greater prize, the presidency of the Reichsbank; by October 1923 it was clear that the ailing Havenstein would soon die. When he finally did die on 20 November (to nearly everyone's secret or open relief),[69] the directors of the Reichsbank unanimously asked for Helfferich as successor. Although the latter was willing to accept, the decision lay in the hands of Stresemann and the Reichsrat, or Federal Council. The other leading candidate was the newly appointed Currency Commissioner and former banker, Hjalmar Schacht. Schacht, who owed his appointment as Currency Commissioner to his close ties to Stresemann, now took care to cultivate the leading Socialists in the Prussian *Land* government, Otto Braun and Carl Severing.[70] In the Reichsrat, Braun's Prussians plumped for Schacht, and that decided the matter. Although he was not Helfferich's equal as an economist, Schacht held remarkably similar views on many economic questions.[71] He was, however, much

[68] Lumm, *Helfferich*, 124. It is most unlikely that the government would in any case have offered him the position; Schacht, *Stabilisierung*, 64-65. See also n.70 below.

[69] Stresemann had earlier attempted unsuccessfully to force Havenstein to resign; "Kabinett-Protokoll," 20 Aug. 1923, "Valuta," Bd. 5.

[70] According to Stresemann himself, he had wanted to appoint Schacht as Finance Minister at the time Hilferding resigned, but some old scandals about Schacht's wartime activities in Belgium had made this impossible because there was insufficient time to check out the charges before an appointment had to be made; Stresemann, *Vermächtnis*, I, 147-48. See also *ibid.*, 257; Luther, *Politiker*, 119, 150-52, 204; D'Abernon, *Ambassador*, III, 110-11. For Schacht's wooing of the Socialists, see Braun, *Weimar*, 143; Carl Severing, *Mein Lebensweg* (2 vols., Cologne, 1950), I, 552-53.

[71] On monetary questions, however, Schacht's views were closer to Hilferding's than they were to Helfferich's: like Hilferding, Schacht had earlier wished to return immediately to gold and had come out sharply against the *Rentenmark*; Schacht currency memorandum, 6 Oct. 1923, "Wertbeständigen Geldes," Bd. 1; Beusch, *Währungszerfall*, 56, 170; Luther,

more skillful in the management of his personal relationships and politically had the saving grace of belonging to the Democratic Party.

Under the energetic and ruthless direction of Luther and Schacht, the stabilization plan succeeded beyond all expectations.[72] The key to its success was not Helfferich's spurious convertibility features but the prohibition against discounting treasury bills at the Reichsbank and the strict limitation placed on the Rentenbank credits the government was to receive. There was, in other words, a foreseeable limit to the amount of the new currency, and people became willing once again to hold both the new *Rentenmark* and the old paper mark as a store of value. As a result, the *Rentenmark* came under attack only for a short time after January 1924, when Schacht's Reichsbank was overly generous with paper-mark credits to business. The government's financial position benefited almost immediately from stabilization. The real value of revenues increased sharply, which, combined with drastic cuts in expenditures, made it possible to balance the budget for the first time since the beginning of the war.

Credit for the "fatherhood of the *Rentenmark*," a question much fought over at the time, undoubtedly ought to go principally to Helfferich. His great contribution was that he recognized the psychological imponderables upon which stabilization depended and then drafted a law which took account of them. He cut off the new issuing institution from the old, which was discredited. He made the economic interests of the country the apparent guarantors of the new currency; Luther said that people accepted the new *Rentenmark* notes precisely because they bore the names of leading industrial and agricultural figures.[73] On the other hand, the limits placed on government borrowing reassured the more astute who believed that the original inflation had come about because of the government's excessive resort to the presses. Last, of all of the many plans for stabilization, Helf-

---

Politiker, 150. Schacht was also a metallist; see Schacht, *Confessions*, 152. On Schacht, see also the very unfavorable assessment of him in Widmaier and Netzband, *Ära Luther*, 50-57, 224-27, *et passim*.

[72] See also the more detailed discussion in *ibid.*, 72-83.

[73] Luther, *Politiker*, 148-55.

ferich's alone had been thought out to the point where it could be reduced to the articles and paragraphs of a law. Hilferding's failure to present his own plans in such a form, with the lack of concreteness that that implied, was one of the things that doomed his rival scheme. Helfferich is also due credit for the energy with which he pushed his plan along. Older Germans who remember Helfferich at all usually remember him as the *Erfinder der Rentenmark*, and, if this gives Luther and Schacht less than their due, it is on the whole a not unjust appreciation.

Toward the Future

Helfferich's willingness to assume the presidency of the Reichsbank may mean that he was not altogether happy with his life as a deputy. Long accustomed to being at the center of things, he may have found a life of perpetual opposition, with only occasional opportunities for the kind of backstairs influence he is said to have had over Cuno, somewhat frustrating. Then too, the chance to supervise the stabilization of the mark and thus to win a permanent place in history as a savior of his country must have appealed to Helfferich, who had a strong sense of the historical. Another more personal reason for wishing to escape from the hurly-burly of party life (if a wish it was) may have been his poor health, which forced him to spend much of the fall and winter of 1923-1924 in the south. He was apparently afflicted with severe sinus headaches, which sessions in smoke-filled Reichstag committee rooms aggravated.[74]

Helfferich's importance to the Nationalist Party was such that it could ill afford to lose him, especially with new elections foreseeable in the not-too-distant future. In the fall of 1923, he had warned that the Reichstag no longer represented political opinion in the country at large, and the elections of May 1924 were to bear him out.[75] For the Left the main issue was the measures which Stresemann and Wilhelm Marx, his successor on 30 November 1923 as Chancellor, had taken under the enabling act to restore Germany's economic health. The principal point of con-

[74] *Reichstagsreden 1922-1924*, 23.
[75] "Helfferich und die 'Morning Post,'" *VZ*, No. 498, 20 Oct. 1923.

tention was the abolition of the eight-hour day, the same issue on which the first Stresemann cabinet had fallen the previous October, and the issue over which the Socialists were in the end to force dissolution. Helfferich, on the other hand, sharply attacked some of the new foreign-policy developments in speeches which were clearly aimed at the coming elections.

His arguments against Stresemann's foreign policy—the latter had remained Foreign Minister in the new Marx government—differed little from his earlier arguments against fulfillment for the simple reason that, as he correctly noted, Stresemann's policy was " 'the policy of fulfillment' rechristened as the 'policy of national liberation [of the occupied areas].' " His bitterest attack on Stresemann came on 6 March.[76] It matched in violence his earlier tirades against Rathenau. Referring to the efforts of the Dawes Committee, a group of Allied economic and financial experts, to arrive at a workable reparations settlement, he chastised Stresemann for encouraging unduly optimistic hopes about the outcome of the committee's deliberations. A more probable outcome, Helfferich warned, was a "new and worse Versailles." He hammered away at the need to combat "the war-guilt lie" and to force a cut in occupation costs. He reiterated that Germany could pay no cash reparations. He harped upon the need to take a more energetic line toward France, particularly in matters having to do with the occupied areas. At this point Erich Koch-Weser of the Democratic Party interrupted to ask Helfferich just what practical steps he would recommend. The latter lamely replied that he would be willing to "draw the most extreme consequences" from France's continual treaty violations. When pressed to reveal what he considered these to be, he could only answer, "I refuse to describe them here in detail."

Helfferich's other remarks were on about the same level. They covered a variety of subjects. Although according to Frau Helfferich he had in the fall of 1923 called Hitler's *Putsch* a *Schweinerei*, by spring he was nevertheless willing to break a lance for

[76] *RTV*, Vol. 361, 6 March 1924, 12,620-33. See also his speech of 21 Feb.; *ibid.*, 12,417-24. It was generally understood at the time of Helfferich's 6 March speech that dissolution was in the offing; *ibid.*, 12,640 (Stresemann).

Hitler, who was then on trial.[77] Calling on his audience not to judge before all the evidence was in, he said motives, too, were important: "a hot love for the fatherland and a burning shame over the dishonor done it" were the grounds for Hitler's act. By 1924, this excuse was becoming more than a little shopworn. Helfferich also had some warm words for his stabilization plan, which he called a "bold and unprecedented construction." He also emphasized that the "initiative for the act of salvation had come from the opposition."[78] He accused the Stresemann government of delaying the introduction of the plan "unnecessarily"; it had supposedly abandoned the passive resistance on 26 September 1923 for fiscal reasons, yet the *Rentenmark* did not enter circulation until 15 November. This account was very misleading. When he had first devised his stabilization plan in July, Helfferich had tacitly admitted that the passive resistance had to be ended, because, until it was, the government could not possibly manage with the 2 billion mark transition credit which he had foreseen.[79] Indeed, it is difficult to see how stabilization could have gone ahead much more rapidly than it did, even had Hilferding accepted Helfferich's plan when it was first offered in August, because the critical delays were those connected with ending the passive resistance.

Although Stresemann's annihilating rebuttal exposed Helfferich's speech for the preelection tub-thumping that it was, the election results of May indicate that the rebuttal had more effect on the liberal press—and on later readers—than on the country at large. A week after, the Reichstag was dissolved and the new elections set for 5 May. The Nationalists began readying their campaign at a great Party Congress in Hamburg during the first

[77] Interview with Annette Helfferich, 11 July 1962.

[78] Much has been made, even by Helfferich's political opponents, of the fact that he "unselfishly" contributed his plan for stabilization to the opposition; Stresemann, *Vermächtnis*, III, 81-82; Rheinbaden, *Versailles*, 77. Perhaps Stresemann wished to encourage the Nationalists once again to follow the "unselfish" line that Helfferich had in the past. To me, the political capital which Helfferich derived from the successful stabilization seems more than adequate recompense for his "unselfishness."

[79] Helfferich was, however, a consistent opponent of ending the passive resistance, which he opposed in the Foreign Affairs Committee as late as September 1923; Stresemann, *Vermächtnis*, I, 135.

week of April. Helfferich received a tumultuous reception from the assembled delegates as the father of the *Rentenmark*, the foremost guardian of German honor during the dark days of the Ruhr occupation, and the prophet who had shown the way to the Promised Land.[80] When he spoke on Bismarck's birthday, the first day of the congress (1 April 1924), we are told that the "enthusiastic crowd shouted 'Heil Helfferich' again and again" after he had finished speaking. Although himself momentarily carried away by this roaring approval, he was finally able to quiet the crowd. He then said: "If you must shout 'Heil,' then don't shout 'Heil Helfferich,' but 'Heil to our German *Volk* and fatherland.'"[81] His audience's extravagant thanksgiving was in a sense no more than appropriate, because the party intended to base its election campaign on its record of opposition to fulfillment and to extoll Helfferich, the creator of the *Rentenmark*, as the savior of his country. The campaign leaflets read: "Helfferich's money put your household planning back on a sound basis. Helfferich's Party can also give your people a strong, reliable leadership."[82]

After the Party Congress was over, Helfferich retired to the Villa Siemens, a vacation house belonging to his wife's family on the shores of Lake Maggiore. He had already spent much of the winter there, recovering his health and making at least one trip to Rome, where he had an interview with Mussolini.[83] During his April stay at the Villa Siemens, the first concrete information about the results of the Dawes Committee's investigations ap-

[80] For the content of Helfferich's speeches, see "Aus der Opposition zur Regierung: die Deutschnationale Tagung," *VZ*, No. 158, 2 April 1924; "Der deutschnationale Parteitag," *DAZ*, No. 157/8, 3 April 1924.

[81] Weiss, *Wille*, 376.   [82] Hertzman, *DNVP*, 209.

[83] Stresemann, *Vermächtnis*, I, 369-70; letter, Helfferich to Westarp, 10 Jan. 1924, Westarp "Nachlass." According to Helfferich's letter, which is deliberately vague, he discussed the domestic situation and his country's foreign-policy difficulties. Mussolini commented on Italy's relations to a "certain power," presumably France. Helfferich's concluding estimate was: "All in all, what M. was mainly interested in was making a personal tie that —as he expects—could be important for the future." For other contacts between Helfferich and the Italians during the winter of 1923-1924, see Klaus-Peter Hoepke, *Die deutsche Rechte und der italienische Faschismus: ein Beitrag zum Selbstverständnis und der Politik von Gruppen und Verbänden der deutschen Rechte* (Düsseldorf, 1968), 269, 272-75.

peared in the press. The experts had proceeded with the aim of creating a workable reparations settlement which did justice both to Germany and her creditors and which would not endanger the newly stabilized currency.[84] Their plan ratified the failure of both the passive resistance and the occupation of the Ruhr. On the one hand, it provided the "productive pledges" which Poincaré had so long demanded, and, on the other, it stated that the plan could succeed only if German territorial integrity were maintained. Without attempting to set a total for reparations, the experts estimated that Germany could eventually pay a total of 2.5 billion gold marks a year, which was to include everything, even occupation costs. The initial payments, however, were to be much smaller, and were to start with 1 billion a year. To assist in making the early payments and in stabilizing the currency, Germany was to receive an international gold loan of 800 million gold marks. The productive pledges consisted of 5 billion marks worth of bonds to be issued against the security of German industrial property and 11 billion in bonds and 2 billion in preferred shares to be issued against the German state railways. To make the latter arrangement possible, the state railways were to be completely reorganized and run by an international commission. (The railways remained the property of the German government, however.) These sources (and the loan) were to provide the money for reparations payments during the first year, with the budget providing increasingly large sums during the subsequent years. The responsibility for transferring payments abroad was given to a special Transfer Committee, which as an agent of the Reparations Commission had the duty of handling the payments in a way which would not endanger the stability of the currency. The victors were also to be given a certain amount of supervisory power over the regulation of those taxes which were reserved for reparations payments (customs, and excises on tobacco, sugar, beer, and alcohol).

Writing from the Villa Siemens, Helfferich lost no time in commenting on the plan in two long *Kreuzzeitung* articles dated 12

[84] For a discussion of the Dawes Plan, see Moulton and Pasvolsky, *War Debts*, 160-69.

and 21 April 1924.[85] Although nearly every provision of the plan either embodied some demand which he had explicitly made or filled some need which he had implicitly recognized as valid, he had nothing good to say about it. He had long called for American assistance in revising the Versailles arrangements, and yet when such assistance came in the shape of the Dawes Committee, he peevishly set the same value on its efforts as he had on the earlier work of the English and French. He had constantly reiterated the need to cut occupation costs, and yet when for the first time an arrangement was established which placed a premium on keeping these costs as low as possible, he refused even to acknowledge it. He had complained about the excessive operating costs of the state railways, and yet, when the experts, proceeding from assumptions similar to his, created arrangements designed to reduce these costs and make the railways pay their way by partially freeing the budget from reparations costs, he then complained the interest charges on the bonds would be so high that foreclosure was virtually certain. In the event, foreclosure never became a serious possibility. Helfferich's criticism was all the more unreasonable because the Cuno government had earlier proposed a railway mortgage scheme to meet the French demands for productive pledges, and he had said nothing.[86] He had explained the inflation by asserting that reparations pressure on the exchanges, combined with the existing unfavorable balance of trade, had caused the collapse of the mark; and yet when a mechanism in the form of the Transfer Committee was created to prevent this from happening in the future, he was so bold as to assert that the committee would acquire "a power over the German economy that has no precedent in economic history. . . . By calling its loans [which was how it was to use funds it could not safely transfer], it will at any moment have the power to completely ruin the German currency and the German firms which

[85] Helfferich, "Das zweite Versailles," 12 April 1924, and "Die Reichseisenbahnen im Expertenbericht: die Darstellung der Regierung konfrontiert mit dem Wortlaut," 21 April 1924, in *Reichstagsreden 1922-1924*, 323-41.

[86] He had even conceded in his speech before the Eisen- und Stahlindustrieller cited in n.28 above, that some kind of foreign budgetary controls might be needed if Germans could not do the job themselves.

have borrowed from it. . . . The system . . . is thus . . . the organization of the *Überfremdung* of the German economy from within." Last, borrowing a theme from his fatal anti-Rathenau speech, he stated that the government had been less than frank in revealing Germany's obligations and had foolishly accepted arrangements which provided Germany with very little in return. He concluded his article of the 12th with the following warning:

> The curse of signing unfulfillable obligations and the curse of transgressing against the spirit of national self-assertion have burdened Germany for five years and led the German people to the edge of destruction. The German people is lost beyond all salvation if today it takes these curses upon itself anew.

The Dawes Plan was, in short, a "second Versailles."

No matter how one interprets Helfferich's excessively unfavorable and bad tempered initial reaction to the Dawes Plan, his response does not place him in a very favorable light. If he really believed all of the things he had to say about the plan, he grossly misunderstood its significance. What was important was not the letter of the plan's provisions but the spirit in which the experts had proceeded with their work and the spirit with which the victor powers had received it. The Ruhr imbroglio had cleared the air. Helfferich quite failed to see, however, that for this reason the Dawes arrangements would be carried out in an altogether more conciliatory spirit than the London Ultimatum and that none of the dire consequences which he forecast would come to pass; the Dawes Plan was not perfect, but neither was it a "second Versailles." Nor does it help to say, as some of his political friends did at the time, that, had he been more completely informed about the plan, his criticisms would have been less harsh.[87] Lacking detailed information, he ought to have followed his own advice at the time of the Hitler trial and not made snap judgments before all the evidence was in. If, on the other hand, his appraisal was nothing more than campaign rhetoric, he was guilty of very great political irresponsibility. His polemical window-smashing was, in fact, to have very serious consequences.

Two days after Helfferich's last article on the Dawes Plan

[87] See, for example, the comments of Otto Hoetzsch; Weiss, *Wille*, 98-99.

appeared, he boarded the evening Milan-Basel express for Germany. The following morning, 24 April, he was to begin the last phase of the Nationalist election campaign by addressing a party rally in Hanau. Before departing he had reiterated to his wife the need to reject the Dawes Plan, and thus we can assume that this was to have been the major theme of his speech.[88] Early on the morning of the 24th, however, the first reports of a horrible railway accident in Bellinzona, Switzerland, began to filter in. By evening, it was certain that Helfferich had been among the victims. A series of switching and scheduling mishaps had carried the southbound Basel-Milan express across the path of Helfferich's northbound train, and they collided at 2:30 in the morning.[89] What happened next is best described by a Frankfurt man who was riding in Helfferich's car, the second behind the engine.[90] After he and his two companions had climbed out, he said, "At that moment, along with a horrible screaming and groaning, I heard a report. The front of the car, which had been pushed high in the air, burst immediately into bright flames, which rapidly raged out of control. There were about five people in the compartment next to ours—Germans—who could not get out because the impact had pushed the compartment together. I had to watch while they were burned alive." Others also reported seeing "human torches vainly attempting to flee." Since few except for the engineers seem to have been killed by the immediate impact, Helfferich presumably also met death by fire.

After a preliminary ceremony for Helfferich and the other victims in Bellinzona, Helfferich's remains were carried to Mannheim, where burial took place. It was a properly impressive occasion, introduced by Beethoven's "Trauermarsch" and dignified by the important personages who spoke. Luther represented the government, Director Stauss the Deutsche Bank, Wild von Hohenborn (a former Prussian Minister of War) the Nationalist Landesverband of Hesse, and Max Wallraf the Nationalist Party

[88] Letter, Annette Helfferich to Westarp, 4 Sept. 1924, Westarp "Nachlass."

[89] The most complete description of the causes of the accident is the final account in the *DAZ*, No. 209/10, 6 May 1924.

[90] "Der Bericht eines Augenzeugen," *Frankfurter Zeitung*, No. 307, 25 April 1924.

as a whole. The Kaiser sent a wreath from Doorn. Impressive memorial ceremonies were also held in Berlin and in Helfferich's native Neustadt a. d. Haardt.[91]

The Deputy in Retrospect

The accounts of Helfferich's career which appeared in the press, written as they were in the shadow of the forthcoming elections, concentrated on his postwar record as deputy and Nationalist leader. The liberal press was of the opinion that the Nationalists had lost "their only talent." As the *Frankfurter Zeitung* put it: "Helfferich was the only man in the party who could have been permitted to appear at an international forum of statesmen."[92] Westarp himself admitted before the election that Helfferich had been the party's choice for Chancellor in the event of victory.[93] As it was, when the voters returned the Nationalists as the largest *bürgerlich* party, the best candidate for Chancellor that the party could think of was the retired Admiral Tirpitz, a choice revealing a lack of imagination and good men. And according to Wilhelm Keil, the party missed Helfferich just as much in the tax and budget committees, where Westarp, Hergt, and Reichert were not adequate replacements.[94]

Yet despite the general agreement that the Nationalists had lost their best man, no one could (or, for that matter, can) really say just what that loss meant in practical political terms. The only certainty is that the Nationalists sorely missed Helfferich's leadership. Later in the summer of 1924, the party faced the hard question of how to vote on the Dawes Plan, which, because constitutional amendments were needed, required a two-thirds majority to pass. Since the Communists were sure to vote against the plan, its fate lay in the hands of the Nationalists. Although the Nationalists had campaigned long and hard against the plan,

---

[91] "Helfferichs Bestattung," *VZ*, No. 206, 1 May 1924. See also *Karl Helfferich zum Gedächtnis*, mainly a collection of letters of condolence to Annette Helfferich.

[92] Ernst Feder, "Helfferich," *BT*, No. 195, 24 April 1924; *Frankfurter Zeitung*, No. 308, 25 April 1924.

[93] *VZ*, No. 200, 27 April 1924, reprinting remarks of Westarp from *Kreuzzeitung*.

[94] Keil, *Erlebnisse*, II, 295-96.

many party members could see numerous and compelling reasons for voting in favor of it; Helfferich's valedictory polemic was proving a troublesome legacy indeed. The entire question was therefore the subject of much debate within the party. Without Helfferich's assistance and support, Hergt mismanaged the situation badly, failing to hold the party to one line or the other. The party split its vote, 52 in favor, 48 against, and the plan passed. Though undoubtedly a blessing for Germany, the vote was a disaster for the party, which never recovered its former unity and finally split in 1928. However Helfferich might have voted, he was the one man who might have held the party together.[95]

After his death, Helfferich became a kind of patron saint of the Nationalist Party. In the *Political Dictionary* which the Nationalists prepared to guide the faithful during the campaigns of 1928, the gospel on an astonishing number of questions is according to Helfferich.[96] He is also one of three accorded the distinction of a full-scale biographical entry. The other two are Erzberger, still in 1928 the devil in Nationalist hagiography, and the exiled William II, the party's figurehead.

How Helfferich would have exploited his party's success is another matter. Some commentators were willing to speculate that Helfferich had played the demagogue in the party in order to bring his party back into the Reichstag with heavy gains, and thus to win office for himself. Having once attained it, he would have become more responsible and statesmanlike.[97] Although he undoubtedly wanted very much to gain office, given his past record it is hard to accept such hopeful appraisals. There is no particular reason to suppose, for instance, that Helfferich would have become a sudden convert to fulfillment after the May elec-

[95] Or such is the opinion of Hertzman, *DNVP*, 215. For the details of the party's difficulty with the Dawes Plan, see *ibid.*, Ch. 7.

[96] Max Weiss (ed.), *Politisches Handwörterbuch (Führer ABC)* (Berlin, 1928).

[97] J.[ulius] E.[lbau], "Dr. Karl Helfferich," *VZ*, No. 195, 24 April 1924. In fairness to Elbau, it should also be noted that he wondered whether Helfferich could have made the transformation from demagogue to responsible statesman, ruled increasingly as he was by his temper. See also *Vorwärts*, No. 194, 24 April 1924, which merely speculated that Helfferich in power might well follow the same policies which he had condemned as treason while in opposition.

tions. Unless he became one, however, he was not destined to remain a member of any cabinet very long. It seems more likely that the victory of 1924 would have confirmed his belief that ultimate success lay in persevering in the pre-1924 policy of opposition. His change of front in 1917 on the submarine warfare question had often been thrown up at him by his Reichstag opponents, with the result, one may speculate, that he had learned if anything too well the dangers of "excessive" political flexibility. Finally, even if Helfferich had overcome his repugnance to fulfillment, it is difficult to picture two such forceful (and by 1924, apparently hostile) personalities as he and Stresemann working amicably for very long in the same cabinet.

In addition to these essentially tactical considerations, there remained Helfferich's fundamental unwillingness to accept the republic. It is true that the longer the republic survived, the more likely he was to acquiesce in it, believing as he did that any system that survived long enough proved its right to existence. His own successes as a politician within a republican framework might also have encouraged him to accept the republic. Nevertheless, for Helfferich the golden age lay in the Imperial past, and his scornful remarks about the shortcomings of democracy in the fall of 1923 seem to show that his monarchist, anti-democratic sentiments were as strong as ever. But monarchism could hardly come to anything after 1918, since there was no politically possible candidate for monarch. In practice, as the earlier experiences of the monarchists in the French Third Republic and Helfferich's own experience revealed, the lack of a suitable pretender reduced the would-be monarchists to a kind of sterile "sentimental monarchism." They could campaign against the existing system, but they had no alternative of their own to offer. Such monarchists were open to the blandishments of any strong man who promised to provide the dynamic leadership which they claimed to seek. It took the searing experience of the Third Reich to convince men of Helfferich's stamp that of the two methods thus far discovered for providing a modern urban, industrial society with forceful popular leadership, it is better provided within the confines of a parliamentary democracy than within a totalitarian state. Helfferich's alternative, a monarchy guided by elitist liberal elements, had really ceased to be practicable by 1918, and perhaps earlier.

In short, it is hard to see why Helfferich's contribution to German political life should have been very much more positive after 1924 than it had been in the previous six years of the republic. Without attempting to weigh very carefully the debits and the credits of his contribution as a deputy, one can say that his criticisms of economic and fiscal policy were on the whole well taken, and far sounder than his criticisms of fulfillment. Some of his objections to the tactics of fulfillment were reasonable enough, but his fundamental assumption, that a policy of defiance offered a real alternative, was not. His greatest contribution, and it was a major one, was his plan for the stabilization of the mark; but balanced against it were his fundamentally irresponsible methods of political campaigning. His favored tactic of identifying the shortcomings of a policy with the moral or intellectual shortcomings of its advocate led him time and time again to overstep the limits of common decency. He must bear a goodly share of the responsibility for helping to create the poisoned political atmosphere which prevailed in Germany after 1918. At the domestic level such an atmosphere delayed the creation of the morally united Germany which Helfferich claimed to seek, and at the international level it perpetuated the wartime hatreds which were the source of many of Germany's postwar difficulties.

CONCLUSION

As the foregoing speculations about Helfferich's political future suggest, it is difficult to sum up a man who dies in mid-career. Too many questions remain unanswered. It is as if we had a group portrait of Helfferich in various guises, but a part of the portrait has been torn away, and that part is of unknown size. Still, what remains of the portrait is clear enough. Although we cannot say what other likenesses Helfferich might have assumed, we can nevertheless say wherein the guises actually portrayed resemble those of contemporaries, and perhaps how our fragment contributes to a larger panorama of the times.

Helfferich was able to combine talents and opportunities most felicitously during the prewar portion of his career. Propelled into the world from a happy home, he made the most of his opportunities from the beginning. He had all of the qualities making for academic success. Brilliant, passionate, and tremendously energetic, he mastered complex material quickly and wrote with ease and vigor. Once he had found his subject, he soon established himself as one of Germany's leading young academic economists. But the same interest in Germany's expanding economy that originally inspired Helfferich to study monetary institutions soon prompted him to leave academe for a more active role in the *Weltwirtschaft*. After being brought into the Colonial Office in late 1901 as an expert on economic development, he rose rapidly to the rank of Vortragender Rat, and, after moving to the Deutsche Bank in 1906, eventually became one of the leading figures in German high finance. Because of his involvement in the Deutsche Bank's multifarious overseas activities, the most important of which was the Bagdad Railway, Helfferich had become by 1914 an important figure in German *Weltpolitik* as well.

He had undertaken these various activities with the ebullience and assurance typical of his generation, perhaps the most self-confident in recent German history. These men, who began to reach positions of power and responsibility in the last prewar decade, had no personal memories of the divided Germany of pre-unification days, and the defeats of two world wars lay in the future. The Wilhelmine period was for Germany one of tremendously rapid material change, a time when industrialization was transforming Germany into the strongest economy of Europe and drastically altering the character of German society. In terms of personal advancement and psychological satisfactions, the group gaining the most from this development was the middle class, which preeminently had the skills (and the outlooks) required to manage the new industrial order. William II, intuitively appreciating the import of the new developments and excited by the *Weltpolitik* they made possible, increasingly opened his councils to such men. The result was that many of the most characteristic personalities of the Wilhelmine era were men such as Tirpitz, Ludendorff, and Helfferich, experts of middle-class origin.

The second phase of Helfferich's career, his wartime service in the bureaucracy, began with his appointment as Treasury Secretary in early 1915. Appointed because of his expert knowledge of finance and his reputation for energy, he soon established the right to be heard on virtually all important questions, frequently with decisive results. Helfferich at first prospered in his new career and was promoted to the office of Interior Secretary and Deputy Chancellor in the spring of 1916. After autumn of 1916, however, he began to encounter increasingly serious political difficulties in the Reichstag, which finally forced him from office in the fall of 1917. He spent the remainder of the war in offices the potential importance of which mocked their actual influence. Even admitting that laurels are hard to win in a country going down to defeat, it would be difficult to characterize Helfferich's wartime record as very successful.

Helfferich was in some ways a personality ill-suited to political office. Lacking much sympathetic insight and of somewhat rigid temperament—a contemporary described him as a "Jesuit in frock-coat"—he was apt to be intolerant of viewpoints very far from his own. He was disinclined to soften his utterances for the sake of being agreeable even when expedient to do so. He did not suffer fools gladly and was generous about whom he included in that category. It is also true that he often seems to have failed to anticipate correctly the reactions of others. Although capable of exhibiting considerable charm among intimates and inspiring the devotion of subordinates, the rather stiff demeanor he presented to the outside world revealed him for what he essentially was, very much the *Verstandesmensch*, the calculating intellectual. He had nothing of the common touch about him, and few of the intuitive abilities that one associates with the more successful politicians of our century.

Helfferich's education and previous career had done little to prepare him for the political responsibilities that faced him after 1915. Neither by precept nor example did German education offer much that was useful for the understanding of any political processes save those of foreign policy. Indeed, the prevailing dominance of the historical approach in all disciplines, with its emphasis on the unique character of national institutions and denial of the possibility of absolutes, strengthened Helfferich's predisposition in favor of existing political institutions and against reform. He thought that with unification the great political tasks had been accomplished. He accordingly showed only sporadic interest in domestic politics before 1914 and opposed steadfastly the Reichstag's wartime efforts at political reform. He was willing in 1917 to grant universal suffrage only because he hoped by granting it to avoid something much worse.

Helfferich's historicist approach to questions had other unfortunate political effects, because it encouraged him to disregard the opinions of those who had not engaged in detailed studies in the discipline encompassing the problem in question. This tendency to confuse history with life explains in part his animus against Erzberger, who persisted in meddling in financial matters which Helfferich considered he could know nothing about. It also explains his infuriating habit while a member of the Bethmann cabinet of lecturing Reichstag deputies as if they were dull schoolboys. He never understood how a man who knew less about the history or grasped fewer of the details of a given economic problem might yet have better ideas than he about the proper solutions because of having a superior understanding of the human values involved. His wish, basically, was to reduce government purely to administration.

But Helfferich's frustrating wartime career represented more than a personal failure. It also symbolized the fate that overtook Wilhelmine political institutions. Helfferich's initial appointment represented a break from tradition only because he was an expert drawn from outside rather than from within the bureaucracy. Such appointments were not unprecedented and did not mean that the problem of governing the new industrial, urban Germany had been solved, for it had not. To make such an assertion is not to say that a more modern political system might have saved Germany from war and defeat. To raise such issues is to open a Pandora's box of unprofitable speculations. It is to say, however, that while Germany produced the needed experts such as Ludendorff and Helfferich, it conspicuously failed to produce the needed Clemenceaus and Lloyd Georges. Germany's political structure was so articulated that Reichstag deputies, the most important potential source of such talents, were effectively cut off from administrative and executive office, while those who filled such offices were isolated from the national constituency needed to give their power the most effective sanction. Thus it availed Bethmann and Helfferich but little to be right on the question of submarine warfare and other matters, because they lacked the popular sanction to oppose Hindenburg and Ludendorff who, though lacking constitutional responsibility for such matters, could justly claim a degree of popular support that the civilians lacked.

The end of the war inaugurated the third and final phase of Helfferich's career, the years of his active opposition to the republic and its leaders. His political accomplishments during these years deserve a very mixed verdict, and his difficulties in coming to grips with Germany's new situation were rather typical of those of many contemporaries. Unlike many of his fellow businessmen, however, who retreated the fastnesses of their *Konzerne* and made the best terms possible with the new order, Helfferich determined to take a more active role. A state which Helfferich had once seen as the benign patron of German industrial development, intent on fostering a salubrious climate for business while allowing management freedom of action, now appeared as the agent of hostile groups. Thus stimulated, Helfferich skillfully transformed himself into a republican politician, becoming an effective political campaigner and Reichstag man. He revealed that he had learned much from his wartime apprenticeship in politics. It cannot be said, however, that he ever fully grasped the essential weaknesses of the old system or saw the potential of the new, as Stresemann came to do; but, then, Stresemann was exceptional. Helfferich's reiterated demands for "cabinets of experts" indicate that some of the basic realities of politics in a democratic age still eluded him. Although the republic ultimately disintegrated, it cannot be said that Helfferich's constitutional ideas, which essentially involved a return to bureaucratic monarchy, offered a viable alternative.

On other issues, too, Helfferich's political judgment was curiously uneven. In foreign policy he was perhaps a better strategist than tactician. To consider his ideas on reparations as an example, his basic assumption that Germany could pay no reparations in gold was clearly correct. His demand for a general settlement of war-born financial obligations, which would include the United States as well as England, France, and Germany, was also sound enough. The means he suggested for achieving these ends, to say nothing of the rhetoric in which he clothed most of his foreign-policy utterances, were hardly calculated to assure him a serious hearing in the Anglo-Saxon countries. Stresemann, by contrast, owed the success of his foreign policy in considerable measure to his ability to present German aims in a guise sympathetic to Allied statesmen. He appeared to be a responsible and reasonable man, whereas Helfferich looked like nothing more than a demagogue.

Helfferich's response to domestic problems was characterized, with the conspicuous exception of his fiscal and monetary proposals, by a similar discontinuity between means and ends. He assumed that if the German people would only stop quarreling among themselves, they could have a government strong enough to solve their most pressing problems. Within limits, this was clearly true. He hardly contributed, however, to this process of national reconciliation with his violent attacks against his political opponents, which did much to create the embittered atmosphere in which two of his principal targets, Erzberger and Rathenau, were assassinated. That he himself was the object of violent attacks may explain but does not excuse his intemperance. However one may judge his rhetoric, it scarcely served to knit the German body politic together.

His most positive accomplishment during the postwar years was undoubtedly his mark stabilization plan of 1923, which employed means well calculated to achieve the ends sought and was tactically very astute. But the plan also reflected in its provisions, the general effect of which was to make the private sector the backer of the new currency, the common view among businessmen that the economy was what really mattered, the republic being merely an unfortunate constitutional accident. Given the high survival rate of the barons of German industry, one cannot say that this opinion was altogether incorrect, but its political consequences were almost uniformly unfortunate. Having lost in 1918 the only state for which they had ever had much regard, businessmen were to see their economic fortresses breached by the world-wide depression of the thirties. Unlike the inflation, the depression profited none and was beyond ingenious solutions such as Helfferich had provided for inflation. Men who confidently opposed the republic thus lost the inner conviction to oppose Hitler when he appeared.

Although Helfferich was capable of supporting while in office political decisions in which he had no confidence, such as that in favor of unrestricted submarine warfare, on most substantive issues his stands were remarkably consistent both in themselves and in terms of the *Weltanschauung* that emerges from his early writings. That is particularly true of his stands on economic issues, where he has most often been accused of double-dealing and special pleading. The most questionable acts of Helfferich's career, such as his campaign against Erzberger, seem to stem from an excess of self-righteousness rather than being primarily the result of calculated demagoguery. His style was Calvinist and puritanical. He was ambitious for his cause, the enhancement of German greatness, rather than for himself. He was perhaps a little too apt to consider himself one of the elect and to confuse his own best interests with those of the nation, but those are delusions common to the Calvinist temperament and public men generally. Altogether, he represents a type that is rather out of fashion these days. If he seems not always to have served the fatherland well, it was not through want of zeal and honest, self-sacrificing effort.

In sum, Helfferich's career perhaps better than any other reflects the interplay of political and economic interests in the later years of the Wilhelmine Empire and the early years of the republic. Undoubtedly one of the more influential men of his era, he remained to the end of his life essentially the expert, the master of detail and the fabricator of solutions.

BIBLIOGRAPHICAL NOTE

A full reference to all works cited may be found by looking up the italicized short title (under the author's name, if any) in the index. As the usefulness of the more important works cited has already been indicated where appropriate in the notes, or in the case of the more important documentary sources in the list of abbreviations, it seems superfluous to make additional comments here. For the sake of future Helfferich biographers, however, I have included a brief survey of the more important books and biographical articles about Helfferich. A list of Helfferich's works, the more important of which have already been discussed in the text, follows this survey.

There are only four book-length studies of Helfferich besides this one. All are short. Only one carries the Helfferich-biographer very far, and that is the appreciation of his lifelong friend, Karl von Lumm: *Karl Helfferich als Währungspolitiker und Gelehrter: Erinnerungen* (Leipzig, 1926). Lumm makes no claim to present a full or scholarly account of his friend's life, but he does provide indispensable information about Helfferich's academic years, 1895-1902, and some useful details about the years thereafter. As a banker who, like Helfferich, also wrote on controversial matters for the financial press, Lumm brought a degree of insight to bear in considering his friend's career unmatched by Helfferich's other German biographers. Lumm also provides a list of Helfferich's writings that is fairly complete. The next two biographies may be considered together. Adolf Scheffbuch, *Helfferich: ein Kämpfer für Deutschlands Grösse* (Stuttgart, 1934), is merely a somewhat longer version of Rudolf Fischer, *Karl Helfferich* (Berlin, 1932), entire pages of which Scheffbuch incorporates verbatim in his own book. Both are tendentious and laudatory but do provide some helpful information from Helfferich's family not readily available elsewhere. The last biography is an attack by an unrepentant old-school conservative of

415

Otto Arendt's stamp: Konrad Wahrmund [pseud.?], *Dr. Karl Helfferich als Gelehrter, Wirtschaftspolitiker und Staatsmann: ein Beitrag zur Geschichte des Unterganges des Bismarckschen Reiches* (Leipzig, 1938). The contrast between Fischer-Scheffbuch, who present Helfferich as a precursor to the new Nazi day, and Wahrmund, who attacks Helfferich as an honorary Jew, may serve as further illustration of how difficult it is to predict the course Helfferich might have taken after 1924.

The best short sketch of Helfferich is that of his Nationalist Party colleague, the historian Otto Hoetzsch, "Karl Helfferich 1872-1924," in *Die Grossen Deutschen: neue deutsche Biographie*, eds. Willy Andreas and Wilhelm von Scholz (5 vols., Berlin, 1937), IV, 552-62. As useful in its way on Helfferich's Reichstag career as Lumm on the scholarly years is Kuno von Westarp's "Lebensbild des Staatsministers a. D. Dr. Helfferich," in *Reichstagsreden 1922–1924*, 7-42. Also helpful on Helfferich's Reichstag career are Westarp's briefer "Helfferich," in Below and Arnim, *Deutscher Aufstieg*, 371-85, and Jacob Reichert, "Karl Helfferich," in *Handwörterbuch der Staatswissenschaften*, eds. Johannes Conrad *et al.* (4th edn., 8 vols., Jena, 1923-1928; "Ergänzungsband," 1929), Ergänzungsband, 492-503, which include bibliographies with some items not on Lumm's longer list. Less helpful but providing some information not found elsewhere is Kurt Singer's brief sketch in Helfferich, *Georg von Siemens: ein Lebensbild aus Deutschlands grosser Zeit*, ed. Kurt Singer (abridged edn., Krefeld, 1956), and the somewhat longer account of Kurt von Raumer, "Karl Helfferich," in Kurt von Raumer and Kurt Baumann (eds.), *Deutscher Westen-Deutsches Reich: Bd. I: Saarpfälzische Lebensbilder* (Kaiserslautern, 1938), 185-220. Although Raumer used some of Helfferich's papers since lost, he provides no novelties and is generally disappointing. One or two new details are in the Helfferich entry in the collection of biographies by Felix Pinner [Frank Fassland], *Deutsche Wirtschaftführer* (Berlin, 1925), hostile in tone. Finally, there is the helpful genealogical article of Friedrich Riehm, "Zur Geschichte des Neustadter Geschlechts Helfferich," *Die Pfalz am Rhein*, 16 (1933), 213-16.

In ordering the list of Helfferich's works which follows, it seemed most useful to group them chronologically by years and alphabetically within years. This scheme provides a capsule survey of what his interests were at various points in his career. Since the amount he wrote was in a rough way inversely proportional to the amount of time his business and administrative concerns were taking, the list also indirectly records how actively he was wielding the levers of power. For the sake of completeness, some items have been included which I have been unable to obtain. Periodical articles have proved the most troublesome to locate, because, particularly in the twenties, Helfferich wrote for a number of periodicals not commonly found in libraries. I have omitted newspaper articles and items included in collected works.

1891

"Abend" and "Am Friedhofe," poems appearing in *Die Gesellschaft: Monatsschrift für Literatur, Kunst und Sozialpolitik*, 1891 (1891).

1893

Ulrich von Hutten: Trauerspiel in fünf Aufzügen von F. Erich Helf (Dresden and Leipzig, 1893).

1894

Die Folgen des deutsch-österreichischen Münzvereins von 1857: ein Beitrag zur Geld- und Währungstheorie (Strassburg, 1894). The first 41 pages constitute Helfferich's doctoral dissertation.

1895

"Adam Riese und Herr Wülfing der Bimetallist," *Die Nation: Wochenschrift für Politik, Wirtschaft und Literatur*, 12 (1895).

Bimetallistische Kampfesart: eine Auseinandersetzung mit Herrn Dr. Otto Arendt (Neustadt a. d. Haardt, 1895).

Gegen den Währungsumsturz (Berlin, 1895).

Der gegenwärtige Stand der Währungsfrage (Berlin, 1895).

417

Währung und Landwirtschaft: gemeinfasslich dargestellt (Stuttgart, 1895).

Die Währungsfrage: gemeinfasslich dargestellt von K. H. (Stuttgart, 1895).

1896

"Die Erklärung des deutschen Reichskanzlers und die Währungsfrage," *Reuters Finanzchronik*, 1896 (1896).

Germany and the Gold Standard ("Gold Standard Defense Association," No. 15) (London, 1896).

Zur Geschichte der Goldwährung (Berlin, 1896).

"Die indische Baumwollespinnerei und die Silberentwertung," *Reuters Finanzchronik*, 1896 (1896).

Die Währungs-Debatte im englischen Unterhaus vom 17. März 1896 (Stuttgart, 1896).

1897

"Bankdiskont und Notensteuer," *Die Nation*, 14 (1897).

1898

Deutschlands Münzreform und die Silberentwertung: einige Worte über bimetallistische Geschichtsschreibung (Stuttgart, 1898).

"Erneuerung des Privilegiums der Reichsbank," *Die Nation*, 15 (1898).

Das neue Fiasko der internationalen Doppelwährung: englischer Parlamentsbericht vom 22. Oktober 1897 (Stuttgart, 1898).

Die Reform des deutschen Geldwesens nach der Gründung des Reiches (2 vols., Leipzig, 1898).

Die Reichsbank: Verhandlungen der Plenarversammlung des deutschen Handelstages vom 14. März 1898: mit einer Einleitung von Karl Helfferich (Stuttgart, 1898). Helfferich was also one of four speakers.

1899

Der Abschluss der deutschen Münzreform (Berlin, 1899).

Die Malthussche Bevölkerungslehre und der moderne Industriestaat (Munich, 1899).

Zur Erneuerung des deutschen Bankgesetzes (Leipzig, 1899).

1900

"Bamberger als Währungspolitiker," in Helfferich (ed.), *Ausgewählte Reden und Aufsätze über Geld- und Bankwesen von Ludwig Bamberger* (Berlin, 1900).

Studien über Geld- und Bankwesen (Berlin, 1900). A collection of ten articles.

1901

"Einleitung," "Notenausgabe," "Diskontpolitik," "Reglung [*sic*] des Geldumlaufs," "Die Banknovelle vom 7. Juni 1899 als Ergebnis der bisherigen Entwicklung," in Germany, Reichsbank, *Die Reichsbank 1876–1900* (Berlin, 1901). Lumm attributes the foregoing articles to Helfferich.

Handelspolitik: Vorträge gehalten in Hamburg im Winter 1900/ 1901 im Auftrag der Hamburgischen Oberschulbehörde (Leipzig, 1901).

1902

"Goldproduktion, internationale Goldbewegungen, inländischer Geldbedarf und Diskontsatz," *Bank-Archiv*, 1 (1902).

1903

"Der deutsche Geldmarkt 1895-1902," *Schriften des Vereins für Sozialpolitik*, 110 (1903).

Das Geld (Leipzig, 1903).

"Opinions of Professor Helfferich, Legationsrat of the Colonial Department of the Imperial Foreign Office [about the Stabilization of Exchange-rates Between Gold and Silver Standard Countries]," in U.S., Commission on International Exchange, *Stability of International Exchange: Report on the Introduction of the Gold Exchange Standard into China and Other Silver-using Countries* (Washington, D.C., 1903).

1904

"Baumwollefrage: ein weltwirtschaftliches Problem," *Marine Rundschau*, 15 (1904).

"Martin Friedrich Rudolf von Delbrück," *Biographisches Jahrbuch und deutscher Necrolog*, 9 (1904).

1905

"Bedeutung der Kolonieen für die deutsche Volkswirtschaft," in *Verhandlungen des Deutschen Kolonialkongresses zu Berlin am 5., 6., 7. Oktober 1905* (Berlin, 1905).

"Geld," in Georg Obst (ed.), *Das Buch des Kaufmanns: ein Hand- und Lehrbuch der gesamten Handelswissenschaften in gemeinverständlicher Darstellung* (6th edn., 2 vols, Stuttgart, 1922 [1905]), I, 388-438. The article remained unchanged after the 1905 edition.

Zur Reform der kolonialen Verwaltungs-Organisation (Berlin, 1905).

1906

"Diskontsatz und Geldverfassung," *Bank-Archiv*, 6 (1906).

Das Geld im russisch-japanischen Kriege: ein finanz-politischer Beitrag zur Zeitgeschichte (Berlin, 1906).

1907

"Reichsbankpräsident Richard Koch," *Bank-Archiv*, 7 (1907).

"Revision des Börsengesetzes," *Bank-Archiv*, 6 (1907).

"Am Scheideweg der Weltpolitik," *Deutsche Kolonialzeitung: Organ der deutschen Kolonialgesellschaft* (1907).

1909

"Die Besitzsteuern," *Bank-Archiv*, 8 (1909).

1910

Das Geld (2nd rev. edn., Leipzig, 1910).

1911

"Auslandswerte," *Bank-Archiv*, 10 (1911).

1912

"Deutschlands Finanzkraft in der Marokkokrisis," *Bank-Archiv*, 12 (1912).

"Die zeitweise übermässige Inanspruchnahme der Reichsbank: ihre Ursachen und die Mittel zur Abhilfe," in *Verhandlungen des IV. Allgemeinen deutschen Bankiertages* (Berlin, 1912).

1913

Deutschlands Volkswohlstand 1888–1913 (Berlin, 1913).

"Türkische Staatsschuld und die Balkanstaaten," *Bank-Archiv*, 12 (1913).

1914

The Condition of Belgium under the German Occupation: Impressions of a Voyage (Berlin, n.d. [1914]).

"Hochschulbildung und Auslandsinteressen," *Grenzboten*, 73 (1914).

"Die Kriegsanleihe," *Bank-Archiv*, 14 (1914).

1915

Die Entstehung des Weltkrieges im Lichte der Veröffentlichungen der Dreiverbandmächte (Berlin, 1915).

1917

"Alldeutsche Agitation im Heere und in der Vaterlandspartei in Deutschland," *Politische und wirtschaftliche Chronik der österreichisch-ungarischen Monarchie* (1917).

"Änderungen des Militärstrafgesetzbuches," *Archiv für Militärrecht*, 1916-1917 (1917).

"Zur Frage der staatlichen Aufsicht über die freiwillige Wohlfahrtspflege," *Caritas* (1917).

Reden und Aufsätze aus dem Kriege (Berlin, 1917). Includes most, but not all, of Helfferich's wartime Reichstag speeches and some speeches made on other occasions.

"Verordnung über den Verkehr mit Stroh und Häcksel," *Blätter für Zuckerrübenbau*, 24 (1917).

"Wirtschaftliche Annäherung zwischen Deutschland und Oesterreich-Ungarn," *Politische und wirtschaftliche Chronik* (1917).

1918

England und wir: Rede über den Wirtschaftskrieg und Wirtschaftsfrieden gehalten von Staatsminister Dr. Helfferich vor dem Verband des Einfuhrhandels am 16. März 1918 (Berlin, 1918).

Krieg und Kriegsanleihe: Vortrag gehalten in Stuttgart am 7. April 1918 (Stuttgart, 1918).

Die politische Lage und die Wahlen zur Nationalversammlung: Vortrag gehalten auf der Wählerversammlung in Putbus am 27. Dezember 1918 (place unknown: pub. Deutschnationaler Volksverein, Kreis Rügen, date unknown).

Rede über die deutsche Volkskraft: gehalten am 11. Oktober 1918 vor den Vertretern der Kriegsanleihe-Werbeorganisationen (Berlin, 1918).

1919

Fort mit Erzberger! (Berlin, 1919).

Der Friede von Versailles: Rede an die akademische Jugend gehalten am 26. Juni 1919 im Auditorium Maximum der Berliner Universität (Berlin, 1919).

Die Friedensbedingungen: ein Wort an das deutsche Volk (Berlin, 1919).

Die Friedensbemühungen im Weltkrieg: Vortrag gehalten in der deutschen Gesellschaft 1914 am 1. September 1919 (Berlin, 1919).

Rede am 24. Juli 1919 anlässlich der ersten Versammlung des 'National-Club von 1919' in Hamburg (Hamburg, 1919).

Das Reichsnotopfer (Berlin, 1919).

Versailles und die Kriegsschuld (Berlin, 1919).

Der Weltkrieg (3 vols., Berlin, 1919).

Der wirtschaftliche Hintergrund des Weltkrieges: Vortrag gehalten in der Gehe-Stiftung zu Dresden am 18. Oktober 1919 (Leipzig, 1919).

1920

Gegen Erzberger: Rede vor der Strafkammer in Moabit, 20. Januar 1920 (Berlin, 1920).

"100 Milliarden Reichsausgaben," *Die Woche* (1920).

Vortrag in Bremen am 6. Mai 1920 (Bremen, 1920).

1921

"Die Beteiligung der deutschen Industrie an dem Wiederaufbau Nordfrankreichs," *Industrie-Kurier: Fachblatt für Kohle, Erze, Eisen, Metalle, Machinen,* 6 (1921).

Die deutsche Türkenpolitik (Berlin, 1921).

Deutschland in den Ketten des Ultimatums (Berlin, 1921).

Erzberger redivivus? Die Steuern und die Eide des Herrn Erzberger (Sonderdruck aus der *Neuen Preussischen (Kreuz-) Zeitung*) (Berlin, 1921). Lumm attributes this pamphlet to Helfferich.

Die Lage der deutschen Finanzen: Rede am 3. September 1921 auf dem 3. deutschnationalen Parteitag in München (Berlin, 1921).

"Mark und Dollar," *Die Woche* (1921).

"Die Neugestaltung der Reichseinkommensteuer," *Bank-Archiv*, 20 (1921).

"Das Problem der Reparation," *Wirtschaftliche Nachrichten aus dem Ruhrbezirk: Amtliches Blatt der Handelskammer Bochum, usw.* (1921).

"Die Wiesbadener Abkommen," *Wirtschaftliche Nachrichten aus dem Ruhrbezirk* (1921).

1922

"Die Autonomie der Reichsbank," *Bank-Archiv*, 21 (1922).

"Die Bilanz der Erfüllungspolitik," *Der deutsche Führer: nationale Blätter für Politik und Kultur*, 1 (Dec. 1922).

"Deutschlands Entmündigung," *Der deutsche Führer*, 1 (Aug. 1922).

"Die Frage der Reparationen," *Der deutsche Führer*, 1 (Jan. 1922).

"Lehrer und Schüler," in Kurt Singer (ed.), *Georg Friedrich Knapp: ein literarisches Bildnis* ("Sonderheft des *Wirtschaftsdiensts*") (Hamburg, 1922).

"Die neue Kapitulation: Notenwechsel zwischen Reichsregierung und Reparationskommission vom 29. und 31. Mai 1922," *Wirtschaftliche Nachrichten aus dem Ruhrbezirk* (1922).

"Die Note der Reparationskommission: Entmündigung und Zwangsvollstreckung," *Wirtschaftliche Nachrichten aus dem Ruhrbezirk* (1922).

Die Politik der Erfüllung (Munich, 1922).

Reichstagsreden 1920 bis 1922: mit einem Anhang: Reden vom 12. und 14. November 1919 vor dem Untersuchungsausschuss der Nationalversammlung (Berlin, 1922).

1923

"Dies Irae," *Der deutsche Führer*, 2 (Jan. 1923).

Das Geld (6th rev. edn., Leipzig, 1923).

Georg von Siemens: ein Lebensbild aus Deutschlands grosser Zeit (3 vols., Berlin, 1923).

"Um Leben und Tod," *Der deutsche Führer*, 2 (Feb. 1923).

Das neue Steuergesetz von 20. März 1923 über die Berücksichtigung der Geldentwertung in den Steuergesetzen (Berlin, 1923).

1924

"German Currency and Finance," *The Statist*, 103 (1924).

"The Gold-Discount Bank and the Proposed Gold-note Bank," *The Statist*, 103 (1924).

"Die Spaltung des Geldbegriffs," *Wirtschaftliche Nachrichten aus dem Ruhrbezirk* (1924).

"The Success and Prospects of the Rentenmark," *American Monthly* (March 1924).

Die Wahrheit über die Rentenmark (Berlin, 1924), a collection of newspaper articles mainly by Helfferich.

1925

Reichstagsreden 1922–1924, ed. Jacob W. Reichert (Berlin, 1925).

INDEX